UNDERSTANDING the NEW TESTAMENT USE of the OLD TESTAMENT

UNDERSTANDING the NEW TESTAMENT USE of the OLD TESTAMENT

Forms, Features, Framings, and Functions

Douglas S. Huffman

Baker Academic
a division of Baker Publishing Group
Grand Rapids, Michigan

Published by Baker Academic
a division of Baker Publishing Group
Grand Rapids, Michigan
www.bakeracademic.com

Printed in the United States of America

Library of Congress Cataloging-in-Publication Data
Names: Huffman, Douglas S., 1961– author.
Title: Understanding the New Testament use of the Old Testament : forms, features, framings, and functions / Douglas S. Huffman.
Description: Grand Rapids, Michigan : Baker Academic, a division of Baker Publishing Group, [2024] | Includes bibliographical references and index.
Identifiers: LCCN 2023058384 | ISBN 9781540966407 (paperback) | ISBN 9781540967763 (casebound) | ISBN 9781493446087 (ebook) | ISBN 9781493446094 (pdf)
Subjects: LCSH: Bible. New Testament—Relation to the Old Testament.
Classification: LCC BS2387 .H84 2024 | DDC 225.6/6—dc23/eng/20240223
LC record available at https://lccn.loc.gov/2023058384

Cover image from Chronicle, Alamy Stock Photo

Baker Publishing Group publications use paper produced from sustainable forestry practices and post-consumer waste whenever possible.

24   25   26   27   28   29   30   7   6   5   4   3   2   1

Contents

Illustrations

Tables

Figures

Sidebars

Preface

Unsurprisingly, the title of this little volume portrays it to be an introduction to the New Testament's use of the Old Testament. This rich area of study has been of tremendous interest among biblical scholars in the last century and has seen particularly increasing scholarly traffic since the 1952 publication of C. H. Dodd's lectures on the subject titled *According to the Scriptures*. My aim here is that this brief book would serve as a guide to others who want to enter this significant field of investigation. The first chapter offers an overview of the relationship between the Old and New Testaments and the value of studying how the New Testament uses the Old. It surveys some key issues for this particular theological discipline, suggests a procedure for approaching it, and introduces some key concepts that are discussed more thoroughly in the subsequent chapters. Throughout the chapters, several charts and diagrams illustrate the concepts. A final chapter provides an analysis of the use of the Old Testament in Luke-Acts as a model of examining one New Testament author's use of Scripture, and a glossary at the end of the volume offers basic definitions to fundamental terms in the field (which occur in boldface type at their first significant mention as the book unfolds). Such is this book's introductory tactic to the discipline of the New Testament use of the Old.

But more than an introduction, this book also takes aim at contributing something new to the ongoing discussion of the New Testament's use of the Old Testament. As I have become more involved in the scholarly investigations in this area—a field of (unsurprisingly) significantly varied views—I have found it helpful to utilize taxonomies, that is, the classification of things into ordered categories. The book distinguishes eight forms—four different "citation" classifications and four different "allusion" classifications—on a multi-level continuum (see esp. chaps. 2 and 3), and it offers a rigorous taxonomy of ten overlapping function categories (see esp. chap. 5). These more rigorous taxonomies of the forms and functions of the New Testament use of the Old Testament are the book's primary contributions to this particular theological discipline.

My closest friends and those familiar with my scholarly work are already aware of my penchant for taxonomic thinking in several areas of scholarly discussion. While I find thinking in terms of taxonomies to be a helpful way to explore various subject matters, I am nonetheless aware that a "hardening of the categories" is an occupational hazard for such approaches. And again, those who know me are aware of my penchant for thinking in terms of continuums and overlapping categories rather than categories with firm borders; this is my way of protecting against overly strict and artificial categorizations. Nevertheless, it is by means of this application of taxonomical continuums to the study of the New Testament use of the Old that I hope to prepare the way for further advances in this particular discipline. Of course, the reader will decide how successful I am here at capitalizing on the benefits of a taxonomic approach while avoiding its potential pitfalls.

My thinking about the New Testament use of the Old Testament with the utilization of taxonomical tools goes back several decades, and various friends have been helpful along the way. Among my research assistants over these years, two in particular deserve mention. Justine (née Lund) Carlson was a student in the mid 1990s at the University of Northwestern-St. Paul when she sorted through Old Testament citations and allusions in Acts for me according to a preliminary taxonomy. Similarly, while an undergraduate at Biola University graduating in 2017, Jordan Cardenas was my research assistant sorting through many Old Testament citations and allusions in the New Testament and locating dozens of books and articles for me related to this project (and other projects!). Influential friends impacting my work include Ardel Caneday, Jon Lunde, Ken Berding, and Darian Lockett, each of whom has served as a conversation partner on things related to the New Testament use of the Old and sometimes as a source for books and articles in this field. I am grateful for their help in sparing me from errant ways; naturally, any remaining errors of scholarship in this work are my own responsibility.

This particular project began as an attempt to write three paragraphs about Luke's use of the Old Testament in Acts for another publication. It wasn't long before those three paragraphs were ten pages, so I thought it should probably be a journal article. Indeed, several of the chapters of this book were presented as papers at annual meetings of the Evangelical Theological Society (ETS) over the past several years; a refined version of one of those papers was published as an article titled "A Two-Dimensional Taxonomy of

Forms for the NT Use of the OT," in *Themelios* 46 (2021): 306–18 and, with a few revisions, is reprinted here with permission. But it was when this project hit thirty pages with still more to cover that I considered the possibility of it becoming a book, and the folks at Baker Academic agreed that this would be a worthwhile pursuit. In particular, Baker's Bryan Dyer—a scholar who has himself published on the New Testament's use of the Old—was influential in getting this project adopted. I am grateful for the kind services of Bryan and the Baker team.

Large portions of the work on this project were accomplished during a sabbatical and a research leave from my regular labors as professor of New Testament and associate dean of biblical and theological studies for Talbot School of Theology at Biola University. I am grateful for the institutional support of such scholarship development opportunities and am especially indebted to those who filled in for me—fellow deans, department chairs, and administrative staff—while I was enjoying research and writing adventures. Lastly, my own life and ministry is so much better because of my dear wife, Deb, who has been with me for nearly four decades of professional biblical studies. Thank you all.

It goes without saying that this project is certainly not the first word on the New Testament's use of Scripture, and it doesn't pretend to be the last. But it has been an informative adventure to follow those who have gone before in studying the New Testament use of the Old Testament and to engage with those who are currently working in the field. Now I pray that reading this book will be as helpful to its readers as writing it has been to its writer.

Soli Deo gloria.

Abbreviations

1–2 Cor.	1–2 Corinthians	1–2 Tim.	1–2 Timothy	1–3 John	1–3 John
Gal.	Galatians	Titus	Titus	Jude	Jude
Eph.	Ephesians	Philem.	Philemon	Rev.	Revelation
Phil.	Philippians	Heb.	Hebrews		
Col.	Colossians	James	James		
1–2 Thess.	1–2 Thessalonians	1–2 Pet.	1–2 Peter		

Old Testament Apocrypha / Deuterocanonical Works

Bar.	Baruch	Sir.	Sirach
Bel	Bel and the Dragon	Sus.	Susanna
1–2 Esd.	1–2 Esdras	Tob.	Tobit
Jdt.	Judith	Wis.	Wisdom
1–4 Macc.	1–4 Maccabees		

Old Testament Pseudepigrapha

As. Mos.	Assumption of Moses	Pss. Sol.	Psalms of Solomon
2 Bar.	2 Baruch (Syriac Apocalypse)	T. Ben.	Testament of Benjamin
1 En.	1 Enoch (Ethiopic Apocalypse)	T. Iss.	Testament of Issachar
2 En.	2 Enoch (Slavonic Apocalypse)	T. Jos.	Testament of Joseph
Jub.	Jubilees	T. Naph.	Testament of Naphtali
Mart.	Martyrdom and Ascension	T. Zeb.	Testament of Zebulun
Ascen. Isa.	of Isaiah		

Qumran / Dead Sea Scrolls

1QpHab	Pesher Habakkuk
4Q37	Deut^j, the text of Deuteronomy

Other Jewish and Patristic Sources

Abbreviations appearing before tractate names indicate the following sources: Mishnah (m.), Tosefta (t.), Babylonian Talmud (b.), and Jerusalem/Palestinian Talmud (y.).

'Abot R. Nat.	'Abot de Rabbi Nathan	Pesah.	tractate Pesahim
Ag. Ap.	Josephus, *Against Apion*	Sanh.	tractate Sanhedrin
1 Clem.	1 Clement	Tg. Isa.	Targum Isaiah
Herm. Mand.	Shepherd of Hermas, Mandate(s)	Tg. Neof.	Targum Neofiti
		Tg. Ps.-J.	Targum Pseudo-Jonathan
Hor.	tractate Horayot		

Bible Texts and Versions

ASV	American Standard Version (1901)
CEB	Common English Bible (2011)
CEV	Contemporary English Version (1995)
CJB	Complete Jewish Bible (1998)

CSB	Christian Standard Bible (2017)
ESV	English Standard Version (2001)
KJV	King James Version (1611)
LXX	Septuagint, Greek Old Testament
MT	Masoretic Text
NA[28]	Nestle-Aland, *Novum Testamentum Graece*, 28th rev. ed., ed. E. and E. Nestle, B. and K. Aland, J. Karavidopoulos, C. M. Martini, and B. M. Metzger (Stuttgart: Deutsche Bibelgesellschaft, 2012)
NASB	New American Standard Version (2020)
NET	New English Translation (2006)
NIV	New International Version (2011)
NKJV	New King James Version (1982)
NLT	New Living Translation (2015)
NRSV	New Revised Standard Version (1989)
OG	Old Greek
SBLGNT	*The Greek New Testament: SBL Edition*, ed. Michael Holmes (2010)
Theod.	Theodotion's Greek translation of the Hebrew Bible (ca. 150 CE)
UBS[5]	United Bible Society, *The Greek New Testament*, 5th rev. ed., ed. B. Aland, K. Aland, J. Karavidopoulos, C. M. Martini, and B. M. Metzger (Stuttgart: Deutsche Bibelgesellschaft, 2014)
WEB	World English Bible (2000)

Modern Secondary Sources

AB	Anchor Bible
AGJU	Arbeiten zur Geschichte des antiken Judentums und des Urchristentums
AnBib	Analecta Biblica
ASNU	Acta Seminarii Neotestamentici Upsaliensis
AUS	American University Studies
AUSS	*Andrews University Seminary Studies*
BAFCS	The Book of Acts in Its First Century Setting
BBR	*Bulletin for Biblical Research*
BBRSup	Bulletin for Biblical Research Supplement
BDAG	W. Bauer, F. W. Danker, W. F. Arndt, and F. W. Gingrich, *Greek-English Lexicon of the New Testament and Other Early Christian Literature*, 3rd ed. (Chicago: University of Chicago Press, 2000)
BETL	Bibliotheca Ephemeridum Theologicarum Lovaniensium
BibInt	Biblical Interpretation Series
BR	*Biblical Research*
BSac	*Bibliotheca Sacra*
BZNW	Beihefte zur Zeitschrift für die neutestamentliche Wissenschaft
CBET	Contributions to Biblical Exegesis and Theology
CBQ	*Catholic Biblical Quarterly*
ConBNT	Coniectanea Biblica: New Testament Series
CSEL	Corpus Scriptorum Ecclesiasticorum
CurBR	*Currents in Biblical Research*

DBCI	*Dictionary of Biblical Criticism and Interpretation*, ed. S. E. Porter (New York: Routledge, 2007)
DJG¹	*Dictionary of Jesus and the Gospels*, ed. J. B. Green, S. McKnight, and I. H. Marshall (Downers Grove, IL: InterVarsity, 1992)
DJG²	*Dictionary of Jesus and the Gospels*, 2nd ed., ed. J. B. Green, J. K. Brown, and N. Perrin (Downers Grove, IL: IVP Academic, 2013)
DLNT	*Dictionary of the Later New Testament and Its Developments*, ed. R. P. Martin and P. H. Davids (Downers Grove, IL: InterVarsity, 1997)
DNTB	*Dictionary of New Testament Background*, ed. C. A. Evans and S. E. Porter (Downers Grove, IL: InterVarsity, 2000)
DPL	*Dictionary of Paul and His Letters*, ed. G. F. Hawthorne and R. P. Martin (Downers Grove, IL: InterVarsity, 1993)
DTIB	*Dictionary for Theological Interpretation of the Bible*, ed. K. J. Vanhoozer, C. G. Bartholomew, D. J. Treier, and N. T. Wright (Grand Rapids: Baker Academic, 2005)
ECL	Early Christianity and Its Literature
EGGNT	Exegetical Guide to the Greek New Testament
EncJud	*Encyclopedia Judaica*, ed. F. Skolnik and M. Berenbaum, 2nd ed., 22 vols. (Detroit: Macmillan Reference USA, 2007)
EvQ	*Evangelical Quarterly*
HNTC	Harper's New Testament Commentaries
ICC	International Crititcal Commentary
Int	*Interpretation*
ISBE	*International Standard Bible Encyclopedia*, ed. G. W. Bromiley, 4 vols. (Grand Rapids: Eerdmans, 1979–88)
ISBL	Indiana Studies in Biblical Literature
JAJSup	Journal of Ancient Judaism Supplements
JBL	*Journal of Biblical Literature*
JE	*The Jewish Encyclopedia*, ed. C. Adler and I. Singer, 12 vols. (New York: Funk & Wagnalls, 1901–6)
JETS	*Journal of the Evangelical Theological Society*
JSNT	*Journal for the Study of the New Testament*
JSNTSup	Journal for the Study of the New Testament Supplement Series
JTI	*Journal of Theological Interpretation*
JTS	*Journal of Theological Studies*
LHB	The Library of Hebrew Bible
LNTS	The Library of New Testament Studies
NDBT	*New Dictionary of Biblical Theology: Exploring the Unity & Diversity of Scripture*, ed. B. S. Rosner, T. D. Alexander, G. Goldsworthy, and D. A. Carson (Downers Grove, IL: InterVarsity, 2000)
Neot	*Neotestamentica*
NICNT	New International Commentary on the New Testament
NIDNTTE	*New International Dictionary of New Testament Theology and Exegesis*, ed. M. Silva, 5 vols. (Grand Rapids: Zondervan, 2014)
NIGTC	New International Greek Testament Commentary
NovT	*Novum Testamentum*
NovTSup	Supplements to Novum Testamentum

NSBT	New Studies in Biblical Theology
NTS	*New Testament Studies*
NTSI	New Testament and the Scriptures of Israel
RBS	Resources for Biblical Study
SBL	Society of Biblical Literature
SBLMS	Society of Biblical Literature Monograph Series
SBLSP	Society of Biblical Literature Seminar Papers
SBLStBL	Society of Biblical Literature Studies in Biblical Literature
SCS	Septuagint and Cognate Studies
SNT	Studien zum Neuen Testament
SNTA	Studiorum Novi Testamenti Auxilia
SNTSMS	Society for New Testament Studies Monograph Series
SSEJC	Studies in Scripture in Early Judaism and Christianity
StBibLit	Studies in Biblical Literature (Lang)
STDJ	Studies on the Texts of the Desert of Judah
SymS	Symposium Series
TENTS	Texts and Editions for New Testament Study
Them	*Themelios*
ThTo	*Theology Today*
TNTC	Tyndale New Testament Commentaries
TOTE	Through Old Testament Eyes
TSAJ	Texte und Studien zum antiken Judentum
VCSup	Supplements to Vigiliae Christianae
VTSup	Supplements to Vetus Testamentum
WUNT	Wissenschaftliche Untersuchungen zum Neuen Testament
ZAW	*Zeitschrift für die alttestamentliche Wissenschaft*
ZEB	*Zondervan Encyclopedia of the Bible*, ed. M. C. Tenney and M. Silva, rev. ed. (Grand Rapids: Zondervan, 2009)
ZECNT	Zondervan Exegetical Commentary on the New Testament
ZTK	*Zeitschrift für Theologie und Kirche*

1

Introduction to Studying the New Testament Use of the Old Testament

You search the Scriptures because you think that in them you have eternal life; and it is they that bear witness about me.

John 5:39

And beginning with Moses and all the Prophets, he interpreted to them in all the Scriptures the things concerning himself.

Luke 24:27

The Relationship between the Testaments

When considering the diverse elements of the First Testament—what Christians call the Old Testament (OT) and what others call the Hebrew Bible—the first-century Jewish historian Josephus commented that "we do not possess myriads of inconsistent books, conflicting with each other. Our books, those which are justly accredited, are but two and twenty, and contain the record of all time" (Josephus, *Ag. Ap.* 1.8 §38).[1] His people, Josephus claims, are

1. Josephus's count of twenty-two books is a variation of the more standard number of twenty-four books in the Hebrew Bible, but it is possible to consider both numbers as actually referring to the same contents as the thirty-nine books of the Protestant OT. The Hebrew Bible simply keeps together as single books what the Protestant canon separates into individual

devoted to the unity of their Scriptures. Even more so, the Christian church has embraced such a commitment to the unity of the whole Bible, that is, a commitment not only to the unity of the OT but also to its unity with the New Testament (NT) as the testimony about Jesus, the fulfiller of the OT.[2] The connections between the OT and the NT as the two major portions of the Christian Scriptures is not as self-evident as people might expect. The connections may well seem more obvious to the one holding a Bible and looking at its table of contents than it does to one actually reading its diverse contents or hearing people talk about the Bible. There is, in fact, a long history—on both the popular and the scholarly levels—of denying any real integration of the two Testaments despite the centuries of their being bound between the same two covers.

In antiquity, Marcion of Sinope (ca. 85–160 CE) rejected the deity described in the Hebrew Scriptures (i.e., the OT) as a warring creator god who had to be lower than the God of the NT. He preferred to give his allegiance to the NT God for exhibiting love and mercy and for sending Jesus as the Christ. Rather than holding to the complete **canon of Scripture**,[3] Marcion's convictions led him to reject the whole of the OT, and his unique theological perspective led him to adopt a canon of Scripture containing only eleven books. Thus, Marcion is the first person known to us today to have published what might be called a NT canon, but he referred to it in two parts as "Gospel" and "Apostle." Marcion's "Gospel" was an otherwise unnamed and modified version of what we call the Gospel of Luke, and his "Apostle" was a collection of ten modified letters of Paul, whom he claimed was the only faithful apostle of Christ. In both his "Gospel" and "Apostle," Marcion simply removed references to the Hebrew Scriptures and that which might give hint to the correctness or authority of the old ways. Despite the fact that

---

volumes. So counting 1 and 2 Samuel, 1 and 2 Kings, 1 and 2 Chronicles, Ezra–Nehemiah, and the Book of the Twelve (Minor Prophets) as single books brings the number to twenty-four; reckoning Judges–Ruth and Jeremiah–Lamentations as compound books brings the number to twenty-two ($\approx$ the number of letters in the Hebrew alphabet); see Roger T. Beckwith, "The Canon of Scripture," *NDBT*, 29.

2. On the complex question of when the canon of the Hebrew Bible was finalized, see such works as John W. Wenham, *Christ and the Bible*, 3rd ed. (Grand Rapids: Baker, 1994; reprint, Eugene, OR: Wipf & Stock, 2009), 128–53; Roger T. Beckwith, *The Old Testament Canon of the New Testament Church and Its Background in Early Judaism* (Grand Rapids: Eerdmans, 1985; reprint, Eugene, OR: Wipf & Stock, 2008); F. F. Bruce, *The Canon of Scripture* (Downers Grove, IL: InterVarsity, 1988), 27–114; E. Earle Ellis, *The Old Testament in Early Christianity: Canon and Interpretation in the Light of Modern Research* (Tübingen: Mohr Siebeck, 1991; reprint, Eugene, OR: Wipf & Stock, 2003), 3–50; and the essays in Lee Martin McDonald and James A. Sanders, eds., *The Canon Debate: On the Origins and Formation of the Bible* (Peabody, MA: Hendrickson, 2002).

3. Terms marked with boldface appear in the glossary at the end of the book.

Marcion's views were adduced to be heretical and unaligned with true faith in Christ and led to his excommunication ca. 144 CE, Marcionite theology maintained official followers for years and led to written responses by early Christian apologists Justin Martyr, Irenaeus, and Tertullian.[4]

And still today, there are scholars suggesting that the OT and the NT have little in common. Furthermore, at the popular level, whether officially or unwittingly, there are congregations calling themselves Christian that prove to be Marcionite in their theology and practice, given their rejection of the OT (in either active dismissal or passive neglect) and their favoring of the NT. Sometimes one even hears the label "New Testament Christians" as if it were possible to be a Christian without the OT. Surely this brings about an oxymoronic situation. That is, many believers who claim the name of Christ have, in fact, rejected the Scriptures that Christ himself claimed hold some kind of permanent authority (e.g., Matt. 5:17). Can a person be a "New Testament Christian" without embracing the OT Scriptures that the Messiah in the NT actually cites approvingly?

Instructively, the Gospel of Luke reports that Jesus scolded the disciples on the road to Emmaus, "O foolish ones, and slow of heart to believe all that the prophets have spoken! Was it not necessary that the Christ should suffer these things and enter into his glory?" And Luke adds, "And beginning with Moses and all the Prophets, he interpreted to them in all the Scriptures the things concerning himself" (24:25–27). Then with intentional repetition a couple of paragraphs later, Luke recounts Jesus addressing a larger group of followers, "These are my words that I spoke to you while I was still with you, that everything written about me in the Law of Moses and the Prophets and the Psalms must be fulfilled." And again Luke adds, "Then he opened their minds to understand the Scriptures, and said to them, 'Thus it is written, that the Christ should suffer and on the third day rise from the dead, and that repentance for the forgiveness of sins should be proclaimed in his name to all nations, beginning from Jerusalem'" (24:44–47). In other words, Jesus clearly saw a connection between the Hebrew Scriptures and the events of his life. This necessitates a connection between what we now call the OT and the NT. Later I will touch on Jesus's rationale for this correlation, but at this juncture we should realize that we make ourselves vulnerable to a rebuke from Jesus himself if we refuse to recognize a connection between

---

4. The classic work on Marcion is that by Adolf von Harnack, *Marcion: The Gospel of the Alien God*, trans. John E. Steely and Lyle D. Bierma (Durham, NC: Labyrinth, 1990 [German original 1921]). For brief introductions to Marcion, see Bruce, *Canon of Scripture*, 134–44; Robert McLachlan Wilson, "Marcion," *ZEB* 4:74–75. See also Joseph B. Tyson, *Marcion and Luke-Acts: A Defining Struggle* (Columbia: University of South Carolina, 2006).

the OT and the NT. There is a unity of Scripture, and somehow Jesus is that unity.[5]

Fortunately, a number of scholarly treatments in the past seventy years help us explore and envision the unity of the Christian Scriptures.[6] Of course, there is hardly unanimity on the question, and even among those who view the OT and NT as united, there is great diversity regarding how to think about that unity.[7] Nevertheless, the possibility of unity is being repeatedly, if also robustly, affirmed. This unity is not one where either Testament is thought to have been merely added to the other, as if by some stroke of luck enough empty chairs were discovered so that more books could be invited to join the party. The NT was not simply added to the OT, nor was the OT somehow later remembered as something to be added to the NT. Given the actions of God in the world, the one Testament grew out of the other, but not merely as part of the other. As Bernd Janowski describes it,

> While in the process of its own canonization, the Bible of Israel was appropriated by the authors of the New Testament. Only through this appropriation, and not in any other way, was the foundation laid on which the Christian Bible took its shape. . . . Throughout this process, it became clear that the New Testament, considered from its own biblical hermeneutic, did not understand itself to constitute an autonomous canon, independent of the reading of the Old Testament. Only together with that first part was the New Testament seen to constitute the one Christian Bible that was composed of two parts. The New Testament was conceived as a separate unit; it was not, however, conceived

5. But I want to be quick to point out that, even as the Jesus of the NT alone makes sense of the OT, it is also the case that the OT alone makes sense of the Jesus of the NT. Brevard Childs observes that "it was not by chance that the witness to Jesus Christ in the New Testament was shaped by the study of the Old Testament"; Brevard S. Childs, "The Nature of the Christian Bible: One Book, Two Testaments," in *The Rule of Faith: Scripture, Canon, and Creed in a Critical Age*, ed. Ephraim Radner and George Sumner (Harrisburg, PA: Morehouse, 1998), 120.

6. See the "Resources on the Unity of the Old and New Testaments as Christian Scripture" section of the bibliography in app. B of this book. For bibliographic references to earlier works, see Floyd V. Filson, "The Unity of the Old and New Testaments: A Bibliographical Survey," *Int* 5 (1951): 134–52.

7. As John Barton sees it, for example, some seek to reconcile differences within Scripture that turn out to be only apparent conflicts, others search for a higher unity that is tolerant of discrepancies (such as a developmental history-of-salvation approach), and still others simply seek to read the Bible as if it is unified in some higher way by the reading of it as Scripture; see Barton, "Unity and Diversity in the Biblical Canon," in *Die Einheit der Schrift und die Vielfalt des Kanons = The Unity of Scripture and the Diversity of the Canon*, ed. John Barton and Michael Wolter, BZNW 118 (New York: De Gruyter, 2003), 11–26. For a recent treatment of the unity of the NT with the OT that properly stresses the newness of the NT, see Donald A. Hagner, *How New Is the New Testament? First-Century Judaism and the Emergence of Christianity* (Grand Rapids: Baker Academic, 2018), esp. 1–21 and 169–79.

as a book independent of the Old Testament, simply to be placed externally facing it.[8]

The two Testaments of the Christian Bible are organically interrelated. The very development of the NT is dependent on the OT, even as faith in Jesus as the Christ of the NT is dependent on what the OT said about the Christ who was coming. We must recognize, in the words of Alexander Kirkpatrick, "Without the New Testament the Old Testament would be a magnificent failure; without the Old Testament the New Testament would be an inexplicable phenomenon. The New Testament presumes and explains the Old Testament. The Old Testament lays the foundations and provides the pre-suppositions for the New Testament. The New Testament does not supersede, but illuminates the Old Testament."[9] This has been the case since the beginnings of Christianity, such that seventy years ago R. V. G. Tasker referred to the recent increased interest in the OT's importance for Christianity as "a rediscovery of the obvious."[10]

But what might be less obvious is the observation that, for the first Christians, the canonical continuity between the OT and the NT was not a mere matter of prequel and sequel but one of secure foundation and intended development.[11] Indeed, the manner in which the NT writers recount the story of Jesus betrays their work to come from a context of believers reflecting on the stories of Israel's Scriptures. The earliest Christian communities viewed the Jesus story as not only deeply rooted in the OT but also as a flowering of the Hebrew Scriptures such that the Scriptures bear a new yet organic and climactic fruit. And in the Gospels in particular, the NT writers have indicated for us that this view of things goes back to Jesus himself.[12] Yes, the NT becomes a continuation of the OT, and yes, there is a significant break—and

8. Bernd Janowski, "The One God of the Two Testaments: Basic Questions of a Biblical Theology," *ThTo* 57 (2000): 305, cf. 297–324; this article was translated by Christine Helmer from its German original, "Der eine Gott der beiden Testamente," *ZTK* 95 (1998): 1–36.

9. Alexander F. Kirkpatrick, "How to Read the Old Testament," in *Critical Questions*, ed. James Adderley (London: Brown, Langham, 1903), 8–9. This is reminiscent of a dictum assigned to Augustine: "The New Testament lies hidden in the Old, and the Old is made plain in the New"; cited in Archibald M. Hunter, *The Work and Words of Jesus* (Philadelphia: Westminster, 1950), 71. See Augustine, *Quaestiones in Heptateuchum* 2.73 (CSEL 28.2:141): ". . . et in vetere novum lateat et in novo vetus pateat." See also Anthony Tyrrell Hanson, *The Living Utterances of God: The New Testament Exegesis of the Old* (London: Darton, Longman & Todd, 1983), 214–20.

10. R. V. G. Tasker, *The Old Testament in the New Testament*, 2nd ed. (Grand Rapids: Eerdmans, 1954), 10.

11. Janowski, "One God," 308.

12. See Richard B. Hays, *Echoes of Scripture in the Gospels* (Waco: Baylor University Press, 2016), 5.

development—moving from one Testament to the next. But these two large sections of the Christian Scriptures are united in Christ and inevitably must be considered together.

The OT and NT are organically and inextricably intertwined. And to read the NT well, we must recognize this intricate indivisibility of the Bible. All this to say, as Grant Osborne phrases it, "It is impossible to overstate the importance of understanding the use of the Old Testament for New Testament research."[13]

The Richness of This Study

Exploring the relationship between the OT and the NT actually has a long history, dating back to the patristic church of the second century.[14] Even so, the theological unity of the Bible has experienced a particularly fertile theological discussion in the last few decades.[15] The concepts proposed for consideration in the exploration of this unity include Christology, salvation history, typology and *sensus plenior*, promise and **fulfillment**, continuity and discontinuity, and covenant.[16] These kinds of theological connections between the OT and the NT that presume the two to be bound together as Holy Scripture are, in fact, testified to by studying the ways the NT uses the Old. And while the theological connections are important, the task of this volume has the narrower goal of examining the ways in which the OT makes appearances in the NT.

Specifically studying the NT use of the OT has seen a renewal of interest in recent years.[17] Reasons for this renewal include (a) an increase in biblical

13. Grant R. Osborne, "The Old Testament in the New Testament," in *The Hermeneutical Spiral: A Comprehensive Introduction to Biblical Interpretation*, rev. ed. (Downers Grove, IL: InterVarsity, 2006), 343.

14. For a brief but thorough history of research on the NT use of the OT from the patristic church to the twentieth century, see E. Earle Ellis, "Quotations in the NT," *ISBE* 4:18–22.

15. It is almost an oddity that Jewish scholars rarely engage in investigating the theological unity of the Hebrew Scriptures themselves. Thus, even apart from the Christian embrace of the NT over against its rejection by Judaism, the concern to uncover the scriptural unity of the Bible—both Old and New Testaments—is a particularly Christian concern; see Graeme L. Goldsworthy, "Relationship of Old Testament and New Testament," *NDBT*, 82.

16. For a brief treatment of these kinds of concepts, see Goldsworthy, "Relationship of Old Testament and New Testament," 86–89. These ideas receive a fuller treatment in the modern classic, David L. Baker, *Two Testaments, One Bible: The Theological Relationship between the Old and New Testaments*, 3rd ed. (Downers Grove, IL: InterVarsity, 2010); Baker provides his own summary of these concepts in a section titled "Towards a 'Biblical' Solution" on 271–76 of his concluding chapter.

17. See esp. Steve Moyise, *The Old Testament in the New*, 2nd ed., T&T Clark Approaches to Biblical Studies (New York: Bloomsbury T&T Clark, 2015); G. K. Beale and D. A. Carson, eds., *Commentary on the New Testament Use of the Old Testament* (Grand Rapids: Baker

theology studies seeking to understand the unity of Scripture (as just mentioned above), (b) an increase in studies examining the **Septuagint** (i.e., the Hebrew Scriptures that were translated into Greek in the third century BCE), (c) an increase in studies examining the NT in light of literary theory, and (d) the continuation of studies of the **Dead Sea Scrolls** and the use of the OT · in those first-century documents.[18] This matrix of Scripture-related investigations has naturally led to an increase in examinations of the OT as used in the NT.

The richness of this topic has resulted in various foci in studies of the use of the OT in the NT. Some have examined Jewish exegetical practices in the Second Temple and post-NT eras.[19] Others focus primarily on textual matters analyzing questions about the most likely text forms used by the NT authors, such as, whether a citation is dependent upon a source text written in Hebrew (the **Masoretic Text**, or **MT**), Greek (the Septuagint, or **LXX**), or something else.[20] Still others attend to theological matters and, of course, hermeneutical issues.[21] My intention here is to examine some of the basic elements in studying the use of the OT in the NT, and in doing so, I will touch on many of the issues just mentioned.

Academic, 2007); and G. K. Beale, *Handbook on the New Testament Use of the Old Testament: Exegesis and Interpretation* (Grand Rapids: Baker Academic, 2012).

18. Steve Moyise, *Evoking Scripture: Seeing the Old Testament in the New* (London: T&T Clark, 2008), 1–2.

19. See Ellis, *Old Testament in Early Christianity*; Richard N. Longenecker, *Biblical Exegesis in the Apostolic Period*, 2nd ed. (Grand Rapids: Eerdmans, 1999); Craig A. Evans, "The Old Testament in the New," in *The Face of New Testament Studies: A Survey of Recent Research*, ed. Scot McKnight and Grant R. Osborne (Grand Rapids: Baker Academic, 2004), 130–45; Craig A. Evans, "Jewish Exegesis," *DTIB*, 380–84.

20. See Moisés Silva, "The New Testament Use of the Old Testament: Text Form and Authority," in *Scripture and Truth*, ed. D. A. Carson and John D. Woodbridge (Grand Rapids: Zondervan, 1983), 147–65; and R. Timothy McLay, *The Use of the Septuagint in New Testament Research* (Grand Rapids: Eerdmans, 2003). On Paul's use of various text forms, see particularly Moisés Silva, "Old Testament in Paul," *DPL*, 630–42, esp. 630–34 and the extensive charting of OT citations in Paul sorted by text form on 631. See also the discussion by Karen H. Jobes, "'It Is Written': The Septuagint and Evangelical Doctrine of Scripture," in *Evangelical Scholarship, Restrospects and Prospects: Essays in Honor of Stanley N. Gundry*, ed. Dirk R. Buursma, Katya Covrett, and Verlyn D. Verbrugge (Grand Rapids: Zondervan, 2017), 137–55.

21. Important volumes covering a variety of debated issues related to the OT in the NT include G. K. Beale, ed., *The Right Doctrine from the Wrong Texts? Essays on the Use of the Old Testament in the New* (Grand Rapids: Baker Academic, 1994); and Kenneth Berding and Jonathan Lunde, eds., *Three Views on the New Testament Use of the Old Testament*, Counterpoints: Bible and Theology (Grand Rapids: Zondervan, 2008). Regarding the problematic implications that the use of the OT in the NT has on the trustworthiness of Scripture, see esp. Douglas J. Moo and Andrew David Naselli, "The Problem of the New Testament's Use of the Old Testament," in *The Enduring Authority of the Christian Scriptures*, ed. D. A. Carson (Grand Rapids: Eerdmans, 2016), 702–46.

Issues Involved in This Study

There are a number of methodological issues and presuppositional matters to consider when studying the rich field of the NT use of the OT. Dennis Stamps has outlined ten issues under the headings of terminology, hermeneutics, and theology (see table 1.1). Some of these matters are narrow in focus (e.g., the kind of citation), and others are broader (e.g., Jewish background) or more sweeping (e.g., historical factors). I have already addressed above one of the theological issues Stamps mentions (i.e., the relationship between the OT and the NT), and I will address several of the other matters in chapters yet to come. But the first terminological issue Stamps discusses is quite fundamental and worth addressing here.[22]

Stamps notes that it is somewhat anachronistic to use the term *Old Testament* when discussing the first-century time period. The NT did not exist yet, so none of the NT writers regarded the Scripture they were citing as the Old Testament. The label **First Testament** is not much better, since it begs for a second. Some scholars prefer the label **Hebrew Bible** or **Hebrew Scriptures**, but this is likewise unfitting for this specific field in view of how often the NT writers are actually quoting from the Old Greek translation of the Scriptures (the Septuagint, or LXX), and some citations are even related to Aramaic targumic traditions.[23] Using a label like "Scriptures of Israel" is somewhat better, but this tag can have unhelpful (albeit unintended) nationalistic vibes. Thus, Stamps suggests that "Jewish sacred writings" may be the more accurate way to refer to the Scriptures cited by the early followers of Jesus. Nonetheless, rather than use awkward and cumbersome phraseology in the name of precision, I adopt here the parlance common among scholars today and refer simply to "the Old Testament in the New Testament" and "the New Testament use of the Old Testament." Scholars understand this way of speaking as a fitting truncation without ignoring this particular methodological concern.[24]

---

22. Dennis L. Stamps, "The Use of the Old Testament in the New Testament as a Rhetorical Device: A Methodological Proposal," in *Hearing the Old Testament in the New Testament*, ed. Stanley E. Porter, McMaster New Testament Studies (Grand Rapids: Eerdmans, 2006), 9–37; for the following discussion, see 10–12.

23. On the technical differences between the Septuagint (LXX) and the Old Greek (OG), see McLay, *Use of the Septuagint*, 1–16. Following conventional usage, I will use LXX to refer to the Greek translation of the Jewish Scriptures in general. Donald Hagner quips, "The use of the Septuagint is so prevalent throughout the New Testament that we would not be far off the mark in referring to the Septuagint as the Bible of the early Church. In addition to the actual quotations, the influence of the Septuagint upon the New Testament in terms of allusory language, specific vocabulary, and conceptuality is incalculable"; Donald A. Hagner, "The Old Testament in the New Testament," in *Interpreting the Word of God: Festschrift in Honor of Steven Barabas*, ed. Samuel J. Schultz and Morris A. Inch (Chicago: Moody, 1976), 87.

24. Cf. Hanson, *Living Utterances of God*, 1.

TABLE 1.1

Methodological Issues for Studying
the New Testament Use of the Old Testament

A. Terminology	B. Hermeneutics	C. Theology
1. Definition of "Old Testament"	4. Historical factors	7. Relationship between the OT and the NT
2. Kind of citation	5. Literary dimensions	8. Theological implications of the form of text cited (MT, LXX, targum)
3. Jewish background	6. Interpretive issues	9. Canonical implications of apocryphal and pseudepigraphical citations
		10. Theological implications of creative citations (e.g., contextual adherence)

Adapted from Dennis L. Stamps, "Use of the Old Testament in the New Testament," 10–23.

After discussing several methodological matters similar to those mentioned by Stamps, Darrell Bock, in one of his several contributions to this field of study, outlines six theological presuppositions or hermeneutical axioms that lay behind the NT use of the OT (see table 1.2).[25] Three of the six presuppositions held by the writers of the NT were shared with Judaism and the other three were not shared with Judaism. Foundational for both is that (what we now call) the OT is God's Word that forms a unified message, maintains relevance through the ages, and is true (i.e., its promises will eventually be fulfilled). Given this mutual view of the OT as Scripture from God, it is not surprising that early Christians shared other theological convictions with first-century Judaism. In addition to their shared view of (1) Scripture as God's communication to humanity, Bock points out that Judaism and the early Christians also shared belief in (2) community representation, meaning that a single member can represent the whole community so that what is said of one member can be applied to another who fits the community identity, and (3) the conviction that God works in history via escalating patterns of realization. On the other hand, the early Christians held three convictions in distinction from Judaism: (4) that the time of scriptural fulfillment had begun with the life, death, and resurrection of Jesus; (5) that fulfillment can

25. Darrell L. Bock, "Scripture Citing Scripture: Use of the Old Testament in the New," in *Interpreting the New Testament Text: Introduction to the Art and Science of Exegesis*, ed. Darrell L. Bock and Buist M. Fanning (Wheaton: Crossway, 2006), 261–68. Bock gives credit to the similar discussion of such presuppositions in E. Earle Ellis, "How the New Testament Uses the Old," in *New Testament Interpretation: Essays on Principles and Methods*, ed. I. Howard Marshall (Grand Rapids: Eerdmans, 1977), 199–219.

come in stages (the now and the not yet)—God's promises had their inaugural fulfillment in Jesus but have a still greater consummation yet to come; and (6) that Jesus is the Christ, the goal and culmination of God's promises in Scripture. Given this array of theological convictions, it should not be surprising to find the NT writers using interpretive methods that are similar to first-century Judaism. Conversely, given their convictions, it should not be surprising to find the NT writers reaching conclusions that differ from first-century Judaism.

Now, it is worth noting here that the christological presuppositions about which Christianity and Judaism have disagreed may be too strongly stated as *pre*suppositions. That is to say, the Christians writing the NT documents could be charged with circular reasoning if they conclude that Jesus is the Messiah by presuming at the very beginning that Jesus is the Messiah. Similarly, the first-century Jews who did not believe in Jesus could be charged with circular reasoning by concluding that Jesus is not the Messiah from the presumption that Jesus is not the Messiah. So if we are speaking of strict *pre*suppositions, it might be better to word the contrasting commitments like this: The NT writers presumed that God could indeed fulfill Scripture by sending his Son as the prophesied messianic figure, and the first-century Jews presumed that God would not/could not fulfill Scripture by sending his Son as the Messiah. This nuance makes better sense of the noncircular arguments that are offered in the NT to prove (i.e., not merely to presume) that Jesus is the Christ. After all, Apollos "vigorously refuted his Jewish opponents in public debate, proving from the Scriptures that Jesus was the Messiah" (Acts 18:28 NIV; cf. 9:22).

G. K. Beale likewise discusses the theological presuppositions held by NT writers, but he does not make as strong a distinction between those held by the early Christians and those held by non-Christian Jews in the first century. The presuppositions that Beale outlines are five in number and in an overlapping fashion correspond somewhat to those Bock presents (the two are compared in table 1.2). Beale's list is as follows: (1) there is the apparent assumption of corporate representation (cf. Bock's presup. 2); (2) Jesus as the Messiah is representative of the true Israel of the OT and the true Israel (the church) in the NT (cf. Bock's presups. 2 and 6); (3) history is unified by a wise and sovereign plan so that the earlier parts are designed to correspond and point to the later parts (cf. Bock's presup. 3); (4) the era of eschatological fulfillment has come in Christ but has not been fully consummated (cf. Bock's presups. 4 and 5); and, as a consequence of the preceding presupposition, it follows that (5) the later parts of biblical history function as the broader context for interpreting earlier parts because they all have the same ultimate divine author who inspires the various human authors of Scripture. One deduction from this premise is that Christ is the goal toward which the OT pointed and is the end-time center of redemptive history, which is the key to interpreting the earlier portions of the OT and its promises (cf. Bock's presups. 1 and 6).[26]

In a footnote referencing Bock's discussion of these presuppositions, Beale suggests that Bock does not include his presupposition 5 (canonical contextual interpretation as the key to interpreting the NT and Christ as the key to interpreting the OT), but this seems to overlook how Bock's presuppositions 1 and 6 combine to address this.[27] More fittingly, Beale notes that Bock does not include his presupposition 2 (Christ and the church as true Israel) and comments on how scholars (like Bock) who hold to a dispensational theology of some kind try to avoid a "replacement theology" that removes hope for the salvation of Israel as a nation. But Beale himself offers a brief and helpful explanation that a person can hold to the idea of Christ as the true Israel and still have room for a nationalist hope for Israel's salvation, noting, "Any such salvation would be in their identification with Christ as true Israel."[28] This observation actually draws on the corporate representation presupposition held by both Bock (2) and Beale (1), so I suggest that even here Beale's presupposition 2 is sufficiently paralleled by the overlap of Bock's presuppositions 2 and 6.

One additional feature of Beale's discussion, which differs from Bock, is worth commenting on here. While Bock appreciably distinguishes between presuppositions that the NT writers shared with first-century Judaism and those not shared with them, Beale is more nuanced and suggests that the early Christian community's presuppositions may not have been radically new and distinguishable from the broader Jewish community with their dependence on the Hebrew Scriptures. He observes how the Qumran community held to some version of the first four of the five presuppositions he identifies.[29] This helps correct for the concern mentioned above that these presuppositions can be over-emphasized as foregone conclusions (i.e., *pre*suppositions). That the writers of the NT were so rooted in the OT and shared the same general

---

26. Beale, *Handbook*, 53 and 96–97. In addition to Bock's work, Beale notes other scholarly discussions of these presuppositions; see Ellis, *Old Testament in Early Christianity*, 101–16; Longenecker, *Biblical Exegesis*, 76–79, 126–27, 134, 155; and Klyne Snodgrass, "The Use of the Old Testament in the New," in *Interpreting the New Testament: Essays on Methods and Issues*, ed. David Alan Black and David S. Dockery, 2nd ed. (Nashville: Broadman & Holman, 2001), 214–18.

27. Beale, *Handbook*, 97n10.

28. Beale, *Handbook*, 97n11.

29. Beale, *Handbook*, 101.

TABLE 1.2

Presuppositions behind the New Testament Use of the Old Testament

Bock	Beale
A. Christian presuppositions shared with Judaism: 1. The Bible is God's Word	1. There is corporate representation.
2. A single member can represent the whole community.	2. Christ as the Messiah is representative of the true Israel.
3. God works in similar patterns in history.	3. History is unified (cf., e.g., Matt. 5:17; 11:13; 13:16–17).
B. Christian presuppositions not shared with Judaism:	4. Eschatological fulfillment has come in Christ but has not been fully consummated.
4. These are the days of fulfillment.	5. The same divine author inspires the various authors of Scripture such that Christ turns out to be the ultimate goal and end-time center of redemptive history.
5. Fulfillment can come in stages.	
6. Jesus is the Christ, the culmination of God's promises in Scripture.	

Note: This table summarizes the views found in Bock, "Scripture Citing Scripture," 261–68; and Beale, Handbook, 95–102; cf. 53.

worldview of the OT writers makes it difficult to claim that the first Christians were from an interpretive community bent on distorting the meaning of the OT texts.[30] That the NT writers' conclusions about Jesus Christ differed from non-Christian Judaism does not in itself entail the interference of illegitimate hermeneutical presumptions.

Various Perspectives on This Study

In light of the various ways to outline the methodological and presuppositional issues involved, scholars have gravitated toward different perspectives on studying the NT use of the OT. By "perspectives" I refer not to the step-by-step methodologies utilized by scholars (for this, see the next section below) but to the various sets of perceptions that affect their approaches to interpreting the NT's use of the OT. A scholar's perspective involves a wider realm of factors, including the methodological issues and presuppositions mentioned above and how those matters affect one's understanding of exegesis and divine involvement in interpretation.

Taking these kinds of factors into account, Michael Vlach presents a taxonomy of seven different perspectives to NT citations of the OT.[31] For each

---

30. Beale, Handbook, 102.

31. Michael J. Vlach, The Old in the New: Understanding How the New Testament Authors Quoted the Old Testament (The Woodlands, TX: Kress Biblical Resources, 2021; Sun Valley, CA: The Master's Seminary Press, 2021), 1–58.

view, Vlach describes the perspective, names representative adherents, and offers a brief discussion of problematic issues. Table 1.3 displays these seven different perspectives. Those interested in a closer analysis of the various perspectives outlined by Vlach are encouraged to engage in the brief and accessible presentation in his book as well as the other comparative analyses

TABLE 1.3

Seven Perspectives on Studying
the New Testament Citations of the Old Testament

1. Single meaning / multiple implications view (or consistent contextual use of the OT by the NT writers approach). Capitalizing on the difference between the meaning of a text and the significance (or applications) of a text, this view suggests that the NT use of the OT is always consistent with the OT author's intended meaning (even if the specific NT application was not in his mind). Representative scholars include Walter C. Kaiser, Abner Chou, and Michael J. Vlach.

2. Human meaning plus fuller divine meaning view (or *sensus plenior* approach). With Scripture resulting from a confluence of human and divine authorship, this view suggests that some OT passages have an additional divinely intended "fuller sense" (*sensus plenior*) hidden from the OT writer (and not found in the OT context) but revealed to NT writers. Representative scholars include Raymond E. Brown, Graeme Goldsworthy, and J. I. Packer.

3. Second Temple Judaism view (or NT writers used Jewish interpretive principles of their day approach). This view suggests that the exegetical procedures of the NT writers exhibit, at least sometimes, the noncontextual hermeneutical methods common in the Second Temple era, which led them to use the OT out of context on occasion. Representative scholars include Richard N. Longenecker and Peter Enns.

4. Canonical interpretation view (or broader canon as basis for understanding the OT approach). This view suggests that the earlier parts of Scripture (e.g., the OT) must always be interpreted in light of later revelation (e.g., the NT); thus, the whole canon of Scripture is the proper context for interpreting any part of it. Representative scholars include Bruce Waltke, G. K. Beale, and Douglas A. Oss.

5. Inspired *sensus plenior* application view (or inspired subjectivity approach). This view suggests that the NT writers interpreted the OT in a literal way via grammatical-historical methods and also on occasion, apart from the OT contextual meaning, unveil new and nonliteral fuller-sense applications by way of divine inspiration. Representative scholars include Robert L. Thomas.

6. Historical-exegetical and theological-canonical view (or eclectic approach). Rather than an either/or approach, this view takes a both/and perspective by applying solutions from several of the other views to problematic citations of the OT in the NT. Representative scholars include Darrell L. Bock and Douglas J. Moo.

7. NT reinterpretation of the OT view (or NT priority over the OT approach). This view suggests that the OT must be reinterpreted by the NT, a reinterpretation that may well change the referents of an OT passage to something entirely different. Representative scholars include George E. Ladd, Kim Riddlebarger, and Stephen Sizer.

Note: This table provides a summary of Michael J. Vlach, *Old in the New*, 1–58.

he mentions.[32] It is important to note that Vlach's seven-part taxonomy is concerned specifically with citations of the OT found in the NT.[33] When discussing how NT authors use the OT, however, we must acknowledge that OT citations, though numerous, are not the only way that NT authors make use of the OT Scriptures.

An examination of the use of the OT in the New can go far beyond looking merely at citations, so it is not necessary at this juncture to select a particular perspective from the seven Vlach lists. Some of the ideas I offer in the present volume may cause certain perspectives to be seen more favorably, others to be ruled out altogether, and still others to be blended together somehow. In fact, when taking into consideration several other kinds of uses of the OT by NT authors beyond citations, a broader eclectic approach may be deemed most helpful.[34] But how should one go about examining a particular instance of the NT using an OT passage? Let us consider the issue of a procedure for this kind of study.

Procedures Used in This Study

Informed by the methodological and presuppositional issues and guided by the theological convictions of their perspectives, various scholars suggest specific procedures for how one might study the use of the OT in the NT. As is true in explanations of biblical hermeneutics in general, scholars working on the NT use of the OT are often quick to describe their procedures less as scientific stages to be completed in precise order and more as important facets to be included in the artistic endeavor of proper interpretation. Some scholars explain the process in a general manner; others are more detailed in their descriptions, including discussions of methodological concerns. Some are more directive in giving steps to follow; others are more suggestive by encouraging particular avenues of inquiry.

32. Vlach refers to the analyses offered by Darrell L. Bock, "Evangelicals and the Use of the Old Testament in the New: Parts 1 and 2," *BSac* 142 (1985): 209–23, 306–19; Robert L. Thomas, "The New Testament Use of the Old Testament," in *Evangelical Hermeneutics: The New versus the Old* (Grand Rapids: Kregel, 2002), 241–69; Berding and Lunde, eds., *Three Views*; and Rynold D. Dean, *Evangelical Hermeneutics and the New Testament Use of the Old Testament* (Iron River, WI: Veritypath, 2009).

33. Vlach (*Old in the New*, 72) counts 357 "quotations of the OT in the NT," and other scholars count a few more or a few less than him; see the discussion toward the end of chap. 2 below.

34. Note that the sixth perspective in Vlach's citation taxonomy is an "eclectic" category for blended approaches. I suggest here that, even among those of us insisting that the NT authors always *cited* the OT with a proper respect for its context, we must acknowledge that the NT authors also *use* the OT in ways other than citation. I think this recognition goes a long way to address the in-or-out-of-context debate regarding the NT use of the OT.

TABLE 1.4

Various Avenues of Inquiry for Studying the New Testament Use of the Old Testament

Johnson

1. Study the NT context.

2. Study the OT context.

3. Compare the citation text in the NT with the text of the OT.

4. Examine the hermeneutical use of the OT citation in the NT.

5. Examine the theological use of the OT citation in the NT.

Evans

1. What OT text(s) is (are) being cited?

2. Which text type is being followed (Hebrew, Greek, Aramaic), and how does the version that the NT has followed contribute to the meaning of the citation?

3. Is the OT citation part of a wider tradition or theology in the OT?

4. How did various Jewish and Christian groups and interpreters understand the passage in question?

5. In what ways does the NT citation agree or disagree with the interpretations found in the versions and other ancient exegeses?

6. How does the function of the citation compare to the function of other citations in the NT writing under consideration?

7. What contribution does the citation make to the argument of the NT passage in which it is found?

Beale & Carson

1. What is the NT context of the citation or allusion?

2. What is the OT context from which the quotation or allusion is drawn?

3. How is the OT quotation or source handled in the literature of Second Temple Judaism or (more broadly yet) of early Judaism?

4. What textual factors must be borne in mind as one seeks to understand a particular use of the OT?

5. What is the nature of the connection to the OT text as the NT writer sees it?

6. To what theological use does the NT writer put the OT quotation or allusion?

Note: This table summarizes the views found in Johnson, *Old Testament in the New*; Evans, "Function of the Old Testament in the New," 170–71; and Beale and Carson, "Introduction," xxiv–xxvi.

For example, without discussing them as "steps," S. Lewis Johnson consistently models five basic aspects in examining the NT use of the OT in several specific instances.[35] Also without referring to them as steps per se, Craig Evans discusses seven questions to ask. Similarly, Beale and D. A. Carson suggest six questions to consider.[36] The approaches of Johnson, Evans, and Beale and Carson can be easily compared and contrasted (see table 1.4).

35. See S. Lewis Johnson, *The Old Testament in the New: An Argument for Biblical Inspiration* (Grand Rapids: Zondervan, 1980).

36. See Craig A. Evans, "The Function of the Old Testament in the New," in *Introducing New Testament Interpretation*, ed. Scot McKnight, Guides to New Testament Exegesis (Grand

With a little more defined sequence, some scholars studying the NT use of the OT suggest step-by-step procedures of examination. For example, Klyne Snodgrass outlines seven steps, Bock recommends a five-step procedure, Beale suggests a nine-step approach, and Greg Lanier commends a simple three-step process for interpreting the use of the OT in the NT. For ease of comparison, these step-by-step approaches of Snodgrass, Bock, Beale, and Lanier are laid out in table 1.5.

These diverse avenues of inquiry and step-by-step procedures endorsed by various scholars for studying a particular occurrence of the OT in the NT epitomize the artistic variety that is ever present in interpretation. Reflecting on these approaches and incorporating many elements from them, I offer here a recommended procedure of my own for studying a place where a NT author utilizes the OT. Without denying the artistic endeavor that interpretation always is, I offer here five numbered steps to studying the use of the OT in the NT. They are numbered in a sensible order, but this does not preclude the possibility that an interpreter might occasionally have sufficient cause to follow a different order, invest disparate amounts of time and energy to different steps, and in the cases of some NT passages, might even be able to remove a step. Such flexibility is on the "artistic" side of the interpretation process and will differ with the varying levels of preparedness of individual interpreters. Nevertheless, it seems reasonable (on the "scientific" side of hermeneutics) to offer a standard procedure for approaching the study of how a particular NT passage references an OT passage. Let me describe in greater detail each of the five steps I am recommending (and then a summary listing of the steps is offered in table 1.6).

1. Identify the OT reference and the form it takes, including the relevant textual traditions (MT, LXX, targums) and textual variants. This step refers not only to identifying the OT reference but also distinguishing its form, that is, the means by which the NT author references the OT passage(s), specifically whether it is a **citation** (per the discussion above) or one of several other kinds of uses: a **recollection**, a **specific allusion**, or a **thematic echo**.[37] While I utilize the term **form** primarily in the sense of means, it is important to note that scholars sometimes employ this same term when referring to the textual *model* or tradition (aka **text type** or **text form**) for an OT passage, that is, whether it comes from the Hebrew MT type, from the Old Greek translation of the Hebrew text, now generally called the LXX, or

Rapids: Baker, 1989), 170–71; and G. K. Beale and D. A. Carson, "Introduction," in *Commentary on the New Testament Use of the Old Testament*, ed. G. K. Beale and D. A. Carson (Grand Rapids: Baker Academic, 2007), xxiv–xxvi.

37. Chapter 2 below goes into detail about these different forms for the NT use of the OT.

from the Aramaic tradition represented in the paraphrases of the **targums.** Determining the form of a reference in the first sense—that is, the means by which the NT author references an OT passage (e.g., citations, specific

TABLE 1.5

Various Step-by-Step Procedures for Studying the New Testament Use of the Old Testament

Snodgrass

1. Determine the original intent of the OT passage.
2. Analyze the form of the text (precise quotation, quotation from memory, paraphrase, or an allusion) and its text agreement (MT, LXX, or some other witness).
3. Determine, if possible, how the OT text was understood and used in Judaism.
4. Determine the hermeneutical or exegetical assumptions that enabled the use of the OT text.
5. Analyze the way the NT writer uses the OT text.
6. Determine the theological significance and relevance of the use of the OT text.
7. Note which OT texts are used in the NT and which are not and inquire what theological conclusions should be drawn from such observations.

Bock

1. Examine the passage in its OT context.
2. Study how the OT text was read in its historical Jewish context.
3. Compare the citation text in the NT with the text of the OT.
4. Examine the passage in its NT context.
5. Consider the type of usage the NT author is making of the OT text.

Beale

1. Identify the OT reference. Is it a quotation or an allusion?
2. Analyze the broad NT context where the OT reference occurs.
3. Analyze the OT context both broadly and immediately, especially thoroughly interpreting the paragraph in which the quotation or allusion occurs.
4. Survey the use of the OT text in early and late Judaism that might be of relevance to the NT appropriation of the OT text.
5. Compare the texts (including their textual variants): NT, LXX, MT, and targums, early Jewish citations (DSS, Pseudepigrapha, Josephus, Philo).
6. Analyze the author's textual use of the OT.
7. Analyze the author's interpretive (hermeneutical) use of the OT.
8. Analyze the author's theological use of the OT.
9. Analyze the author's rhetorical use of the OT.

Lanier

1. Distinguish between a citation, quotation, and allusion.
2. Compare the wording and explore the OT context.
3. Examine how the NT author interprets the OT text.

Note: This table summarizes the views found in Snodgrass, "Use of the Old Testament in the New," 222–24; Bock, "Scripture Citing Scripture," 261–68; Beale, *Handbook*, 41–54; and Greg Lanier, *Old Made New: A Guide to the New Testament Use of the Old Testament* (Wheaton: Crossway, 2022), 19–39.

allusions, recollections, and thematic echoes)—may very well necessitate a consideration of text forms, that is, the form in the second sense of model (i.e., MT, LXX, or targums). Model text forms for any ancient text (i.e., those written prior to the print press) must be reconstructed from examining the extant **manuscripts** (handwritten copies) of that text and sorting through any **variant readings** among those manuscripts—a process called **textual criticism**. So, for example, a particular citation under examination might be closer to a variant reading of the OT text; and likewise, the NT passage may have variant readings that more closely match one of the OT textual traditions. The freedom with which NT authors cite the OT text is its own area of scholarly discussion.[38] But the point here is that what looks like a loose rendering might not look as loose if the NT author was using a different text type. Chapter 2 discusses further the particular form (in the sense of means) by which a NT author references the OT.

2. Analyze the NT context where the OT reference occurs. While a more detailed contextual analysis comes in step 5 below, it is helpful to put into words the broad NT context early in the examination process. Understanding the broad intentions of the NT document and the narrower intentions of the specific chapter will aid in making connections between the NT passage and the OT passage being drawn upon. Identifying the pertinent presuppositional matters at this early stage (e.g., as outlined above; see table 1.2) can also prove enlightening for understanding the NT context. At this stage also, it might prove helpful to analyze other uses of the same OT text elsewhere in the NT (i.e., in the larger NT context).

3. Analyze the OT context from which the reference is drawn. Understanding the broad intentions of the OT document and the narrower intentions of the specific chapter from which the reference is drawn will aid in making connections to the NT passage utilizing it. Understanding something in its original context is a basic principle of human communication.

4. Examine possible framing devices for the OT passage by surveying the use of the OT text in later OT Scripture and in early and late Judaism. These other possible uses of the specific OT passage elsewhere in the OT can be relevant to its use by the NT authors. Beale and Carson observe, "Sometimes a NT author may have in mind the earlier OT reference but may be interpreting it through the later OT development of that earlier text, and if the lens of that later text is not analyzed, then the NT use may seem strange or may

---

38. For a brief introduction to the issue of NT authors alternating text forms, see Susan E. Docherty, "New Testament Scriptural Interpretation in Its Early Jewish Context: Reflections on the *Status Quaestiones* and Future Directions," *NovT* 57 (2015): 3–7; cf. Silva, "New Testament Use of the Old Testament," 147–65.

not properly be understood."[39] This study of how the particular text was interpreted by later Scripture writers is a larger contextual issue that can provide important insight. For example, the Gospel writers appeal to Isaiah as they begin narrating how God will rescue his people (see Matt. 3:3//Mark 1:2–3//Luke 3:4–6//John 1:23 citing Isa. 40:3[–5]), and Isaiah appeals to the exodus event even as he writes about God rescuing his people from exile (see Isa. 11:15–16; cf. Exod. 14:21–31; 23:20–33). Tracing this stream of scriptural exegetical dependence can bring a larger contextual understanding to the NT writers' message about God rescuing his people.

Gary Schnittjer pushes this larger contextual matter further in his exhaustive study of the OT use of the OT, encouraging the consideration of **networks** of OT passages. Rather than a "single-stream" of one OT text being interpreted by another OT text that can shed light on a NT writer's use of the first text, networks can be uncovered where a significant OT passage is referenced (and re-referenced) by multiple OT writers producing a group of intentionally interconnected interpretive passages. A NT writer may cite one of the OT texts while having the whole network in mind, so uncovering that network may well provide insight for properly understanding the NT author's use of a particular OT passage.[40]

Similarly, and possibly with less magnitude, other uses of the OT passage in the writings of the Dead Sea Scrolls, the Apocrypha, the Pseudepigrapha, Josephus, Philo, and/or the **rabbinic writings** may provide some insight. Chapter 4 below discusses first-century Jewish exegetical practices as framing devices.

5. Analyze the NT author's functional use of the OT, including theological and rhetorical concerns. This is one of the central concerns in discussions of the OT in the NT, but it best follows upon examination of the NT and OT contexts (steps 2 and 3) informed by the larger scriptural and first-century

---

39. Beale and Carson, "Introduction," xxiv.

40. Gary Edward Schnittjer, *Old Testament Use of Old Testament: A Book-by-Book Guide* (Grand Rapids: Zondervan Academic, 2021), 852–56. Schnittjer offers more than a dozen samples of what might be called "single-stream" scriptural exegesis (including the Exodus-Isaiah-Gospels example above; 865–68) but also provides a chapter that graphically lays out twenty-one different sample networks and a Scripture index to these networks (873–87). The sample networks include subjects such as various covenants (e.g., Abrahamic, Davidic, and new), theme concepts (e.g., branch, seventy years), worship components (e.g., collective confession, temple vessels, place Yahweh chooses for his name, Sabbath), persons (e.g., Judah-king, prophet like Moses, teachers), and others.

Having mentioned the OT use of the OT, I can note here that there is also evidence of the NT use of the NT; e.g., 2 Pet. 1:17 refers to the event of Matt. 17:5//Mark 9:7//Luke 9:35 (cf. Matt. 3:17//Mark 1:11//Luke 3:22); 1 John 3:23 refers to the command in John 13:34–35; 1 Tim. 5:18 appears to cite Luke 10:7; 2 Pet. 3:15–16 refers to the letters of Paul; and of course, there is the discussion of the interdependence of the Synoptic Gospels.

TABLE 1.6

Recommended Steps for Studying
the New Testament Use of the Old Testament

1. Identify the OT reference and the form it takes, including the relevant textual traditions (MT, LXX, targums) and textual variants.

2. Analyze the NT context where the OT reference occurs.

3. Analyze the OT context from which the reference is drawn.

4. Examine possible framing devices for the OT passage by surveying the use of the OT text in later OT Scripture and in early and late Judaism.

5. Analyze the NT author's functional use of the OT, including theological and rhetorical concerns.

context (step 4). Chapter 5 below offers a taxonomy of possibilities for the consideration of how an OT reference is intended to function in the NT author's use of it.

After his discussion of the NT's use of the OT—including a similar, albeit abbreviated, method for studying an individual occurrence—Osborne closes with sound advice that reflects the various elements of the procedure I am recommending here. I think it is worth quoting in full:

> So when we study quotes or allusions, we must look at all levels, the Old Testament context from which they come, the Jewish theology and techniques in their own appropriation of the particular text or story, and the explicit use of that passage in the New Testament context. The writers both expected the reader to understand the original context and to see what aspect of it is utilized in the new context. There is both faithfulness to the original and a transformation of it in its new context. Both aspects must be understood for a true understanding of the use of the Old Testament in the New Testament.[41]

Forms, Framings, and Functions

The procedure for analyzing the use of the OT in the NT recommended above names three different but interrelated elements that deserve a few more comments: forms, framings, and functions. As already noted, by forms I refer to the means by which a NT writer references an OT passage or theme (e.g., a citation, a specific allusion, a recollection, or a thematic echo). By **functions** I refer to the discourse purpose for which a NT writer intends to utilize an OT passage or theme (e.g., making a declaration, referring to history, dem-

---

41. Osborne, *Hermeneutical Spiral*, 343–44.

FIGURE 1.1

Forms, Framings, and Functions

The subject matter can take different forms in different framings for different functions.

Form: the item on display

A wedding photo   A wedding sketch

Framing: how the item is displayed

Rectangular matted   Oval unmatted
frame on the desk   frame on the wall

Function: why the item is displayed here

To remember   To honor
a happy event   the artist

onstrating fulfillment of prophecy, etc.). The various options within these categories have their own disputes and discussions, which I will cover in the corresponding chapters below. But the remaining term, *framings*, warrants a greater introduction here.

My concern with the **framing** of a NT reference to the OT is intended to focus more distinctly on the means by which a NT author displays a particular form of referring to an OT passage, and yet I propose that it is also distinct from the way in which the NT author intends the OT passage to function in his argument. To craft an analogy, let me suggest that the form is like the kind of artwork on display referencing a particular subject matter (e.g., a photograph, a drawing, a finger painting, etc.), the framing is like the means by which the artwork is put on display (e.g., wood or plastic, matted or not, glass-covered or plexiglass, etc.), and the function is the reason this particular item is put on display (e.g., to decorate a room, to recall an event, to honor the artist, etc.). Two different pieces of art can reference the same subject matter even while taking different forms in different framings for different functions (see fig. 1.1).

In keeping with the analogy of this illustration, I will utilize the label *framing* for the means by which an OT passage is displayed in the NT. Even as selection of artwork forms and functions have an influence on the methods by which the artwork is framed, so also a NT author's selection of a particular form and function for an OT reference may very well influence his choice for framing it. Nevertheless, while they might exercise an overlapping influence on each other, these aspects remain distinct from one another, each in its own right.

Thus, in separate chapters below I describe these areas of classification in greater detail, hoping to move the scholarly discussion along just a bit in each realm. Chapter 2 suggests a taxonomy of forms, working with such labels as citations, allusions, recollections, and thematic echoes. As is fitting, I also

---

SIDEBAR 1.1

Intertextuality and Studying the New Testament Use of the Old Testament

Scholars sometimes use the term **intertextuality** in discussions of NT references to the OT (as well as the occurrence of references to earlier OT passages in later OT texts). The history and connotations of this term are complex, and this means that there is some debate about the appropriateness of the term in discussions of the NT use of the OT. The term *intertextuality* was coined in wider postmodern reader-oriented literary studies to refer to the creation of new contexts for understanding previous texts when they are referenced by later texts.[1] This kind of intertextuality examines how a prior text is reinterpreted by a later text so as to allow the reader to reinterpret the two texts together in one's own context. In the more specific field of biblical studies, however, the term *intertextuality* is more often (although not exclusively) used merely as a summary way to refer to the fact of one text using another text.[2] When studying how the NT uses the OT, biblical scholars are typically curious to discover the intentions of the biblical authors and not current-day readers. Stanley Porter suggests that use of the term *intertextuality* in biblical studies is merely a fad and even an intrusion from postmodern literary studies.[3] Rather than intertextuality, Beale suggests that terms like **inner-biblical exegesis** or **inner-biblical allusion** be used for discussions of the use of prior Scripture in later Scripture.[4]

Where the term *intertextuality* is used in this book, I mean it in the narrower sense more common in biblical studies—that is, to refer to one text using another text.

1. See Kevin J. Vanhoozer, *Is There a Meaning in This Text? The Bible, the Reader, and the Morality of Literary Knowledge* (Grand Rapids: Zondervan, 1998), 132–33. Coinage of the term *intertextuality* in wider literary studies is usually credited to Julia Kristeva; see Julia Kristeva, *Desire in Language: A Semiotic Approach to Literature and Art*, ed. Leon S. Roudiez (New York: Columbia University Press, 1980), esp. 15.

2. See Willard M. Swartley, "Intertextuality in Early Christian Literature," *DLNT*, 536–42, where the term *intertextuality* is not defined, and the dictionary entry simply describes how various NT authors use the OT. Compare this with the more nuanced definition of Robert W. Wall, "Intertextuality, Biblical," *DNTB*, 541–51.

3. Stanley E. Porter (with Bryan R. Dyer), *Sacred Tradition in the New Testament: Tracing Old Testament Themes in the Gospels and Epistles* (Grand Rapids: Baker Academic, 2016), 11–13.

4. G. K. Beale, *Handbook*, 39–40.

address the taxonomical area of **features** or characteristics for determining whether or not a reference of some kind to the OT is actually occurring in a NT passage; this subdivision concern over the criteria used for identifying forms is taken up in chapter 3. Chapter 4 outlines various framings, the means by which a NT author puts an OT passage on display. Chapter 5 discusses a variety of functions, the various discourse purposes for which NT writers use OT texts. Finally, as an example of assessing one NT author's overall purposes in his many uses of the OT, in a separate chapter (chap. 6) I address Luke's program for using the OT in Luke-Acts.

All of this to note that the NT's use of the OT—or as some reference it, the intertextuality of the two Testaments (see sidebar 1.1)—demonstrates that the two parts of the Christian Bible belong together. We must stress the continuity between the OT and the NT so as to avoid all versions of Marcionism that would seek to destroy the unity of Scripture.[42] Thus, without denying their differences, the two Testaments must be valued together, for as the NT's use of the OT makes clear, they work together. It is the "unity of the subject matter" that ultimately connects the OT and the NT.[43] While the work the Testaments do together cannot be sufficiently defined merely by examining how the one utilizes the other or by noting their common interests and themes, seeing how the OT is employed by NT authors does in fact move us toward a greater recognition of their unity. So let us now apply ourselves to this task.

42. Janowski, "One God," 309.
43. Janowski, "One God," 322.

2

Form Classifications
for the New Testament Use
of the Old Testament

Long ago, at many times and in many ways, God spoke to our fathers
by the prophets, but in these last days he has spoken to us by his Son,
whom he appointed the heir of all things, through whom also he created
the world.

Hebrews 1:1–2

When I speak of the form of a passage, I am referring to the means by which
a NT writer refers to an OT text.[1] Scholars working in this field disagree
about the kinds of forms observed and what to call them, and many readily
admit that the terminology in use can be confusing because of ambiguous
definitions.[2] This is particularly the case when it comes to such form labels

1. An earlier version of this chapter was titled "A Two-Dimensional Taxonomy of Forms
for the NT Use of the OT" (paper presented remotely for the seventy-second annual meeting
of the Evangelical Theological Society, November 17, 2020), and a refined version of it was
published as an article of the same title in *Them* 46 (2021): 306–18. With gratitude to *Themelios* editor Brian Tabb, that article, with several revisions and additions, is reprinted here with
permission.
2. Regarding confusion of terms among scholars for various categories for the NT use of
the OT, see chap. 1 of Stanley E. Porter (with Bryan R. Dyer), *Sacred Tradition in the New
Testament: Tracing Old Testament Themes in the Gospels and Epistles* (Grand Rapids: Baker

as *citation, quotation, paraphrase, allusion, echo,* and the like. Most might agree that the noun *use* is the broadest label and that it encompasses all of the forms descriptive of how the NT engages with the OT.[3] But other labels are also employed at this largest umbrella level, including the terms *citation* and *echo*. There is even the proposal that the label *allusion* be the broadest umbrella term—equivalent to *use*—and that an introduced quotation be recognized as a specific kind of allusion.[4] Thus, even though many scholars might prefer to employ the terms *citation, quotation, paraphrase, allusion,* and *echo* as specific labels for different, mutually exclusive categories underneath the broad umbrella term *use*, the English language allows for overlap in the semantic domains of these terms, even to the extent that each can be (and has at times been) employed at the highest level.

To address this kind of confusion, I suggest employing a refinement of the labels used for the different forms. Furthermore, I suggest thinking in terms of a taxonomy about the overlapping relationships of these different forms and suggest that this will be helpful to scholarly interaction. But before I discuss form taxonomies further—and recommend a particular two-dimensional taxonomy of forms—I first want to emphasize the importance of refining the definitions of the forms.

Disambiguation of Form Labels

The importance of distinguishing between forms is for gaining clarity on what one is attempting to study. If one wishes to study, for example, Luke's use of the OT (i.e., "use" in the broadest sense of the term), but then proceeds to examine only Luke's explicit biblical citations, there is some self-deception afoot. Luke's use of Scripture is much more involved than can be discovered by simply examining his limited explicit citations of it. While many scholars (of course, not all) dwell on citations of the OT in the New, and while this may well prove valuable to the discussion, we must not assume that this gives us the whole picture concerning a NT author's use of the Scriptures.[5] To assume so

---

Academic, 2016), 3–25; see esp. 16–22, where Porter cites some specific examples of debated and confused terminology.

3. But I hasten to note that the noun *use* is employed not only in reference to the form of NT use of the OT, but it is also employed when scholars discuss the completely different taxonomical realm of function for the occurrence of an OT reference in a NT passage. I discuss function classifications in chap. 5 below.

4. David McAuley, *Paul's Covert Use of Scripture: Intertextuality and Rhetorical Situation in Philippians 2:10–16* (Eugene, OR: Pickwick, 2015), 73–74.

5. So also Porter, *Sacred Tradition,* 17, 22–24.

is perhaps another version of the old assumption that NT authors always cite (i.e., in a quotation or a paraphrase) everything from the Scriptures that they are thinking about; nothing in the OT context is to be considered if the NT author does not explicitly cite it. But this **prooftexting** assumption is surely as wrongheaded as such prooftexting accusations. For example, the book of Revelation is clearly steeped in OT imagery and contains dozens of allusions and verbal parallels to the OT even though it has not a single clear citation of OT Scripture.[6] The NT authors use Scripture in a variety of forms to serve their purposes, so an assessment of their use of Scripture should be informed by that same variety of forms.

Thus a certain amount of disambiguation of terms can be helpful to the general discussion of the NT use of the OT. This is especially the case if one wishes to investigate a NT author's particular kinds of uses of the OT Scriptures. Thus, a taxonomy of forms with clear definitions for the labels can only be of service to the discussion.

Taxonomies of Forms

Some scholars take up the discussion of the NT use of the OT with the assumption that everyone agrees with their definitions for terms like *citations* and *allusions*, without explicitly defining their use of form labels. Some suggest—or rather, appear to be working with—two basic forms: quotations and allusions.[7] With more overt intention and by making more fine-tuned distinctions, some scholars distinguish three forms of reference (e.g., quotations, allusions, and **echoes**)[8] or four forms of reference (e.g., quotations, allusions, recollections,

---

6. See Brian J. Tabb, *All Things New: Revelation as Canonical Capstone*, NSBT 48 (Downers Grove, IL: InterVarsity, 2019), 15–17; Jon Paulien, "Elusive Allusions: The Problematic Use of the Old Testament in Revelation," *BR* 33 (1988): 37–53; Steve Moyise, *The Old Testament in the Book of Revelation*, JSNTSup 115 (Sheffield: Sheffield Academic, 1995), 11–20; and G. K. Beale, *John's Use of the Old Testament in Revelation*, JSNTSup 166 (Sheffield: Sheffield Academic, 1998), 60–128.

7. The UBS[5] has one index of "quotations" of the OT (857–63) and another index of "allusions and verbal parallels" (864–83). Interestingly, the introduction to UBS[5] (56*) has a brief section describing the cross-references given at the bottom of each page of its text, and rather than two, it numbers and describes three categories: (1) quotations, (2) definite allusions, "where it is assumed that the writer had in mind a specific passage of Scripture," and (3) literary and other parallels (i.e., presumably unintentional and/or referencing broad themes). The index of "allusions and verbal parallels" combines the latter two categories.

8. Perhaps most notable for distinguishing "echoes" from "allusions," albeit with great flexibility, is Richard B. Hays, *Echoes of Scripture in the Letters of Paul* (New Haven: Yale University Press, 1989), esp. 23 and 29; see also the three-part system in Michael B. Thompson, *Clothed with Christ: The Example and Teaching of Jesus in Romans 12.1–15.13*, JSNTSup 59 (Sheffield: Sheffield Academic, 1991; reprint, Eugene, OR: Wipf & Stock, 2011), 30.

and motifs).[9] And of course, some have more complex taxonomies that discern various subcategories.[10] Employing subcategories can be helpful for clarifying definitions. For example, a broad twofold division can be spread into a more complex sixfold taxonomy with the category called "citations" divided into three subcategories (formulaic quotation, direct quotation, and paraphrase) and the category called "allusions and verbal parallels" divided into three categories (allusion, recollection, and thematic echo).

This sixfold taxonomy can be placed on a linear continuum or line with formulaic quotation as the most explicit and thematic echoes as the least explicit.[11] With such a continuum, the categories overlap or blur into one another, such that some scholars might label a particular usage a paraphrase while others label the same passage an allusion. These labeling differences are more tolerable when the linear continuum is recognized (see table 2.1). A linear continuum acknowledges that some passages can be clearly labeled paraphrases and other passages can clearly be labeled allusions, while a third set of passages is best mapped to the border between those two labels, with scholars pushing them to one side or the other (and thus in table 2.1, broken lines represent permeable borders between categories).

9. Without introduction or explication of the categories, Wilcox simply states, "Old Testament quotations and allusions, reminiscences and motifs appear in some profusion throughout much of the NT." See Max Wilcox, "On Investigating the Use of the Old Testament in the New Testament," in *Text and Interpretation: Studies in the New Testament Presented to Matthew Black*, ed. Ernest Best and R. M. Wilson (New York: Cambridge University Press, 1979), 231. See also the four numbered (but otherwise unnamed) "classes" used by Henry M. Shires, *Finding the Old Testament in the New* (Philadelphia: Westminster, 1974), 65–72.

10. For example, MacDonald presents a taxonomy of seven form categories in Dennis MacDonald, "A Categorization of Antetextuality in the Gospels and Acts: A Case for Luke's Imitation of Plato and Xenophon to Depict Paul as a Christian Socrates," in *Intertextuality of the Epistles: Explorations of Theory and Practice*, ed. Thomas. L. Brodie, Dennis R. MacDonald, and Stanley E. Porter, New Testament Monographs 16 (Sheffield: Sheffield Academic, 2006), 213–14. Some of MacDonald's seven categories (i.e., citation, paraphrase, reference, allusion, echo, redaction, and imitation) have subcategories (i.e., marked vs. unmarked citations, and conforming vs. transforming allusions, redactions, and imitations). Marshall offers a taxonomy of four large groupings (i.e., actual citations, allusions, echoes, and language) containing a total of nine form categories: (1) summary references, (2) citations with formulas, (3) citations without formulas, (4) paraphrases, (5) allusions, (6) echoes, (7) scriptural terminology, (8) language, and (9) motifs and structures; I. Howard Marshall, "Acts," in *Commentary on the New Testament Use of the Old Testament*, ed. G. K. Beale and D. A. Carson (Grand Rapids: Baker Academic, 2007), 518–19. Marshall admits that the boundaries between his echo and language groupings are rather fluid (519).

11. This is very similar to the suggestion of Porter's continuum of five categories moving from explicit to nonexplicit: i.e., formulaic quotation to direct quotation to paraphrase to allusion to echo; Porter, *Sacred Tradition*, 33–47. See also Hays, *Echoes of Scripture in the Letters of Paul*, 23. Hays has a three-realm continuum moving from more explicit to more subliminal: quotation to allusion to echo.

TABLE 2.1

A Linear Layout of Form Classifications
for the New Testament Use of the Old Testament

Citations			Allusions and Verbal Parallels		
Formulaic quotation	Direct quotation	Paraphrase	Allusion	Recollection	Thematic echo

Nevertheless, while such a diagram is helpful in some respects, this linear system of classification fails to account for some passages that seem to fit two categories that are not next to one another on the linear continuum. For example, sometimes a paraphrase of an OT passage occurs after the NT author makes a formulaic introduction of the text (e.g., Amos 9:11–12 in Acts 15:15–18). Thus, such a citation can be labeled formulaic, but it is not technically a quotation; the passage falls into two quite separate sectors of the linear continuum. I would like to propose a two-dimensional taxonomy that can address this problem.

Recommended Labels for Forms

Before describing my recommended two-dimensional taxonomy, I need to define my form labels with a bit more clarity. In commenting on his taxonomy of terminology (which is much like the linear continuum just discussed), Stanley Porter remarks, "I have tried to define the categories used to describe the use of the OT in the NT. I realize that these categories themselves are problematic, yet I offer them as an incentive for further discussion of what continues to be a problematic area of NT studies, both methodologically and in terms of the actual results."[12] What I offer here is a taxonomy that is similar to Porter's, but a bit more specific at points. Mine utilizes a few more categories (eight over against Porter's five) and suggests some changes in label titles. Naturally, I want to utilize some of the same labels already utilized in the discussion; but in hopes of greater clarity at the lowest levels of the taxonomy of labels, I have tried to avoid using single-word labels that might be mistaken for an unintended category. Furthermore, my recommendation is that the taxonomy be envisioned on a multilevel continuum so as to overcome some of the drawbacks of envisioning the taxonomy on a linear continuum. In doing all this, I mean to take up Porter's invitation to offer further refinement of the language used in this field of study.

12. Porter, *Sacred Tradition*, 46.

I distinguish eight basic form classifications for the NT's use of the OT grouped under the two broad categories of *citations* and *allusions and recollections*. I will provide here brief definitions for each of these broad and more specific categories.

Citations

Citations are quotations and paraphrases of prior texts. I use the term *citation* to describe when a NT author, in order to move his argument or narrative forward, was specifically setting out to cite a particular passage of the OT. Most citations in the NT are introduced in some fashion (e.g., "It is written" or "David said about him"), which confirms the author's intention to cite a specific OT passage.[13] But some citations are not formally introduced.

Furthermore, I label some citations **quotations** where the OT vocabulary and word order are largely preserved; and other citations are labeled **paraphrases** where the NT author appears to be rephrasing the OT passage using synonyms, different verb tenses, altered word order, and so on.[14] This has led to four subcategories for the citations form classification section of my taxonomy, with two kinds of **formal citations** (i.e., those with introductory statements) and two kinds of **informal citations** (i.e., those without introductory statements).[15]

1. **Introduced quotations** largely retain the wording of the source text and are introduced by the NT author as citations of a prior text. For example, the citation of Isa. 61:1–2 in Luke 4:17–19 matches the OT text precisely (LXX) and has a rather formal introductory statement (i.e., "the scroll of the prophet Isaiah").[16]

2. **Introduced paraphrases** are introduced by the NT author as citations of a prior text, but reformulate the source text by means of synonym substitutions, changes to case endings, altered word order, and so on. For example,

---

13. See the further discussion of introductory formulas in chap. 3 below.

14. I recognize that some differentiate between citations and quotations as parallel categories, with a citation having an introduction (e.g., "it is written") and a quotation lacking such an introduction; e.g., Kenneth Duncan Litwak, "The Use of the Old Testament in Luke-Acts: Luke's Scriptural Story of the 'Things Accomplished among Us,'" in *Issues in Luke-Acts: Selected Essays*, ed. Sean S. Adams and Michael Pahl, Gorgias Handbooks 26 (Piscataway, NJ: Gorgias, 2012), 148. Nevertheless, I prefer to use the labels *quotations* and *paraphrases* as parallel subcategories of citations and to recognize the presence of an introduction as a separate factor.

15. See the discussion of the labels *formal* and *informal* in Christopher A. Beetham, *Echoes of Scripture in the Letter of Paul to the Colossians*, BibInt 96 (Leiden: Brill, 2008), 16–17.

16. I originally used the label *formulaic quotations* for this first category, but after further reflection, I think that it is better to keep the labels parallel between *introduced / unintroduced quotations* and *introduced / unintroduced paraphrases*. And at this juncture I want to avoid discussing how "formal" an introduction must be in order for a citation to be dubbed a formulaic quotation as a potential subcategory of introduced quotations.

the citation of Isa. 42:1–4 in Matt. 12:18–21 clearly paraphrases the OT text (scholars discuss the differences of the text form from both the LXX and the MT), and yet the citation has a formal introductory statement (Matt. 12:17).

3. **Unintroduced quotations** largely retain the wording of their source texts but lack any introductory formulas identifying the citations as coming from a prior author; the NT author simply quotes the prior text directly as part of his own text. For example, Jesus's citation of Ps. 118:26 [117:26] in Luke 13:35 matches the OT text of the LXX precisely but lacks an introductory statement.

4. **Unintroduced paraphrases** are places where a source text is clearly utilized in a reformulated way by means of synonym substitutions, changes to case endings, altered word order, and so on, but lack any introductory formulas identifying the citations as coming from a prior author. For example, Jesus's last words on the cross in Luke 23:46 are a recognizable paraphrased citation of Ps. 31:5 [30:6] even though they have no introduction.

Allusions and Recollections

Allusions and recollections are places in the NT that indirectly borrow from the words and/or ideas of OT passages.[17] As a broad grouping, this category in my recommended taxonomy is (unsurprisingly) divided into two categories that are each divided into two subcategories with more precise definitions that are of greater importance. The first two subcategories are kinds of recollections; the last two subcategories are kinds of allusions. Because it is somewhat cumbersome, this broad category is often simplified by many to the single-term label *allusions*, but to my way of thinking, there is a distinct grouping of references to prior texts worthy of a more precise label: *recollections*.[18]

What I call "recollections" are passages that do not have any blatantly shared language structures with the prior text, but where the NT author, nevertheless, makes his intentional references to prior texts clear enough with

---

17. My broad category of allusions and recollections is not merely a substitute title for the category called "allusions and verbal parallels" in the UBS⁵ critical text. That is, what I call "recollections" are not what UBS⁵ calls "verbal parallels." In fact, the verbal parallels of UBS⁵ appear to be broader and/or unintentional (see n. 7 of the present chapter), whereas recollections in my taxonomy are narrower and decidedly intentional by the NT authors. See the detailed descriptions below.

18. The stretchiness of labels in the field has already been noted, and any reference to a prior text that is not a citation (of some kind) is often simply referred to as an allusion. Concerning a broad use of the label *allusions*, see the definition in William Harmon and Clarence H. Holman, *A Handbook to Literature*, 10th ed. (Upper Saddle River, NJ: Pearson/Prentice Hall, 2006), 15. Porter (*Sacred Tradition*, 37) identifies five significant elements in the Harmon/Holman definition for allusions: the reference (1) may be to historical or literary entities, (2) is indirect, (3) is intentional, (4) might go unrecognized by a reader, and (5) is most effective when the author and reader share the body of knowledge involved with the allusion.

some sort of introduction. Thus, a recollection is something akin to a kind of authorially intended cross-reference, and the category is further divided into the subcategories of Scripture summaries (focused on teaching content) and historical reminiscences (focused on people and/or events).

Unlike recollections, which are kinds of introductions without any blatantly shared language structures with the prior text, the last two subcategories belong to a converse grouping that I call "allusions" (in a narrow sense of the term), which do have limited borrowed language from a prior text but without any introductory statements. Allusions in this narrower sense are shorter and subtler references to prior texts than citations are. Some scholars suggest that, in order to qualify as an allusion, a text must contain at least three but no more than five words in a combination unique to the prior text.[19] But instead of counting the number of words, I follow the more general suggestion of G. K. Beale: "The telltale key to discerning an allusion is that of recognizing an *incomparable or unique parallel in wording, syntax, concept, or cluster of motifs in the same order or structure.*"[20] The two subcategories of allusions that I recommend have the labels *specific allusions* and *thematic echoes.* I suggest that a specific allusion contains wording parallel to a *specific* prior text (similar to a citation but less extensive), whereas a thematic echo more subtly shares an idea or thematic parallel with a network of multiple prior texts.

Here then are the more precise definitions of the four form classifications under the broad category of allusions and recollections (numbered here as 5–8 so as to distinguish them from the four form classifications of the broad citations category that are numbered 1–4 above).

5. Scripture summaries are recollections of the teachings of prior Scriptures with a very limited use of similar language but with some kind of introductory statement. For example, Luke 24:25–27 records Jesus's interactions with the disciples on the road to Emmaus with one Scripture summary in the mouth of Jesus and another in the words of the narrator: "'O foolish ones, and slow of heart to believe all that the prophets have spoken? Was it not necessary that the Christ should suffer these things and enter into his glory?' And beginning with Moses and all the Prophets, he interpreted to them in all the Scriptures the things concerning himself" (cf. 24:44, 46–47). Paul similarly tries to convince those in the audience with Festus and Herod Agrippa II that he is saying "nothing but what the prophets and Moses said would come to pass: that the Christ must suffer and that, by being the first to rise from the

---

19. See Beetham, *Paul to the Colossians,* 17–20; cf. Porter, *Sacred Tradition,* 35–36.
20. G. K. Beale, *Handbook on the New Testament Use of the Old Testament: Exegesis and Interpretation* (Grand Rapids: Baker Academic, 2012), 31 (emphasis original).

dead, he would proclaim light both to our people and to the Genitles" (Acts 26:22–23).[21]

6. Historical reminiscences are recollections of people and/or events recorded in prior texts with a very limited use of similar language but with some kind of introductory statement. For example, in Luke 6:3–4 Jesus introduces a particular event (i.e., "Have you not read what David did?") reminiscing about David eating the bread of the Presence (see 1 Sam. 21:1–6), but he does so without any quotation or even paraphrase of that prior Scripture.[22]

7. Specific allusions involve intentional references to specific OT passages by means of borrowed phrases or similar wording but without any introduction. For example, when Jesus references "the Son of Man" coming in "a cloud" with "power and great glory" in Luke 21:27, it is difficult not to think specifically of Dan. 7:13–14, even though Jesus is not quoting or even paraphrasing that passage. With this restricted use of the label *specific allusion*, if the collocation is not specific enough to identify just one OT passage, I give it the label *thematic echo*.

8. Thematic echoes are allusions using themes or ideas or structures that occur in multiple prior texts. For example, the narrative of John the Baptist's birth to Elizabeth and Zechariah in Luke 1 echoes the OT stories about divine intervention in the pregnancies of Sarah and Abraham in Gen. 18, of Rebekah and Isaac in Gen. 25, of Rachel and Jacob in Gen. 30, of Manoah and his wife in Judg. 13, and of Elkanah and Hannah in 1 Sam. 1–2.[23] Thus,

---

21. Cf. Steve Moyise, *Evoking Scripture: Seeing the Old Testament in the New* (London: T&T Clark, 2008), 130. What I call "recollections," MacDonald calls the "reference" category; MacDonald, "Categorization of Antetextuality," 212. Hays and Green have something similar to my recollections category that they title "summaries of OT history and teaching" (a title that apparently allows for two subcategories akin to what I call historical reminiscences for historical events and Scripture summaries for teaching); Richard B. Hays and Joel B. Green, "The Use of the Old Testament by New Testament Writers," in *Hearing the New Testament: Strategies for Interpretation*, ed. Joel B. Green, 2nd ed. (Grand Rapids: Eerdmans, 2010), 127.

22. Albeit in a broader sense, Bovon also uses the label *reminiscence* in distinction from *quotations*; François C. Bovon, *Luke the Theologian: Fifty-Five Years of Research (1950–2005)*, rev. ed. (Waco: Baylor University Press, 2006), 118. Likewise, Berding uses the term *reminiscence* more broadly, covering this sixth category together with our eighth category of thematic echoes; Kenneth Berding, *Polycarp and Paul: An Analysis of Their Literary & Theological Relationship in Light of Polycarp's Use of Biblical & Extra-biblical Literature*, VCSup 62 (Leiden: Brill, 2002), 32. Thompson (*Clothed with Christ*, 30) also lumps together "echo" with "reminiscence." My classification of recollections (with both historical reminiscences and Scripture summaries) is perhaps most similar to what Porter calls in a narrow sense "allusion"; Porter, *Sacred Tradition*, 36–37; cf. "the indirect invoking of a person, place, literary work, or the like, designed to bring the external person, place, literary work, or similar entity into the contemporary material" (39).

23. See Kenneth Duncan Litwak, *Echoes of Scripture in Luke-Acts: Telling the History of God's People Intertextually*, JSNTSup 282 (London: T&T Clark, 2005), 55. Hays and Green

as the metaphor implies, thematic echoes are ideas heard over and over again in prior texts.

While used in earlier works, the metaphorical term *echoes* for references to the OT found in the NT has come to the fore with the 1989 publication of Richard Hays, *Echoes of Scripture in the Letters of Paul*, where Hays tends to utilize the label *echo* in a broad manner as if it were synonymous with the label *allusion*.[24] I prefer the approach of Christopher Beetham, however, who distinguishes between allusions and echoes.[25] But such an approach fails to account for those (like Hays) who use those terms interchangeably and even more broadly. So in this work, by using the more detailed, two-term labels *specific allusion* and *thematic echo* I intend to maintain a distinction between these form classifications even while acknowledging them as subcategories of what scholars often refer to more broadly as allusions.

A Two-Dimensional Taxonomy of Forms

Given my eight specific classifications under two broad categories, for greater clarity I have employed a diagram to illustrate the relationships between the various form classifications in the taxonomy. The diagram attempts to represent the complexity of relationships between the forms on a multilevel continuum rather than on a line (see fig. 2.1). That is, rather than merely moving left and right, classification categories also move up and down. Like the simple linear diagram, this diagram has left-and-right movement according to the similarity of wording with the OT passage: quotations have much the same wording, paraphrases and allusions have similar wording, and recollections and thematic echoes have somewhat different wording. This diagram, however, adds another level of complexity based on the presence or absence of an introductory formula, or (in recognition of a continuum) the degree to which the reference is introduced. The more extensive the introduction, the

---

use the label *type-scenes* for such thematic echoes; Hays and Green, "Use of the Old Testament," 127–28.

24. In developing his system, Hays leans upon the work of John Hollander, where echo is a distinct "mode of allusion"; see John Hollander, *The Figure of Echo: A Mode of Allusion in Milton and After* (Berkeley: University of California Press, 1981), ix, 75, 103, 125, passim; esp. 72: "Echo, allusion, and quotation, then, are forms of citation that are clearly related and clearly distinct." Hays, however, uses echo in a broader sense. The impact of Hays's book is evidenced by the fact that it precipitated the publication of an interactive set of essays from the Scripture in Early Judaism and Christianity section of the Society of Biblical Literature: Craig A. Evans and James A. Sanders, eds., *Paul and the Scriptures of Israel*, JSNTSup 83, SSEJC 1 (Sheffield: Sheffield Academic, 1993).

25. See Beetham, *Paul to the Colossians*, 20–24; cf. 34. See also Porter's plea to distinguish between these labels; Porter, *Sacred Tradition*, 46–47.

higher the citation would be plotted on the diagram. Finally, the diagram's dotted lines between classification regions acknowledge that scholars differ on such things as the number of same words required for using the label *quotation* instead of *allusion* and how formal an introduction must be worded.

It will be helpful to plot some instances of the different forms on this recommended two-dimensional continuum. Leading toward my illustrative

FIGURE 2.1

A Two-Dimensional Continuum of the Form Classifications for the New Testament Use of the Old Testament

		WORDING	
	Same	**Similar**	**Different**
INTRODUCTION **YES**	Introduced Quotations	Introduced Paraphrases	Scripture Summaries / Historical Reminiscences
INTRODUCTION **NO**	Unintroduced Quotations	Unintroduced Paraphrases / Specific Allusions	Thematic Echoes

Note: New Testament passages using the OT can be mapped according to the similarity of their wording (left-to-right movement) and according to the degree to which the reference is introduced (up-and-down movement). The more similar the wording, the further left the passage is plotted on the diagram; the more extensive the introduction, the higher the passage is mapped on the diagram. The broad category of "Citations" (with its various subcategories) is to the left, and the broad category of "Allusions and Recollections" (with its various subcategories) is to the right. The more debated texts tend to be at the borders of various classification sectors.

KEY

CITATIONS: The label covering authorially intended quotations or paraphrases of specific OT passages, whether they occur with formulaic introductions (i.e., "Introduced Quotations" and "Introduced Paraphrases") or without (i.e., "Unintroduced Quotations" and "Unintroduced Paraphrases").

ALLUSIONS and RECOLLECTIONS: The broad use of this category label covers authorially intended references to specific OT passages that nevertheless are not citations (i.e., "Specific Allusions"), recollections of particular OT people or events (i.e., "Historical Reminiscences") or of scriptural teaching (i.e., "Scripture Summaries"), as well as references to broader scriptural themes (i.e., "Thematic Echoes"). Some scholars use the term *echoes* for this broad category.

RECOLLECTIONS: A subcategory of "Allusions and Recollections" for items that have introductions but very limited similarities of language such that they refer to people or events (i.e., "Historical Reminiscences") or to summaries of scriptural teaching (i.e., "Scripture Summaries").

study of one NT writer's use of the OT (see chap. 6), I have plotted sample passages from Luke-Acts demonstrating how one author utilizes all eight different forms (see fig. 2.2).

FIGURE 2.2

Plotting Some Examples on the Two-Dimensional Continuum of Form Classifications for the New Testament Use of the Old Testament

		WORDING		
		Same	Similar	Different
INTRODUCTION	YES	★ Introduced Quotations	Introduced Paraphrases ✳	● Scripture Summaries ‡ Historical Reminiscences
	NO	✦ Unintroduced Quotations	Unintroduced Paraphrases † / ◆ Specific Allusions	Thematic Echoes ■

   CITATIONS

   ALLUSIONS and RECOLLECTIONS

   RECOLLECTIONS

Note: Using this more complex diagram of the various form classifications for the NT use of the OT, I offer here some examples of these forms. Some of these are clear examples of particular forms and plotted accordingly; others are debated examples and are thus plotted along the borders between the various form sectors on the chart.

★ The introduced citation at Luke 4:18–19 is a quotation of Isa. 61:1–2.

✦ The unintroduced citation in Luke 13:35 is a quotation of Ps. 118:26 [117:26].

✳ The introduced paraphrase in Acts 15:15–18 is a paraphrase of Amos 9:11–12.

† The unintroduced paraphrase in Luke 23:46 is a paraphrase of Ps. 31:5 [30:6].

● Luke 24:46–47 has an introductory formula but no clearly referenced OT passage; some suggest that it is a very free paraphrase of Hosea 6:1–2 (i.e., an introduced paraphrase) and others suggest that it is a Scripture summary of passages like Isa. 52:13–53:12 along with Hosea 6:1–2 (i.e., a kind of recollection).

‡ Luke 6:3–4 has an introduction reminiscing about David in 1 Sam. 21:1–6.

◆ The vocabulary of Luke 21:27 indicates a specific allusion to Dan. 7:13.

■ The narrative of John the Baptist's birth to Elizabeth and Zechariah in Luke 1 evidences a thematic echo to the childbearing themes in the OT stories of Sarah and Abraham (Gen. 18), Rebekah and Isaac (Gen. 25), Rachel and Jacob (Gen. 30), Manoah and his wife (Judg. 13), and Elkanah and Hannah (1 Sam. 1–2).

Because the citation of Isa. 61:1–2 in Luke 4:18–19 matches the OT text precisely as we have it in the LXX along with a rather formal introductory statement, that citation would be plotted in the "Introduced Quotations" sector of the diagram. Similarly, the citation of Ps. 118:26 [117:26] in Luke 13:35 also matches the OT text as we have it in the LXX, but it lacks an introductory formula and would thus be plotted in the "Unintroduced Quotations" sector. Even so, both citations are labeled as quotations because they have the same wording as the LXX.

On the other hand, Jesus's unintroduced citation of Ps. 31:5 [30:6] in Luke 23:46 might be labeled an unintroduced quotation by some, but because it has one tense form change when compared to the LXX text, it might be labeled an unintroduced paraphrase by others. Thus, it can be plotted near the border between the sectors called "Unintroduced Quotations" and "Unintroduced Paraphrases." Meanwhile, the clearly paraphrased citation of Amos 9:11–12 in Acts 15:15–18 has an equally clear formal introductory statement, so it can be firmly plotted in the "Introduced Paraphrases" zone. With or without introductions, each of these sample passages falls into the same general area for citations of the OT (the light gray zone in fig. 2.2).

Outside of the citations area and within the allusions and recollections area of the chart (the darker zone in figs. 2.1 and 2.2), a text such as Luke 6:3–4 has an introduction but no citation (reminiscing about David in 1 Sam. 21:1–6), so it can be firmly plotted with recollections, specifically in the "Historical Reminiscences" sector. On the other hand, Luke 24:46–47 is less firmly plotted, for it is clear that the introductory formula has led some scholars to suggest that it is a paraphrase of Hosea 6:1–2 while others regard it as a Scripture summary of the teaching of several OT texts (e.g., Isa. 52:13–53:12 along with Hosea 6:1–2). Thus, Luke 24:46–47 might best be plotted on the border between the light gray zone and the darker gray zone, between the "Introduced Paraphrases" sector and the "Scripture Summaries" sector.[26] Clearer is Luke 21:27, which has no introductory formula but enough shared vocabulary with Dan. 7:13 to recognize it as a specific allusion. And the birth narrative of John the Baptist in Luke 1 has a clear thematic echo of several OT birth narratives (e.g., those in Gen. 18, 25, 30, Judg. 13, and 1 Sam. 1–2).

In this manner, my recommended charting gives space to plot clear examples of the NT's use of the OT as well as allows the illustrative plotting of debated passages. It is also worth noting that the two-dimensional diagram has intentionally made room for the specific allusion classification to touch directly the unintroduced quotation classification even as does the

---

26. For more on Luke 24:46–47, see app. A.

unintroduced paraphrase classification, as this area is a nexus of discussion for assigning particular passages.[27] While this organizational charting of the forms for the NT use of the OT may need further refinement, it attempts to go beyond overly simplistic explanations such as systems that suggest all quotations have introductions and those without introductions are to be classified as allusions and echoes.[28]

One issue to be faced in charting a taxonomy of forms is the question of where to slot **compressed citations**, that is, when a NT author quotes several key phrases from a particular OT source text while eliminating certain parts of the quotation. For example, Heb. 7:1–2 reorders and compresses Gen. 14:17–20 into a briefer citation: "For this Melchizedek, king of Salem, priest of the Most High God, met Abraham returning from the slaughter of the kings and blessed him, and to him Abraham apportioned a tenth of everything." More dramatically, Acts 7:33–34 contains a string of phrases from Exod. 3:5, 7, 8, and 10, and yet it reads as if one passage: "Then the Lord said to him, 'Take off the sandals from your feet, for the place where you are standing is holy ground. I have surely seen the affliction of my people who are in Egypt, and have heard their groaning, and I have come down to deliver them. And now come, I will send you to Egypt.'" Ken Berding distinguishes between a "true citation" (what I call here a "quotation"), a "loose citation" (what I call here a "paraphrase"), and a "compressed citation."[29] For convenience some might consider all compressed citations to be a kind of paraphrase, particularly when word order is changed and synonyms are used (such is the case with Heb. 7:1–2 mentioned above). But when the word order remains the same and the volume of material warrants the recognition, I am content to dub such a compressed citation as a quotation, much as we do in modern quotations that use ellipses (. . .) for the intentionally excluded words (so Acts 7:33–34). Perhaps the most compressed passages would best be placed near the dotted line between the "Quotations" and "Paraphrases" sectors of the two-dimensional continuum diagram.

Likewise problematic is the question of **composite citations** or **conflation**, when a NT author cites two (or more) different passages (even from different

27. Of course, I readily admit that this charting has difficulty capturing all the complexities in the discussion of form classifications for the NT use of the OT. For example, differences between the classifications of specific allusion, thematic echo, and unintroduced paraphrase seem related to intention as much as to form.

28. E.g., Peter R. Rodgers, *Exploring the Old Testament in the New* (Eugene, OR: Resource, 2012), 11; cf. Thompson, *Clothed with Christ*, 30; Travis B. Williams, "Intertextuality and Methodological Bias: Prolegomena to the Evaluation of Source Materials in 1 Peter," *JSNT* 39 (2016): 175–76.

29. See Berding, *Polycarp and Paul*, 31.

OT books) as if they were one passage (e.g., 1 Cor. 15:54–55 cites together Isa. 25:8 and Hosea 13:14 as "the saying that is written"). Linking texts on similar subjects is not merely an ancient practice (commonly identified with rabbinic exegetical methods discussed in chapter 4 below); modern interpreters regularly engage in this practice as part of "doing theology." Pragmatically, I treat such conflated passages in separate fashion, according to their forms. For example, the introduced quotation of Isa. 40:3 in Mark 1:2–3 has a specific allusion to Mal. 3:1 (and perhaps a thematic echo; cf. esp. Exod. 23:20), so I simply acknowledge them each in their own form categories.

A Comparison of the Forms

In sorting through the differences between the proposed eight different form categories, it can be especially helpful to see a comparison of NT authors using the same OT passage but in the various different forms. Unfortunately, there is no one OT passage that is used in all eight of the forms in my recommended taxonomy. But examples of all eight forms are covered in looking at just two OT passages. There are five different forms in which NT authors have utilized Ps. 118:22 [117:22], "The stone that the builders rejected has become the cornerstone" (items 1, 3, 4, 7, and 8). And there are three different forms in which NT authors have utilized 2 Sam. 7:12–14, "When your days are fulfilled and you lie down with your fathers, I will raise up your offspring after you, who shall come from your body, and I will establish his kingdom. . . . I will be to him a father, and he shall be to me a son. When he commits iniquity, I will discipline him with the rod of men, with the stripes of the sons of men" (items 2, 5, and 6). To illustrate the differences in the forms in action, below I cite the NT passages using these two OT texts in a comparative manner. Naturally, other texts can be compared in a similar fashion to assist in distinguishing between the forms of this recommended taxonomy.[30]

1. Introduced quotation: A citation of Ps. 118:22 is introduced in Luke 20:17 and largely retains the wording: "What then is this that is written: 'The stone that the builders rejected has become the cornerstone'?"

2. Introduced paraphrase: A paraphrase of 2 Sam. 7:14 is introduced in 2 Cor. 6:16, 18, but the source text is reformulated by means of synonym

---

30. For example, Ps. 110:1 [109:1]—arguably the most referenced OT passage in the NT—is used in at least five different forms: (1) an introduced quotation in Luke 20:42–43 and Acts 2:34b–35, (2) an introduced paraphrase in Matt. 22:43–44 and Mark 12:36, (3) an unintroduced quotation in Heb. 1:13, (7) a specific allusion in 1 Cor. 15:25), and (8) a thematic echo (i.e., "seated at the right hand") in Matt. 26:64; Mark 14:62; 16:19; Luke 22:69; Rom. 8:34; Eph. 1:20; Col. 3:1; Heb. 1:3; 8:1; and 10:12; cf. Pss. 16:11 [15:11]; 80:17 [79:18]; 1 Kings 2:19; 1 Chron. 6:39.

substitutions, altered tenses, and so on: "As God said, . . . 'I will be a father to you, and you shall be sons and daughters to me,' says the Lord Almighty."

3. Unintroduced quotation: The wording of Ps. 118:22 is largely retained in 1 Pet. 2:7, but it is not introduced as a citation: "So the honor is for you who believe, but for those who do not believe, 'The stone that the builders rejected has become the cornerstone.'"

4. Unintroduced paraphrase: Without any introduction, a paraphrase of Ps. 118:22 occurs in Acts 4:11 but in a reformulated way by means of synonym substitutions, altered tenses and word order, and so on: "Jesus is 'the stone you builders rejected, which has become the cornerstone'" (NIV).

5. Scripture summary: Hebrews 12:7 recollects the teaching of 2 Sam. 7:14 but with a limited use of similar language: "It is for discipline that you have to endure. God is treating you as sons. For what son is there whom his father does not discipline?" The Father-Son imagery for God and his people and/or their king appears in several OT passages (e.g., Exod. 4:22; Pss. 2:7; 89:26–27; Isa. 43:6; Jer. 31:9; and 2 Sam. 7:14).

6. Historical reminiscence: Acts 13:36 recollects the people and/or events of 2 Sam. 7:12 with a limited use of similar language: "For David, after he had served the purpose of God in his own generation, fell asleep and was laid with his fathers and saw corruption."

7. Specific allusion: Wording similar to Ps. 118:22 but not necessarily a contextual citation of it is found in Mark 8:31, "And he began to teach them that the Son of Man must suffer many things and be rejected by the elders and the chief priests and the scribes and be killed, and after three days rise again."

8. Thematic echo: Themes or ideas or structures that occur in Ps. 118:22 are found in 1 Pet. 2:4, "As you come to him, a living stone rejected by men but in the sight of God chosen and precious." That this is a thematic echo is confirmed by Peter's subsequent citations of other "stone texts" in this same passage: Isa. 28:16 (v. 6); Ps. 118:22 (v. 7); and Isa. 8:14 (v. 8).

A Summary on Forms

Generally speaking, the following broad guidelines provide helpful distinctions between the form classifications that I have suggested for the NT's use of the OT. A *citation* (whether formally introduced or directly cited without introduction) is an intentional excerpt of a specific passage in a prior text—whether that is a word-for-word rendering (i.e., an introduced quotation or an unintroduced quotation) or a reworded rendering (i.e., an introduced paraphrase or an unintroduced paraphrase) of that prior text.[31] Over against the extended shared wording found in citations is the broad category of *allusions and recollections*, which has the two bifurcated subcategories. *Recollections* are references to prior texts—introductions, if you will—but without much borrowed language, and they come in two varieties: a Scripture summary recollects the teaching of a collection of OT texts, and a historical reminiscence recollects a person and/or event found in a prior text. Finally, the common and perhaps overly stretchy term *allusions*—variously vague references without introduction—has two varieties: a specific allusion involves enough minimal borrowed OT language pointing to a specific OT passage, and a thematic echo is less particular and carries forward ideas and themes found in multiple places in the OT. Identifying this variety of forms in which NT authors use OT texts contributes to the study of biblical intertextuality by giving scholars more nuanced categories in which to classify and examine the NT use of the OT, an important improvement upon merely counting the number of OT quotations in the NT.

Indeed, how the forms are defined certainly affects the counting of the citations versus the non-citations in the NT. Beale opines, "Most commentators agree on the vast majority of what should be recognized as quotations from the OT."[32] That this is an overstatement is easily demonstrated given the disagreements on the definitions for what is to be reckoned as a citation and by the variations in enumerations of them. For example, Henry Shires counts 239 OT quotations in the NT, E. Earle Ellis numbers them at 250, Roger Nicole calculates 295, and Michael Vlach counts 357.[33] Even the standard critical editions of the Greek NT disagree on OT citations in the NT. For example, the NA[28] sees OT citations at Luke 1:15; 9:54; 12:35, 53; 13:27; 19:46; 23:34; and Acts 14:15 that the UBS[5] recognizes only as allusions. Conversely, the UBS[5] sees OT citations at Luke 8:10; 20:28; 22:69; Acts 2:30, 31; 4:11; 7:7, 30–31; and 13:22 that the NA[28] recognizes only as allusions (see app. C).[34]

---

31. One rule of thumb might be to note that a citation is intentional enough that it would be placed within quotation marks (" ") in modern English translations. But, of course, there are differences between modern English translations on what OT citations are to be recognized in the NT with quotation marks.

32. Beale, *Handbook*, 29.

33. See Shires, *Finding the Old Testament*, 15; E. Earle Ellis, "Quotations in the NT," *ISBE* 4:18; Roger R. Nicole, "New Testament Use of the Old Testament," in *The Right Doctrine from the Wrong Texts? Essays on the Use of the Old Testament in the New*, ed. G. K. Beale (Grand Rapids: Baker Academic, 1994), 13; and Michael J. Vlach, *The Old in the New: Understanding How the New Testament Authors Quoted the Old Testament* (The Woodlands, TX: Kress Biblical Resources, 2021; Sun Valley, CA: The Master's Seminary Press, 2021), 72.

34. This naturally also shows up in differences between modern English translations regarding which NT passages have quotation marks (" ") identifying OT citations.

To Beale's point, however, such variations become somewhat ameliorated when the differences in form definitions are factored into the discussion. In fact, Nicole makes several refinements to his count of 295 OT citations: 224 are quotations with introductions, 7 are second quotations added with "and" to a prior introduced quotation, 19 are introduced paraphrases, and 45 are unintroduced citations and paraphrases. Robert Bratcher likewise makes similar distinctions listing 242 quotations (close to the counts of Shires and Ellis) and 40 additional paraphrases (bringing his total of 282 citations close to the total count of Nicole).[35] While text-critical considerations may sometimes come into play, scholars differ in their counts of OT citations in the NT primarily because of differences in the precise definitions of what they are counting.

Another factor in counting the NT's OT citations is the question of whether one is counting the NT passages or the OT passages. So, for example, the "Index of Quotations" in the UBS[5] text has an "Old Testament Order" section that lists 260 OT passages cited in 350 NT passages; but the "New Testament Order" section lists 317 NT passages citing 343 OT passages. These differences are due to such phenomena as single OT passages being cited by more than one NT passage and composite citations where a NT passage cites more than one OT passage. Thus, combining differences in definitions and differences in counting methods, it is no surprise that scholars arrive at different totals for the number of OT citations in the NT. Furthermore, even two scholars agreeing on the same number might still differ in their specific identification of individual quotations.[36] These kinds of issues make for variations in scholars' counts of NT citations of the OT.

Nevertheless, despite these variations—and scholars vary on whether the variations are major or minor issues—those in the conversation tend to address most of the same passages. And if the discussion partners don't classify each of the same passages as OT citations, they at least classify them as OT allusions of some kind. But here we can make the oxymoronic observation that, when scholars all agree that a particular reference to the OT is *not* to be classified as a citation, they are more prone to disagreement about what kind of non-citation form classification best applies in that particular instance. It is the area of non-citations that sees the greater discussion, especially regarding (using my terms) specific allusions and thematic echoes. Thus, the discussion of form definitions narrows to determining the criteria by which one recognizes a particular kind of form.

---

35. Robert G. Bratcher, *Old Testament Quotations in the New Testament*, 3rd ed. (New York: United Bible Societies, 1984).

36. Gert Jacobus Steyn, *Septuagint Quotations in the Context of the Petrine and Pauline Speeches of the Acta Apostolorum*, CBET 12 (Kampen: Kok Pharos, 1995), 29n37.

Not surprisingly, and as already indicated in the discussion above, some texts are difficult to classify because they have features that seem to qualify them for two different form classifications. My layout of the forms on a multilevel continuum is an attempt to allow for some of this ambiguity. For example, how dissimilar must the wording of a citation be before it moves from being labeled a quotation to being labeled a paraphrase? How dissimilar must the wording of an unintroduced paraphrase be before it is classified as a specific allusion instead? How many borrowed words and phrases must a specific allusion have? The nature of such questions about a particular text may push the charting of that text to the fuzzy boundary between two neighboring zones of the chart.

Indeed, the primary contribution of this chapter is the visual charting of form classifications of the NT authors' use of the OT on a two-dimensional continuum that clarifies the potential overlap between classifications. The two-dimensional continuum charts the presence of an introductory formula on one axis and the level of verbal similarities on the other axis. On the one hand, this layout of the forms on a multilevel continuum is an attempt to allow for some of the ambiguity that seems inherent in discussions of particular NT passages. On the other hand, this charting of the different form categories in their overlapping spatial interrelations may well help scholars see that their differences in classifying certain NT uses of the OT may not be as far apart as previously imagined. Thus, the recommended two-dimensional continuum gives scholars the opportunity to map their disagreements in such a way as to discover more agreement. If nothing else, one benefit of the suggested multilevel continuum for plotting these forms is having a playing field for scholarly discussions regarding the proper application of their form classification labels.

3

Features for Form Identification in the New Testament Use of the Old Testament

Do your best to present yourself to God as one approved, a worker who has no need to be ashamed, rightly handling the word of truth.

2 Timothy 2:15

With the previous chapter distinguishing eight different kinds of forms in which NT authors reference the OT, clearly some description of the differing features of those forms has already entered the discussion. In this chapter I discuss in greater detail the criteria for recognizing particular forms of the NT's use of the OT. For citations, introductory statements are a significant and frequent feature of references to the OT, so treatment of these will occupy a significant portion of the chapter. While somewhat briefer here, the discussion of other features for identifying non-citation references to the OT is no less colorful, as it is an area of some debate among scholars. Nevertheless, the very existence of a taxonomy of forms calls for the specification of meaningful criteria by which to discern a NT author's form of reference to the OT. I begin here by offering a system of features for identifying citations.

Features for Identifying Citations

While most scholars can agree on the identification of the vast majority of which NT passages are citations of the OT (i.e., either quotations or paraphrases), there are several debated passages. These debates are perpetuated in part by ambiguous definitions for what counts as a citation. Some scholars suggest that only passages with introductory formulas should be identified as citations. But given that some recognizable and lengthy OT verses appear in the NT without introduction (e.g., Gen. 2:24 in Eph. 5:31), other scholars have a broader definition so as to allow for greater inclusion. For example, Darrell Bock has two criteria for recognizing a NT quotation of the OT: either the statement is introduced by a formula or it is "a substantial reproduction (more than a phrase) of a passage" such that by either or both of these criteria the reader can deduce that the NT author intended the citation to be understood as a quotation.[1]

Christopher Stanley, however, has argued for a narrower approach, one that disallows Bock's flexible "substantial reproduction" criterion. Stanley suggests that the citation label be applied to a passage only if it meets one or more of three criteria: (a) it must have an introductory formula, or (b) it must be accompanied by a clear interpretive gloss (e.g., Rom. 4:22; 13:9a; 1 Cor. 15:27), or (c) it must stand in syntactical tension with its new location in the NT writing (e.g., Rom. 9:7; 10:18; Gal. 3:8, 12).[2] In my desire to clarify the definitions of forms in order to improve discussions of the NT's use of the OT, I can appreciate Stanley's careful set of criteria for identifying OT citations. In particular, his allowance for citations apart from those with introductory formulas is laudable. Nevertheless, Stanley readily admits that his criteria will still rule out passages that many scholars prefer to read as NT citations of the OT. Given that Stanley's criteria disallow recognizing passages such as Rom. 12:20 as an OT citation ("If your enemy is hungry, feed him; if he is thirsty, give him something to drink. In doing this, you will heap burning coals on his head"), which is almost word-for-word from Prov. 25:21–22, some might suggest that Stanley's criteria fail the "common sense" test.[3] Thus, I find it valuable to tweak Stanley's three criteria a bit and to add a fourth.

---

1. Darrell L. Bock, *Proclamation from Prophecy and Pattern: Lucan Old Testament Christology*, JSNTSup 12 (Sheffield: Sheffield Academic, 1987), 47; cf. Charles A. Kimball, *Jesus' Exposition of the Old Testament in Luke's Gospel*, JSNTSup 94 (Sheffield: Sheffield Academic, 1994), 47.

2. Christopher D. Stanley, *Paul and the Language of Scripture: Citation Technique in the Pauline Epistles and Contemporary Literature*, SNTSMS 74 (Cambridge: Cambridge University Press, 1992), 33–37; cf. 66. See the somewhat related criteria for recognizing biblical quotations in the OT defined by Michael V. Fox, "The Identification of Quotations in Biblical Literature," *ZAW* 92 (1980): 416–31.

3. Stanley acknowledges that his criteria rule out recognizing as citations such passages as Rom. 10:13; 11:34, 35; 12:20; 1 Cor. 2:16; 5:13; 10:26; 15:32; 2 Cor. 9:7; 10:17; 13:1; and Gal. 3:11, all of which are "normally regarded as Pauline citations"; Stanley, *Paul and the Language of Scripture*, 37.

a. **Introductory formula:** The passage has an introductory formula.

Regarding Stanley's first criterion, I have an expanded sense of introductory formula that includes specific and more formal references (e.g., mentioning "Scripture," "the prophets," etc.), the use of verbs of speech, writing, or fulfillment (e.g., "God says," "Moses writes," "it is written," "in order that it would be fulfilled," etc.), and even simple and less official references that nevertheless indicate crediting a source, particularly when the formula can be rendered as a shortened version of a more official reference (e.g., "as it says," "in order that," etc.).

b. **Parallel wording:** The passage has substantial parallel wording with the OT text.

This is the criterion that I am adding to Stanley's three (and putting into the second position), one that is in line with Bock's suggested "substantial reproduction" criterion. This parallel wording is more than a simple phrase, although the wording may incorporate synonyms and other paraphrasing alterations. The addition of this criterion goes a long way toward overcoming the failure of Stanley's system to recognize commonly agreed upon OT citations in the NT that lack introductory statements.[4]

c. **Interpretive gloss:** In its NT context, the passage is accompanied by the NT author's clear attempt to interpret and/or apply the text and/or is used to explain his comments.

For example, Paul's paraphrase of Ps. 68:18 [67:19] in Eph. 4:8 is confirmed as a citation by Paul's parenthetical commentary on the passage in Eph. 4:9–10. I have refined Stanley's second criterion to include not only interpretive glosses about the OT text but also to include the NT writer's use of the OT passage to explain his own comments. For example, Paul's command in Eph. 4:25 that his readers put away falsehood is immediately followed by an unintroduced citation of Zech. 8:16, "Let each one of you speak the truth with his neighbor," after which Paul continues, "for we are members of one another."

d. **Syntactical tension:** The passage has a grammatical or syntactical mismatch to the NT author's (or the NT speaker's) linguistic style.

Even if the wording is not completely parallel between the NT text and the purported OT source text, the grammatical or syntactical mismatch is such that rendering it a citation makes better sense of the passage. This is Stanley's third criterion, and it is worth noting that the NT author gets to control this. So, when a NT author changes such things as the specific vocabulary

---

4. With this inclusion of parallel wording, the criteria that I am suggesting result in recognizing as citations (either as quotations or as paraphrases) all the passages excluded by Stanley mentioned in the previous footnote (so also NA[28]; UBS[5] includes all but 2 Cor. 9:7 as citations).

and word order of an OT text but maintains the OT text's syntactical point of view (e.g., with its verb tenses and pronominal references) as something separate from his own syntactical point of view, I call this a paraphrase that can still be recognized as a citation. For example, while talking about Abraham in the third person in Gal. 3:8, with syntactical tension Paul employs a second-person pronoun to say, "In you shall all the nations be blessed." Having earlier referenced the Scripture preaching (an introduction) and coming across this retention of the OT text's point of view (syntactical tension), we easily recognize that Paul is citing Gen. 12:3, even if paraphrasing with the synonym "the nations" instead of "the families of the earth" (cf. Gen. 18:18).

On the other hand, however, when a NT author changes such things as the verb tenses and pronominal references to render the wording and point of view of an OT text more fitting with the grammatical and syntactical point of view of his own writing (or the speaker in his writing), what might have otherwise been a citation has now become allusive. For example, while speaking in his own voice, Paul's particular combination of vocabulary in Rom. 4:9, "For we say that faith was counted to Abraham as righteousness," evidences a specific allusion to Gen. 15:6. The NT author could have referenced the OT text with a citation (either as a quotation or as a paraphrase) had he wanted to do so, but we must allow him to reference the OT text as a specific allusion instead—and we can certainly allow him to do so without thinking that he thereby is mishandling the OT or weakening his reference to the prior text.

Given these four criteria—which I put into a natural observational order—I suggest that a NT passage must have at least two of the four criteria in order to be counted as a citation proper (see table 3.1). One the one hand, to be labeled a citation of the OT, a NT passage needs to have more than a mere introductory formula; on the other hand, it need not have any introductory statement to be labeled a citation as long as it has at least two of the other criteria. Applying these criteria in this manner includes many more NT passages as citations than Stanley's (admittedly) more narrow criteria.[5] Applying these criteria for identification of citations helps recognize a function for introductory formulas

5. In addition to the excluded passages mentioned earlier, in a footnote (*Paul and the Language of Scripture*, 37n14), Stanley lists additional Pauline passages excluded from his study: Rom. 2:6; 3:20; 4:9; 9:20; 11:2, 25; 12:16, 17; 1 Cor. 10:5; 14:25; 15:25; 2 Cor. 3:16; 8:21; 9:10; Gal. 2:16; Eph. 1:22; 4:8, 25, 26; 5:14, 18, 31; 6:2–3; Phil. 1:19; 2:10–11, 15; 1 Tim. 5:18, 19; and 2 Tim. 2:19. Of these, the criteria that I outline include as citations (either as quotations or as paraphrases) Rom. 2:6; 9:20; 11:2; Eph. 4:8, 25, 26; 5:31; 6:2–3; 1 Tim. 5:18; and 2 Tim. 2:19 (so also NA[28]). The remaining passages I reckon to be recollections, specific allusions, or thematic echoes. Additionally, NA[28] also includes 1 Cor. 14:25; 15:25; 2 Cor. 9:10; Eph. 1:22; and 1 Tim. 5:19 as citations. Differently, UBS[5] omits Rom. 2:6, 9:20, and 11:2 from its citations index but includes Rom. 4:9.

TABLE 3.1

Criteria for Identifying a New Testament Citation of the Old Testament

If a NT passage evidences at least two of the following four criteria, I recommend that it be recognized as a citation of the OT. These are placed here in a natural observational order.

    a. Introductory formula

    b. Parallel wording

    c. Interpretive gloss

    d. Syntactical tension

Introductory formulas (criterion *a*) followed by clear parallel wording (criterion *b*) are the most common indicators of intended citations of the OT in the NT. When an introductory formula is lacking, the presence of at least two of the remaining three criteria assist in identifying a passage as an OT citation. In this way, citations can be sorted according to the following four subcategories (discussed in chap. 2):

    1. Introduced quotations—criterion *a* + criterion *b*

    2. Introduced paraphrases—criterion *a* + criterion *c* and/or criterion *d*

    3. Unintroduced quotations—criterion *b* + criterion *c* and/or criterion *d*

    4. Unintroduced paraphrases—criterion *c* + criterion *d*

Note: If a suspected citation meets only one of the four criteria, with an introduction formula it may well be classified as a recollection (i.e., a Scripture summary or a historical reminiscence), but with any of the others it may be an allusion (i.e., a specific allusion or a thematic echo).

apart from announcing citations (i.e., where there is a lack of parallel wording, interpretive gloss, and syntactical tension). So, if a suspected citation has only an introduction formula, it may well be classified as a recollection (i.e., a Scripture summary or a historical reminiscence). On the other hand, if a suspected citation has no introduction and meets only one of the other criteria (i.e., some parallel wording, an interpretive gloss, or syntactical tension), it may be a specific allusion or a thematic echo (I say more about this below).

As mentioned in chapter 2, I also extend the definition of citation in another direction by making two additional label distinctions—quotations versus paraphrases—and each of these is notably nevertheless still acknowledged as a citation proper by application of my proposed criteria. Thus, a citation with an introductory formula and at least one of the other three criteria might be reckoned either as a quotation (with substantial parallel wording) or as a paraphrase (if meeting one of the remaining two criteria) and respectively labeled an introduced quotation or an introduced paraphrase. And a citation without an introductory formula but with at least two of the other three criteria might be reckoned either as a quotation (with substantial parallel wording and at least one of the remaining two criteria) or as a paraphrase (if only meeting both of the last two criteria) and respectively labeled an unintroduced quotation or an unintroduced paraphrase.

The Vocabulary of Introductory Formulas for Quotations and Paraphrases

Despite the complications indicated above, fortunately most citations of the OT in the NT have introductions of some kind. Some NT introductions to Scripture citations are more explicit or descriptive than others. For example, Acts 1:16 contains one of the NT's most descriptive introductory statements (i.e., "the Scripture had to be fulfilled in which the Holy Spirit spoke long ago through David" [NIV]), which is then recapitulated with increasingly less detailed secondary introductions to the actual citations (i.e., "it is written in the Book of Psalms" introduces a paraphrase of Ps. 69:26 in Acts 1:20a, and simply the word "and" introduces a quotation of Ps. 109:8 in Acts 1:20b). Some introductions are rather vague (e.g., with reference to God in the prior verse, 2 Cor. 6:2 begins with "For he says" to introduce a quotation of Isa. 49:8), and others are more precise (e.g., Acts 13:33b introduces a quotation of Ps. 2:7 with the words "as also it is written in the second Psalm").[6] This wide-ranging assortment of introductory statements is present throughout the NT. Even so, no matter their level of decorum or descriptiveness, for the sake of convenience, I refer to all such introductory statements as introductory formulas.[7]

Unsurprisingly, a wide variety of vocabulary is reflected in the wide-ranging assortment of introductory formulas. Scripture is mentioned in general (e.g., "Scripture," "the Law," "the Law of the Lord," "the prophets," etc.), OT writers are identified by name (e.g., "Moses wrote," "David says," "in the book of Isaiah," etc.), and sometimes God is noted as the speaker (e.g., "God says," "the Lord said," "the Holy Spirit says"). While the wide assortment of introductory formulas is almost as numerous as the actual number of OT citations in the NT, the introductions can nonetheless be sorted into some basic vocabulary groupings.[8]

6. Metzger notes that the introduction to the citation of Ps. 2 in Acts 13:33b is the most precise introduction in the NT; Bruce M. Metzger, "The Formulas Introducing Quotations of Scripture in the NT and the Mishnah," *JBL* 70 (1951): 305.

7. Cf. Stanley, *Paul and the Language of Scripture*, 66n5.

8. Regarding the various introductory formulas used in the NT citations of the OT, see Henry M. Shires, *Finding the Old Testament in the New* (Philadelphia: Westminster, 1974), 65–72; Shires counts 169 different introductory formulas used to introduce (his count of) 239 citations of the OT in the NT, including several different variations of "it is written" (55×), several variations of "God/Scripture says" (70×), various references to the prophets (22×), references to fulfillment (17×), introductions to a psalm (12×), six different one-word introductions (36×), two different two-word introductions (5×), rhetorical questions about reading the OT passage (6×), and a few other formulas (69–70). See also Metzger, "Formulas Introducing Quotations," 297–307.

Citation introductions using the γραφή / γράφω word group. The most basic term used for referencing the Israelite written Scriptures is (unsurprisingly) "the writing(s)" (γραφή, 50× in the NT). This noun is used 20× to introduce a citation of the OT.[9] As might be expected, naturally the term γραφή is used to reference Scripture apart from introducing citations (30×),[10] but it is never used in the NT to reference any other "writings."

Like the noun, the corresponding verb, γράφω ("I write"; 191× in the NT), also occurs in the NT with reference to Scripture outside of introducing citations (20×);[11] but it is also used 100× for writing activities apart from referencing the OT. Nevertheless, the verb γράφω is frequent in introducing Scripture citations. In introductory formulas γράφω occurs most often (55×) in the perfect passive indicative spelling, γέγραπται ("it is written").[12] It occasionally occurs in the perfect passive participle, γεγραμμένος (11×: Luke 4:17; 20:17; 22:37; John 2:17; 6:31, 45; 10:34; 12:14; 15:25; 1 Cor. 15:54; 2 Cor. 4:13), the aorist passive indicative, ἐγράφη (2×: Rom. 4:23; 1 Cor. 9:10), the aorist active indicative, ἔγραψεν (2×: Mark 12:19; Luke 20:28), or the present active indicative, γράφει (1×: Rom. 10:5).[13]

Citation introductions using λέγω. In addition to "it is written," several verbs of speech are used to introduce OT citations. The common verb of speech λέγω ("to say"; 2353× in the NT) is frequently utilized in NT introductory formulas, and it has various subjects. The present tense of λέγω with θεός, for "God says," occurs in a few citation introductions (e.g., Acts 2:17; 3:25; Rom. 9:14–15), and its present participle with θεός for "said by God" is also evidenced (e.g., Matt. 22:31). More commonly, the aorist tense of λέγω with θεός, for "God said," occurs in citation introductions of quotations (e.g., Matt. 15:4; Mark 12:26) and of paraphrases (e.g., Acts 7:3, 7; 13:22; 2 Cor. 4:6; 6:16).[14]

---

9. See Matt. 21:42; Mark 12:10; John 7:38; 13:18; 19:24, 36, 37; Acts 1:16; 8:32; Rom. 4:3; 9:17; 10:11; 11:2; Gal. 3:8; 4:30; 1 Tim. 5:18; James 2:8, 23; 4:5; 1 Pet. 2:6. Acts 8:32 is the only citation introduction in the NT with περιοχὴ τῆς γραφῆς for "passage of Scripture."

10. See Matt. 22:29; 26:54, 56; Mark 12:24; 14:49; Luke 4:21; 24:27, 32, 45; John 2:22; 5:39; 7:42; 10:35; 17:12; 19:28; 20:9; Acts 8:35; 17:2, 11; 18:24, 28; Rom. 1:2; 15:4; 16:26; 1 Cor. 15:3, 4; Gal. 3:22; 2 Tim. 3:16; 2 Pet. 1:20; 3:16.

11. See Matt. 26:24; Mark 9:12, 13; 14:21; Luke 18:31; 21:22; 24:44, 46; John 1:45; 5:46; 8:17; 12:16; Acts 13:29; 24:14; Rom. 15:4; 1 Cor. 4:6; 10:11; Gal. 3:10b; 4:22; Heb. 10:7.

12. See Matt. 2:5; 4:4, 6, 7, 10; 11:10; 21:13; 26:31; Mark 1:2; 7:6; 11:17; 14:27; Luke 2:23; 3:4; 4:4, 8, 10; 7:27; 10:26; 19:46; Acts 1:20; 7:42; 13:33; 15:15; 23:5; Rom. 1:17; 2:24; 3:4, 10; 4:17; 8:36; 9:13, 33; 10:15; 11:8, 26; 12:19; 14:11; 15:3, 9, 21; 1 Cor. 1:19, 31; 2:9; 3:19; 9:9; 10:7; 14:21; 15:45; 2 Cor. 8:15; 9:9; Gal. 3:10, 13; 4:27; 1 Pet. 1:16.

13. Noteworthy are the two times Luke's narrative has questions utilizing γράφω verb forms that introduce citations of Scripture: in Luke 10:26–27 a question receives as a response a paraphrase of Deut. 6:5 and/or Deut. 10:12 (with allusion to Josh. 22:5 [21:5]) and a quotation of Lev. 19:18; and in Luke 20:17 a question introduces a quotation of Ps. 118:22 [117:22].

14. For more on Acts 13:22 and 2 Cor. 4:6, see app. A.

Examples of introductory formulas using λέγω with the Lord (κύριος) as the subject or the agent also occur for "the Lord says" (e.g., 1 Cor. 14:21; 2 Cor. 6:17, 18), for "the Lord said" (e.g., Acts 7:33), and for "spoken by the Lord" (e.g., Matt. 1:22; 2:15). Some introductory formulas utilize variations of λέγω, to report what David "said" (e.g., Matt. 22:43; Mark 10:43; 12:36; Luke 20:42; Acts 2:25, 34; 4:24–25; Rom. 4:6; 11:9; Heb. 4:7). Likewise, some introductory formulas name Isaiah as the one who "said" (e.g., Matt. 3:3; 4:14; 8:17; 12:17; 13:14; 15:7; 12:38, 39; Rom. 10:16, 20; 15:12; cf. Mark 7:6); some name Moses (e.g., Matt. 22:24; Mark 7:10; Acts 3:22; 7:37; Rom. 10:19; Heb. 12:21); twice Jeremiah is named (Matt. 2:17; 27:9); one names "the prophet Joel" (Acts 2:16); one has "he says in Hosea" (Rom. 9:25); and others state more generically, "the prophet(s) says/said" (e.g., Matt. 1:22; 2:15; 13:35; 21:4; Acts 7:42; 48; 13:40; 15:15).

Moving away from persons, "Scripture says" (γραφή with λέγω) introduces some citations (e.g., Rom. 4:3; 9:17; 11:2; James 2:23), and the perfect passive participle of λέγω introduces "what is said in the Law" (e.g., Luke 2:24). Even without explicitly named subjects or agents, "he/it says," λέγω introduces citations (e.g., Matt. 19:5; Luke 4:12; 20:37b;[15] Acts 13:34, 35; Rom. 9:12; 10:8; Heb. 1:5; 8:8; James 4:5–6),[16] sometimes in participle verb forms (e.g., Acts 7:26, 35; Rom. 4:18; Heb. 2:12; 7:21; 10:30).

Citation introductions using λαλέω. A less common verb of speaking, λαλέω ("I speak"; 296× in the NT), is used proportionately less in introductory formulas. The subject/agent of the action varies widely: "And God spoke thus that" (Acts 7:6); "Well the Holy Spirit spoke" (Acts 28:25); "the one who spoke to him" (Heb. 5:5); "about whom it was spoken" (Heb. 11:18).

Citation introductions using the "to fulfill" word group. Over against terms of speech and writing, which emphasize the production of statements on the OT side of this field of study, the "to fulfill" word group (i.e., πίμπλημι, πληρόω, τελειόω, and τελέω), when used by NT authors to introduce OT citations, seems to emphasize the NT side of the investigation. These "to fulfill" terms are not used uniformly, however. The term πίμπλημι (24× in the NT) is used only once to mean "to fulfill" Scripture but not in a citation introduction (Luke 21:22). Similarly, τελειόω (23× in the NT) is used only once to mean "to

---

15. Some might suggest that the introductory formula in Luke 20:37 includes the phrase "Moses . . . at the bush, as he says" (Μωϋσῆς . . . ἐπὶ τῆς βάτου, ὡς λέγει). See the English versions that render this phrase something like "in the passage about the bush": e.g., CSB, ESV, NASB, NIV, NKJV, NLT. However, I am rendering "at the bush" as a recollection of an event (see KJV, WEB; cf. CEV, NRSV), so I list Luke 20:37a among the Lukan historical reminiscences (see app. C), and I render "as he says" in Luke 20:37b as a separate introductory statement to a paraphrase of Exod. 3:6, 15, 16 (cf. 3:2).

16. For more on James 4:5–6, see app. A.

fulfill" Scripture (John 19:28), but that usage is in a Scripture summary, not a citation (see below). On the other hand, τελέω (28× in the NT) is used five times to affirm that Scriptures are to "be accomplished," but it is used only once in a citation introduction (Luke 22:37), with the remaining four occurrences in other kinds of comments (Luke 18:31; Acts 13:29; Rev. 10:7; 17:17).

In this "to fulfill" word group, πληρόω (86× in the NT) is the more commonly used term in introductory formulas (18×), especially in Matthew (Matt. 1:22; 2:15, 17, 23; 4:14; 8:17; 12:17; 13:35; 21:4; 27:9) and in John (12:38; 13:18; 15:25; 19:24, 36), but only twice elsewhere in the NT (Acts 1:16; James 2:23) and never in Paul as part of an introductory formula (cf. Gal. 5:14). And unsurprisingly, the term πληρόω is used on several occasions meaning "to fulfill" Scripture without actually introducing a citation (Matt. 5:17; 26:54, 56; Mark 14:49; Luke 4:21; 24:44; John 17:12; Acts 3:18; 13:27; cf. "to fulfill all righteousness" in Matt. 3:15; and John 18:9, 32 speaking of Jesus's words being "fulfilled").

Citation introductions using other verbs. Several other verbs are used in NT citation introductions. Among them are verbs of speech such as προλέγω, "say beforehand, predict" (e.g., Acts 1:16; Rom. 9:29; cf. Heb. 4:7); φημί, "say" (e.g., 1 Cor. 6:16; Heb. 8:5); ἐντέλλω, "command" (Acts 13:47);[17] κράζω, "cry out" (Rom. 9:27);[18] διαμαρτύρομαι, "testify" (Heb. 2:6); and μαρτυρέω, "bear witness" (Heb. 7:17). Others are various collocations with verbs of being used to introduce a citation; for example, with a demonstrative pronoun ("this is"; e.g., Matt. 11:10; 27:46; Luke 7:27; 20:17; Acts 2:16; 4:11; 8:32); with a substantive adjective ("the most important is"; e.g., Mark 12:29); with a conjunction ("and it will be"; e.g., Acts 3:23); in a question (e.g., Matt. 12:7); and once to say "there came the voice of the Lord" (Acts 7:31). And other descriptive clauses are also in use for citation introductions; for example, "having this seal" (ἔχων τὴν σφραγῖδα ταύτην; 2 Tim. 2:19) and clauses about reading (ἀναγινώσκω; e.g., Matt. 19:4; 21:16, 42; 22:31; Mark 12:10, 26; Luke 10:26; Acts 8:32).[19]

Non-verb citation introductions. NT writers occasionally utilize non-verb citation introductions. Some of these might be clauses with a presumed verb of being (e.g., Mark 12:31). But other citations are introduced by being placed

---

17. While Matt. 19:7//Mark 10:3 and John 8:5 use ἐντέλλω in reference to commands of Moses in their NT contexts, these NT passages are best classified as specific allusions to the teaching in Deut. 24:1 and in Lev. 20:10; Deut. 22:22, respectively. Similarly, the use of ἐντέλλω in Heb. 11:22 is part of a historical reminiscence to the event in Gen. 50:24–25.

18. Rather than the psalmist, the occurrence of κράζω in the accounts of the triumphal entry (Matt. 21:9//Mark 11:9//[Luke 19:18 has λέγω]//[John 12:13 has κραυγάζω] has the crowd as the subject of the verb, even though their words are from Ps. 118:25–26; I count these as unintroduced citations.

19. With regard to reading, one of the two Greek nouns for "book" (βιβλίον or βίβλος) are utilized in citation introductions in six places with γράφω (written) or λέγω (says) verbs: Matt. 12:26; Luke 3:4; 4:17; 20:42; Acts 1:20; 7:42.

in discourse apposition to a noun like "commandment" (ἐντολή; e.g., Matt. 15:3; 19:17; 22:36, 38; Mark 10:19; 12:28; Luke 18:20; Rom. 13:9; Heb. 9:19). And in some of these, the short phrase "and the second is like it" (Matt. 22:39//Mark 12:31) introduces a second commandment, borrowing on the mention of the "greatest commandment" introducing the previous citation that is followed by an interpretive gloss (Matt. 22:36–38//Mark 12:28–32). A similar appositive introduction occurs with "the word of promise" (Rom. 9:9). In 1 Pet. 1:24–25, immediately subsequent to a mention of "the living and abiding word of God" (v. 23), Peter uses the simple subordinating conjunction διότι ("for") to introduce a quotation of Isa. 40:6–8, which he then follows with an interpretive gloss saying, "And this word is the good news that was preached to you" (v. 25).

There are other examples of simple conjunctions and conjunctive phrases used to hearken back to the immediately preceding and more fully introduced citation; for example, καί, "and" (e.g., Luke 10:27); ἀλλά, "but" (e.g., Rom. 9:7); ἤ, "or" (e.g., Rom. 10:7); γάρ, "for" (e.g., Rom. 10:13); καὶ πάλιν, "and again" (Rom. 15:11; cf. 15:10, 12; 1 Cor. 3:20; Heb. 1:5; 2:13; 10:30);[20] διότι καὶ ἐν ἑτέρῳ, "and in another" (Acts 13:35); καὶ ὅτι, "and that" (Luke 4:11); ἵνα, "in order that" (e.g., Luke 8:10); ἄχρι οὗ, "until which time" (Acts 7:18); and ὥσπερ γάρ, "for just as" (Matt. 12:40).

Regarding this variety of vocabulary, it is important to note that these terms are not always used individually in citation introductions. That is to say, these terms are sometimes used in combinations with each other in a single introduction to a citation. For example, the introduction to the citation of Hosea 11:1 in Matt. 2:15 is a rather formal combination of terms: "This was to fulfill what the Lord had spoken by the prophet." A similar decorum results from a different combination of terms in the introduction to the citation of Isa. 40:3–5 in Luke 3:4, "As it is written in the book of the words of Isaiah the prophet." Hebrews 1 has a string of variously introduced citations, and the series of two dozen or more citations in Rom. 9–11 displays a wide variety of citation introductions, including some with no introductory statements. And the lack of introductory statements is a worthy topic for examination.

Quotations and Paraphrases without Introductions

Sometimes a NT author clearly quotes (or even paraphrases) an OT passage without introducing it as a citation at all. As already noted, some scholars

---

20. Interestingly, John 19:37 utilizes both a recapitulating καὶ πάλιν (referring back to the "that Scripture be fulfilled" in 19:36) and ἑτέρα γραφὴ λέγει ("another Scripture says") to immediately introduce a second citation.

operate with the assumption that all citations have introductory formulas, but several rather blatant examples in the NT counter this assumption. The blatant instances of unintroduced citations might be identifiable by way of a single criterion: the sheer volume of parallel wording, that is, if an overwhelming number of words match the OT text, then it can be considered a citation (e.g., Luke 13:35b; 19:38; 23:30, and 46). But I have also suggested two more criteria—interpretive glosses and syntactical tension—and the notion that any passage without an introductory formula but containing at least two of these three additional criteria can be properly considered a citation (labeled as either an unintroduced quotation or an unintroduced paraphrase; see table 3.1 above).

On these latter two criteria for identifying citations apart from introductory formulas and parallel wording, let me make a couple of additional comments. As to the presence of an interpretive gloss, what I mean by this is a NT author's attempt to interpret and/or apply what appears to be a cited passage and/or his use of a prior text to explain (or otherwise ground) his own comments. In a sense, these additional comments appear to be something like citation introductions that occur after the citation is made instead of beforehand. For example, Rom. 2:6 has wording clearly parallel to Ps. 62:12 [61:13] (and/or to Prov. 24:12), and the fact that Paul goes on to apply the text in Rom. 2:7–8 confirms it to be a citation—which I label an unintroduced quotation—in view of its meeting at least two of the four criteria: the criteria of parallel wording and interpretive gloss. Likewise, after quoting Deut. 5:16 without introduction in Eph. 6:2, Paul adds the interpretive gloss ("this is the first commandment with a promise") before continuing with the citation of Deut. 5:16 in Eph. 6:3. So even without an introductory statement, by the criteria of parallel wording and interpretive gloss, we can recognize in Eph. 6:2–3 a citation of Deut. 5:16 as an unintroduced quotation.

Regarding syntactical tension, I can say here a bit more about the grammar of a passage serving as a factor to consider. On the one hand, a NT author can intend a brief phrase (e.g., of less than three words) to serve as a citation rather than a specific allusion, even without an introductory formula. Such is the case with John 8:58, where Jesus's grammar feels a bit awkward in his declaration, "Truly, truly, I say to you, before Abraham was, I am" (Ἀμὴν ἀμὴν λέγω ὑμῖν, πρὶν Ἀβραὰμ γενέσθαι ἐγὼ εἰμί). But recognizing that the two words "I am" (ἐγὼ εἰμί) are parallel to those in Exod. 3:14, where God offers to Moses a name for himself, helps us excuse the odd grammar and identify the unintroduced quotation. Indeed, the listeners in John 8 recognized Jesus's claim and responded by preparing to dispense the capital punishment of stoning for blasphemous claims to be God (John 8:59; cf. 10:31–33).[21]

On the other hand, a NT author can intend a lengthy phrase (e.g., of five words or more) to serve as a specific allusion rather than a quotation, and his grammatical (re)phrasing of the OT text is informative of his intention. Along these lines, it might be instructive to compare the use of Isa. 45:23 ("To me every knee shall bow, every tongue shall swear allegiance") in Rom. 14:11 and in Phil. 2:10–11. In both cases seven or more words are the same, and yet both NA[28] and UBS[5] consider Rom. 14:11 to be a citation of Isa. 45:23 but Phil. 2:10–11 a specific allusion. The fact that Rom. 14:11 has an introductory formula and eight contiguous words with only one out of order warrants recognizing it as a citation, more specifically, an introduced quotation (ὅτι ἐμοὶ κάμψει πᾶν γόνυ καὶ πᾶσα γλῶσσα ἐξομολογήσεται τῷ θεῷ compared to Isa. 45:23 LXX: ὅτι ἐμοὶ κάμψει πᾶν γόνυ καὶ ἐξομολογήσεται πᾶσα γλῶσσα τῷ θεῷ). Philippians 2:10–11, however, has no introductory formula and utilizes a total of seven words from Isa. 45:23 in two clauses with altered word order (πᾶν γόνυ κάμψῃ . . . καὶ πᾶσα γλῶσσα ἐξομολογήσηται) interrupted by an intervening string of adjectives (ἐπουρανίων καὶ ἐπιγείων καὶ καταχθονίων). The wording of Isa. 45:23 is so reworked into Paul's description of Jesus in Phil. 2:10–11 that I dub it a specific allusion. Thus, Paul references Isa. 45:23 in both epistles; he simply decided to use the passage differently in the two letters: an introduced quotation in Romans and a specific allusion in Philippians.

Apart from altered word order and intervening phrases, a NT author can also transform what might have been a citation into a specific allusion by means of other grammatical and syntactical changes. For example, while both NA[28] and UBS[5] consider Acts 7:5 to contain a quotation of Gen. 17:8 and/or 48:4, I argue that the word order and the pronominal references in Acts 7:5 have been adjusted so as to transform the quotation into a specific allusion (see table 3.2). Rather than calling his listeners' attention to a directly cited passage, Luke (or Stephen, the speaker in Acts 7) has adjusted the syntax of the Genesis text so much—by removing the syntactical tension, in this case by adjusting the word order and the pronouns—that it becomes part of his own speech and is thus better recognized as a specific allusion.

21. On the grammar of John 8:58, see Daniel B. Wallace, *Greek Grammar beyond the Basics: An Exegetical Syntax of the New Testament* (Grand Rapids: Zondervan, 1996), 515, 530–31. The "I am" saying is appealed to elsewhere in the OT and thus, beyond a simple two-word citation, it becomes something of a thematic echo as well: see esp. the "I am he" sayings (Greek: ἐγώ εἰμί; Hebrew: אֲנִי הוּא) in such places as Deut. 32:39; Isa. 41:4; 43:10; 46:4; 48:12; 52:6; cf. the Hebrew of Isa. 42:8; 43:13. Neither UBS[5] nor NA[28] list John 8:58 as a citation of, or as even an allusion to, Exod. 3:14, but NA[28] lists allusions to Isa. 43:10, 13.

TABLE 3.2

An Example of Differentiating a Citation from a Specific Allusion

With the change of grammatical features such as pronominal references, a NT author can transform what would be an OT citation into a specific allusion. Recognition of the specific OT text is still the author's goal in using a specific allusion; it simply is not set up as a citation. The grammar flows with the NT setting differently for a specific allusion than for a citation. Thus, while some might consider Acts 7:5 to contain a quotation of Gen. 17:8 and/ or Gen. 48:4 (e.g., both NA²⁸ and UBS⁵ suggest this), Luke's word order and pronominal adjustments indicate his intention to transform the wording into a specific allusion rather than to maintain the wording as a citation (compare here the bolded words for similar terms and the underlined portions of the texts for vocabulary changes).

Gen. 17:8	καὶ <u>δώσω σοι</u> **καὶ τῷ σπέρματί** <u>σου</u> **μετὰ** <u>σὲ</u> τὴν γῆν, ἣν παροικεῖς, πᾶσαν τὴν γῆν Χανααν, **εἰς κατάσχεσιν** αἰώνιον καὶ ἔσομαι αὐτοῖς θεός.
	And <u>I will give to you</u> **and to** <u>your</u> **descendants after** <u>you</u> the land where you live as a stranger, the whole land of Canaan, **as a possession** forever and I will be their God. (my translation)
Gen. 48:4	καὶ εἶπέν μοι Ἰδοὺ ἐγὼ αὐξανῶ σε καὶ πληθυνῶ σε καὶ ποιήσω σε εἰς συναγωγὰς ἐθνῶν **καὶ** <u>δώσω σοι</u> τὴν γῆν ταύτην **καὶ τῷ σπέρματί** <u>σου</u> **μετὰ** <u>σὲ</u> **εἰς κατάσχεσιν** αἰώνιον.
	And he said to me, "Behold, I will cause you to grow and I will multiply you and I will make you a community of peoples **and** <u>I will give to you</u> this land **and to** <u>your</u> **descendants after** <u>you</u> **as a possession** forever." (my translation)
Acts 7:5	καὶ οὐκ ἔδωκεν αὐτῷ κληρονομίαν ἐν αὐτῇ οὐδὲ βῆμα ποδός, **καὶ** <u>ἐπηγγείλατο δοῦναι αὐτῷ</u> **εἰς κατάσχεσιν** αὐτὴν **καὶ τῷ σπέρματι** <u>αὐτοῦ</u> **μετ'** <u>αὐτόν</u>, οὐκ ὄντος αὐτῷ τέκνου.
	And he gave him no inheritance in this place, not even a foot's step, **and** <u>promised to give it</u> **as a possession** <u>to him</u> **and to** <u>his</u> **descendants after** <u>him</u>, even though he had no child. (my translation)

I must be quick to note here, however, that pronominal shifts may be sufficient for signaling the author's intention to allude to, rather than to cite, an OT passage, but such shifts on their own do not always necessitate a change in discourse perspective. Indeed, some pronominal shifts are intended to amplify and apply the citation. For example, in Acts 4:11, Peter paraphrases Ps. 118:22 [117:22] not to change the discourse posture so as to make his reference a specific allusion, but to apply the citation to Jesus ("this one") and to his immediate listeners (adding the pronoun "you"): "This one is 'the stone you builders rejected, which has become the cornerstone'" (my translation). Similarly, in John 1:23 John the Baptist shows recognition of his identity when he leads his citation of Isa. 40:3 with the added first-person pronoun (ἐγώ): "I am the voice of one crying out in the wilderness, 'Make straight the way of the Lord,' as the prophet Isaiah said." Both of these citations have pronominal shifts that do not disqualify them from being recognized as citations (both meet the criteria of an introductory formula and parallel wording). Thus, while pronominal shifts can be the means for shifting the discourse perspective from citation to specific allusion, as always, the context will help the reader ascertain the author's intention.[22]

Nevertheless, my point here is that, in addition to the presence of parallel wording and the presence or absence of an introductory formula, the grammar of a passage can help us determine the author's intentions for the form in which he utilizes an OT passage. So when the NT author maintains the original discourse posture (evidenced by such features as word order and pronominal references, etc.), even in an otherwise paraphrased representation of the OT, this makes clear his intention to offer a citation even when he does not include an introductory formula of some kind.

With this perspective on identifying unintroduced citations, I suggest that Luke-Acts offers only four unintroduced citations, and all four are in the Third Gospel: Luke 13:35b quotes Ps. 118:26 [117:26]; Luke 19:38a paraphrases Ps. 118:26 [117:26] (cf. Zech. 9:9 for the word "king"); Luke 23:30 paraphrases Hosea 10:8 LXX; and Luke 23:46 paraphrases Ps. 31:5 [30:6]. All four of these passages in Luke evidence parallel wording (criterion *b*); in fact, the parallel wording is so extensive in each of these instances that it would seem irresponsible not to identify them as citations of some kind. But I have suggested that candidates for recognition as citations should also meet a second of the four criteria. And admittedly with some difficulty, it appears that all four of these unintroduced citations of the OT in Luke fulfill a second criterion for indicating citations with a kind of interpretive gloss or commentary on the suspected citation and/or what might be called a kind of discourse syntactical tension—that is, a grammatical or syntactical mismatch to the NT author's (or the NT speaker's) linguistic style.

Interestingly, all four Lukan passages utilize the term λέγω in a non-introductory way that may be viewed as calling attention to an OT citation. The quotation of Ps. 118:26 [117:26] in Luke 13:35 follows Jesus's remarking "I tell [λέγω] you . . . until you say [εἴπητε, 2nd person plural of λέγω]." This double use of λέγω is not a citation introduction about Scripture "saying," but it nevertheless signals the hearers to notice the OT quotation. Likewise, the quotation of the same Ps. 118:26 [117:26] in Luke 19:38 follows Luke's

---

22. A more difficult situation is the citation of Ps. 68:18 [67:19] in Eph. 4:8, which contains several paraphrasing alterations including the pronominal changes from second-person to third-person perspective ("When he ascended on high he led a host of captives, and he gave gifts to men"). Nevertheless, its simple introductory formula ("therefore it says," διὸ λέγει), its parallel wording, and Paul's interpretive gloss in Eph. 4:9–13 (my criteria *a*, *b*, and *c* in table 3.1) render it a citation, and it is reckoned as such by the common English versions (e.g., CEB, CSB, ESV, NASB, NET, NKJV, NIV, NLT, WEB, etc.).

narrative use of three verbs of speech in verse 37—χαίροντες (present active participle of χαίρω, "rejoice"), αἰνεῖν (present active infinitive of αἰνέω, "praise"), and the pleonastic λέγοντες (present active participle of λέγω)—to introduce the chanting of the people at Jesus's arrival to Jerusalem. This piling up of verbs of speech does not form a citation introduction about Scripture "saying," but again it may well signal Luke's reader to notice the OT quotation (along with the facts that the Pharisees complain about the chanting in 19:39 and that the chanting fulfills Jesus's words in the previous unintroduced citation of Luke 13:35). Similarly, in the crucifixion scene Luke piles up some speaking terms in Luke 23:46 to introduce Jesus's final words, "Then Jesus, calling out with a loud voice, said . . ." (καὶ φωνήσας φωνῇ μεγάλῃ ὁ Ἰησοῦς εἶπεν . . .). His dying words turn out to be an otherwise unintroduced paraphrase of Ps. 31:5 [30:6], which Luke encloses with another use of λέγω (εἰπών) commenting, "And having said this he breathed his last." Lastly, rather than piling up verbs of speech in Luke 23:30 leading to the paraphrase of Hosea 10:8 LXX, Luke reports Jesus remarking to the Jerusalem women about their children, "Then they will begin to say . . ." (τότε ἄρξονται λέγειν . . .). In Luke 23:30, the third-person future construction ἄρξονται λέγειν replaces the third-person future tense ἐροῦσιν in Hosea 10:8, but then follow the ten words of the citation with the phrases reordered. The collocation of ἄρχομαι + λέγειν is common in Luke's narrative to introduce speech (i.e., Luke 3:18; 4:21; 7:24, 49; 11:29; 12:1; 20:9), and occurs only one other time in the mouth of Jesus (i.e., Luke 13:26). While not a proper citation introduction, it nevertheless would signal the OT citation for the women listeners.

The Pauline corpus contains a number of unintroduced citations—both quotations and paraphrases—of the OT Scriptures as judged by the presence of parallel wording, interpretive glosses, and/or syntactical tension. I already mentioned the quotation of Ps. 62:12 [61:13] and/or Prov. 24:12 in Rom. 2:6 where Paul offers an interpretive gloss in Rom. 2:7–8. Other Pauline examples are easily noticed in Romans and in Ephesians. Romans 9:20 contains a paraphrase of Isa. 29:16, with Paul offering an interpretive gloss in Rom. 9:21–23. Ephesians 4:25 contains a quotation of Zech. 8:16, with Paul offering an interpretive gloss in the second half of the verse. Ephesians 4:26 contains a quotation of Ps. 4:4 [4:5], with Paul offering an interpretive gloss in Eph. 4:26b–27. It is noteworthy that, in addition to Paul offering specific interpretive glosses on unintroduced citations, he sometimes uses an OT passage as something of an interpretive comment on his own remarks. For example, Rom. 11:2 contains a paraphrase of Ps. 94:14 [93:14] that serves as an interpretive gloss on Paul's own comment in Rom. 11:1, and Eph. 5:31

contains a quotation of Gen. 2:24 that serves as an interpretive gloss for applying Paul's own comments in Eph. 5:28–30.

Some have suggested additional unintroduced citations in Paul's letters. For example, while they don't fit my criteria, NA[28] includes as citations 1 Cor. 14:25; 15:25; 2 Cor. 9:10; Eph. 1:22; and 1 Tim. 5:19, and UBS[5] renders Rom. 4:9 as a citation.[23] Stanley questions what to do with the following Pauline passages, but when I apply my criteria, each of these would be reckoned as specific allusions, recollections, or thematic echoes and not as citations: Rom. 11:25 (at best a thematic echo of texts like Prov. 3:7); Rom. 12:16 (a specific allusion to Prov. 3:7); Rom. 12:17 (a specific allusion to Prov. 3:4); 1 Cor. 10:5 (a recollection of Num. 26:64–65; cf. Num. 14:16); 2 Cor. 3:16 (a specific allusion to Exod. 34:34); 2 Cor. 8:21 (a specific allusion to Prov. 3:4); Phil. 1:19 (a specific allusion to Job. 13:16); Phil. 2:10–11 (specific allusions to Isa. 45:23); and Phil. 2:15 (a specific allusion to Deut. 32:5).[24] More will be said below about the criteria for specific allusions and thematic echoes, but let me first say something about recollections, the category containing the classifications of Scripture summaries and historical reminiscences.

Recollections: Introductions without Citations

Scholars have puzzled over the handful of introductory formulas in the NT that mention the Scriptures but don't seem to introduce any recognizable citations. But my contention is that these introductory formulas do serve recognizable purposes. In chapter 2, I suggested the label *recollections* for NT references to OT content that do not otherwise quote or even use much of the language of the relevant OT passages. The label *historical reminiscences* is used for the classification of recollections about OT people and/or events, and the label *Scripture summaries* is used for the classification of recollections about OT teachings and/or customs. My suggestion is that the reminiscent references to OT people and/or events are too general to be considered mere specific allusions (i.e., with shared wording), and yet they are hardly paraphrases of the OT passages, much less citations. Similarly, Scripture sum-

23. UBS[5] leaves out of its listed citations Rom. 2:6; 9:20; 11:2, all three of which I (and NA[28]) reckon as citations.

24. Stanley, *Paul and the Language of Scripture*, 34n7. Using form definitions that differ slightly from mine, Porter suggests that Phil. 1:19 should be reckoned as an unintroduced quotation (which he labels a "direct quotation") of Job 13:16 and that Phil. 2:15 should be reckoned as an unintroduced quotation of Deut. 32:5. See Stanley E. Porter with Bryan R. Dyer, *Sacred Tradition in the New Testament: Tracing Old Testament Themes in the Gospels and Epistles* (Grand Rapids: Baker Academic, 2016), 18–22, 24, 35.

maries mention the message of the OT but with such non-specific wording that they too fall short of being considered citations.

Examples of Scripture summaries are found in such passages as Matt. 7:12, where Jesus summarizes OT teaching by saying, "So whatever you wish that others would do to you, do also to them, for this is the Law and the Prophets," and in John 1:45, where Philip declares, "We have found him of whom Moses in the Law and also the prophets wrote, Jesus of Nazareth, the son of Joseph." Examples of historical reminiscences can be illustrated here with Luke 4:27, where Jesus clearly references 2 Kings 5:1–19 by commenting, "And there were many lepers in Israel in the time of the prophet Elisha, and none of them was cleansed, but only Naaman the Syrian," and with Gal. 4:22, where Paul references the historical events recorded in Genesis, saying, "For it is written that Abraham had two sons, one by a slave woman and one by a free woman."

So it is that such recollections of OT people/events (i.e., historical reminiscences) or recollections of OT teachings/customs (Scripture summaries) can appear as something like introductions without citations. The content of recollections tends to be even freer than paraphrases (recall the variability of the continuum diagram of fig. 2.1). As with citations, the introductions to recollections can be placed on something of a continuum. That is, on the one hand, introductions to Scripture summaries range from the more official (e.g., "But all this has taken place that the Scriptures of the prophets might be fulfilled" in Matt. 26:56; and "he promised beforehand through his prophets in the holy Scriptures, concerning his Son, who was descended from David" in Rom. 1:2–3) to the less official (e.g., "for he [Moses] wrote of me" in John 5:46; and "as he promised" in Acts 13:23). On the other hand, the "introductions" for historical reminiscences are usually the mere mention of the people and/or events involved, whether complex (e.g., "Long ago, at many times and in many ways, God spoke to our fathers by the prophets" in Heb. 1:1), or candid (e.g., "As an example of suffering and patience, brothers, take the prophets who spoke in the name of the Lord" in James 5:10), or curt (e.g., "Remember Lot's wife" in Luke 17:32).

Scholars may vary on whether 2 Pet. 1:21 is a Scripture summary or a historical reminiscence: "For no prophecy was ever produced by the will of man, but men spoke from God as they were carried along by the Holy Spirit." While I think of this as a recollection of the events of history, some may consider it to be more of a summary of OT teaching regarding the many scriptural statements about what "the Lord says." Perhaps 2 Pet. 1:21 would best be mapped on the two-dimensional form continuum (fig. 2.1) somewhere along the line between Scripture summary and historical reminiscence.

The Vocabulary of Scripture Summary Introductions

Because they are identified by key terms regarding the people and/or events being referenced, I won't offer any discussion of the vocabulary of the introductions for the historical reminiscences of the NT. But because the introductions to Scripture summaries tend to be worded more like citation introductions, we can more easily examine their vocabulary. And in doing so, Scripture summary introductions can be grouped into some of the same basic vocabulary groupings.

Scripture summary introductions using the γραφή / γράφω word group. As in citation introductory formulas, several NT Scripture summary statements utilize the noun γραφή for "Scripture." With diverse subjects and verbs, γραφή appears in fourteen Scripture summaries (Matt. 26:54, 56; Mark 14:49; Luke 24:27, 45; John 5:39; 7:42; 17:12; 19:28; 20:9; Acts 17:2; Rom. 1:2; 1 Cor. 15:3, 4). Similarly, the verb γράφω ("I write") is utilized in Scripture summary statements in fifteen assorted ways. The perfect passive, "it is written," occurs seven times (Matt. 26:24; Mark 9:12, 13; 14:21; Luke 24:46; John 8:17; Gal. 4:22), and the aorist active, "he wrote," occurs twice (John 1:45; 5:46). The perfect passive participle, "what has been written," occurs six times (Luke 18:31; 21:22; 24:44; John 12:16; Acts 13:29; 24:14) with all five Lukan instances in construction with the adjective πᾶς, "all, every."

Scripture summary introductions using λέγω. Unlike its use in citation introductions, λέγω ("I say") is much less common in Scripture summaries, but it does occur. People wondering about Jesus's identity state in a clear Scripture summary in John 7:42, "Has not the Scripture said that the Christ comes from the offspring of David, and comes from Bethlehem, the village where David was?" It also occurs in two NT introductory statements that have made scholars scramble in search of possible OT citation candidates. Matthew 2:23 says, "And he went and lived in a city called Nazareth, so that what was spoken by the prophets might be fulfilled, that he would be called a Nazarene"; and Luke 11:49 states, "Therefore also the Wisdom of God said, 'I will send them prophets and apostles, some of whom they will kill and persecute.'" My suggestion is that these somewhat formal introductions are not to mysterious, lost, or otherwise unknown citations; rather, these are Scripture summaries.[25]

Scripture summary introductions using λαλέω. Even more so than the citation introductory formulas, a significant number of Scripture summary introductions utilize the common verb of speech λαλέω ("I speak") in a variety of constructions. The "prophets" are sometimes mentioned as the subject or

25. For more on Matt. 2:23 and Luke 11:49, see app. A.

agent of the verb (e.g., Luke 1:70; 24:25; Acts 3:21, 24; 26:22). Both David (Acts 2:34) and Moses (Heb. 7:14; 9:19) are explicitly named as speakers.

Scripture summary introductions using the "to fulfill" word group. Even as they are utilized in citation introductions, the "to fulfill" word group (i.e., πίμπλημι, πληρόω, τελειόω, and τελέω) makes disproportionate appearances in NT Scripture summary statements. The term τελέω (28× in the NT) is used twice (with γράφω) regarding how what was written "will be accomplished" (Luke 18:31) or had been "carried out" (Acts 13:29) regarding Jesus. The term τελειόω (23× in the NT) is used only once meaning "to fulfill" Scripture, and that single use is in a Scripture summary (along with γραφή) in John 19:28, "After this, Jesus, knowing that all was now finished, said (to fulfill the Scripture), 'I thirst'" (summarizing passages such as Ps. 22:15 and 69:21). Similarly, πίμπλημι (24× in the NT) is used only once meaning "to fulfill" Scripture, and that (along with γραφή) is in a Scripture summary (Luke 21:22). The more common "to fulfill" term, πληρόω (86× in the NT), occurs in seven Scripture summary statements, with the Gospel instances also using γραφή or γράφω (Matt. 26:54, 56; Mark 14:49; Luke 24:44; John 17:12; Acts 3:18; 13:27).

Scripture summary introductions using other verbs. As with citations, some NT introductory statements to Scripture summaries use several other verbs of speech attributed to God, Moses, and/or the OT prophets. These include προστάσσω, "to command" (Matt. 8:4//Mark 1:44//Luke 5:14); ἐντέλλω, "to command" (Matt. 19:7–9//Mark 10:3–4; John 8:5); προλέγω, "to foretell" (2 Pet. 3:2); προκαταγγέλλω, "to announce beforehand" (Acts 3:18); μαρτυρέω, "to bear witness" (John 5:39; Acts 10:43; Rom. 3:21); παραδίδωμι, "to deliver, hand over" (Acts 6:14); and χαρίζομαι, "to give, favor with" (Gal. 3:18). In two instances the verb of being γίνομαι ("to be, become, happen") is used with the noun ἐπαγγελία ("promise") to summarize scriptural teaching: "the promise that was made to our ancestors" (Acts 13:32 CSB); "the promise made by God to our fathers" (Acts 26:6–8); and in one instance the verb of being εἰμί ("to be") is likewise used with ἐπαγγελία (Rom. 4:13).

Non-verb Scripture summary introductions. Sometimes the NT authors refer to scriptural teaching without using verbs; these are primarily prepositional phrases with objects such as "Moses," "law," "commandment," "customs," "prophets," and combinations of these. Most common is the use of κατά ("according to"): "according to the Law of Moses" (Luke 2:22); "according to the custom of the Law" (Luke 2:27); "everything according to the Law of the Lord" (Luke 2:39); "according to the commandment" (Luke 23:56); "according to promise" (Acts 13:23; Gal. 3:29); "according to that law" (John 19:7); "a commandment in the law" (Heb. 7:5); and "according to the law" (Heb. 8:4; 9:22; 10:8). Luke also utilizes περὶ ("concerning, about"): "For what is [written] about me" (Luke 22:37; cf. 24:44); and "in all the Scriptures the things concerning himself" (Luke 24:27); and he twice uses ἀπό ("from"): "from the Law of Moses and the Prophets" (Acts 28:23); and "from the Scriptures" (Acts 17:2–3). Paul uses διά ("through"): "through promise" (Gal. 4:23).

Furthermore, occasionally summaries of scriptural teachings are announced with nouns alone; for example, "the custom of Moses" (Acts 15:1); "Moses" (Acts 15:20–21); "Moses . . . [according to our] customs" (Acts 21:21). Similar to the author of Hebrews (e.g., Heb. 6:12, 15, 17; 7:6; 11:17), note Paul's preference for using the noun ἐπαγγελία ("promise") in various references to OT teaching, for example, "the promise" (Rom. 4:14; 9:8); "the promise of God" (Rom. 4:20; 2 Cor. 1:20); "the promises to the fathers" (Rom. 15:8); "these promises" (2 Cor. 7:1); "the covenants of promise" (Eph. 2:12). And Paul has a string of nouns in Rom. 9:4 recalling OT teaching about the Israelites: "the adoption, the glory, the covenants, the giving of the law, the worship, and the promises."

As with citation introductions, it is important to note that the diverse vocabulary used in introducing Scripture summaries occurs in a variety of combinations with each other. This is seen in some of the examples given above. What is significant here, however, is that many of the same terms (and combinations of terms) employed for citation introductions are also employed for Scripture summary recollections where no citation is intended. This was apparently not problematic for the NT authors, and we should not see it as some sort of problem in sorting out their various references to the OT.

Summary on Identifying Citations and Recollections

Recognizing that a wide variety of NT introductory statements can serve as preludes to recollections of OT teaching rather than to citations offers a model for solving some difficulties in NT exegesis. There are several places in the NT that have introductory statements followed by apparent citations that have no clear counterpart in the OT. The suggestion is that some of the debated passages might be explained as Scripture summaries of OT teaching or historical reminiscences about OT people or events. Nevertheless, this suggestion has been particularly problematic for places where the introductory formulas are more formal than many of those found in the typical recollection passages. Scholars have offered various explanations for these difficult cases (see table 3.3 and my solutions in app. A), but work is likely to continue on these matters.

TABLE 3.3

Apparent Citations Introduced in the New Testament but Difficult to Locate in the Old Testament

The following fourteen NT passages have introductory statements for apparent citations that scholars have difficulty locating in the OT. They are cited here along with some of the solutions of possible OT references proposed by others. For my specific solutions to each of these, see appendix A.

Matt. 2:23	"And he went and lived in a city called Nazareth, so that what was spoken by the prophets might be fulfilled, that he would be called a Nazarene." Proposed referents: Judg. 13:3–7; Isa. 4:2–3; 11:1; 52:13–53:12; Jer. 23:5; 33:15
Luke 11:49	"Therefore also the Wisdom of God said, 'I will send them prophets and apostles, some of whom they will kill and persecute.'" Proposed referents: Jer. 7:25–26; 25:3–7; 2 Chron. 36:15–16
Luke 24:46–47	"Thus it is written, that the Christ should suffer and on the third day rise from the dead, and that repentance for the forgiveness of sins should be proclaimed in his name to all nations, beginning from Jerusalem." Proposed referents: Deut. 18:15; Pss. 22:1–11 [21:1–12]; 69:1–36 [68:1–36]; Isa. 49:6; 50:6; 52:13–53:12; Dan. 9:24–27; 12:2; Mic. 5:2 [5:1]; Zech. 12:10; 13:7; Hosea 6:1–2
John 7:38	"Whoever believes in me, as Scripture has said, 'Out of his heart will flow rivers of living water.'" Proposed referents: Zech. 14:8; Ezek. 47:1–12; Isa. 44:3; Joel 2:28 [3:1]; Ezek. 36:25–27; cf. Neh. 9:15, 19–20; Prov. 18:4; Song 4:15; Isa. 43:19–20; 55:1; 58:11; Joel 3:18 [4:18 MT]; Sir. 24:19–21, 30
John 12:34	"We have heard from the Law that the Christ remains forever. How can you say that the Son of Man must be lifted up? Who is this Son of Man?" Proposed referents: 2 Sam. 7:12–16; Pss. 89:4–5, 36 [88:5–6, 37]; 110:1–4 [109:1–4]; Isa. 9:7; Ezek. 37:25; Dan. 7:13–14
Acts 7:26	"And on the following day he appeared to them as they were quarreling and tried to reconcile them, saying, 'Men, you are brothers. Why do you wrong each other?'" Proposed referent: Exod. 2:13–14
Acts 13:22	"And when he had removed him, he raised up David to be their king, of whom he testified and said, 'I have found in David the son of Jesse a man after my heart, who will do all my will.'" Proposed referents: Ps. 89:20 [88:21]; 1 Sam. 13:14; 16:1, 12–13; Isa. 44:28; cf. 1 Clem. 18.1
1 Cor. 2:9	"But, as it is written: 'What no eye has seen, nor ear heard, / nor the heart of man imagined, / what God has prepared for those who love him.'" Proposed referents: Isa. 64:4 [64:3 LXX, MT]; 65:16–17; cf. Exod. 20:6; Jer. 3:16
1 Cor. 9:10	"Does he not certainly speak for our sake? It was written for our sake, because the plowman should plow in hope and the thresher thresh in hope of sharing in the crop." Proposed referents: Deut. 25:4; Sir. 6:19
2 Cor. 4:6	"For God, who said, 'Let light shine out of darkness,' has shone in our hearts to give the light of the knowledge of the glory of God in the face of Jesus Christ." Proposed referents: Gen. 1:2–3; Ps. 112:4 [111:4]; Job 37:15; Isa. 9:2 [9:1]
Eph. 5:14	"Therefore it says, 'Awake, O sleeper, / and arise from the dead, / and Christ will shine on you.'" Proposed referents: Isa. 26:19; 51:17; 52:1; 60:1–2; nonbiblical sources (e.g., a Christian hymn or apocryphal work)
1 Tim. 5:18b	"For the Scripture says, 'You shall not muzzle an ox when it treads out the grain,' and 'The laborer deserves his wages.'" Proposed referents: Lev. 19:13; Deut. 24:15; Luke 10:7
2 Tim. 2:19b	"But God's firm foundation stands, bearing this seal, 'The Lord knows those who are his,' and, 'Let everyone who names the name of the Lord depart from iniquity.'" Proposed referents: Lev. 24:16; Num. 16:26–27; Job 36:10; Pss. 6:9 [6:8]; 34:14 [33:15]; Prov. 3:7; Isa. 26:13; 52:11; Sir. 17:26; 23:10; 35:3
James 4:5	"Or do you suppose it is to no purpose that the Scripture says, 'He yearns jealously over the spirit that he has made to dwell in us'?" Proposed referents: Exod. 20:5; 34:14; Deut. 4:24; 32:11; Pss. 42:1 [41:2]; 84:2 [83:3]; 119:20, 131, 174 [118:20, 131, 174]; Prov. 3:34

Nonetheless, apart from the fourteen most difficult cases (and perhaps a few other debated passages), generally speaking there is a lot of agreement among scholars regarding the identification of citations. Due to differences in precise definitions for citation subcategories, however, scholars can exhibit substantial disagreement in identifying which citations are quotations and which are paraphrases. Similar differences of opinion exist regarding the broader classification category that I label "recollections" with its two subcategories of Scripture summaries and historical reminiscences. I have discussed these here with the citations classification because recollections (as I define them) typically exhibit some kind of introductory statement. Other scholars, however, simply include these OT forms as versions of specific allusions.

As noted in chapter 2, my grouping of the various form classifications for uses of the OT in the NT is mapped on a two-dimensional continuum, which illustrates visually the proximity relations of the various forms with citations and recollections regularly displaying introductory statements of some kind (see figs. 2.1 and 2.2). Although other scholars using definitions different from mine might offer slightly altered outlines of the examples provided here, I suspect there would be substantial agreement once the merely definitional differences are accounted for.

Features of Specific Allusions and Thematic Echoes

I have noted that there are several features to observe when attempting to identify the OT passage(s) being utilized by a NT writer. The clearer the features of a particular form (e.g., the introductory formulas in introduced quotations and introduced paraphrases), the easier it is for us to identify the prior text being referenced. Similar to introduced citations, recollections are easier to identify given their introductory formulas and corresponding OT passages. On the other hand, scholars discuss and debate the proper means for identifying the much more difficult concepts of allusions to, and echoes of, a prior text (aka a source text). What is an "allusion," and what evidence exists to indicate when an author is intentionally but allusively referring to a prior text in his present text? Nevertheless, in the words of Michael Thompson, "Despite their differences, literary critics concur that allusion involves (1) the use of a sign or marker that (2) calls to the reader's mind another known text (3) for a specific purpose."[26]

---

26. Michael B. Thompson, *Clothed with Christ: The Example and Teaching of Jesus in Romans 12.1–15.13*, JSNTSup 59 (Sheffield: Sheffield Academic, 1991; reprint, Eugene, OR:

Thompson has offered eleven criteria for identifying allusions to, and echoes of, a Gospel saying in the text of a NT epistle, and these can be refashioned to apply to the search for allusions to the OT in the NT (see in table 3.4). The desire for precision, especially regarding the difficult concept of allusion, is appreciable, but Thompson's approach might be considered overkill or even unworkable by some.[27] Thompson admits that some of his criteria "are weightier than others," naming specifically verbal, conceptual, and formal agreement over against the presence of other contextual indicators. And he is clear about the level of certainty his criteria can or cannot provide: "Criteria such as these cannot be expected to *prove* dependence in a mathematical way." Rather, the use of such criteria simply assists the interpreter in judging relative probability of allusions or echoes, and Thompson suggests a six-point sliding scale of certainty: virtually certain—highly probable—probable—possible—doubtful—incredible.[28]

Perhaps the most notable list of criteria for identifying intertextual references is that provided by Richard Hays. Technically, Hays's criteria—which he calls more fully "criteria for testing claims about the presence and meaning of scriptural echoes"—apply to citations (both quotations and paraphrases) as well as to what I have dubbed specific allusions and thematic echoes. With regard to citations, the passages being tested will simply offer that much more evidence in the criteria categories (e.g., in volume of parallel wording). But the place where Hays's suggested criteria get more attention in scholarly discussion is in their helpfulness for identifying uses of the OT in the NT other than citations. Hays's tests consist of questions to ask in relation to passages in Paul's letters that allegedly echo particular passages of the OT. While aimed at the Pauline literature, Hays's questions can be rephrased for use when examining any NT passage suspected of alluding to the OT (see the sketch of them in table 3.4). As have many other scholars, I discuss Hays's seven criteria here with specific notes on the application of each.[29]

Wipf & Stock, 2011), 29. Thompson appeals to the assessment of Carmela Perri, "On Alluding," *Poetics* 7 (1978): 289–307.

27. So Porter, *Sacred Tradition*, 13–15, 39. In an earlier version of his evaluation of Thompson, Porter suggests that much of Thompson's criteria for "allusions" better fits what Porter terms "paraphrase." See Stanley E. Porter, "Further Comments on the Use of the Old Testament in the New Testament," in *Intertextuality of the Epistles: Explorations of Theory and Practice*, ed. Thomas. L. Brodie, Dennis R. MacDonald, and Stanley E. Porter, New Testament Monographs 16 (Sheffield: Sheffield Academic, 2006), 109n41.

28. Thompson, *Clothed with Christ*, 36 (the emphasis in the quotation is his); Thompson notes that his sliding scale of certainty is adapted from E. P. Sanders, *Jesus and Judaism* (Philadelphia: Fortress, 1985), 321.

29. See Richard B. Hays, *Echoes of Scripture in the Letters of Paul* (New Haven: Yale University Press, 1989), 29–32; cf. Richard B. Hays, *The Conversion of the Imagination: Paul as*

TABLE 3.4

Various Criteria for Identifying Specific Allusions and Thematic Echoes

Thompson

1. Verbal agreement—similar words in both texts

2. Conceptual agreement—similar themes in both texts

3. Formal agreement—similar structure and number of elements

4. Place of the saying in the tradition—availability to the author

5. Common motivation, rationale for both texts

6. Dissimilarity to outside traditions or other sources (e.g., Greco-Roman)

7. Contextual indicators (e.g., named characters from the source text)

8. Traditional indicators (e.g., interruptions in the grammar, style, or context flow)

9. Shared word/concept clusters in the immediate context

10. Likelihood the author knew the saying—the author uses the source elsewhere

11. Exegetical value—acknowledging the allusion advances the author's argument

Hays

1. Availability—that the author had access to the source text

2. Volume—the amount of the source text reproduced

3. Recurrence—repeated use of the same passage

4. Thematic coherence—similar topic, wording, and images

5. Historical plausibility—the likelihood that the reference could be intended

6. History of interpretation—that others have recognized the reference

7. Satisfaction—acknowledging the allusion makes better sense of the text

MacDonald

1. Accessibility—that the author had access to the source text

2. Analogy—to what extent other authors utilized the same source text

3. Density—the volume of similarities between the texts

4. Order—similar order of elements between the texts

5. Distinctive trait—anything unusual that is in both texts

6. Interpretability—the value of acknowledging the dependence

Note: These criteria lists are adapted from Thompson, *Clothed with Christ*, 28–36; cf. 20–21; Hays, *Echoes of Scripture in the Letters of Paul*, 29–32; Dennis R. MacDonald, "A Categorization of Antetextuality in the Gospels and Acts: A Case for Luke's Imitation of Plato and Xenophon to Depict Paul as a Christian Socrates," in *Intertextuality of the Epistles: Explorations of Theory and Practice*, ed. Thomas L. Brodie, Dennis R. MacDonald, and Stanley E. Porter, New Testament Monographs 16 (Sheffield: Sheffield Academic, 2006), 212.

Interpreter of Israel's Scripture (Grand Rapids: Eerdmans, 2005), 34–45. In the following discussion, the label for each criterion is that of Hays, but the discussion of each is my own. This section draws upon some suggestions of Kenneth Duncan Litwak, *Echoes of Scripture in Luke-Acts: Telling the History of God's People Intertextually*, JSNTSup 282 (London: T&T Clark,

1. Availability: Was the proposed source of the echo available to the author and/or original readers?

Certainly, it makes sense that an author must have access to a source text (and perhaps presume that readers have some level of access to that text) in order for the author to make use of it in some fashion in the subsequent text. There is little question that the Scriptures of Israel were available to the NT authors and their readers in the first-century Mediterranean world. We can agree that readers' familiarity with the prior text increases their ability to understand and appreciate the author's intended meaning.[30] Nevertheless, Porter is correct that the *author's* familiarity with the prior text—not the readers' familiarity with it—is ultimately what makes the reference to that prior text possible.[31]

2. Volume: What is the degree of explicit repetition of words or syntactical patterns, how distinctive or prominent is the precursor text within Scripture, and how much rhetorical stress does the echo receive in the NT passage?

Volume has to do primarily with the amount of wordings and structures from the source text that are taken over into the successive text, but also includes the level of prominence the proposed source text has in the successive text.[32] For example, Luke-Acts contains about ten explicit citations of Isaiah that are so extensive (i.e., "voluminous") that few would dispute Luke's dependence on the OT prophet at those points, even when he does not explicitly introduce the quotation as coming from Isaiah. But going farther, Luke-Acts has many easily recognized specific allusions to Isaiah, some occurring in the same contexts, which raises the likelihood of Luke's intentional use of Isaiah; for example, after Acts 7:49–50 cites Isa. 66:1–2, then Acts 7:51 contains a specific allusion to the rebellious activity of the Israelites mentioned in Num. 27:14 and in Isa. 63:10–11. Recent works have argued for Isaiah having a formative influence on the structure and message of the whole of Luke-Acts.[33]

2005), 62, but I offer a number of my own examples. See also G. K. Beale, *Handbook on the New Testament Use of the Old Testament: Exegesis and Interpretation* (Grand Rapids: Baker Academic, 2012), 33–35; and Christopher A. Beetham, *Echoes of Scripture in the Letter of Paul to the Colossians*, BibInt 96 (Leiden: Brill, 2008), 27–35.

30. With reference to the work of Stefan Alkier, Hays mentions this issue of a reader's "encyclopedia of reception" containing the necessary information to recognize allusions; Richard B. Hays, "The Liberation of Israel in Luke-Acts: Intertextual Narration as Countercultural Practice," in *Reading the Bible Intertextually*, ed. Richard B. Hays, Stefan Alkier, and Leroy A. Huizenga (Waco: Baylor University Press, 2009), 104.

31. See Porter, *Sacred Tradition*, 18–24; cf. 41–43, 47.

32. With "echo" and "volume" both having aural applications, the wordplay here is appreciable; even so, complaints about Hays's use of a metaphorical label seem to forget that "volume" has a more basic (and here, fitting) meaning about the amount or quantity of something.

33. See particularly David W. Pao, *Acts and the Isaianic New Exodus*, WUNT 2/130 (Tübingen: Mohr Siebeck, 2000; reprint, Biblical Studies Library, Grand Rapids: Baker Academic, 2002);

3. Recurrence: How often does the NT author elsewhere cite or allude to the same scriptural passage?

When the author of a successive text repeatedly and explicitly uses a source text, additional allusions and echoes to that source text can also be expected. For example, given that Paul twice cites Lev. 19:18 (in Rom. 13:9 and Gal. 5:14), it is no surprise that he would allude to it elsewhere in his letters (e.g., in Rom. 12:19). On a larger scale, the author of Hebrews cites several verses from Ps. 95 five times (i.e., Heb. 3:7–11, 15; 4:3, 5, 7), so it is no surprise to find a specific allusion to Ps. 95:11 in Heb. 3:18. On a still larger scale, because Luke-Acts contains more than a dozen explicit citations of Exodus, it would not be surprising for Luke to utilize Exodus in more subtle specific allusions and thematic echoes as well; indeed, some count more than fifty specific allusions and thematic echoes to Exodus in Luke-Acts. Thus, with the emphasis upon repeated use, recurrence can be understood as a form of volume.[34]

4. Thematic coherence: How well does the alleged echo fit into the line of argument that the NT author is developing?

When the topic, wording, and images of the present text are covering the same or similar material as a prior text, an echo to that prior text would not be surprising in the present text. For example, given the interest that both Matthew and Luke have in Jesus's genealogy (i.e., Matt. 1:1–17 and Luke 3:23–38), it is unsurprising that they both have echoes of the genealogical material in 1 Chron. 1–3 and Ruth 4.

5. Historical plausibility: Could the NT author have intended the alleged meaning effect, and could his readers have understood it?

If a particularly slanted treatment of a source text were historically unavailable to the author of the successive text, any suggested echoes of the source text with that particular slant are less likely. So, for example, it is probably correct to note echoes of Isa. 42:5 in the references to "God who made the world and everything in it" and "gives to all mankind life and breath" in Acts 17:24–25. But it is unconvincing to suggest that this echo proves Luke held an evolutionary view of the creation process because of Isaiah's wording "who spread out the earth and what comes from it." Even if such an evolutionary

---

Bart J. Koet, "Isaiah in Luke-Acts," in *Dreams and Scriptures in Luke-Acts: Collected Essays* (Leuven: Leuven University Press, 2006), 51–79; Peter Mallen, *The Reading and Transformation of Isaiah in Luke-Acts*, LNTS 367 (New York: T&T Clark, 2008); Holly Beers, *The Followers of Jesus as the 'Servant': Luke's Model from Isaiah for the Disciples in Luke-Acts*, LNTS 535 (New York: Bloomsbury T&T Clark, 2015); and see the critical analysis by Ben Witherington III, "Isaiah the Architect: The Use of Isaiah by the Evangelists to Structure their Gospels (and Acts)," in *Isaiah Old and New: Exegesis, Intertextuality, and Hermeneutics* (Minneapolis: Fortress, 2017), 477–96.

34. So Litwak, *Echoes of Scripture in Luke-Acts*, 63.

reading of Isaiah might be questioned on other grounds, such a suggestion is simply not historically plausible for Luke.

6. History of interpretation: Have other readers, both critical and precritical, heard the same echoes?

While an echo may seem unlikely to a current-day reader, if other informed interpreters of the text under consideration have recognized in it an echo to a particular prior text, the presence of that echo is more likely. For example, current-day readers may find odd the common suggestion that the account of the Ethiopian eunuch worshiping in Jerusalem (Acts 8:27) echoes OT passages mentioning worshipers coming from "beyond the rivers of Cush" (e.g., 1 Kings 8:41–43; Pss. 68:29–31 [67:30–32]; 87:4 [86:4]; Isa. 18:7; 56:3–7; Jer. 38:7 MT; Zeph. 3:10). But this historical connection makes better sense when readers learn that the upper Nile region was called "Cush" in the OT era and "Ethiopia" in the NT era, referring to the Nubian Empire in what is now southern Egypt and northern Sudan (not today's Ethiopia).

7. Satisfaction: With or without clear confirmation from the other criteria listed here, does the proposed reading make sense? Does it illuminate the surrounding discourse? Does it produce for the reader a satisfying account of the effect of the intertextual relation?

If a proposed echo to a source text makes better sense of the successive text in its context (and to its original readers), then the proposed echo is said to be satisfying. For example, Luke introduces his account of the transfiguration with the words "about eight days after" (Luke 9:28), while Matthew and Mark each introduce the same story with "after six days" (Matt. 17:1; Mark 9:2). Although some readers will be unnecessarily distracted by the apparent discrepancy—but note that eight does indeed come "after six"!—it is better to suggest that Luke prefers to use the number eight here as one of his many echoes in this passage to the Festival of Tabernacles, which was an eight-day celebration of the exodus event (Lev. 23:36). This suggested echo is particularly satisfying when noting that Luke alone (and not Matthew and Mark) actually uses the Greek term "exodus" (ἔξοδος, Luke 9:31) in his account.

Summary on Identifying Specific Allusions and Thematic Echoes

Hays's criteria for identifying allusions and echoes have met with much discussion and debate, and this has resulted in various suggested modifications.[35]

---

35. For critiques of Hays's criteria, see esp. Porter, *Sacred Tradition*, 9–11, 43–46; see also Matthew Bates, "Beyond Hays's *Echoes of Scripture*," in *Paul and Scripture: Extending the Conversation*, ed. Christopher D. Stanley, Early Christianity and Its Literature 9 (Atlanta: Society

Dennis MacDonald suggests a simpler list of six criteria for identifying the use of prior texts (what he calls "antetexts"; see in table 3.4, above).[36] G. K. Beale's analysis reduces Hays's seven criteria to only five, suggesting that "thematic coherence" and "satisfaction" be combined and that "availability" and "historical plausibility" be combined.[37] Thomas L. Brodie, Dennis R. MacDonald, and Stanley E. Porter reduce the number further and suggest three criteria that coordinate somewhat with that of Hays (particularly his first two) and other scholars: the criterion of "initial external plausibility" ($\approx$ availability), the criterion of "significant similarities" (which covers genre, themes, style, plot, motifs, structure, order, and wording, thus $\approx$ volume), and the criterion of "classifiable and interpretable similarities and differences" (i.e., the ability to describe "what is going on between the texts," thus $\approx$ satisfaction).[38] Some scholars suggest that Hays's first two criteria of availability and volume are the most useful for identifying echoes of Scripture, and others suggest altogether different repackaging approaches.[39] As the examples above illustrate, however, each of the criteria Hays suggests—admittedly, to varying degrees—can have its helpful application. Thus, even for scholars who use fewer of them, Hays's list of seven criteria remains the primary set of tools for recognizing (and/or confirming) specific allusions and thematic echoes referencing OT Scripture.[40]

---

of Biblical Literature, 2012), 263–91; Alex J. Lucas, "Assessing Stanley E. Porter's Objections to Richard B. Hays's Notion of Metalepsis," *CBQ* 76 (2014): 93–111; and David Allen, "The Use of Criteria: The State of the Question," in *Methodology in the Use of the Old Testament in the New: Context and Criteria*, ed. David Allen and Steve Smith, LNTS 579 (New York: Bloomsbury T&T Clark, 2020), 129–41.

36. MacDonald, "Categorization of Antetextuality," 212.

37. Beale, *Handbook*, 35.

38. Thomas L. Brodie, Dennis R. MacDonald, and Stanley E. Porter, "Conclusion: Problems of Method—Suggested Guidelines," in *Intertextuality of the Epistles: Explorations of Theory and Practice*, ed. Thomas. L. Brodie, Dennis R. MacDonald, and Stanley E. Porter, New Testament Monographs 16 (Sheffield: Sheffield Academic, 2006), 292–95.

39. For examples of those preferring Hays's first two criteria, see Litwak, *Echoes of Scripture in Luke-Acts*, 63–65; Robert Lawson Brawley, *Text to Text Pours Forth Speech: Voices of Scripture in Luke-Acts*, ISBL (Bloomington: Indiana University Press, 1995), 13–14; and Joel B. Green, *The Gospel of Luke*, NICNT (Grand Rapids: Eerdmans, 1997), 13. For an altogether different repackaging example, see the suggestion of Steve Smith, "The Use of Criteria: A Proposal from Relevance Theory," in *Methodology in the Use of the Old Testament in the New*, ed. David Allen and Steve Smith, LNTS 579 (New York: Bloomsbury T&T Clark, 2020), 142–54.

40. Given my two-out-of-four criteria approach to identifying NT citations of the OT, I can be grouped among those scholars who prefer to reduce the Hays criteria to a smaller number of tests. But I am willing to admit that Hays's longer list of criteria can be useful in identifying the more difficult specific allusions and thematic echoes that reference OT Scripture.

4

Framing Classifications for the New Testament Use of the Old Testament

Therefore, beloved, since you are waiting for these, be diligent to be found by him without spot or blemish, and at peace. And count the patience of our Lord as salvation, just as our beloved brother Paul also wrote to you according to the wisdom given him, as he does in all his letters when he speaks in them of these matters. There are some things in them that are hard to understand, which the ignorant and unstable twist to their own destruction, as they do the other Scriptures.

2 Peter 3:14–16

How Framing Overlaps with Form and Function

As with other terminology used in the field of the NT's use of the OT, the term *framing* needs some definition, particularly in distinction from the terms *form* and *function*. In chapter 1, I defined framing as the means by which a NT writer presents the OT passage and not merely the characteristics of his OT reference (i.e., the form) or his motives for appealing to that particular OT passage (i.e., the function). That is to say, if the function refers to the NT author's motives and the form refers to the characteristics of the OT reference, then the framing is the setting in which the NT author places the OT reference.[1]

While the realm of framing is somewhat distinct from the realm of form (discussed in chaps. 2 and 3 above) and from the realm of function (discussed in chap. 5 below), an important complicator needs to be examined at this juncture. As has already been suggested in previous chapters, among scholars working in this field, there is some overlap not only in the use of various labels but also in the concepts themselves. Thus, the realm I am calling framing overlaps with the realms of form and of function. This is particularly the case when considering the phenomena of paraphrases and typology. Is a paraphrase a form of referring to an OT text (e.g., over against quotations, allusions, etc.), or is it a framing in order to set an OT passage in a particular light? Is typology a framing in order to set an OT passage in a particular light, or is it a function regarding the purpose the NT author has for referring to an OT text? Similarly, every instance of the form I call "historical reminiscences" certainly has the function of recalling a particular person or event history.[2] Thus, there is an overlap of concepts as well as labels when considering the various realms of concern in examining the NT's use of the OT, an overlapping phenomenon that can be pictured in figure 4.1.

Given this overlap of classification realms, I readily admit that my various taxonomical categories are somewhat artificial. Yet I want to argue that they remain helpful in analyzing the NT authors' use of the OT. Having such taxonomical tools available assists modern-day interpreters in seeing the complexity of the ancient authors' thinking and may restrain us from making unwarranted assumptions about the first-century use of prior texts.

Nevertheless, despite a few areas of conceptual overlap, it is important to consider a distinct place for various kinds of framings for the NT authors' display of OT references. In this regard, the classification realm that I call framings is the place to discuss matters of first-century Jewish exegetical practices. Here scholars make distinctions between various first-century practices such as **targum** (interpretive paraphrases), **midrash** (interpretation and/or commentary from searching the text itself), **pesher** (explaining eschatological mysteries), **allegory** (extracting symbolic meanings), and **typology** (noticing how historical events, institutions, places, and figures function as divinely

---

1. An earlier version of this chapter was titled, "A New Taxonomy of Framing Classifications for the NT Use of the OT" (paper presented at the seventy-third annual meeting of the Evangelical Theological Society, Fort Worth, November 16, 2021).

2. Furthermore, while scholars primarily discuss introductory formulas in the realm of *forms* (as I did in chap. 3 above), introductory formulas can also be viewed as ways for NT authors to frame their use of OT passages.

FIGURE 4.1

Taxonomical Overlap of Forms, Framings, and Functions

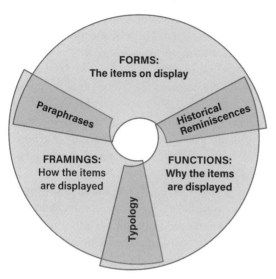

FORMS:
The items on display

Paraphrases

Historical Reminiscences

FRAMINGS:
How the items are displayed

FUNCTIONS:
Why the items are displayed

Typology

In studying the NT use of the OT, some elements seem to fall into more than one category. Thus the same reference to an OT passage in the NT might be seen as a form from one angle but as a framing from another angle (e.g., a paraphrase). Another reference to an OT passage in the NT might be viewed as a framing in one sense but as a function in another sense (e.g., typology). And another reference to an OT passage in the NT might be considered a form in one sense but as a function in another sense (e.g., a historical reminiscence).

ordained symbols of subsequent, greater realities).[3] These first-century exegetical practices are among the framings under consideration in this chapter.

Respect for the Old Testament Context in First-Century Jewish Exegetical Methods

That NT writers used Jewish exegetical methods is accepted by virtually all NT scholars, and virtually all expect that this at least partially explains some of their uses of the OT. It is the extent to which the NT writers used these various exegetical methods that has been a matter of voluminous research and scholarly discussion. This particular question is utilized to address what Beale calls "the most important debate" about the use of the OT in the NT: "whether the NT interprets the Old in line with the original OT

---

3. These five practices are discussed in this order by Craig A. Evans, "The Old Testament in the New," in *The Face of New Testament Studies: A Survey of Recent Research*, ed. Scot McKnight and Grant R. Osborne (Grand Rapids: Baker Academic, 2004), 131–34; Longenecker discusses literalist, *midrashic, pesher,* and allegorical interpretations; Richard N. Longenecker, *Biblical Exegesis in the Apostolic Period*, 2nd ed. (Grand Rapids: Eerdmans, 1999), 14–33. Approaching the Jewish exegetical methods as framing devices provides assistance in treating the NT authors with the respect they deserve.

meaning."[4] Does their utilization of first-century Jewish exegetical practices lead the NT authors to interpret the OT out of context?

Rather than directly engaging in such a debate at this juncture, I want to suggest a way forward. Admittedly, this suggestion puts me firmly in the camp of those who understand the NT authors as entirely faithful to the OT contexts in their use of the Scriptures, but my proposal here fleshes out the sensibility of such a conclusion. There are two points to this proposal.

First, I don't want to deny that the NT authors used first-century Jewish exegetical methods. Jan Willem Doeve (1918–1979), a pioneer in the modern study of the NT use of the OT, argues that the NT authors use the same Jewish exegetical practices found in **rabbinic literature** (i.e., interpretations of Jewish law collected and eventually written down in the centuries after Jerusalem was destroyed). But Doeve recognizes a (rather obvious) difference between the early Christians, who believed in Jesus as Messiah, and the rabbinic Jews, who denied Jesus to be Messiah. This significant difference, claims Doeve, is due not to dissimilarities in interpretation methodology (strictly speaking) but to things like the presence of the Holy Spirit and the modeling of Jesus himself.[5] More recently Douglas Moo and Andrew Naselli suggest something similar by distinguishing "appropriation techniques" from "hermeneutical axioms."[6] The ways in which NT authors select OT texts and set them up in their NT writings are indeed similar to Jewish **appropriation techniques**. But the very different convictions about God's Word and work held by the NT authors distance them from rabbinic interpreters, as their **hermeneutical axioms** (i.e., their underlying theological commitments) lead them to utilize the selected Scriptures differently.

Thus, we must recognize that it is possible for different interpreters to appeal to some of the same interpretation tools and yet for them to reach different—even opposing—conclusions due to how they utilize those interpretation tools

---

4. G. K. Beale, *Handbook on the New Testament Use of the Old Testament: Exegesis and Interpretation* (Grand Rapids: Baker Academic, 2012), 1.

5. Jan Willem Doeve, *Jewish Hermeneutics in the Synoptic Gospels and Acts* (Assen: Van Gorcum, 1954), 91–118. In the century prior, Patrick Fairbairn made similar remarks; see Patrick Fairbairn, *The Typology of Scripture*, 2 vols. in 1 reprint ed. (Grand Rapids: Zondervan, 1956 [6th ed., 1882]), 1:395. Most recently, reflecting on the NT use of Isaiah, Witherington remarks, "What sets the NT readings of Isaiah apart from those in general in early Judaism is they are Jesus-focused readings of Isaiah"; Ben Witherington III, "Isaiah the Architect: The Use of Isaiah by the Evangelists to Structure Their Gospels (and Acts)," in *Isaiah Old and New: Exegesis, Intertextuality, and Hermeneutics* (Minneapolis: Fortress, 2017), 496. This recalls the discussion of presuppositions in chap. 1 above (see esp. table 1.2).

6. Douglas J. Moo and Andrew David Naselli, "The Problem of the New Testament's Use of the Old Testament," in *The Enduring Authority of the Christian Scriptures*, ed. D. A. Carson (Grand Rapids: Eerdmans, 2016), 716.

in light of some of their other commitments. As Moo and Naselli state it, "Scholars often exaggerate the influence of Jewish exegetical methods on the NT. A vast gulf separates the often fantastic, purely verbal exegeses of the rabbis from the NT's sober, contextually oriented interpretations. Indeed, the NT differs most from Jewish literature when the latter strays furthest from what we would consider sound hermeneutics."[7]

Moreover, the sensible similarities between the NT writers and the rabbinic interpreters may well be because those same elements are found in their mutually authoritative source: the Hebrew Scriptures. That is to say, the normal, sober, and contextually oriented exegetical methods of the NT writers that appear similar to many rabbinic techniques are actually interpretation elements found within the OT Scriptures themselves. This is uncovered in studying the OT's use of the OT.[8] After his most thorough examination of the use of Scripture within the OT itself, Gary Schnittjer observes, "Since these interpretive tendencies are not unusual but widely disseminated in the Hebrew Scriptures it [is] not clear why the authors of the New Testament would need to consult proto-rabbinic exegetical scholarship or vice versa. It seems entirely natural that those who studied the Hebrew Bible, like the authors of the New Testament and the Judaic scholars of late antiquity, could independently and coincidentally emulate the sorts of interpretive interventions found within Israel's Scriptures."[9] The NT writers did not use fantastical methodologies to interpret Scripture; rather, examples of their methods are found within the OT Scriptures themselves.

This brings me to my second point here: I want to suggest that there may well be proper ways to use what scholars have dubbed first-century hermeneutical tools. If there are proper ways to use first-century tools, there are also improper ways to use them, which means that varying degrees of errant interpretation could occur among ancient writers (even as they do among scholars today!). Nevertheless, while hermeneutical practices in any age can be misapplied—even when well-intended—each and every use of a first-century interpretational practice need not be deemed illegitimate. But more to the point, I want to suggest that the "Jewish exegetical methods" under discussion here, in the hands of the best interpreters, were utilized for faithful exposition

7. Moo and Naselli, "Problem," 716.

8. On this specific field, see the definitive work of Gary Edward Schnittjer, *Old Testament Use of Old Testament: A Book by Book Guide* (Grand Rapids: Zondervan Academic, 2021). For a very brief description of the OT's use of the OT, see C. John Collins, "How the New Testament Quotes and Interprets the Old Testament," in *Understanding Scripture: An Overview of the Bible's Origin, Reliability, and Meaning*, ed. Wayne Grudem, C. John Collins, and Thomas R. Schreiner (Wheaton: Crossway, 2012), 185–86.

9. Schnittjer, *Old Testament Use of Old Testament*, 860–61.

of the true theology of the Scriptures. Rather than merely *exegetical* methods, these were *expositional* methods and *application* methods. These were not merely ways of exegesis; they were ways of what we call today "doing theology."[10] And these practices were not merely ways of finding theology in the text; they were also ways of communicating and applying the theology of the text.[11] They were ways of presenting—or framing—the theological message of Scripture.

A Taxonomy of Framings

With this framing perspective, I offer a taxonomy of fifteen distinct ways—but not necessarily mutually exclusive ways—that NT authors would frame their uses of the OT Scriptures.[12] While the fifteen are numbered consecutively, the various entries in the taxonomy are collected into two commonly discussed groupings of Jewish exegetical practices, with a few in a third, "other" grouping at the end.

Midrashic Exegetical Framings

The Jewish exegetical practices known by the Hebrew term *midrash*, which resulted in commentary from searching the scriptural text itself, were not designated as such until the early fourth century CE. So in considering them as potential patterns used by NT authors, we risk slipping into anachronism. Nevertheless, many of the practices so labeled appear to be present much earlier. For example, in 2 Chronicles the word *midrash* is used to refer to "the annotations of the prophet Iddo" (13:22 NIV) and "the annotations on the book of the kings" (24:27 NIV), and a cognate Hebrew term is used for "study" in Ezra 7:10, "For Ezra had devoted himself to the study and

10. For a cautious but decidedly positive view of midrashic interpretation—as Jewish exegetical methods per se—see Martin Pickup, "New Testament Interpretation of the Old Testament: The Theological Rationale of Midrashic Exegesis," *JETS* 51 (2008): 353–81; see his cautions on 380–81.

11. Grant Osborne similarly suggests that at least some of the first-century Jewish interpretation practices should be reckoned as "appropriation techniques." He distinguishes "hermeneutical methods for understanding the text" from "the means of appropriating the text for community use"; Grant R. Osborne, *The Hermeneutical Spiral: A Comprehensive Introduction to Biblical Interpretation*, rev. ed. (Downers Grove, IL: InterVarsity, 2006), 327–28. Osborne credits Douglas Moo for the label "appropriation techniques"; see Douglas J. Moo, *The Old Testament in the Gospel Passion Narratives* (Sheffield: Almond, 1983), 25.

12. By saying the various methods are not mutually exclusive, I mean, of course, that a NT author can use multiple framing methods at the same time, even as a photograph can be displayed with multiple matting frames.

TABLE 4.1

The Seven Rules of Hillel (First Century BCE) and Old Testament Examples

1. *Qal wa-ḥomer* (light and heavy): Lesser to greater
   OT Examples: Lev. 19:33–34 → 19:18; and Exod. 23:4–5 → Deut. 22:1–4

2. *Gezerah shawah* (an equivalent regulation): Meaning deduced by analogy
   OT Examples: Exod. 22:21–23 → Deut. 24:17–19 (cf. Exod. 3:7); and Deut. 14:29; 26:13

3. *Binyan 'ab mikkatub 'eḥad* (constructing a father [i.e., a principal rule] from one passage): Application transcends individual mandate to all kindred mandates
   OT Example: Lev. 13:45–46 → Num. 5:1–4

4. *Binyan 'ab mishene ketubim* (constructing a father [i.e., a principal rule] from two passages): Application deduced from two passages
   OT Example: 1 Sam. 21:4 → Lev. 24:9 + Deut. 23:14

5. *Kelal uperat uperat ukelal* (the general and the particular; and the particular and the general): Particular to general, general to particular
   OT Examples: Exod. 13:12–13 → Num. 18:15; and Exod. 23:19; 34:22; Lev. 23:10–11 → Num. 15:18–21 → Num. 18:12–13

6. *Kayotse bo bi-maqom 'aher* (to which something is similar in another place): Similarity in content from elsewhere
   OT Example: Exod. 33:9 vs. 40:34–35 ← 1 Kings 8:11

7. *Dabar halamed me'inyano* (a word of instruction from the context): Meaning deduced from context
   An OT Example: Gen. 11:7 ← Deut. 32:8 LXX / 4Q37 (Deutʲ)

Note: Each of Hillel's rules has a transliterated Hebrew name, a rough translation, and a more user-friendly title. This listing is dependent on Instone Brewer, *Techniques and Assumptions*, 226. The user-friendly titles and examples from the OT are the suggestions of Schnittjer, *Old Testament Use of Old Testament*, 860n69.

observance of the Law of the LORD" (NIV). The first-century Jewish writer Philo, a contemporary of the NT authors, also exhibits comparable methods. Thus, there is good reason to compare NT use of the OT with such rabbinic procedures. Yet, while such comparisons are legitimate, we must caution ourselves against assuming that all of the later developments of the third and fourth centuries were necessarily present in their first-century uses.[13] Thus, I prefer to stick as close to the first century as I can.

One of the most influential Jewish religious leaders of the first century BCE was Hillel the Elder (sometimes anachronistically referred to as Rabbi Hillel). Hillel is often associated with the development of midrash, and seven "rules" (or *middot*) of exegesis are attributed to him (see table 4.1). Hillel's

---

13. Longenecker, *Biblical Exegesis*, 19. See also E. Earle Ellis, "How the New Testament Uses the Old," in *New Testament Interpretation: Essays on Principles and Methods*, ed. I. Howard Marshall (Grand Rapids: Eerdmans, 1977), 203.

relationship to the seven rules is not clear in the rabbinic literature; he might not have originated them himself, and the rules may well predate his famous application of some of them to a question about Sabbath observance.[14] Moreover, basic examples of each of these principal methodologies can be found with the OT itself where one OT writer appeals to an earlier Scripture.[15] But the rules are said to be Hillel's if for no other reason than that he is the first one known to have recorded them.

Furthermore, Hillel's seven rules were later modified and expanded to thirteen by Rabbi Ishmael ben Elisha (ca. 90–135 CE; see table 4.2), and then in the mid-second century to thirty-two separate rules by Rabbi Eliezer ben Jose ha-Galili (ca. 130–160 CE).[16] Such expansion continued in the twelfth-century when Karaite Jewish scholar Judah ben Elijah Hadassi, in his treatise on the Ten Commandments titled *Eshkol ha-Kofer* (or *Sefer ha-Peles*), offered 140 guidelines divided into two groups of 60 and 80 each (with a nod to the "sixty queens" and "eighty concubines" of Song 6:8!).[17] By the nineteenth century, in his commentary on the Sifra (midrashic comments on Leviticus), Rabbi Meir Leibush ben Yehiel Michel Wisser (1809–1879), better known as Malbim, had stretched the "rules" of exegesis to 613 in number—the same as the recognized number of precepts in the Torah.[18] But these expansions seem to have brought more and more excesses in fanciful interpretations and applications of Scripture.[19]

---

14. See b. Pesah. 66a; y. Pesah. 6.1; t. Pesah. 4.1–3. For a brief discussion of the debate about assigning the rules to Hillel, see David Instone Brewer, *Techniques and Assumptions in Jewish Exegesis before 70 CE*, TSAJ 30 (Tübingen: Mohr Siebeck, 1992), 5–7.

15. See esp. Schnittjer, *Old Testament Use of Old Testament*, 860n69; and the OT examples in table 4.1.

16. The Baraita of Rabbi Yishmael, which forms the introduction to the rabbinic Sifra, outlines his thirteen rules and can be read at https://www.sefaria.org/Sifra%2C_Baraita _DeRabbi_Yishmael?lang=bi. See also S. Mendelsohn, "Ishmael B. Elisha," *JE* 6:648–50; S. Mendelsohn, "Eliezer B. Jose Ha-Gelili," *JE* 5:117; and Louis Ginzberg, "Baraita of the Thirty-Two Rules," *JE* 2:520–21; cf. Abraham Zimels, "Bible Exegesis and Study: Talmudic Literature," *EncJud* 3:641; and Doeve, *Jewish Hermeneutics*, 61. The writings of Rabbi Eliezer ben Jose "the Galilean" were long lost, and his thirty-two rules—sometimes called the Baraita of the Thirty-Two Rules or the Baraita of R. Eliezer ben Jose ha-Gelili—were known only from being referenced by others (e.g., the medieval French rabbi Rashi in his commentaries on Gen. 2:8; Exod. 14:24; cf. b. Hor. 3a). But the rules are now available at the beginning of the *Midrash Mishnat R. Eli'ezer*, discovered and published by Hyman Gerson Enelow (New York: Bloch, 1933); see Barnet David Klien, "Baraita of 32 Rules," *EncJud* 3:129. David Instone Brewer offers a clear listing of the 32 rules; see Brewer, *Techniques and Assumptions*, 228–31.

17. Max Seligson, "Hadassi, Judah ben Elijah Habel," *JE* 6:132–33; see Judah ben Elijah Hadassi, *Sefer Eshkol ha-Kofer* (Gozlow: Bi-defus M. Tirishken, 1836), esp. 54–96.

18. Instone Brewer, *Techniques and Assumptions*, 4.

19. See Longenecker, *Biblical Exegesis*, 21–22.

TABLE 4.2

The Thirteen Rules of Rabbi Ishmael Ben Elisha (ca. 90–135 CE)

1. Inference from minor to major, or major to minor.

2. Inference from similarity of phrases in texts.

3. A comprehensive principle derived from one text, or from two related texts.

4. A general proposition followed by a specifying particular.

5. A particular term followed by a specific proposition.

6. A general law limited by a specific application and then treated again in general terms must be interpreted according to the tenor of the specific limitation.

7. A general proposition requiring a particular or specific term to explain it, and conversely, a particular term requiring a general one to complement it.

8. When a subject included in a general proposition is afterward particularly excepted to give information concerning it, the exception is made not for that one instance only, but to apply to the general proposition as a whole.

9. Whenever anything is first included in a general proposition and is then excepted to prove another similar proposition, this specifying alleviates and does not aggravate the law's restriction.

10. But when anything is first included in a general proposition and is then excepted to state a case that is not a similar proposition, such specifying alleviates in some respects and in others aggravates the law's restriction.

11. Anything included in a general proposition and afterward excepted to determine a new matter cannot be applied to the general proposition unless this be expressly done in the text.

12. An interpretation may be deduced from the text or from subsequent terms of the text.

13. In like manner when two texts contradict each other, we follow the second, until a third text is found which reconciles the contradiction.

Note: As outlined in Instone Brewer, *Techniques and Assumptions*, 227–28; for the Hebrew text and an English translation, see the Baraita of Rabbi Yishmael, which forms the introduction to the rabbinic Sifra, available electronically at https://www.sefaria.org/Sifra%2C_Baraita_DeRabbi_Yishmael?lang=bi.

Concerned here primarily with the NT use of the OT and not with later practices, I limit my list of midrashic framings to Hillel's seven rules.[20] "Rules" seems a fitting term to describe Hillel's seven midrashic exegetical framings, since they operate as syllogistic deductive schemes for drawing conclusions and applying Scripture.

20. In the rabbinic literature, Hillel's seven rules are found in 'Abot R. Nat. 37 and in t. Sanh. 7.11. My discussion of them here utilizes such works as Doeve, *Jewish Hermeneutics*, 60–72; John W. Bowker, *The Targums and Rabbinic Literature: An Introduction to Jewish Interpretation of Scripture* (Cambridge: Cambridge University Press, 1969), 315; E. Earle Ellis, *The Old Testament in Early Christianity: Canon and Interpretation in the Light of Modern Research* (Tübingen: Mohr Siebeck, 1991; reprint, Eugene, OR: Wipf & Stock, 2003), 87–91 and 130–32; Craig A. Evans, "Jewish Exegesis," *DTIB*, 381–82; and Instone Brewer, *Techniques and Assumptions*, 226.

1. Hillel's rule 1: *Qal wa-ḥomer* (light and heavy). If something is true or applicable in a lesser (light) case, then it must be just as true or applicable in a greater (heavy) case.

This syllogistic method of theological application is evident in passages like Matt. 6:30 (//Luke 12:28), where Jesus shows God's concern for his people by comparing the adornment of lilies with a historical reminiscence about the surprising riches of Solomon (cf. 1 Kings 10:4–7; 2 Chron. 9:3–6): "But if God so clothes the grass of the field, which today is alive and tomorrow is thrown into the oven, will he not much more clothe you, O you of little faith?"

2. Hillel's rule 2: *Gezerah shawah* (an equivalent regulation). If two passages utilize the same term or idea, they may explain or interpret one another.

This method of linking two texts that share a common word or phrase or idea is utilized as a means of exposition so as to have one text inform the other or to expand upon it or even to explain it. Jesus uses this method of "doing theology" in Matt. 12:1–8 (//Mark 2:23–28//Luke 6:1–5), comparing himself as Son of Man in God's "presence" (cf. Dan. 7:13–14) eating grain on the Sabbath to King David eating the priestly bread of the "presence" (1 Sam. 21:1–7). Ellis explains, "David, who received a kingdom from God (1 Sam. 15:28), was blameless when he and those with him violated the law in eating the bread of the Presence. Therefore, the Son of Man, who has also received a kingdom from God (Dan. 7:13f.), is equally blameless when those with him violate the sabbath law in similar circumstances."[21]

3. Hillel's rule 3: *Binyan 'ab mikkatub 'eḥad* (constructing a father [i.e., a principal rule] from one passage). A theological truth can be inferred from a single text.

In responding to a trick question from some Sadducees in Mark 12:18–27 (//Matt. 22:23–33//Luke 20:27–40), Jesus utilizes a single passage from the Pentateuch, knowing that the Sadducees viewed the writings of Moses as more authoritative. From God's self-identifying declaration, "I AM WHO I AM . . . The LORD, the God of your fathers, the God of Abraham, the God of Isaac, and the God of Jacob . . ." in Exod. 3:14–15, Jesus infers biblical support for the truth of the general resurrection. "And as for the dead being raised, have you not read in the book of Moses, in the passage about the bush, how God spoke to him, saying 'I am the God of Abraham, and the God of Isaac, and the God of Jacob'? He is not God of the dead, but of the living" (Mark 12:26–27; cf. Matt. 22:31–32//Luke 20:37–38).

---

21. Ellis, *Old Testament in Early Christianity*, 131.

4. Hillel's rule 4: *Binyan 'ab mishene ketubim* (constructing a father [i.e., a principal rule] from two passages). A theological truth can be inferred from two passages working together.

This extension of Hillel's third rule seems to be at work in the gospel invitation in Peter's Pentecost sermon, "For the promise is for you and for your children and for all who are far off, everyone whom the Lord our God calls to himself" (Acts 2:39). This invitation utilizes the words of two separate OT passages—or perhaps two separate OT themes—addressing those whom the Lord desires to save. In one passage the LORD says, "Peace, peace, to the far and to the near" (Isa. 57:19; cf. Zech. 6:15; 10:9; Sir. 24:32), and in the other passage is the promise, "And it shall come to pass that everyone who calls on the name of the LORD shall be saved. For in Mount Zion and in Jerusalem there shall be those who escape, as the LORD has said, and among the survivors shall be those whom the LORD calls" (Joel 2:32 [3:5]; cf. Isa. 43:1; Mic. 6:9). From these two passages (or perhaps two sets of passages) Peter infers the single truth that the Lord calls people to salvation from far and near.

5. Hillel's rule 5: *Kelal uperat uperat ukelal* (the general and the particular; and the particular and the general). A general principle can be restricted by a specific particularization elsewhere; and a particular principle can be used to make general application to unspecified instances.

This seems to be the point of the common practice in Jesus's day of discussing the identity of the greatest commandment in Scripture. "You shall love the LORD your God with all your heart and with all your soul and with all your might" (Deut. 6:5) and "you shall love your neighbor as yourself" (Lev. 19:18) are commended by Jesus as the greatest commandments precisely because they nicely summarize and generalize all of the particular commandments of the law (Matt. 22:34–40//Mark 12:28–34//Luke 10:25–28).[22] A common suggestion is that love for God is a summary extension of the first table of the Ten Commandments (i.e., the first four particular commandments directed toward honoring God) and that love for neighbor is a summary extension of the second table (i.e., the six particular commandments directed toward honoring others).

6. Hillel's rule 6: *Kayotse bo mi-maqom 'aḥer* (to which something is similar in another place). Difficulty in one passage can be cleared up by a theological truth inferred from an analogous passage.

In Matt. 26:64 (//Mark 14:62//Luke 22:69) Jesus remarks, "But I tell you, from now on you will see the Son of Man seated at the right hand of Power

---

22. On the addition of "and with all your mind" in Mark 12:30 and Luke 10:27, see the relevant literature.

and coming on the clouds of heaven," a comment that draws primarily upon the OT imagery of "one like a son of man" who came with "the clouds of heaven" to "the Ancient of Days" (Dan. 7:13–14). While God is seated on his throne among several thrones (Dan. 7:9), the Son of Man figure is not explicitly said to be seated in the Daniel passage. But another messianic passage has the LORD inviting the Davidic Messiah figure, "Sit at my right hand" (Ps. 110:1 [109:1]), so Jesus's inference that the Son of Man figure will be seated at God's right hand (i.e., one of the neighboring thrones of Dan. 7:9) is entirely fitting.[23]

7. Hillel's rule 7: *Dabar halamed me'inyano* (a word of instruction from the context). Relevant instruction can be found in the greater context of a passage.

With two introduced quotations in Acts 3:22–23, Peter reports the prophetic remark of Moses, "The Lord your God will raise up for you a prophet like me from among your own people; you must listen to everything he tells you. Anyone who does not listen to him will be completely cut off from their people" (NIV). The close of Peter's citation of Moses's remarks (Deut. 18:15–16) actually paraphrases the more general warning from God a few verses later in Deuteronomy ("And whoever will not listen to my words that he shall speak in my name, I myself will require it of him"; Deut. 18:19), and this functions as Peter's opportunity to move to the greater context of the Pentateuch. Leviticus describes the punishment for not properly keeping the Day of Atonement: "Those who do not deny themselves on that day must be cut off from their people" (Lev. 23:29 NIV), and Peter paraphrases this warning in Acts 3:23b as applicable consequences for not heeding the Messiah Jesus.[24]

Midrashic Homiletical Framings

This second subcategory addresses homiletical structures found in Rabbinic midrash on the text of Scripture. Because these structures are for the presentation of lessons, they serve as additional outline framing options that can incorporate rather than replace the other framings mentioned above.

---

23. In the next verse of Luke's account, in response to the council's question, "Are you the Son of God, then?" Jesus replies, "You say that I am" (Luke 22:70; cf. Mark 14:62). If this reference to "I am" (ἐγώ εἰμι) is an appropriation of the divine name in the Pentateuch (Exod. 3:14), then Luke 22:69–70 (as well as Mark 14:62) contains specific allusions to all three sections of Israel's Scriptures (Torah, Prophets, and Writings; see also Luke 24:44); cf. Peter R. Rodgers, *Exploring the Old Testament in the New* (Eugene, OR: Resource, 2012), 53–54.

24. Hillel's first rule, *Qal wa-ḥomer* (light and heavy), may be at work in Peter's remark as well; i.e., if not observing the Day of Atonement properly results in being cut off from God's people, then certainly refusing God's Moses-like messiah who provides atonement will likewise result in separation from God's people.

These sermonic literary structures are most noted in the rabbinic era, centuries after the NT was written; thus, they are evidently not devised from Christian practice, and yet they do occur in NT documents.[25] Two such homily formats are known by the names **proem** and *yelammedenu rabbenu*.[26] Examples of these sermon formats in the NT have some variations from the strict rabbinic layouts; but even when leaving out one or two elements, the formats remain recognizable.

8. Proem ("introduction"): A homiletical format for discussing several Scripture passages together.

The sermonic format for this approach generally had the following outline (with an example from Rom. 9:6–29):

    a. An initial text for the day, usually from the Pentateuch—Gen. 21:12 in Rom. 9:6–7.

    b. A second text in the introduction to the discourse—Gen. 18:10 in Rom. 9:8–9.

    c. The exposition including supplementary quotations, parables, and other commentary with verbal links to both the initial text and the final text—citations in Rom. 9:13, 15, 17, 25, 26, 27–28 (note καλέω in vv. 7, 12, 24, 25, 26 and υἱός in vv. 9, 26, 27).

    d. A final text, usually alluding to the initial text and sometimes adding a concluding application—Isa. 1:9 in Rom. 9:29 (note σπέρμα in vv. 7, 8, 29).

New Testament examples of this format regularly lack a secondary text, occasionally lack verbal links between the texts, and regularly have some eschatological orientation and/or application. Variations on proem framings are recognizable in Luke 20:9–19 (cf. //Matt. 21:33–46//Mark 12:1–12) and Acts 3:11–26; 7:2–53; 13:17–41.[27]

9. *Yelammedenu rabbenu* ("let our master teach us"): A dialogical homiletical format for discussing several Scripture passages in a dialogue setting.

---

25. Ellis, *Old Testament in Early Christianity*, 96; my descriptions of these homiletical patterns are dependent on the presentation of Ellis (96–100).

26. See esp. John W. Bowker, "The Speeches in Acts: A Study in Proem and Yelammedenu Form," *NTS* 14 (1967–68): 96–111. See also the caution of I. Howard Marshall, "Acts," in *Commentary on the New Testament Use of the Old Testament*, ed. G. K. Beale and D. A. Carson (Grand Rapids: Baker Academic, 2007), 521.

27. See other examples outlined in Ellis, "How the New Testament Uses the Old," 203–5; Ellis, *Prophecy & Hermeneutic in Early Christianity: New Testament Essays* (Grand Rapids: Eerdmans, 1978; reprint, Eugene, OR: Wipf & Stock, 2003), 155–58; and Ellis, *Old Testament in Early Christianity*, 96–100.

This sermonic format was similar to that of the proem, the difference being that it began with something of a dialogue structure (i.e., as if with a teacher), posing an initial question or problem that the exposition would answer. Luke 10:25–37 exhibits this framing and can be laid out as follows:[28]

> a. Dialogue with a question and initial text(s) usually from the Pentateuch—Deut. 6:5 and Lev. 19:18 are engaged in Luke 10:25–27.
>
> b. A second text—an allusion to Lev. 18:5 in Luke 10:28.
>
> c. The exposition utilizing parables, commentary, and verbal links—Luke 10:29–36 has a parable with verbal links to the initial text (note πλησίον in vv. 27, 29, 36).
>
> d. A concluding application with verbal links to one of the texts—Luke 10:37 has verbal links to the second text (ποιέω in vv. 28, 37a, 37b).

Notice that Luke 10:25–27 contains the framing described by Hillel's rule 5 (see above) as do the Synoptic parallels of Matt. 22:34–40 and Mark 12:28–34. But Luke continues the story (Luke 10:28–37), providing an additional full *yelammedenu* framing (an argument can be made that Mark also provides this homiletical framing albeit with different emphases).

See also the use of this *yelammedenu* framing method elsewhere in the Synoptic Gospels: in Matt. 12:1–8//Mark 2:23–28//Luke 6:1–5; and in Matt. 22:23–33//Mark 12:18–27//Luke 20:27–40; as well as in Acts 15:14–21. Interestingly, the *yelammedenu* framing present in the Synoptic tradition in Matthew and Mark is sometimes absent from Luke: compare Matt. 15:1–9//Mark 7:1–23 with Luke 11:37–41; and Matt. 19:3–12//Mark 10:2–12 with Luke 16:18; cf. Matt. 21:10–17//Mark 11:15–17//Luke 19:45–46.

Other Sermonic Framings

Several other sermonic approaches are collected together in this third grouping. These are sometimes dubbed "ancient interpretation practices," but they are nonetheless easily recognized as methods of framing for a speaker/author's presentation of truths from the OT.

10. Targum or paraphrasing translation: Translating a passage into another language with an applicational paraphrase.

After the Babylonian exile of the sixth century BCE, Aramaic became the lingua franca of the Hebrew people. Thus, there was a need for the Hebrew OT to be rendered into the language of the people. Nehemiah 8:8 gives

---

28. Ellis, *Prophecy & Hermeneutic*, 158.

evidence of this custom in public readings, "They read from the book, from the Law of God, clearly, and they gave the sense, so that the people understood the reading."[29] The term *targum* is used to refer to this practice of making an interpretive paraphrase of an OT passage, translating it from Hebrew into Aramaic (when referencing the written Aramaic translation of the Hebrew Bible, the term is capitalized as Targum). John Bowker explains that the translator worked closely with the original Hebrew text of Scripture with no intention of changing its message. The purpose of targum was to interpret the text so as to communicate its meaning to the congregation. "That explains why the Targums lie half-way between straightforward translation and free retelling of the biblical narrative: they were clearly attached to the Hebrew text, and at times translated it in a reasonably straightforward way, but they were also prepared to introduce into the translation as much interpretation as seemed necessary to clarify the sense."[30]

The Targum of Pseudo-Jonathan on Lev. 22:28 provides an example of such an applicational translation. Leviticus 22:28 reads, "But you shall not kill an ox or a sheep and her young in one day," whereas Tg. Ps.-J. Lev. 22:28 renders it with an application principle, "Sons of Israel, my people, as our Father in heaven is merciful, so shall you be merciful on earth: neither cow, nor ewe, shall you sacrifice along with her young on the same day." Evans suggests that this targumic tradition is reflected in Luke 6:36, "Be merciful, even as your Father is merciful."[31] Following Hillel's rule 5, Luke 6:36 is more particular than the general version in Matt. 5:48, "You therefore must be perfect, as your heavenly Father is perfect," which reflects Lev. 19:2, "You shall be holy, for I the LORD your God, am holy." But certainly (following Hillel's rule 7) the emphasis on mercy in the greater context of Leviticus (and in the Sermon on the Mount) can explain why Luke emphasizes a mercy application of Lev. 19:2.

From this example we see that use of the OT in the NT can be set up in several layers of framings. This is especially the case with paraphrasing, and recognition of different framings can help us see why a NT author might slant his paraphrase in a particular direction. While we have already discussed paraphrase as a form for the NT use of the OT, here we see a clear example of the aforementioned taxonomical overlap of the realms of forms and framings.

29. Perhaps somewhat ironically, targums exist for every book of the Hebrew Bible except for Nehemiah, Ezra, and Daniel—three books associated with the need for translation—possibly because portions of Ezra (sometimes joined as one book with Nehemiah) and portions of Daniel were already composed in Aramaic; Christian M. M. Brady, "Targum," *DTIB*, 780.

30. Bowker, *Targums and Rabbinic Literature*, 13. Brady remarks, "The *targumim* are at once both translation and commentary"; Brady, "Targum," 780.

31. Evans, "Old Testament in the New," 131. Evans also suggests similarities in comparisons of Mark 4:12 with Tg. Isa. 6:10 and of Rom. 10:6–8 with Tg. Neof. Deut. 30:11–14.

11. Pesher ("solution" or "interpretation"): Explaining the eschatological mysteries referenced in a passage.

Interpretation techniques labeled with the Aramaic term *pesher* are associated with the manner in which the members of the **Qumran** community read the OT Scriptures as reflected in the Dead Sea Scrolls. The first-century separatist community of Jews living on the western shores of the Dead Sea was highly eschatologically oriented, viewing themselves as the divinely appointed people of God attending to the consummation of the present age and ushering in the age to come. Their interpretive framings were much like the rabbinic midrashic framings already discussed. But despite common habit, pesher should not be defined merely as a more extreme version of midrashic exegesis with an apocalyptic orientation.[32] It is better to understand pesher as something additional to midrash. More than apocalyptic midrash, pesher is particularly caught up with interpreting eschatological mystery.

With the words for mystery (*rāz*) and interpretation (pesher) occurring in the commentary on Habakkuk found at Qumran, Longenecker uses it as an illustration of the central way the Qumran community consciously approached the text: with a *rāz-pesher* revelational motif.[33]

> God told Habakkuk to write the things that were to come upon the last generation, but he did not inform him when that period would come to consummation. And as for the phrase, "that he may run who reads," the interpretation [*pesher*] concerns the Teacher of Righteousness to whom God made known all the mysteries [*rāzim*] of the words of his servants the prophets.[34]

Thus, it is better to define pesher as "explaining eschatological mysteries" of the text perhaps not known even to the original author of the text (cf. the various pesher word forms in such places as Eccles. 8:1 and Dan. 5:12–17). Here is how F. F. Bruce describes it.

> This principle, that the divine purpose cannot be properly understood until the *pesher* has been revealed as well as the *rāz*, underlies the biblical exegesis in the Qumran commentaries. The *rāz* was communicated by God to the prophet, but the meaning of that communication remained sealed until its *pesher* was made known by God to His chosen interpreter. The chosen

---

32. Longenecker, *Biblical Exegesis*, 26.
33. Longenecker, *Biblical Exegesis*, 26–27.
34. This is the commentary on Hab. 2:1–2 found in 1QpHab 7.1–5 as cited by Longenecker, *Biblical Exegesis*, 26–27.

interpreter was the Teacher of Righteousness, the founder of the Qumran community.[35]

Akin to the scrolls found at Qumran and their focus on the Teacher of Righteousness, the NT documents betray an eschatological orientation about faith in Jesus Christ, a faith based in the fulfillment of the OT Scriptures seen with fresh insight (e.g., Mark 1:14–15; 1 Cor. 10:11; Heb. 1:2; 9:26; 1 Pet. 1:5, 9–12). The scholarly community has often discussed Paul's approach to the explaining of mystery because Paul actually uses the Greek term *mystery* (μυστήριον) twenty-one of the twenty-eight times it occurs in the NT. While less commonly discussed with regard to other NT authors, this kind of orientation is nevertheless evidenced in several places. The Synoptics each use the term *mystery* where Jesus explains his use of parables (Matt. 13:10–17// Mark 4:10–12//Luke 8:9–10). Specifically referencing Isa. 6:9–10, the idea that Jesus communicates sounds very much like pesher: the teacher reveals the mysteries of God to his select people.[36] In this regard, even apart from specific vocabulary, Luke offers many summary statements about the OT (arguably more than any other NT writer) that reflect the Christian realization that Jesus is the intended culminating focus of Scripture (among his many Scripture summaries, see esp. Luke 24:25–26, 27, 44, 46–47; Acts 3:18, 21; 10:43; 13:27, 29; 17:2–3; 26:22–23; 28:23; cf. Acts 8:35; 9:22; 18:28). In one such passage Jesus remarks that "everything written about me in the Law of Moses and the Prophets and the Psalms must be fulfilled" (Luke 24:44), to which Luke adds, "Then he opened their minds to understand the Scriptures" (Luke 24:45).

Again, apart from the term *mystery*, some identify pesher interpretation by the introductory formula "the interpretation [pesher] is . . ." and its apparent equivalent "this is . . ." found in the Qumran writings.[37] Thus, NT authors have pesher-like leanings when they utilize a "this is . . ." type of introduction to discuss an eschatological fulfillment of the OT. Luke reports Peter utilizing a "this is . . ." introduction in Acts 2:16–21 (quoting Joel 2:28–32 [3:1–5]) and in Acts 4:10–11 (quoting Ps. 118:22 [117:22]). See also Paul's several uses of "this is . . ." statements (Rom. 9:7–9; 10:6–8; 1 Cor. 10:1–6; and Eph. 5:31–32).

The similarities of Christian interpretation of the OT with Qumranic pesher, however, are not complete.[38] While the Qumran commentators are

---

35. F. F. Bruce, *Biblical Exegesis in the Qumran Texts* (Grand Rapids: Eerdmans, 1959), 8; cf. George J. Brooke, "Pesher," *DBCI*, 273; and Evans, "Jewish Exegesis," 383.

36. Cf. Bruce, *Biblical Exegesis*, 67.

37. E.g., Ellis, *Prophecy & Hermeneutic*, 160; and Brooke, "Pesher," 273–74.

38. Brooke refers to the NT's use of the OT as "pesheresque" at best; Brooke, "Pesher," 274. See esp. the discussion of Schnittjer on how the NT use of pesher interpretation is more like

concerned to find mysterious contemporary applications of each detail of an OT passage, the NT emphasizes how the permanent principle properly found in an OT passage reaches the zenith of its fulfillment in Christ. Rather than a mysterious fulfillment of the OT that may seem to defy its context, for the NT authors Jesus is the fulfillment that makes sense of the OT context. Jesus is the focus.[39]

12. Allegory: Finding spiritual symbolism in a passage that does not seem to indicate such symbolism.

The use of allegory in interpretation seeks to extract symbolic meanings that are thought to be buried deep beneath the obvious surface meaning of a text. Without necessarily denying the historical and literal meanings of a text, allegorists appear far more interested in symbolic (and arguably "more spiritual") uses of a passage, even if the passage gives no hints of having such intentions. While evidenced in early Hellenistic writings, in the scrolls found at Qumran, and among the later rabbis and Christian interpreters (e.g. Origen, ca. 185–254 CE), allegorical interpretation is most famously associated with the first-century allegorist Philo of Alexandria. Philo's writings abound in allegorical suggestions for deeper meanings to be found in Scripture, especially the Pentateuch. Influenced by Platonic thought, Philo tended to set aside literal interpretation, viewing the literal meaning of the Law, which is akin to the visible body, as merely representative of the more spiritual meaning of the words, which is akin to the invisible soul. Thus, symbolic value could be assigned to any and every detail of the text.[40]

Paul actually uses the word *allegorize* to describe his discussion of Hagar and Sarah (Gal. 4:21–31; "Now this may be interpreted allegorically [ἀλληγορέω]," v. 24). But rather than a method for interpreting the Genesis narrative, Paul seems to be constructing his own illustration by using characters familiar to his audience; perhaps his use of the passive periphrastic construction—"can

---

that found in the OT than like that found in the Qumran writings; Schnittjer, *Old Testament Use of Old Testament*, 861–65.

39. Bruce remarks, "The early Christians, then, like the men of Qumran, recognized that the Old Testament writings pointed forward to the emergence of a great prophet, a great priest and a great king at the end-time; but whereas the men of Qumran thought of three distinct personages, the early Christians looked to their Lord as the one in whom all three figures were realized and transcended" (*Biblical Exegesis*, 75; cf. 66–77).

40. Annewies Van Den Hoek, "Allegorical Interpretation," *DBCI*, 11. Some might try to distinguish "allegory" as the discovery of legitimate symbolic values (i.e., not intended by the original author but not contradicting the original intent and perhaps even recognizable as authentic by the original author after the fact) from "allegorism" as the illegitimate attachment of outlandish symbolisms to texts that cannot bear them; cf. Leopold Sabourin, *The Bible and Christ: The Unity of the Two Testaments* (New York: Alba House, 1980), 145. Such a distinction, however, is not at all pervasive in the literature.

be allegorized"—indicates his role in *creating* the allegory rather than a claim about *finding* a (divinely) intended allegory in Genesis. There is no hint that Paul is unconcerned with an accurate reading of the Genesis account or the historical figures of the OT.[41]

In the NT, Jesus's parables come closest to being open for allegorical interpretation, in which characters and events in a simple story seem to represent the interactions of higher spiritual realities.[42] For example, the parable of the wicked vineyard tenants in the Synoptic Gospels (Matt. 21:33–46// Mark 12:1–12//Luke 20:9–19) is ripe with fruitful allegory. As Jesus tells the story, it is evident that the vineyard owner is God, the vineyard itself is God's people, the wicked tenants are the religious leaders, the rejected servants are God's prophets, and the murdered son is Jesus. All three Synoptics record that the religious leaders listening to Jesus "perceived that he had told the parable against them" (Mark 12:12; cf. Matt. 21:45; Luke 20:19). But even here, rather than assigning symbolic values to story elements that are otherwise unconnected to their original context, Jesus's parable seems to be faithfully representing the intention of the parable in Isa. 5:1–7, where the interpretation is clear,

> For the vineyard of the LORD of hosts
> is the house of Israel,
> and the men of Judah
> are his pleasant planting;
> and he looked for justice,
> but behold, bloodshed;
> for righteousness,
> but behold, an outcry! (v. 7)

It is also worth noting that Jesus's telling of this parable fits into a variation of the proem homiletical framing (mentioned above) as follows in Luke's account:

a. Luke 20:9—An opening parable makes specific allusion to the vineyard parable regarding the people of God in Isa. 5:1–7.

b. Luke 20:10–12—The telling of the parable makes specific allusion to a second text, 2 Chron. 36:15–16, which is about the people's responses to God's repeatedly sent messengers.

---

41. Some suggest that Paul is here utilizing typology (see below) rather than what is to be labeled with our modern terminology "allegory"; Gerald Bray, "Allegory," *DTIB*, 34.

42. Bray, "Allegory," 34.

c. Luke 20:13–16—The parable begun in the specific allusion of the initial text reaches a climactic point, and the listeners give a verbal response.

d. Luke 20:17–18—The citation of a final text, Ps. 118:22 [117:22], draws on a second image for Israel, that of a building, and challenges the listeners to make the correct choice.[43]

13. Typology: Divinely intended symbolism in history whereby historical figures, places, events, or institutions (the "types") foreshadow subsequent greater realities (the "antitypes").[44]

Typological thinking is similar to, or perhaps underlies, the representational thinking behind pesher and allegorical ways of interpretation, except that typology is directly tied to history. Craig Evans remarks, "Unlike midrash, pesher, or even allegory, typology is primarily interested in biblical events and not in the biblical text."[45] In order to avoid abusive interpretive methodologies that sometimes get attached to the term *typology*, some scholars have shifted to using the term **figural reading** to refer to the proper use of typological considerations.[46] At this juncture, however, I am content to continue using the term *typology* but want to be understood as referring only to its reputable connotations.[47]

Properly understood, typology sees actual historical figures and events portrayed in the OT as symbolic foreshadows of subsequent historical figures and events. There is thus a necessary continuity between the referenced OT element in its context and its partner in the NT passage. The NT element reveals an escalated (but not necessarily new) sense of the OT element. As Leonard Goppelt says it, "For our understanding of the OT, typology provides a framework that is determined not only by the NT but also by the OT itself; one that unites the two Testaments with one another and that facilitates the understanding of each by pointing to the other."[48] What is debated among

---

43. Ellis offers a proem outline of the parable of the wicked vineyard tenants in the parallel text of Matt. 21:33–46 in Ellis, *Old Testament in Early Christianity*, 98; cf. Ellis, *Prophecy & Hermeneutic*, 251.

44. Beale defines typology as "the study of analogical correspondences among revealed truths about persons, events, institutions, and other things within the historical framework of God's special revelation, which, from a retrospective view, are of a prophetic nature and are escalated in their meaning"; Beale, *Handbook*, 14; he points out five "essential characteristics": (a) analogical correspondence, (b) historicity, (c) a pointing-forwardness, (d) escalation, and (e) retrospection.

45. Craig A. Evans, "New Testament Use of the Old Testament," *NDBT*, 79; cf. Evans, "Old Testament in the New," 133; Evans, "Jewish Exegesis," 383–84; Ellis, *Old Testament in Early Christianity*, 106; Ellis, *Prophecy & Hermeneutic*, 168–69.

46. See Schnittjer, *Old Testament Use of Old Testament*, 853–56.

47. For a brief treatment on debates surrounding typology, see Beale, *Handbook*, 13–25.

48. Leonhard Goppelt, *Typos: The Typological Interpretation of the Old Testament in the New*, trans. Donald H. Madvig (Grand Rapids: Eerdmans, 1982 [German original, 1939]; reprint, Eugene, OR: Wipf & Stock, 2002), 237.

scholars is the extent to which the typological nature of the person, place, event, or institution must be anticipated in the OT context over against being merely recognized retrospectively by NT writers.[49]

Found among the rabbis and in early Christianity, typology is often discussed as a Jewish exegetical method.[50] But typology is not really an exegetical method per se (i.e., focused on interpreting texts), because typology is concerned with the actual people and events in history more so than the (necessary) texts about those people and events.[51] As others, this homiletical framing device is also evidenced within the OT itself where former events in history are retrospectively viewed as prefiguring promises of future events. For example, God's redemption of Israel from Egypt (narrated in Exodus–Deuteronomy) is later taken as something of a foreshadowing of God's redemption of Israel from Babylonian exile (e.g., Isa. 43:14–21; 48:20–21).

This focus on historical realities is continued in the NT. For example, Luke extends this exodus typology to the redemption that God provides through Jesus (see Luke 9:28–36, which contains more exodus images than its Synoptic parallels in Matt. 17:1–9 and Mark 9:2–10). In Acts 7 we see Stephen make a specific connection between Moses's own claim to be a messianic type (Deut. 18:15 in Acts 7:37) and Jesus's more general reference to the prophets being types of him and his ministry (Acts 7:51–52; cf. Acts 3:17–26, where Peter does something similar).[52] On two occasions Paul actually uses the Greek term "type" (τύπος) when making such comparisons: Adam was a type foreshadowing Jesus (Rom. 5:14), and the exodus events are types for us (1 Cor. 10:1–11 with several images suggested). Twice in the NT the matching term "antitype" (ἀντίτυπος) is used in typological discussions: in 1 Pet. 3:21 of baptism in correspondence to the Noahic flood; and in Heb. 9:24 of man-made sanctuaries in correspondence to the realities of heaven itself (which

---

49. See the discussions in Walter C. Kaiser Jr., *The Uses of the Old Testament in the New* (Chicago: Moody, 1985; reprint, Eugene, OR: Wipf & Stock, 2001), 103–10; and in David L. Baker, *Two Testaments, One Bible: The Theological Relationship between the Old and New Testaments*, 3rd ed. (Downers Grove, IL: InterVarsity, 2010), 179–89.

50. See esp. Goppelt, *Typos*, 1–58.

51. See R. T. France, *Jesus and the Old Testament: His Application of Old Testament Passages to Himself and His Mission* (Grand Rapids: Baker, 1971), 41, "But while strict exegesis is a prerequisite of typology, it is not correct to describe typology itself as a method of exegesis"; cf. Baker, *Two Testaments, One Bible*, 181–82. Most insightful is the argument of Ardel Caneday that typology is a function of divine revelation and not of human interpretation; see Ardel B. Caneday, "Biblical Types: Revelation Concealed in Plain Sight to Be Disclosed—'These Things Occurred Typologically to Them and Were Written Down for Our Admonition,'" in *God's Glory Revealed in Christ: Essays in Honor of Tom Schreiner*, ed. Denny Burk, James M. Hamilton Jr., and Brian Vickers (Nashville: B&H Academic, 2019), 135–55.

52. Goppelt, *Typos*, 121; cf. 107–24 on typology in Luke-Acts.

thus reverses the expected use of the labels "type" and "antitype"). The most extensive use of typological imagery from the OT in the NT is found in the Letter to the Hebrews.[53] Such comparisons are thus framing devices: a particular figure or event in an OT passage is set out as a comparison to some greater figure or event in the NT era.

As utilized in the NT, typology is sometimes viewed not merely as a framing device for citing an OT passage but as the reason why a NT author cites that particular passage. That is, the message that the NT author wants to portray is precisely that the OT passage portraying a **type** (i.e., a historical figure, place, event, or institution) now has its **antitype** (i.e., a later and greater historical figure, place, event, or institution) in the Jesus event. In this way typology is viewed as having a kind of fulfillment role for the function of the OT in the New. Darrell Bock has tried to allow for this kind of overlap by offering two different usage (or function) subcategories related to typology. When a fuller, more extensive fulfillment of some kind is already anticipated at the initial appearance of the type in its written OT context, Bock labels it a "typological-PROPHETIC" usage; the use of Joel 2:28–32 [3:1–5] in Acts 2:17–21 can be slotted here as well as the christological uses of the Servant Songs of Isaiah, fulfilled first in Israel and now in Jesus (e.g., Isa. 49:6 in Acts 13:47; Isa. 53:7–8 in Acts 8:32–33; and Isa. 53:12 in Luke 22:37). But when the typological imagery is hidden until its escalated fulfillment is realized, as pointed out by a NT author, Bock labels it a "TYPOLOGICAL-prophetic" usage; the clearest suggestion for this classification is the citation of Hosea 11:1 in Matt. 2:15, and the use of the righteous sufferer psalms also fit here (e.g., Ps. 16:8–11 [15:8–11] in Acts 2:25–28; Ps. 22:1 [21:2] in Matt. 27:46 and Mark 15:34).[54] In my terms here, Bock's former category stresses the NT author's use of the OT passage functioning as a prophecy that is fulfilled, and Bock's latter category stresses the NT author's framing of the OT passage as having a typological setting.[55] Thus, typology falls into the region where the taxonomical realms of framings and functions overlap (see fig. 4.1 above).

53. On Hebrews, see esp. Goppelt, *Typos*, 161–78.
54. Darrell L. Bock, "Single Meaning, Multiple Contexts and Referents: The New Testament's Legitimate, Accurate, and Multifaceted Use of the Old," in *Three Views on the New Testament Use of the Old Testament*, ed. Kenneth Berding and Jonathan Lunde, Counterpoints: Bible and Theology (Grand Rapids: Zondervan, 2008), 118–20; see also Darrell L. Bock, "Scripture Citing Scripture: Use of the Old Testament in the New," in *Interpreting the New Testament Text: Introduction to the Art and Science of Exegesis*, ed. Darrell L. Bock and Buist M. Fanning (Wheaton: Crossway, 2006), 271–73.
55. From another vantage point, Bock's "typological-PROPHETIC" label corresponds to my promising patterns function classification, and his "TYPOLOGICAL-prophetic" label corresponds to my typological correlation function classification; see the discussion of the functions of the NT use of the OT in chap. 5 below.

14. *Peshat*, or literal interpretation: Understanding a passage to mean plainly and exactly what it says.

Longenecker notes that the Hebrew word **peshat** ("to strip off, to flatten, to rush out, to flay") has been associated with plain interpretation since at least the fourth century CE and came to be used somewhat synonymously (even if not by all commentators) with the word "to interpret."[56] Even though the NT authors do not use such a label to describe any of their references to the OT, their simple framing of a passage to be understood literally is everywhere attested. Naturally this is especially evident in the places where they recall historical events from the OT Scriptures (e.g., in the form that I call historical reminiscences).[57]

15. Conflation: When two (or more) different passages of Scripture are referenced together as if they are one passage.

While not specifically named as a Jewish method of exegesis, conflation can occur in several first-century framings (e.g., Hillel's rules 4 and 6, and both midrashic homiletical framings; see table 4.3 below); scholars sometimes refer to this as a form of "implicit *midrash*" or more colorfully "chain-quoting."[58] The conflation of two or more different passages into one composite citation is distinct from a compressed citation, which is the abbreviation of a single passage by leaving portions out. In modern times authors use ellipses (. . .) to mark compression in their quotations of a source, but ancients did not have such punctuation conventions (or even basic punctuation!). Conflations are likewise unmarked in ancient texts. An example of conflation occurs in Luke 4:17–19, which contains a quotation of Isa. 61:1–2 that largely fits with the wording of the LXX. With an introduction in verse 17, this is a clear instance of an introduced quotation. Nevertheless, one line of the citation makes a specific allusion to Isa. 58:6: "to release the oppressed." Thus, with allusive insertion, this introduced quotation (a form classification) takes the framing of a conflation of OT texts. Another example occurs in Matthew's

---

56. Longenecker, *Biblical Exegesis*, 17–18. See Instone Brewer's discussion of *peshat* ("plain") as distinguished from *derash* ("hidden") and his suggestion that two other modes of exegesis be defined somewhere between *peshat* and *derash*: nomological (i.e., reading Scripture as though it were a legal document) and ultra-literal (i.e., refusal to recognize idiomatic language, even when the context explains the words to be other than literal); see Instone Brewer, *Techniques and Assumptions*, 14–17.

57. Perhaps in pressing the metaphor of framings for presenting Scripture snapshots, the *peshat* approach might be considered the absence of a frame: it is simply a raw presentation of a particular OT passage.

58. For "implicit *midrash*," see, e.g., Ellis, "How the New Testament Uses the Old," 201–3; Ellis, *Prophecy & Hermeneutic*, 151–54; and Ellis, *Old Testament in Early Christianity*, 92–96; for "chain-quoting," see, e.g., Robert H. Gundry, "Quotations in the New Testament," *ZEB* 5:13.

TABLE 4.3

A Taxonomy of Framing Techniques
for the New Testament Use of the Old Testament

Midrashic Exegetical Framings

1. Hillel's rule 1: Lesser to greater
2. Hillel's rule 2: Meaning deduced by analogy
3. Hillel's rule 3: Application transcends individual mandate to all kindred mandates
4. Hillel's rule 4: Application deduced from two passages
5. Hillel's rule 5: Particular to general, general to particular
6. Hillel's rule 6: Similarity in content from elsewhere
7. Hillel's rule 7: Meaning deduced from context

Midrashic Homiletical Framings

8. Proem
9. *Yelammedenu rabbenu*

Other Sermonic Framings

10. Targum or paraphrasing translation
11. Pesher
12. Allegory
13. Typology
14. *Peshat* or literal interpretation
15. Conflation

account of the words from the cloud at Jesus's transfiguration (Matt. 17:5), which contain allusions to all three sections of the Israelite Scriptures (Torah, Prophets, and Writings): "This is my beloved Son [Ps. 2:7], with whom I am well pleased [Isa. 42:1]; listen to him [Deut. 18:15]."[59]

Final Thoughts on Respect for Old Testament Contexts

As already noted earlier in this chapter, these various framings for citing a text can be abused in such a way as to take an original text out of its proper context. But, of course, the possibility of abuse is not, in itself, proof of abuse. On the contrary, I am suggesting that we recognize that the NT writers used

59. Gundry, "Quotations in the New Testament," 5:11. Similarly, the phenomenon occurs in Acts 20:28 with Paul's challenge to the Ephesian elders: "Be shepherds of the church of God [see Ps. 74:1–2 (73:1–2 LXX) and elsewhere], which he bought [relative pronoun + περιποιέω; see Isa. 43:21; cf. Isa. 31:5] with the blood of his own Son [see Gen. 22:2, 16]" (NIV margin); Rodgers, *Exploring the Old Testament*, 54.

first-century Jewish methodologies (as discussed above and listed in table 4.3) primarily as framing techniques that remain faithful to the OT contexts from which they cite.

Some time ago James Rendel Harris proposed that early Christians maintained "testimony" lists of certain OT passages from which they could make prooftext quotations. The suggestion is that such written *testimonia* collections would help explain NT passages that appear to take OT passages out of context.[60] Taking up the idea of *testimonia* passages, C. H. Dodd, another notable pioneer in the modern study of the NT use of the OT, argues instead that the NT writers cite Scripture passages in keeping with their OT contexts. Dodd observes that only a few OT contexts are repeatedly referenced in the NT but that these OT contexts are rarely referenced by citing the same OT verses from those larger passages. Dodd's proposal is that the NT authors would cite a phrase or sentence from the OT with the intention that those particular lines would bring to their readers' minds the whole OT passage wherein the citation is found. Thus, while the particular OT verse cited in the NT might appear to be taken out of its immediate context, Dodd suggests that it is used in the NT as a signpost pointing to the broader OT passage, which in fact does properly support the NT claim.[61] Thus, Dodd defends the idea that the NT writers cited the Scriptures with proper respect for their OT settings.

Of course, not all scholars are convinced by Dodd's theory.[62] Nevertheless, even some of the more skeptical have come to recognize Dodd's conclusion

60. See James Rendel Harris, with Vacher Burch, *Testimonies*, 2 vols. (Cambridge: Cambridge University Press, 1916, 1920).

61. See C. H. Dodd, *According to the Scriptures: The Sub-structure of New Testament Theology* (London: Nisbet, 1952). Dodd lists the following fifteen OT passages as significantly important to NT writers and as candidates for belonging to a list of *testimonia* passages for the early church: Pss. 2:7; 8:4–6; 110:1 [109:1]; 118:22–23 [117:22–23]; Isa. 6:9–10; 53:1; 40:3–5; 28:16; Gen. 12:2; Jer. 31:31–34 [38:31–34]; Joel 2:28–32; Zech. 9:9; Hab. 2:3–4; Isa. 61:1–2; and Deut. 18:15, 19. But Dodd clarifies that these key passages did not compose an exhaustive list and suggests a four-part broader grouping of Scriptures. Furthermore, in the practice of the early church, these key passages "were understood as *wholes*, and particular verses or sentences were quoted from them rather as pointers to the whole context than as constituting testimonies in and for themselves" (126). Barnabas Lindars suggests that the importance of Dodd's study "can hardly be over-estimated" and that it "has struck the death-blow against the theory of a Testimony Book put forward by Rendel Harris"; Barnabas Lindars, *New Testament Apologetic: The Doctrinal Significance of the Old Testament Quotations* (London: SCM, 1961), 14. Gundry has suggested adding a few more texts to Dodd's list; see Gundry, "Quotations in the New Testament," 5:16.

62. For examples of those against Dodd's thesis (even if not naming Dodd per se), see Albert C. Sundberg, "On Testimonies," *NovT* 3 (1959): 268–81, esp. 275–78; S. L. Edgar, "Respect for Context in Quotations from the Old Testament," *NTS* 9 (1962–63): 55–62; D. Moody Smith Jr., "The Use of the Old Testament in the New," in *The Use of the Old Testament in the New and Other Essays: Studies in Honor of William Franklin Stinespring*, ed. James M. Efird (Durham,

as fitting in at least some instances. For example, in considering the use of the OT in the NT book of Acts, John Carroll willingly admits that "on occasion at least, the quotations in Acts betray considerable reflection on the meanings of the larger passages from which the cited verses are drawn."[63] Perhaps Dodd's theory has a broader application than merely "on occasion."[64] In fact, David Instone Brewer has made an extensive argument that the celebrated examples of fanciful rabbinic exegetical practices—those ignoring the original OT context—come primarily from the post-70 CE era. Instone Brewer combs through all extant examples of Jewish exegesis preserved in the rabbinic literature with the likelihood of having originated prior to 70 CE (approximately one hundred items) and suggests that faithfulness to the original context was the goal of exegesis in the scribal tradition of that era, even in those instances that might be judged as unsuccessful.[65]

In line with such scholars as Dodd and Instone Brewer, my suggestion here is that the NT authors' citations of the OT cannot be passed off as nothing

---

NC: Duke University Press, 1972), 29–30; Morna D. Hooker, "Beyond the Things That Are Written? St. Paul's Use of Scripture," *NTS* 27 (1981): 295–309; Donald Juel, *Messianic Exegesis: Christological Interpretation of the Old Testament in Early Christianity* (Philadelphia: Fortress, 1988), 19–22; Christopher D. Stanley, *Arguing with Scripture: The Rhetoric of Quotations in the Letters of Paul* (New York: T&T Clark, 2004); and Stanley, "Paul's 'Use' of Scripture: Why the Audience Matters," in *As It Is Written: Studying Paul's Use of Scripture*, ed. Stanley E. Porter and Christopher D. Stanley, SymS 50 (Atlanta: Society of Biblical Literature, 2008), 125–55. For a recent revival of the *testimonia* theory, see Martin C. Albl, *"And Scripture Cannot Be Broken": The Form and Function of the Early Christian Testimonia Collections*, NovTSup 96 (Leiden: Brill, 1999); cf. Susan E. Docherty, "New Testament Scriptural Interpretation in Its Early Jewish Context: Reflections on the *Status Quaestiones* and Future Directions," *NovT* 57 (2015): 7–10.

63. John T. Carroll, "The Uses of Scripture in Acts," in *Society of Biblical Literature 1990 Seminar Papers*, ed. David J. Lull, SBLSP 29 (Atlanta: Scholars Press, 1990), 528.

64. For examples of those supportive of Dodd's thesis (even if not naming Dodd per se), see Lindars, *New Testament Apologetic*, 14–17; Robert Rendell, "Quotations in Scripture as an Index of Wider Reference," *EvQ* 36 (1964): 214–21; Lars Hartman, *Prophecy Interpreted: The Formation of Some Jewish Apocalyptic Texts and of the Eschatological Discourse Mark 13 Par.*, trans. Neil Tomkinson, ConBNT 1 (Lund: Gleerup, 1966), 126; France, *Jesus and the Old Testament*; Ellis, "How the New Testament Uses the Old," 201, 208; David Seccombe, "Luke and Isaiah," in *The Right Doctrine from the Wrong Texts? Essays on the Use of the Old Testament in the New*, ed. G. K. Beale (Grand Rapids: Baker, 1994), 248–56; Anthony Tyrrell Hanson, *The Living Utterances of God: The New Testament Exegesis of the Old* (London: Darton, Longman & Todd, 1983), 32–33, 38; Moo, *Old Testament in the Gospel Passion Narratives*, 377–78; Kaiser, *Uses of the Old Testament in the New*, 11, 51, 227; Richard B. Hays, *Echoes of Scripture in the Letters of Paul* (New Haven: Yale University Press, 1989), 157–58, 182; and Beale, *Handbook*, 5–6. See also Doeve, *Jewish Hermeneutics*, 115–16.

65. Instone Brewer, *Techniques and Assumptions*; Instone Brewer states rather strongly, "The results of the present study show that the predecessors of the rabbis before 70 CE did not interpret Scripture out of context, did not look for any meaning in Scripture other than the plain sense, and did not change the text to fit their interpretation, though the later rabbis did all these things" (1, cf. 255).

more than common prooftexting that abuses Scripture by taking it out of context. We should rather recognize them as actual expressions of faithfulness to the original context of the OT writers. If the NT authors intended to reference larger OT passages by mentioning smaller portions of them, their use of the OT is less prooftexting and more theological. Even today scholars still use key phrases to reference whole passages (e.g., "the creation account," "the shepherd's psalm," "the Servant Songs," "the feeding of the 5000," etc.), and they use key terms to evoke whole theological themes and arguments (e.g., "justification by faith," "inspiration of Scripture," "baptism of the Holy Spirit," "priesthood of believers," etc.). Given that we ourselves do this, certainly we cannot begrudge the NT authors their use of the practice.[66] The cited portion is "merely the tip of the iceberg" by which the NT author intends to reference "the larger mass just under the surface."[67]

The extent to which NT authors may have improperly utilized these framings—if at all improperly—continues to be a matter of discussion among biblical scholars. And perhaps very much to this point, we should remind ourselves that during his earthly ministry, Jesus called upon first-century Jewish interpreters to give up their improper readings and challenged them to read Scripture correctly (e.g., Matt. 15:1–9//Mark 7:1–13). In one such interaction recorded solely in John's Gospel, Jesus is rather explicit about the impact of one's theological presuppositions on the ability to read Scripture. "And the Father who sent me has himself borne witness about me. His voice you have never heard, his form you have never seen, and you do not have his word abiding in you, for you do not believe the one whom he has sent. You search the Scriptures because you think that in them you have eternal life; and it is they that bear witness about me, yet you refuse to come to me that you may have life" (John 5:37–40). Another such corrective interaction about properly understanding Scripture is found in the Synoptic Gospels (Matt. 22:23–33//Mark 12:18–27//Luke 20:27–40), and Luke alone adds, "Then some of the scribes answered, 'Teacher, you have spoken well'" (v. 39). And Luke closes his Gospel with the resurrected Lord continuing to challenge his followers to understand Scripture in a way different from the way their previous commitments—or hermeneutical axioms—had led them (Luke 24:25–27, 44–47).

Thus, my suggestion is that the taxonomy of framings for the NT use of the OT need not be seen merely as first-century Jewish hermeneutical methods.

---

66. With examples like "Pearl Harbor," "Watergate," and "9/11," Rodgers notes that the utilization of key terms and phrases to evoke a larger idea or incident "is a common feature of literature in any culture"; Rodgers, *Exploring the Old Testament*, 14–15.

67. So Richard B. Hays, *The Conversion of the Imagination: Paul as Interpreter of Israel's Scripture* (Grand Rapids: Eerdmans, 2005), 27.

As framings, each of these practices has its proper, truthful use. Acknowledging these practices as framings instead of simply exegetical methods makes it possible to recognize the NT authors' faithfulness to the intentions of the original OT authors, even in places where such faithfulness has been previously questioned. So, rather than mere exegetical methods, these techniques were expositional methods and application methods. I suggest that what has commonly been referred to simply as first-century Jewish hermeneutical practices might best be referred to as first-century Jewish homiletical practices. These framings, as I call them, are the methods by which the NT authors put OT passages on display so as to point faithfully to Jesus as the Christ of Scripture.

5

Function Classifications
for the New Testament Use
of the Old Testament

But as for you, continue in what you have learned and have firmly believed, knowing from whom you learned it and how from childhood you have been acquainted with the sacred writings, which are able to make you wise for salvation through faith in Christ Jesus. All Scripture is breathed out by God and profitable for teaching, for reproof, for correction, and for training in righteousness, that the man of God may be complete, equipped for every good work.

2 Timothy 3:14–17

Searching for a Comprehensive, Manageable, and Flexible Taxonomy of Functions

In thinking about the use of the OT in the NT, what I mean by function has to do with how a NT writer uses the OT passage in his argument. A notable NT passage that actually treats the subject of the use of Scripture is 2 Tim. 3:14–17 (cited above). Written before the NT was compiled into Christian Scripture, the referent to "Holy Scriptures" here, or "sacred writings" (ἱερὰ γράμματα), is clearly the OT, and (to the chagrin of people like Marcion mentioned in chap. 1 above) clearly the OT is judged as applicable to the Christian life. Paul outlines here a four-part taxonomy of ways the OT can be used: for teaching, reproof, correction, and training in righteousness, all for the purpose of equipping the person of God for proper living.

While I do not at all disagree with Paul's outline of uses for studying Scripture, this is not what NT scholars typically mean when discussing the "functions" of references to the OT in the NT. Rather, the term *function* refers to the discourse purpose for which the NT writer is using the OT text. That is, we are asking about the role the OT passage plays in the NT writer's literary presentation or argument. Recognizing the various ways in which NT authors use the OT Scriptures in their arguments will help us properly understand the messages that they intend to portray. Without intending to psychologize about the NT authors, some might prefer to think of these as different motivations for various uses of prior texts. Nevertheless, my assumption here is that the NT authors have specific reasons for utilizing OT passages in their writings, and I employ the label *function* for this facet of the discipline. With this understanding of the term, this chapter proposes a new taxonomy of functions for the NT use of the OT.[1]

At the outset of this discussion, we must caution ourselves regarding a specific concern and a general concern. The specific concern is analogous to the discussion in the previous chapters and simply cautions against a "hardening of the categories." The categories that I suggest may not be mutually exclusive, and rather than a single purpose, an author can have multiple intentions for citing a passage. I have even formulated some diagrams to illustrate this flexibility in my proposed taxonomy of functions.

The general caution has to do with a potential misconception that a NT author would be the sole driving force in constructing his text. That is, even in describing our task as an attempt to discover the way an OT text functions in the NT author's argument, it sounds as if we might view the NT author as the creative originator of his argument when it could be that the NT author is himself trying to fit his written work into the larger argument of Scripture. Richard Hays recounts an insightful suggestion from Markus Bockmuehl: "It seems both a matter of fact and part of the biblical authors' intent that their engagement with the Old Testament is at least as much a function of the text's own agency in terms of its (divine) *claim and impact on them*, rather than merely of the 'use' of it. Could one say that that they speak as they do because they are thunderstruck by the pressure that Scripture

---

1. An earlier version of this chapter was titled, "A New Taxonomy of Functions for the NT Use of the OT" (paper presented at the seventy-first annual meeting of the Evangelical Theological Society, San Diego, November 20, 2019).

as a hermeneutical Other exerts on their own view of things?"[2] As Hays suggests elsewhere, rather than plundering the OT for prooftexts taken out of context, the NT authors may well prove to be pondering the OT in its fuller context, a context that includes "a preexisting conceptual/theological structure."[3] Perhaps the NT author, at least in some instances, is not trying to create an argument per se but is simply trying to pass on the argument he finds in Scripture or (as he might view it) the argument that Scripture has forced upon him. Rather than mere supportive roles, references to the OT may well reveal the formative or constitutive role the OT plays in the argument of a NT book.[4] Indeed, the NT authors were followers of arguments as well as makers of arguments.

In all of this, I have tried to create a taxonomy of functions that is comprehensive in its coverage of kinds of usages and yet is both manageable and flexible for those studying the NT use of the OT. To be comprehensive, the taxonomy spells out many different usage classifications; to remain manageable, the many classifications are grouped into like clusters of three under five broader headings; and to stay flexible, I have tried to illustrate areas of overlap for the five broader category assignments. But before outlining my recommended taxonomy, it is helpful to get an overview of several other function taxonomies for the NT use of the OT.

Function Taxonomies Proposed by Others

Various scholars have proposed different lists of ways that references to the OT are set up to function in their NT settings (see table 5.1). For function categories, Walter Kaiser suggests apologetic, prophetic, typological, theological, and practical uses.[5] I. Howard Marshall suggests history uses recounting part of the OT story, promise and fulfillment uses highlighting predictions coming to pass and/or God's faithfulness to keep his promises, pattern and type uses recognizing continuations and/or climaxes in the NT, principles uses identifying divine commands still applicable, characterization uses portraying figures in the NT narrative as standing in line with Scripture, and allegorization uses

---

2. Richard B. Hays, *Echoes of Scripture in the Gospels* (Waco: Baylor University Press, 2016), 7–8 (emphasis original).

3. Richard B. Hays, *Echoes of Scripture in the Letters of Paul* (New Haven: Yale University Press, 1989), 87.

4. Peter R. Rodgers, *Exploring the Old Testament in the New* (Eugene, OR: Resource, 2012), 79.

5. Walter C. Kaiser Jr., *The Uses of the Old Testament in the New* (Chicago: Moody, 1985; reprint, Eugene, OR: Wipf & Stock, 2001). Kaiser has two chapters on each of his proposed functions.

extracting symbolic meanings from Scripture.[6] Reminiscent of some of his predecessors' classifications, Darrell Bock suggests the function categories of prophetic fulfillment, typological-prophetic (of two different kinds), authoritative illustration, and ideas or summaries.[7] In the categories proposed by C. John Collins, there seems to be an inclusion of not only ways the OT references function but also topics that the references address: promise and fulfillment, pattern and fulfillment, analogy and application, eschatological continuity, eschatological discontinuity, development, "fuller sense," and deity of Christ.[8]

Perhaps the most complex taxonomy—one that mixes together the three taxonomical classification areas of forms, framings, and functions (which I have readily acknowledged have overlapping areas)—is that of Brodie, MacDonald, and Porter, who list a total of thirty-nine different techniques for how ancient authors utilized prior texts. They have groupings of eight basic adaptation techniques, four combinations and rearrangements, six focus techniques, sixteen transformation techniques, and five substitution techniques; even so, they suggest that their list "is far from complete."[9] Less complex and

---

6. I. Howard Marshall, "Acts," in *Commentary on the New Testament Use of the Old Testament*, ed. G. K. Beale and D. A. Carson (Grand Rapids: Baker Academic, 2007), 519–20. In an earlier work, Marshall outlines seven functions of the OT in the NT: (1) OT language influences the NT, (2) OT style influences the NT, (3) reference to OT events, (4) reference to divine commands, (5) reference to OT prophecies now fulfilled, (6) typological use showing OT-NT correlation, (7) allegorical use drawing OT-NT parallels; I. Howard Marshall, "An Assessment of Recent Developments," in *It Is Written: Scripture Citing Scripture*, ed. D. A. Carson and H. G. M. Williamson (Cambridge: Cambridge University Press, 1988), 9–10.

7. Darrell L. Bock, "Scripture Citing Scripture: Use of the Old Testament in the New," in *Interpreting the New Testament Text: Introduction to the Art and Science of Exegesis*, ed. Darrell L. Bock and Buist M. Fanning (Wheaton: Crossway, 2006), 271–74.

8. C. John Collins, "How the New Testament Quotes and Interprets the Old Testament," in *Understanding Scripture: An Overview of the Bible's Origin, Reliability, and Meaning*, ed. Wayne Grudem, C. John Collins, and Thomas R. Schreiner (Wheaton: Crossway, 2012), 185–91.

9. In the concluding chapter to their edited collection of articles on intertextuality, they remark (with intentional overstatement?), "Quotations and allusions are, therefore, but a small part of a vast and diverse range of ways in which one text may use another. In fact, the number of potential ways of reworking texts is limitless, spanning an incredibly broad range of possibilities almost too numerous to name." See Thomas L. Brodie, Dennis R. MacDonald, and Stanley E. Porter, "Conclusion: Problems of Method—Suggested Guidelines," in *Intertextuality of the Epistles: Explorations of Theory and Practice*, ed. Thomas. L. Brodie, Dennis R. MacDonald, and Stanley E. Porter, New Testament Monographs 16 (Sheffield: Sheffield Academic, 2006), 287. For the sake of completeness, here is their list of thirty-nine functions (from 288–90):

A. *Basic Adaptation Techniques*: (1) verbatim copying, (2) near-verbatim copying, (3) verbatim or near-verbatim use of a relatively small number of words with or without some introductory formula, (4) explicit or near-explicit reference to a person, place, or writing (aka allusion), (5) paraphrase (i.e., rewording), (6) abbreviation (utilizing compression, compactness, condensing, distillation, or creative summary), (7) expansion or elaboration, (8) omission.

TABLE 5.1

Various Taxonomies for the Functions of the New Testament Use of the Old Testament

Kaiser

1. Apologetic	4. Theological
2. Prophetic	5. Practical
3. Typological	

Marshall

1. History	4. Principles
2. Promise and fulfillment	5. Characterization
3. Pattern and type	6. Allegorization

Bock

1. Prophetic fulfillment	4. Authoritative illustration
2. Typological-PROPHETIC	5. Ideas or summaries
3. TYPOLOGICAL-prophetic	

Collins

1. Promise and fulfillment	5. Eschatological discontinuity
2. Pattern and fulfillment	6. Development
3. Analogy and application	7. "Fuller sense"
4. Eschatological continuity	8. Deity of Christ

Brodie-MacDonald-Porter

1. Basic adaptation (8 kinds)	4. Transformation (16 kinds)
2. Combinations and rearrangements (4 kinds)	5. Substitution (5 kinds)
3. Focus (6 kinds)	

Beale

1. Direct fulfillment of OT prophecy	7. Proverbial
2. Indirect fulfillment of OT typological prophecy	8. Rhetorical
3. Affirmation of yet-to-be fulfilled OT prophecy	9. Prototypical
4. Analogical or illustrative	10. Alternate textual
5. Symbolic	11. Assimilated
6. Abiding authority	12. Ironic or inverted

Note: This table summarizes the views found in Kaiser, *Uses of the Old Testament in the New*, 17–224; Marshall, "Acts," 519–20; Bock, "Scripture Citing Scripture," 271–74; Collins, "How the New Testament Quotes and Interprets," 185–91; Brodie, MacDonald, and Porter, "Conclusion," 288–90; and Beale, *Handbook*, 41–54.

B. *Combinations and Rearrangements*: (1) conflation, (2) dispersal or dividing, (3) rearrangement (reorganization, repositioning, transposition, reshaping), (4) compound allusion.

C. *Focus Techniques*: (1) clarification, explicitation, or preservation, (2) making vivid or graphic, (3) building credibility in narration, (4) intensification, (5) continuity-building, (6) archaism.

perhaps most similar to my taxonomy for functions of the OT in the NT is that of Greg Beale, who suggests direct fulfillment of OT prophecy, indirect fulfillment of OT typological prophecy, affirmation of yet-to-be fulfilled OT prophecy, analogical or illustrative use, symbolic use, abiding authority, proverbial use, rhetorical use, prototypical use, alternate textual use, assimilated use, and ironic or inverted use.[10]

More recently, and choosing an approach different from many others, John Goldingay has offered a five-part taxonomy for the uses that the NT makes of the OT, or in the words of his book's subtitle, *How the New Testament Helps Us Understand the Old Testament*.[11] Taking his cues from the Gospel of Matthew, but surveying the rest of the NT as well, Goldingay examines how the NT explains Jesus and faith in him in light of the OT (or as Goldingay prefers, the First Testament). He suggests the following broad categories: story, promise, ideas, relationship, and life (see table 5.2).

Goldingay is clear on two additional points. First, the OT is intelligible on its own: "We do not need the New Testament to tell us what it means."[12] Second, study of how the NT writers used the OT will be instructive for how we ourselves might approach the OT. These two additional points help us see that Goldingay's approach has somewhat different intentions than the approaches of some of the other scholars mentioned above. Or perhaps it is better to say that Goldingay's approach is differently motivated than the other approaches. But there is no inherent conflict or implied—much less necessary—opposition in these different approaches. Indeed, among those proposing function classifications for the NT use of the OT, few, if any, would suggest that their lists are exhaustive or that their labels for the

---

D. *Transformation*: (1) antithesis (including reversal, dialectic, or contrast), (2) complementarity, in which an image or action balances the original, (3) actualization (e.g., modernization, Christianization, or contemporization), (4) allegorical interpretation, (5) typological interpretation, (6) dramatization, (7) domestication, (8) positivization, (9) meditation, involving rethinking of the antetext, (10) internalization, (11) spiritualization, (12) universalization, (13) theological change, adaptation, or redesigning, (14) inventive imitation, (15) wordplay, (16) deuteronomizing.

E. *Substitution*: (1) character change or adaptation (recasting), (2) form change or adaptation, (3) geographic change or adaptation, (4) image change or adaptation, (5) institutional change or adaptation.

10. G. K. Beale, *Handbook on the New Testament Use of the Old Testament: Exegesis and Interpretation* (Grand Rapids: Baker Academic, 2012), esp. 55–93.

11. John Goldingay, *Reading Jesus's Bible: How the New Testament Helps Us Understand the Old Testament* (Grand Rapids: Eerdmans, 2017).

12. Goldingay, *Reading Jesus's Bible*, 4. He continues immediately, "But it is natural for Christians to assume that the New Testament ought to help us understand the First Testament." See also John Goldingay, *Do We Need the New Testament? Letting the Old Testament Speak for Itself* (Downers Grove, IL: InterVarsity, 2015).

TABLE 5.2

Goldingay's Taxonomy for Functions
of the New Testament Use of the Old Testament

1. Story: The First Testament tells the story of which Jesus is the climax (e.g., Matt. 1:1–17; cf. Romans; 1 Corinthians; and Hebrews).

2. Promise: The First Testament declares the promise of which Jesus is the fulfillment (e.g., Matt. 1:18–2:23; cf. Luke; Acts; Hebrews; and Romans).

3. Ideas: The First Testament provides the images, ideas, and words with which to understand Jesus (e.g., Matt. 3:1–17; cf. Romans; Hebrews; and Revelation).

4. Relationship: The First Testament lays out the nature of a relationship with God (e.g., Matt. 4:1–11; 5:1–16; cf. Ephesians; Revelation; and Hebrews).

5. Life: The First Testament provides the foundation for Jesus's moral teaching, inviting us to study what the Scriptures have to teach us about the way we should live (e.g., Matt. 5:17–48).

Note: Drawn from John Goldingay, *Reading Jesus's Bible*, esp. 3.

various functions are inviolable. Rather, scholars attempt to be both full and flexible, both meaningful and manageable.

A Recommended Taxonomy of Functions

I have adopted and adapted Goldingay's five-part outline as a broad base of usage clusters for my recommended taxonomy of function classifications for the NT use of the OT. Then each of these five areas is divided into several more detailed classifications. For discussing how a particular OT passage functions within the argument of a NT writer, there are some advantages to beginning with a broad base of usage categories. This can help modern readers find general agreement in their perspectives before spelling out possible areas of disagreement in the nuanced details of the discussion.

Five Broad Usage Clusters

In adopting and adapting Goldingay's five-part outline for the NT use of the OT, I make three adjustments. First, I have altered the five titles slightly; Goldingay's titles mix descriptions of content (e.g., story, promise, and ideas) with descriptions of applications (e.g., relationship and life), but I would like the titles to be more parallel in addressing the apparent intentions of the NT authors. Thus, I maintain Goldingay's titles of *story* and *ideas*; but I use the label *fulfillment* for his "promise" grouping, the label *analogy* for his "relationship" grouping, and the label *declaration* for his "life" grouping. Second, I have filled out the taxonomy by using some of the more specific classifications exemplified in the work of other scholars: I am suggesting three such function classifications for each of the five areas Goldingay has identified. Third, while Goldingay's discussion of the five usage clusters follows the order in which he uncovers them in the Gospel of Matthew, I have reordered them into something of a continuum according to their interrelatedness, especially where they begin to overlap with one another.

On this last point, I am suggesting that the three specific function classifications in each of the five broad usage clusters overlap in a circulating continuum in such a way that they number only ten altogether. Thus, the new taxonomy of functions for the NT use of the OT consists of ten function classifications grouped into five overlapping clusters. The overlapping nature of function categories—which is regularly noted by scholars in this field—is more easily visualized when the categories are sketched on a continuum that shows a progression of neighboring usage classifications (e.g., fig. 5.1).

But I also want to acknowledge the possibility that a NT author may intend more than one function for his use of a particular OT text and that those multiple functions may not be next to each other on the continuum as I have

---

FIGURE 5.1

Recommended Taxonomy of Function Classifications for the New Testament Use of the Old Testament

This list of NT usages of the OT attempts to be flexible and comprehensive in its coverage of various functions as well as manageable for those studying the NT use of the OT. The ten individual function classifications aim at being comprehensive; the five broad clusters try to make the list more manageable by grouping together similar functions that vary by nuances along the continuum within the broader cluster; and the overlapping of the five broad clusters demonstrates some of the intended flexibility of this taxonomy. Note that where the continuum moves off the chart to the right, it rejoins the continuum on the left.

DECLARATION	FULFILLMENT	STORY	ANALOGY	IDEAS
1. Ultimate Truth 2. Ethical Wisdom	3. Prophecy Fulfillment 4. Promising Patterns	5. Typological Correlation 6. Historical Backdrop	7. Cultural Background 8. Instructive Exemplars	9. Illustrations & Imagery 10. Vocabulary & Style

sketched it. To address this, the use of a circular, spoked-wheel continuum can help us visualize the potential for overlapping functions that are otherwise not immediate neighbors on the continuum (e.g., fig. 5.2). In my discussion of these ten function classifications grouped into five broader usage clusters, I have numbered the functions consecutively. Before expounding on the ten function classifications, let me first briefly define the five broader usage clusters, some of which warrant more discussion than others.

Declaration usage cluster. I have relabeled Goldingay's "life" category as "declaration" uses. This broad cluster covers the uses of the OT that NT authors employ when they are discussing key truths about reality as we know it

FIGURE 5.2

A Circular Taxonomy of Function Classifications for the New Testament Use of the Old Testament

This spoked-wheel diagram of the recommended taxonomy of function classifications for the NT use of the OT is a way to illustrate the potential overlapping of intended uses that are not immediate neighbors along the circular continuum.

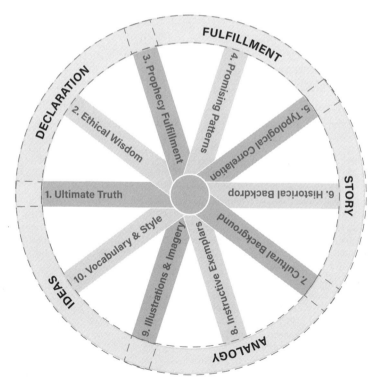

and cite Scripture as an authority on the subject. Sometimes Scripture is used to declare universal truths; sometimes Scripture is appealed to in discussing wisdom for living; and sometimes God's prophetic intentions are the subject being declared. Thus, this broad cluster covers three category classifications that I identify as ultimate truth, ethical wisdom, and prophecy fulfillment function categories.

Fulfillment usage cluster. Focusing on the apparent intentions of the NT authors, I have relabeled Goldingay's "promise" category as "fulfillment" uses. Despite decades of scholarship encouraging otherwise, the all-too-natural assumption in popular theological discussions of the concept of "fulfillment" is that this indicates a specific forward-looking prediction meeting its one-and-only anticipated outcome. While this notion is certainly one possible application of the concept of fulfillment, it is naive to assume that this is the primary one, much less that it is the only employment of the idea. The fulfillment terminology of the NT (i.e., the terms in the πίμπλημι, πληρόω, τελειόω, and τελέω families of words) has a number of different connotations. This variety of nuances is readily recognizable in some of the more mundane contexts, and this should make it easier for us to recognize the differing senses when the NT uses these terms in reflections on the OT.[13]

The use of fulfillment terminology particularly in Matthew and John—with varied nuances—has convinced most that this is an important function classification for these NT authors' use of Scripture. This area of Luke's use of Scripture, however, has seen a lot of scholarly debate. Despite several key voices of dissent, I agree with those who view this as a useful function grouping for assigning at least some of Luke's uses of the OT.[14] And it is Luke's

13. That these words can be used in a variety of other ways—e.g., to speak of a boat being "full" of fish (Matt. 13:48), of a room being "full" of people (Matt. 22:10) or of a fragrance (John 12:3) or of a sound (Acts 2:2), of time being "completed" (Luke 1:23) or forty years "coming to pass" (Acts 7:30), of a ministry being "completed" (Acts 12:25), of a person being "full" of wisdom (Luke 2:40) or of anger (Luke 4:28) or of the Holy Spirit (Acts 2:4), or of Satan (Acts 5:3), and of joy reaching its "completion" (John 16:24)—it should not surprise us that this same group of words would have several different connotations when talking about Scripture being "fulfilled," "filled," "filled up" or "filled out" in the life and ministry of Jesus. See particularly "πληρόω," *NIDNTTE* 3:784–93. Goldingay (*Reading Jesus's Bible*, 65–67) has a brief and helpful discussion about properly widening the sense of "fulfill."

14. A relevant survey of the debate on Luke's prophecy-fulfillment use of the OT is found in Darrell L. Bock, *Proclamation from Prophecy and Pattern: Lucan Old Testament Christology*, JSNTSup 12 (Sheffield: Sheffield Academic, 1987), 27–46; see also Darrell L. Bock, "Proclamation from Prophecy and Pattern: Luke's Use of the Old Testament for Christology and Mission," in *The Gospels and the Scriptures of Israel*, ed. C. A. Evans and W. R. Stegner, JSNTSup 104, SSEJC 3 (Sheffield: Sheffield Academic, 1994), 280–307. With dependence on Bock, Porter offers a brief such survey in Stanley E. Porter, "Scripture Justifies Mission: The Use of the Old Testament in Luke-Acts," in *Hearing the Old Testament in the New Testament*, ed. Stanley E. Porter,

varied employments of the fulfillment terminology that helps me make this recognition.

In the realm of the NT use of the OT, it is better to think of **fulfillment** as having at least three possible nuanced implications. Scripture is fulfilled in one sense when a prediction comes true, in another sense when a promise is still kept or some other pattern is still followed, and in a third sense when a prefigurement comes to light. The three function categories that are grouped together in the fulfillment usage cluster correspond to these differing connotations of the fulfillment concept: prophecy fulfillment (the function category that overlaps with the declaration usage cluster), promising patterns, and typological correlation. And, of course, we should note that NT writers can express these fulfillment concepts without actually using any of the fulfillment terms.

Story usage cluster. Goldingay suggests the category of "story" for when the OT is used in the NT to emphasize that Jesus (and his movement) is the climax to the OT story. Because the NT authors clearly saw Jesus as the fulfillment—in a variety of senses of that word—of the OT story, I map the story usage cluster immediately next to the fulfillment usage cluster. These two broad clusters overlap, both laying claim to the typological correlation category.[15] The other categories here in the story usage cluster that emphasize the connections of Jesus and the church to OT history are the historical backdrop and cultural background function categories.

Analogy usage cluster. I have relabeled Goldingay's "relationship" category as "analogy" uses. In this broad category, Goldingay focuses on the OT as providing the foundation for Jesus's moral teaching, and indeed it is. Some of the specific examples that Goldingay cites, however, might be better slotted in my recommended taxonomy under the ultimate truths classification (the first of the three specific categories in the declaration usage cluster).[16] In my taxonomy, the broad analogy usage cluster is charted next to the story usage cluster. The analogy usage cluster covers instances when the OT is appealed to not simply as the authority pertaining to human relationships, but specifically to the utilizations of the OT that make some comparison of its storyline background, or its characters, or its imagery so as to call for—by

---

McMaster New Testament Studies (Grand Rapids: Eerdmans, 2006), 105–7; Porter likewise sees prophetic fulfillment of the OT as "a useful hypothesis to utilize in Lukan studies" (107).

15. Goldingay (*Reading Jesus's Bible*, 14–16) also includes typology in his broad "story" grouping.

16. Similarly, Bock's broad category of "authoritative illustration" specifically covers some of the same analogy concerns as I have in this analogy usage cluster, but he also includes some of what I label "ethical wisdom functions" (the second of the three specific classifications in the declaration usage cluster); see Bock, "Scripture Citing Scripture," 273–74.

analogy—some similar or more advanced kind of behavior in the NT context. Thus, the three category function classifications of the analogy usage cluster include cultural background (the function category that overlaps with the story usage cluster), instructive exemplars, and illustrations and imagery.

Ideas usage cluster. In this cluster we find images, ideas, and words from the OT that are now applied to the NT extension of the storyline. In his tracing of Matthew's use of the OT in the opening chapters of the First Gospel, Goldingay notes that Matt. 3 moves away from story and promise utilizations for understanding the Jesus event. Now Matthew "provides us with the images, ideas, and words with which to understand Jesus."[17] In my functions taxonomy, the broad ideas usage cluster of the OT is charted next to the analogy usage cluster, with these two clusters overlapping where analogies transition from being examples for mimicking to concepts for understanding. Thus, the first specific category here in the ideas usage cluster (i.e., illustrations and imagery) is shared with the analogy usage cluster. The other specific function categories in the ideas usage cluster are the vocabulary and style classification and the ultimate truths classification. And in my circular continuum, the ultimate truths classification is the function category that overlaps with the declaration usage cluster, moving from ultimate truths to be understood to ultimate truths to be declared.

The taxonomies of other scholars also give recognition to NT writers borrowing and reapplying ideas and vocabulary from the OT.[18] In his earlier taxonomy of function categories, Marshall includes two different idea-related function classifications for NT uses of the OT: "OT language influences" and "OT style influences"; I put these two together under the single function classification label *vocabulary and style* in the ideas usage cluster.[19] And this broad ideas usage cluster is arguably a comfortable beginning point for analyzing the function of many instances of specific allusions to the OT in the New.[20] But I must be quick to note that the specific allusion form can be

17. Goldingay, *Reading Jesus's Bible*, 104. Some specific examples of the OT in the NT that Goldingay places in his broad ideas category I have slotted elsewhere in my taxonomy, but this is partially explainable in terms of the greater detail I propose for the classifications as well as the phenomenon of function classification overlap.

18. Of course, given the flexible application of the term *use*, there is potential for confusion when several different kinds of taxonomies are under discussion. So in contemplating the ideas usage cluster, for example, Bock ("Scripture Citing Scripture," 274) has a broad grouping with a similar label (i.e., "ideas or summaries"), but what he means by this is what I have labeled "Scripture summary" in the form taxonomy, not the function taxonomy.

19. See Marshall, "Assessment of Recent Developments," 9.

20. Brawley makes some insightful comparisons of the use of scriptural allusions in Luke-Acts to the use of metaphors. See Robert Lawson Brawley, *Text to Text Pours Forth Speech: Voices of Scripture in Luke-Acts*, ISBL (Bloomington: Indiana University Press, 1995), 8–10.

utilized with virtually any of the ten function categories across the whole of this taxonomy.

Ten Specific Function Classifications

My recommended taxonomy of functions for the NT use of the OT consists of ten specific function classifications grouped into the five overlapping usage clusters discussed above. As I have sketched it, each of the five usage clusters in the taxonomy contains three specific function classifications. On first blush, of course, five broad clusters with three specific classifications for each implies a total of fifteen different function classifications (i.e., $5 \times 3 = 15$). But as explained above, the five broad usage clusters overlap in a circulating continuum in such a way that the specific function classifications number only ten altogether (see figs. 5.1 and 5.2 above). In the discussion of these ten function categories here, they are numbered consecutively, and several examples are offered for each.

1. Ultimate truths: The author/speaker of the NT text may simply want to declare the message contained in the OT text.

Sometimes this declaration may be simply stated; other times the speaker/author may appeal to the truth stated in the OT text as part of the argument unfolding in the NT text. Gathered here are functions for which other scholars have labels such as "for purposes of argument," "general truth,"[21] "apologetic use,"[22] and "abiding authority."[23] Hebrews 12:5–6 is a fine example of this function category, for it simply declares the truth of Prov. 3:11–12 by citing it as applicable to the NT situation,

> My son, do not regard lightly the discipline of the Lord,
>   nor be weary when reproved by him.
> For the Lord disciplines the one he loves,
>   and chastises every son whom he receives.

So also Prov. 3:34 is cited in James 4:6. In Acts 7:48–50, in order to declare the eternal truth that "the Most High does not dwell in houses made by hands" (v. 48), Stephen cites Isa. 66:1–2. With a bit more sophistication, Rom. 3:2–4 might be slotted here, because, in making an argument that God will be found faithful in new circumstances even as he formerly was, Paul cites Ps. 51:4 [50:6] about God being proved right when he speaks and prevailing

---

21. The first two phrases in quotations are those of Frederic Gardiner, *The Old and New Testaments in Their Mutual Relations*, 2nd ed. (New York: James Pott, 1887), 312.

22. Kaiser, *Uses of the Old Testament in the New*, 17–57.

23. Beale, *Handbook*, 72–73.

when he makes judgments. As I have conceived of it, this classification can also be applied to texts like Luke 20:37, where Jesus references the wording in Exod. 3, "the God of Abraham, and the God of Isaac, and the God of Jacob" (see vv. 6, 15, 16), as a description that can always be declared about God (and therefore has theological implications for the afterlife). In keeping with the continuum idea here, where a NT author refers to the OT so as to declare an eternal truth that is more specifically about ethical behaviors, I suggest a second, but immediately neighboring, function category: ethical wisdom.

2. Ethical wisdom: The author/speaker of the NT text appeals to the ethical directives of the OT text as applicable to the reading/listening audience.

Sometimes the NT author simply makes the declaration of an OT text that is still quite directly applicable to life in the NT era and today. What Marshall calls "principles" fits this particular function category.[24] As declaration of wisdom principles, this category is the heart of the declaration usage cluster. This function is quite evident in the appeals to the Ten Commandments made in the NT (e.g., Matt. 19:16–22; Mark 10:17–22; and Luke 18:18–23, all citing Exod. 20:12–16 and/or Deut. 5:16–20; cf. Rom. 13:9; James 2:11) as well as the appeals to the "greatest commandments" (e.g., Matt. 22:36–40; Mark 12:28–31; and Luke 10:26–27, all citing Deut. 6:5 and Lev. 19:18; cf. Rom. 13:9; Gal. 5:14; James 2:8). And Paul appeals to Deut. 5:16 in Eph. 6:1–3 in addressing the issue of proper behavior for children. Similarly, in Acts 23:5 Luke reports Paul commenting on his own retort against the high priest by citing Exod. 22:28 [22:27], "You shall not speak evil of a ruler of your people." Sometimes the NT has more involved ethical discussions with appeals to the OT as supportive to its arguments. Jesus's use of Deuteronomy in his temptation experiences can be slotted here (Matt. 4:1–11 and Luke 4:1–13 citing Deut. 6:13, 16; and 8:3). Interestingly, in the temptation narratives the devil also appeals to Scripture (i.e., Ps. 91:11–12 in Matt. 4:6 and Luke 4:10–11) to make an ethical argument so as to tempt Jesus to behave poorly.

Ethical appeals in the NT are made not only with citations but also with allusions to the OT. Luke T. Johnson suggests that James reflects Lev. 19:12–18 as one of his key sources for the series of ethical demands he places on his readers. James's interest in declaring the OT law as found in the Holiness Code of Leviticus is seen in his specific allusions and thematic echoes as follows: Lev. 19:12 (in James 5:12); Lev. 19:13 (in James 5:4); Lev. 19:15 (in James

---

24. Marshall, "Acts," 520; he formerly referred to this usage as "reference to divine commands" in Marshall, "Assessment of Recent Developments," 10.

2:1, 9); Lev. 19:16 (in James 4:11); Lev. 19:17 (in James 5:20); Lev. 19:18a (in James 5:9); and Lev. 19:18b (actually cited in James 2:8).[25]

3. Prophecy fulfillment: The event under discussion in the NT is viewed by the author/speaker as somehow fulfilling a prophecy recorded or indicated in the OT.

In the overlapping layout of function categories, the prophecy fulfillment category falls into both the declaration usage cluster and the fulfillment usage cluster. Sometimes NT authors (re)declare the specific truths that God's prophets had declared in the OT and expected to happen in the future, and thus it makes sense to see such functions as falling into the declaration usage cluster (e.g., 2 Pet. 3:11–14 and Rev. 21:1 both draw upon Isa. 65:17 and 66:22 in looking still to the eschatological future; cf. Matt. 19:28).[26] Several of Jesus's allusions to Dan. 7:13–14 are still forward-looking declarations of prophecy about his yet future coming on the clouds (e.g. Matt. 24:30//Mark 13:26//Luke 21:27; Matt. 25:31; Matt. 26:64//Mark 14:62//Luke 22:69). More often, however, NT authors emphasize not only that a particular prophecy was declared in the OT but also that it has found its fulfillment in Jesus and/ or his followers. In such cases as these, we see the NT writers using fulfillment terminology in the familiar sense of a prediction finding its one-and-only anticipated outcome, one of the classifications within the fulfillment usage cluster.

This classification easily applies to passages like Matt. 2:5–6, where the priests and scribes understood Mic. 5:2 as a specific prediction of where the Messiah would be born (cf. the similar expectation evidenced in John 7:41–42). So also Isa. 40:3–5 is understood as a specific prediction of a forerunner like John the Baptist in Matt. 3:3//Mark 1:3//Luke 3:4–6 (cf. John 1:23). Other instances of this function include Jesus's application of Isa. 61:1–2 to himself in Luke 4:17–21; and Paul's use of a string of OT verses (i.e., Hosea 2:23; 1:10; Isa. 10:22–23; 1:9) in Rom. 9:24–29. That first-century Jews were expecting a specific fulfillment of Moses's prediction of a prophet is evidenced not only in explicit mentions of Moses's words from Deut. 18:15 (e.g., Acts 3:22–23a; 7:37) but also in other references to "the Prophet" (e.g., John 1:21; 25; 6:14; 7:40) and "the one who is to come" (e.g., Luke 7:18–35; Matt. 11:2–19). Furthermore, Jesus remarks rather bluntly, "If you believed

---

25. See Luke T. Johnson, "The Use of Leviticus 19 in the Letter of James," *JBL* 101 (1982): 391–401. Kaiser (*Uses of the Old Testament in the New*, 221–24) provides a brief summary of the argument and a nice charting of the parallels between James and Lev. 19.

26. Beale (*Handbook*, 66–67) has a separate usage category for this sense of prophecy declaration, but he notes there that Paul takes an inaugurated view, with the new creation having already begun in some sense in the Jesus event (see 2 Cor. 5:17; Gal. 6:15).

Moses, you would believe me, for he wrote about me" (John 5:45–47). And yet these prophet-like-Moses instances may fit better into the next usage category, that of promising pattern, if the OT context intends a succession of prophets after Moses to which Christians discover Jesus as its climactic expression.[27]

4. Promising patterns: The NT author sees God as continuing to keep to his promised and/or characteristic behavior as reflected or recorded in the OT.

As is readily illustrated by wedding vows, some singular promises have a myriad of applications in patterns of behavior. This illustrates the promising patterns category. Rather than seeing a specific prediction that comes true, this classification applies when a NT author recognizes a pattern in the OT that has continued into the NT era. This function classification is an acknowledgment that such patterns and promises are indicated in the OT and, even if not fully anticipated beforehand, can be discovered in Jesus and the church.[28] This is a "filling out" of Scripture, often in ways that were not specifically anticipated by the writers and readers of the OT but in patterns and promises that are no less recognizable for their lack of full expectation. The concept that a single meaning can have multiple referents helps one grasp the promising patterns function category (see sidebar 5.1). With this wider recognition of fulfillment, this category is the heart of the fulfillment usage cluster.

Darrell Bock argues for the NT's use of the OT in a pattern and promise sense, particularly in Luke-Acts.[29] Isaiah's servant figure (see Isa. 42:1–9; 49:1–13; 50:4–11; 52:13–53:12) provides an important example.[30] The figure has both a national identity (explicitly called "Israel" in Isa. 49:3) and an

27. Marshall ("Acts," 520) indicates the possibility of either classification.

28. My use of the terms *promise* and *pattern* together in this classification label, "promising patterns," places this category between the two different categories that use these terms in the function taxonomy of Collins, "How the New Testament Quotes and Interprets," 187. Collins's category of "promise and fulfillment" is equivalent to my category of prophecy fulfillment, and his category of "pattern and fulfillment" is equivalent to my typological correlation; the classification that Collins calls "development" might be seen as something of an in-between category in his taxonomy. To avoid an overly strict understanding of promise fulfillment functions whereby modern readers assume that a specific prediction lies behind the term *promise*, James Charlesworth has suggested that "promise" be replaced with "expectation"; James H. Charlesworth, "What Has the Old Testament to Do with the New?," in *The Old and the New Testaments: Their Relationship and the "Intertestamental" Literature*, ed. James H. Charlesworth and Walter P. Weaver, Faith & Scholarship Colloquies (Valley Forge, PA: Trinity Press International, 1993), 68–71. But I see a drawback in the use of "expectation" in that some of the scriptural fulfillment occurs in surprising—truly unexpected—ways, apparently recognized by the NT authors only after the fact. So I retain the term *promise* in this function classification label.

29. See esp. Bock, *Proclamation from Prophecy and Pattern*; and Bock, "Scripture Citing Scripture," 271–72.

30. I take my cues here from Bock, "Scripture Citing Scripture," 272.

individual identity (particularly in Isa. 52:13–53:12), reflecting a kind of relationship with God that involves both representation and suffering. The pattern is found in Luke-Acts, where Israel is called the servant (Luke 1:54), and yet

---

SIDEBAR 5.1

Promising Patterns: Single Meaning with Multiple Referents

When a bride and groom promise to be faithful to one another, they are not making a specific prediction that will have a onetime anticipated fulfillment; rather, they are committing to an anticipated pattern of behavior to be repeatedly fulfilled in any and all circumstances, including some that will only be fully recognizable after the fact. This is illustrative of what scholars mean when they refer to NT writers recognizing promising patterns from the OT Scriptures that are continuing to occur. Previous generations of scholars debated the existence of "double meanings" or "double fulfillments" of some OT prophecies, with one side denying such a concept and the other side suggesting that the OT prophets might not have been able to understand the "double sense" of their own words. On this matter, I am inclined to esteem the (rather dated) advice of Franklin Johnson on this matter: "A large part of this controversy might have been avoided had writers on both sides used the term 'double reference' instead of the term 'double sense.'"[1]

Preferring the label "generic fulfillment," Walter Kaiser has a more recent and more wieldy discussion of this matter, explaining, "The fundamental idea here is that many prophecies begin with a word that ushers in not only a climactic fulfillment, but a series of events, all of which participate in and lead up to that climactic or ultimate event in a protracted series that belong together as a unit because of their corporate or collective solidarity." Capitalizing on the shared collectivity as indicative of single meanings, he continues, "In this way, the whole set of events makes up one collective totality and constitutes *only one idea*, even though the events may be spread over a large segment of history by the deliberate plan of God." And he summarizes, "The important point to observe, however, is that all of the parts belong to a single whole. They are generically related to each other by some identifiable wholeness."[2] This is what I intend by the use of such terms as *promise* and *pattern*: a single meaning can have multiple referents, a single promise is kept over and over again in a pattern of multiple applications.

1. Franklin Johnson, *The Quotations of the New Testament from the Old Considered in the Light of General Literature* (Philadelphia: American Baptist Publication Society, 1896), 197; see Johnson's lengthy chapter on double reference, 186–335.

2. See Kaiser, *Uses of the Old Testament in the New*, 61–76; the quotations are from 67–68 (emphasis original).

Jesus is pictured specifically as fulfilling the role (Simeon alludes to Isa. 49:6 in Luke 2:32 as descriptive of Jesus; Jesus cites Isa. 53:12 in Luke 22:37 about himself; and Acts 8:32–33 cites Isa. 53:7–8 as descriptive of Jesus). But Jesus pushes the servant imagery pattern further to include his followers, describing them as his agents to reach "the ends of the earth" (an allusion to Isa. 49:6 in Acts 1:6–8), something that Paul and Barnabas then explicitly apply to themselves (citing Isa. 49:6 as being to "us" in Acts 13:47). Also fitting in this function category are the NT's use of particular psalms as patterns for how to understand Jesus as the Davidic king (e.g., Ps. 110:1 [109:1] in Luke 20:42–43; 22:69; Acts 2:34b–35; and Ps. 118 [117] in Luke 13:35b; 19:38; 20:17; Acts 4:11) and for how to respond to the opponents of the Davidide (e.g., Ps. 69:25 [68:26] and 109:8 [108:8] in Acts 1:20b). Another example is seen in John the Baptist filling out the role of Elijah in the prophecy of Mal. 3:1; 4:4–5 in a beginning sense of the expected pattern (Matt. 11:10–14//Luke 7:27; Matt. 17:10–13//Mark 9:11–13; cf. Luke 1:17, 76) but not yet in the ultimate sense of the pattern (John 1:19–27).[31]

Another, more complex example in the promising patterns category involves the concept of the "day of the Lord." The day of the Lord in the writings of the OT prophets (aka "that day," "the day," etc.) was the anticipated time of God's intervention in human history to bring judgment upon the unfaithful and enemies of the Lord (e.g., Isa. 2:1–22; 13:1–13; Joel 2:1–11; Amos 5:18–20) and blessing upon the faithful (e.g., Isa. 11:10–12; Joel 3:14–18; Amos 9:11–15). While initial fulfillments of this judgment and blessing came to OT Israel, the arrival of the Holy Spirit (see Acts 2:17–21 specifically citing Joel 2:28–32 [3:1–5]) and the spread of the gospel to the gentiles (see Acts 15:16b–17 specifically citing Amos 9:11–12) indicate a further filling out of this pattern, although evidently not yet in its eschatological climactic sense (cf. 2 Pet. 3:10–14).[32]

5. Typological correlation: Divinely intended symbolism in history whereby historical figures, places, events, or institutions (the "types") foreshadow subsequent greater realities (the "antitypes").

Typology was discussed in chapter 4 as a framing technique (i.e., as one way to display particular OT ideas in a NT setting). So here I recall that the concept of typology falls into both the framing realm and the function realm (see fig. 4.1). In examining the various functions of OT references in the NT, typology falls into two broad groupings: the fulfillment usage cluster and the story usage cluster. As a kind of foreshadowing, typological use of the OT fits

31. See Kaiser, *Uses of the Old Testament in the New*, 77–88.
32. See esp. Kaiser's discussion of Joel 2:28–32 [3:1–5] cited in Acts 2:17–21 in Kaiser, *Uses of the Old Testament in the New*, 89–100.

the fulfillment usage cluster with the classifications of prophecy fulfillment and promising patterns. But as a means to point to historical material, typological use of the OT also fits the story usage cluster with the classifications of historical backdrop and cultural background.

While grouped with the other fulfillment uses (i.e., the classifications of prophecy fulfillment and promising patterns), typological correlation is in some ways not as specific as those function categories. As noted in the discussion above, the promising patterns classification applies to uses of the OT that foreshadow some anticipated future fulfillment that unfolds in the NT; the typological correlation category likewise is concerned with foreshadowing, but it applies to uses of the OT in the NT where the pattern is not especially anticipated by the OT language and is largely recognizable only after the decisive pattern occurs.[33] For texts with the typological correlation classification, the person or events under discussion in the NT passage are seen now in retrospect as having been represented by the person or events referred to in the OT, with the NT antitype representing an escalated filling up or filling out of the earlier historic type. In this way, typological correlation has a greater focus on the historical setting and is thus at home with the next broad grouping of functions, the story usage cluster.

Perhaps the clearest suggestion for the typological correlation classification is the rather famously problematic citation of Hosea 11:1 in Matt. 2:15. The Hosea passage is speaking about Israel's historic exodus from the land of Egypt and not predicting that the Messiah would come out of Egypt. Nevertheless, Matthew cites the passage with reference to Jesus being taken into Egypt as an infant as if this were preparation to fulfill predictive prophecy: "This was to fulfill what the Lord had spoken by the prophet, 'Out of Egypt I called my son.'" How can Jesus's coming out of Egypt "fulfill" a prediction that is not really a prediction at all? This has been the problem with understanding Matthew's

---

33. It was noted in chap. 4 above that Bock has two classification labels related to typology: his "typological-PROPHETIC" label corresponds to my promising patterns function classification emphasizing the role of the OT material (i.e., functioning as prophecy), and his "TYPOLOGICAL-prophetic" label corresponds to a Jewish homiletical practice emphasizing the historical framing of the OT material (i.e., set in historical comparison). From another vantage point, however, Bock's "TYPOLOGICAL-prophetic" label could be seen as corresponding to my typological correlation function classification. Interestingly, Bock ("Scripture Citing Scripture," 271–73) even uses the word *typology* in the discussion of a third function category. To minimize confusion of labels for function classifications, I use the word *typological* only in the most central of these categories, which is arguably where typology has the greatest consensus of recognition. For a recent fulsome examination of typology, see James M. Hamilton Jr., *Typology: Understanding the Bible's Promise-Shaped Patterns* (Grand Rapids: Zondervan Academic, 2022); noteworthy, however, is that Hamilton stresses anticipatory typology (which corresponds to my promising pattern classification) over against retrospective recognition of typology.

citation of Hosea 11:1. But given the retrospective nature of typological recognitions, given a broader understanding of the word *fulfill* to include a filling up or filling out (see chap. 3), and given the common presupposition that a single member can represent the whole community (see chap. 1), it seems that Matthew is fittingly correlating two of God's actions in history: God acted once to bring his son (i.e., the nation of Israel) out of Egypt, and now he is acting again in a similar manner to bring his son (i.e., Jesus) out of Egypt. Matthew is not pretending that Hosea 11:1 is fulfilled predictive prophecy; he is simply recognizing a filling out of a typological correlation between two events in history.[34] A few verses later, Matt. 2:18 cites Jer. 31:15 with reference to the slaughter of the innocent children in Bethlehem, and as a retrospective recognition of a pattern, this fulfillment may also best be classified as a typological correlation.

Because they are noted only in retrospect, the NT's use of the psalms about the righteous suffering king as typifying Jesus in his suffering also fits in the typological correlation category. In their OT contexts, such passages describe the suffering of a real historical figure, the righteous king (i.e., anointed one), despite (or perhaps because of) his desire to serve God. Looking back at these figures in the OT story, the NT writers have aha moments recognizing that Jesus is the ultimate righteous suffering King (e.g., Ps. 16:8–11 [15:8–11] in Acts 2:25–32 and 13:35; Ps. 22 [21] in Matt. 27:33–46; Mark 15:22–34; Luke 23:33–38; and John 19:23–24; cf. Heb. 2:12; 1 Pet. 5:8).[35] Similarly, some of the royal psalms describing various kingly activities in the OT story are seen by various NT authors to be filled up in a greater sense by the ultimate King, Jesus (e.g., Ps. 2 in Luke 3:22; 9:35; Acts 4:25–26 and 13:33 of royal crises; Ps. 8 in 1 Cor. 15:26–28 and Heb. 2:5–10 of royal supremacy; and Ps. 45:6–7 [44:7–8] in Heb. 1:8–9 of the royal wedding).[36]

---

34. Craig Blomberg calls the use of Hosea 11:1 in Matt. 2:15 "a classic example of pure typology"; Craig L. Blomberg, "Matthew," in Beale and Carson, *Commentary*, 8. Cautioning against excusing it as an instance of *sensus plenior*, Collins ("How the New Testament Quotes and Interprets," 190–91) suggests that the use of Hosea 11:1 in Matt. 2:15 is an example of "pattern and fulfillment," by which he means typology. While Beale also classifies it as a typological use, he discusses the possibility that the occurrence of Hosea 11:1 in Matt. 2:15 may not be purely a retrospective recognition of a pattern as is expected with typology. Beale notes that the reference in Hosea 11:1 to the historic exodus from Egypt occurs in the discussion of an anticipated future restoration of Israel in Hosea 11:1–11. Thus, Hosea appears to understand that the first exodus is to be recapitulated in some future exodus (e.g., the return from exile) and/or other restorations; see Beale, *Handbook*, 60–64. Thus, if forward-looking, the use of Hosea 11:1 in Matt. 2:15 might be classified as a promising pattern use in my taxonomy.

35. See Joshua W. Jipp, "Luke's Scriptural Suffering Messiah: A Search for Precedent, a Search for Identity," *CBQ* 72 (2010): 255–74.

36. See Bock, "Scripture Citing Scripture," 273. See also Goppelt's description of typology in the early church's preaching as recorded in Acts; Leonhard Goppelt, *Typos: The Typological*

6. Historical backdrop: The NT author/speaker uses an OT text to provide the reader/listener with historical information helpful for understanding the subject under consideration in the NT context.

While the typological correlation function category focuses on correlating particular historical figures, places, events, or institutions with escalated NT historical partners, the historical backdrop function category is concerned with the OT story itself. Rather blandly, Marshall calls this specific category "history," but even with more colorful labels, this is, plain and simple, how many references to the OT function in the NT.[37] To explain Jesus as the climax to the OT story, the NT authors must regularly refer to the OT story. Thus, the historical backdrop function classification is the heart of the story usage cluster.

As might be expected, key examples of the historical backdrop function of the OT in the NT occur in the form realm that I have labeled "historical reminiscences." In fact, as recollections of people and/or events in the OT story, the historical reminiscences form is always utilized for historical backdrop functions of the OT in the NT. This includes the NT genealogies for Jesus (Matt. 1:1–17 and Luke 3:23–38), which might seem like dull reading to many twenty-first-century readers, but in an era without photographs, these lists of names functioned not only as legal records but as something like photo albums or family video montages that provided readers opportunities to reminisce and to reflect on the work of God in history.[38] The speeches of Acts have occasional references to the OT story in citations and in allusions. The longest speech in Acts, that of Stephen in Acts 7, is laden with uses of the OT in a historical backdrop function; the speech is a virtual survey of OT history focused on the patriarchs and Moses, with thirteen citations (primarily from the Pentateuch) interwoven with numerous historical reminiscences.[39] Paul's speech at Pisidian Antioch in Acts 13 likewise recalls the OT story in citations and historical reminiscences, but there the focus is on getting from the patriarchal beginnings to the Davidic part of the story. Of course, the point in telling the OT story is to make the

---

Interpretation of the Old Testament in the New, trans. Donald H. Madvig (Grand Rapids: Eerdmans, 1982 [German original, 1939]; reprint, Eugene, OR: Wipf & Stock, 2002), 121–24.

37. Marshall, "Acts," 520; he formerly referred to this usage as "references to OT events"; see Marshall, "Assessment of Recent Developments," 10. With a little more specificity than my taxonomy, Collins has two function classifications related to how the OT story is continued or not continued in the NT telling of it: "eschatological continuity" and "eschatological discontinuity"; Collins, "How the New Testament Quotes and Interprets," 188–89.

38. See Douglas S. Huffman, "Genealogy," *DJG¹*, 253–59.

39. More than half of the representatives of the historical reminiscences form in Luke-Acts occur in Acts 7.

historical connection to Jesus and his followers (e.g., see Acts 7:52–53; cf. 6:13–14; and 13:23, 26–39).[40]

7. Cultural background: The NT author/speaker uses a reference to the OT in order to explain some cultural behavior in the NT story by its background in the OT story.

The cultural background function category is where we classify NT references to the OT when the OT story itself is not the focus of the reference but some feature of it is used for its explanatory power at a particular juncture in the NT story. This is why this function category is in the overlap region shared by the story usage cluster and the analogy usage cluster. Drawing upon the cultural background from the OT storyline, the NT author offers some kind of explanation for what is happening in the NT storyline or for the proposed action in the NT context.

The infancy narratives in Luke's Gospel contain several examples of the cultural background function classification. In narrating the opening days of Jesus's life, Luke reports that Mary and Joseph took the child to Jerusalem to present him to the Lord as required by the Law of Moses. Three times Luke summarizes the legal requirements (Luke 2:22, 27, 39; cf. Lev. 12:6–8; Exod. 13:2, 11–16), and twice he cites portions of those requirements with introductory formulas (Luke 2:23, 24). These religious cultural references explain for the reader why Jesus's parents had him in the temple area of Jerusalem, where he is the recipient of two words of prophecy regarding his life and ministry (by Simeon in Luke 2:28–35 and by Anna in Luke 2:36–38). Thus, with this explanation, Jesus's life and ministry are proleptically framed as being in keeping with Scripture; the redemption of the child according to the law of the Lord pictures the Lord's provision for the redemption of his people (cf. Luke 2:38).

Another example of the cultural background function classification is found in the Jerusalem Council in Acts 15, where the young church is discussing how Jewish and gentile believers are to interact with one another in an era when God has inaugurated the new covenant with his people. After citing Amos 9:11–12 to demonstrate that God has always intended to bring gentiles into the community of his people (Acts 15:15–18), James outlines for the council the expectations he thinks appropriate for Jews to have of gentiles. The expectations placed upon the new gentile believers (aka "the apostolic decree") clearly reflect the kinds of requirements expected of resident aliens

---

40. Jacob Jervell observes that nowhere else in the NT do we have narrative recitals of OT history like those in Acts 7 and 13; not even the nonnarrative listing of historic figures in Heb. 11 compares; Jacob Jervell, *The Theology of the Acts of the Apostles*, New Testament Theology (Cambridge: Cambridge University Press, 1996), 62.

living in OT Israel (cf. Acts 15:20, 28; 21:25 with Lev. 17–18). Luke reports James's explanation, "For from ancient generations Moses has had in every city those who proclaim him, for he is read every Sabbath in the synagogues" (Acts 15:21). The gentile Christians are aware of the scruples of their Jewish neighbors and should behave with sensitivity for the sake of unity in the worshiping community. Thus, Luke's use of the OT as an explanation of cultural background is not merely for the sake of historical curiosity; it also has some helpfulness for understanding Christian behavior (e.g., here sensitivity for the sake of unity) going forward. Examples like these help us see the cultural background classification as part of not only the story usage cluster but also the analogy usage cluster.

Here also we might slot Paul's cultural references to not muzzling a working ox (Deut. 25:4 cited in 1 Cor. 9:9 and 1 Tim. 5:18). Framed like Hillel's rule 1: *Qal wa-ḥomer* (discussed in chap. 4), Paul makes an argument by analogy from the lesser to the greater: if we are to take care of our animals, certainly we are to care for other people (an argument that the context of Deut. 25 seems to be making as well).

8. Instructive exemplars: The NT speaker/author refers to the OT as giving an example that is to be followed by the listeners/readers of the NT text.

This function category is the heart of the analogy usage cluster and is generally rather straightforward. Perhaps the quintessential instance of a NT writer using the OT in an exemplar manner is Paul in 1 Cor. 10:1–22. After identifying the OT Israelites of the exodus as a community that disobeyed God (vv. 1–5), Paul explains, "Now these things took place as examples for us, that we might not desire evil as they did" (v. 6). He makes several very practical applications from their poor examples—do not be idolaters (v. 7), do not commit sexual immorality (v. 8), do not test Christ (v. 9), and do not grumble (v. 10)—each time referencing "as some of them were/did" (3× καθώς τινες αὐτῶν, and 1× καθάπερ τινὲς αὐτῶν). Then he makes another explanatory statement, "Now these things happened to them as an example, but they were written down for our instruction, on whom the end of the ages has come" (v. 11, followed by further points of application in vv. 12–22).

An example from the life of Christ is seen when, defending the actions of his disciples plucking grain on a Sabbath, Jesus makes reference to David and his companions eating the discarded consecrated bread usually reserved for priests. Thus, Jesus draws an analogy between David with his followers on a kingly mission and himself with his followers on a kingly mission as "Lord of the Sabbath" (Matt. 12:1–8//Mark 2:23–28//Luke 6:1–5; cf. 1 Sam.

21:1–9).[41] Similarly, James makes an argument by analogy, appealing to Abraham (Gen. 22:1–18; cf. 2 Chron. 20:7; Isa. 41:8; and citing Gen. 15:6) and to Rahab (Josh. 2:1–24; 6:25) as examples of exhibiting one's faith in action (James 2:20–26).

9. Illustrations and imagery: The NT speaker/author refers to someone or something in the OT as an illustration of the subject matter under discussion in the NT context or otherwise draws upon imagery from the OT.

The title of this function classification betrays why it would be a category in the analogy usage cluster: illustrations and imagery have analogous appeal to listeners and readers. But illustrations and imagery also draw upon ideas, so the illustrations and imagery function category is also part of the overlapping ideas usage cluster. The point of this particular classification is that sometimes a NT author uses OT figures or ideas to construct an illustration. In doing so, he is not setting out to reinterpret an OT passage in some fuller sense (see sidebar 5.2 on *sensus plenior*). Rather, he simply wants to use some well-known OT components to write his own NT passage. The NT author cannot be charged with disrespecting the OT context, for he is not at all interpreting the OT passage.

This seems to be the best explanation of the illustration Paul constructs in Gal. 4:21–31, using the familiar characters of Hagar and Sarah from the book Genesis. Paul is not uncovering some hidden meaning to the Genesis passage, nor is he taking it out of context.[42] Paul is simply drawing an analogy (he uses the word allegory, ἀλληγορέω, v. 24) creating his own illustration for why his readers should reject the temptation to go back to enslavement under the covenant of the law. Drawing on these images fits the broad ideas usage cluster, and utilizing them as illustrations for expected behaviors fits the broad analogy usage cluster; this is why this specific function classification is placed where these two broad clusters overlap.

Paul provides another such example of this. While he had a messianic view of Isaiah's servant imagery (e.g., Rom. 10:16; 15:21), Paul nevertheless seems to draw upon that imagery as somehow descriptive of his own life (Gal. 1:15 alluding to Isa. 49:1; cf. Acts 13:47 citing Isa. 49:6). Clearly Paul is not claiming

41. See Collins, "How the New Testament Quotes and Interprets," 187; Collins has this example in his "analogy and application" category. Because of its connections to Jesus as the ultimate example of the Davidic king, some interpreters will prefer to classify this instance as having a *promising patterns* function.

42. Cf. Collins, "How the New Testament Quotes and Interprets," 188. But see now Matthew S. Harmon, "Allegory, Typology, or Something Else? Revisiting Galatians 4:21–5:1," in *Studies in the Pauline Epistles: Essays in Honor of Douglas J. Moo*, ed. Matthew S. Harmon and Jay E. Smith (Grand Rapids: Zondervan, 2014), 144–58; Harmon would classify this as an example of typological correlation.

Sensus Plenior: A Hidden/New Meaning with "Fuller Sense"

Readers may notice that the recommended taxonomy of functions here lacks a specifically labeled *sensus plenior* category. The term **sensus plenior** was coined in 1927 to refer to a "fuller sense" that might be divinely intended for Scripture beyond the recognition of its original writers.[1] In its most tame expressions, *sensus plenior* seems to be simply another way to speak about typology under the classification label "typological correlation" in the recommended taxonomy. But there are other nuances associated with the concept of *sensus plenior*.[2] One of the dangers of some expressions of *sensus plenior* is the presumption that OT texts can possess (or can develop) meanings that are completely unconnected to the intentions of the original writers and consequently are undetectable by means of exegesis. In my way of thinking, this kind of departure from the normal use of language goes too far. Rather than recognition of a new *meaning* of the OT text, I understand typological correlation as recognition of a divinely intended *significance* of the historical item (person, event, or institution, etc.) as expressed in the OT text and filled out in the NT context.[3] To protect against confusion with illegitimate connotations, I have here generally avoided using the term *sensus plenior* in my discussion of function classifications.[4]

1. Andrés Fernández is credited with coining the term, perhaps as early as 1925; see Raymond E. Brown, *The* Sensus Plenior *of Sacred Scripture* (Baltimore: St. Mary's University, 1955; reprint, Eugene, OR: Wipf & Stock, 2008), esp. 88; Brown gives his technical definition of *sensus plenior* on 92; cf. Raymond E. Brown, "The *Sensus Plenior* in the Last Ten Years," *CBQ* 25 (1963): 262–85.

2. For a brief survey indicating such varied nuances, see Jonathan Lunde, "An Introduction to Central Questions in the New Testament Use of the Old Testament," 7–41, and Kenneth Berding, "An Analysis of Three Views on the New Testament Use of the Old Testament," 233–43, in *Three Views on the New Testament Use of the Old Testament*, ed. Kenneth Berding and Jonathan Lunde, Counterpoints: Bible and Theology (Grand Rapids: Zondervan, 2008), esp. 13–18 and 233–35. This volume contains interactive essays by Walter C. Kaiser Jr., Darrell L. Bock, and Peter Enns, where they debate, among other issues, the concept of *sensus plenior*.

3. For a more technical expression of this kind of distinction between meaning and significance as it pertains to the concept of *sensus plenior*—one that employs the canonical context as a control on the concept such that the author's original meaning cannot be changed or contradicted—see Kevin J. Vanhoozer, *Is There a Meaning in This Text? The Bible, the Reader, and the Morality of Literary Knowledge* (Grand Rapids: Zondervan, 1998), 263–65, 313–14. For more on canonical considerations pertaining to the NT use of the OT, see also Douglas J. Moo and Andrew David Naselli, "The Problem of the New Testament's Use of the Old Testament," in *The Enduring Authority of the Christian Scriptures*, ed. D. A. Carson (Grand Rapids: Eerdmans, 2016), 734–37.

4. Of the various other function taxonomies consulted, only Collins has a separate *sensus plenior* category, and he highly qualifies it: "It is tenuous, however, to advocate a *sensus plenior* that dispenses with original intent"; Collins, "How the New Testament Quotes and Interprets," 190. It should be noted that the definitive Catholic work on *sensus plenior* by Brown similarly qualifies it as well; Brown, *The* Sensus Plenior *of Sacred Scripture*, 92–93. For other such cautious uses of *sensus plenior*, see J. I. Packer, "Infallible Scripture and the Role of Hermeneutics," in *Scripture and Truth*, ed. D. A. Carson and John D. Woodbridge (Grand Rapids: Zondervan, 1983), 349–50; Richard N. Longenecker, *Biblical Exegesis in the Apostolic Period*, 2nd ed. (Grand Rapids: Eerdmans, 1999), xxxii–xxxiv, 198; Craig A. Evans, "The Old Testament in the New," in *The Face of New Testament Studies: A Survey of Recent Research*, ed. Scot McKnight and Grant R. Osborne (Grand Rapids: Baker Academic, 2004), 145; Darrell L. Bock, "Single Meaning, Multiple Contexts and Referents: The New Testament's Legitimate, Accurate, and Multifaceted Use of the Old," in *Three Views on the New Testament Use of the Old Testament*, ed. Kenneth Berding and Jonathan Lunde, Counterpoints: Bible and Theology (Grand Rapids: Zondervan, 2008), 112–15; and esp. Moo and Naselli, "Problem," 730–34.

to be the Messiah but is seeing that imagery as illustrative of how he is to live his life. Thus, this instance also exemplifies how the specific illustrations and imagery function category lies in the overlapping region between the analogy usage cluster (as an example to be followed) and the ideas usage cluster (as a concept to be understood).[43]

The opening chapters of the Third Gospel contain several examples of OT imagery in terms of ideas. This is especially the case in the songs of the infancy narratives (e.g., Luke 1:46–55, 67–79; 2:25–33; cf. 2:36–38).[44] At the other end of the NT, and quite famously, the book of Revelation has no citations of the OT at all and yet abounds in OT imagery using the forms of specific allusions and thematic echoes; some suggest that Revelation has "hardly a verse without an allusion" to the OT.[45]

On the imagery side of this illustrations and imagery function classification is where the "proverbial use" in Beale's taxonomy fits. Because particular turns of phrase and particular images in the OT had corresponding implications, appeals to those phrases and images would be understood to carry those associated proverbial connotations. As an example, Beale points to the NT use of the term μυστήριον ("mystery, secret"; 27 or 28× in the NT), which is almost always used in the presence of an OT quotation or allusion.[46] The OT use of this term—particularly in Dan. 2, where the LXX uses μυστήριον to translate the Aramaic term *rāz* (רָז) eight times—pictures divine revelation regarding eschatological matters that have been heretofore hidden from human understanding. Thus Jesus's use of the term μυστήριον to describe his teaching in parables about the kingdom of God (Matt. 13:10–17//Mark 4:10–12//Luke 8:9–10) draws on the OT imagery bound up in that word and points the listeners to the beginning of an unexpected fulfillment of such end-time mysteries (see also the use of μυστήριον in Rom. 11:25; 16:25–26; 1 Cor. 2:6–10; 4:1; Eph. 1:7–10; 3:1–12; 6:19; Col. 1:25–2:3; 4:3; and 1 Tim. 3:16).[47]

---

43. Drawing on my placement of NT uses of the Isaiah servant passages in the promising patterns classification (item 4 above), this example also illustrates the possibility that function classifications can overlap in some instances even though they are not next to each other on the continuum in fig. 5.1; the spoked-wheel diagram in fig. 5.2 is designed to illustrate this possibility.

44. See Stephen C. Farris, *The Hymns of Luke's Infancy Narratives: Their Origin, Meaning and Significance*, JSNTSup 9 (Sheffield: Sheffield Academic, 1985); and Chang-Wook Jung, *The Original Language of the Lukan Infancy Narratives*, JSNTSup 267 (New York: T&T Clark, 2004).

45. So Goldingay, *Reading Jesus's Bible*, 153. See also G. K. Beale, *John's Use of the Old Testament in Revelation*, JSNTSup 166 (Sheffield: JSOT Press, 1998).

46. Beale, *Handbook*, 75–78.

47. Beale points to the classic work of George Eldon Ladd, *The Presence of the Future: The Eschatology of Biblical Realism*, 2nd ed. (Grand Rapids: Eerdmans, 1974), esp. 223–25; as well as A. E. Harvey, "The Use of Mystery Language in the Bible," *JTS* 31 (1980): 320–36.

Beale's specific category of "ironic or inverted use" would fit with the illustrations and imagery function classification as well. When Paul cites Deut. 21:23 in Gal. 3:13, he appeals to the scriptural teaching about crucifixion—the punishment for the most vile of criminals—and applies this image to the suffering endured on our behalf by Christ, the most honorable human ever. Similarly, the curse of confusion of language at the tower of Babel leads to the dispersion of humanity in Gen. 10–11, and this confusion seems alluded to in Acts 2 when the diversity of tongues brings the blessing of one message intended to bring God's people together in a whole new sense.[48]

10. Vocabulary and style: The NT writer borrows the vocabulary and style of OT writers without intending particular citations and interpretations.

This is the function category at the heart of the ideas usage cluster. Unsurprisingly, many applications of this particular function classification can be made to occurrences of the thematic echo form. It has long been noted that Luke's writing style appears to be an intentional imitation of the Greek OT.[49] And there has been extended discussion in scholarly circles about the level of influence the LXX has had on Luke's vocabulary.[50] Such vocabulary and style observations are the core of investigations of allusions. And perhaps rhetorical use of language can be included under the vocabulary and style function classification. Beale, for example, suggests that Paul's citation of Deut. 30:12–14 in his argument in Rom. 10:5–9 is meant "to embellish the gospel with OT-sounding language in order to enhance its persuasiveness to the readers" but that he does this with the specific OT contextual meaning in mind.[51] Thus, at times Paul writes with an intentional biblical style.

See also "μυστήριον," *NIDNTTE* 3:350–57; and Markus Bockmuehl, *Revelation and Mystery in Ancient Judaism and Pauline Christianity*, WUNT 2/36 (Tübingen: Mohr Siebeck, 1990; reprint, Eugene, OR: Wipf & Stock, 2009).

48. Beale, *Handbook*, 92–93.

49. In chap. 6 below I comment further on Luke's apparent motives for writing with such a biblical style.

50. E.g., Max Wilcox examines eleven such "septuagintalisms" and offers nuanced conclusions; see Max E. Wilcox, *The Semitisms of Acts* (Oxford: Clarendon, 1965), esp. 56–86.

51. Beale, *Handbook*, 78–79; Beale calls this a "rhetorical use" of the OT (see also his "assimilated use" classification). Other scholars approach the concept of the "rhetorical use" of the OT in the NT with different nuances; see Dennis L. Stamps, "The Use of the Old Testament in the New Testament as a Rhetorical Device: A Methodological Proposal," in *Hearing the Old Testament in the New Testament*, ed. Stanley E. Porter, McMaster New Testament Studies (Grand Rapids: Eerdmans, 2006), 9–37; Christopher D. Stanley, *Arguing with Scripture: The Rhetoric of Quotations in the Letters of Paul* (New York: T&T Clark, 2004); John Paul Heil, *The Rhetorical Role of Scripture in 1 Corinthians*, SBLStBL 15 (Atlanta: Society of Biblical Literature, 2005); and Nicholas G. Piotrowski, *Matthew's New David at the End of Exile: A Socio-Rhetorical Study of Scriptural Quotations*, NovTSup 170 (Leiden: Brill, 2016).

More than just style and even theology, scholars note that the OT also influences the very structure of some of the documents in the NT. Willard Swartley sees something of the OT traditions in each of the four major sections of the Synoptic Gospels: the exodus tradition in the Galilean narrative, the way-conquest tradition in the journey narrative, the temple traditions in the pre-passion narratives, and the kingship traditions in the passion narratives.[52] Focused just on Luke-Acts, some scholars suggest that Luke appears to use whole sections of Deuteronomy, or Isaiah, or the Elijah-Elisha narrative in 1–2 Kings as models for outlining portions of his own writing.[53] Sylvia Keesmaat suggests that Paul is reinterpreting the exodus tradition in Rom. 8 and Gal. 4.[54] Matthew Harmon proposes that Isa. 49–55 serves as the model for Paul's outline of Galatians.[55] Beale points to fourteen shared elements occurring in roughly the same order as evidence that Dan. 7 serves as a model for Rev. 4–5.[56] These extensive uses of Scripture seem too precise and detailed to be accidental.[57]

---

52. See Willard M. Swartley, *Israel's Scripture Traditions and the Synoptic Gospels: Story Shaping Story* (Peabody, MA: Hendrickson, 1994).

53. This was mentioned in the discussion of "volume" in chap. 3 above, with Luke's extensive use of Isaiah supported by the works of Pao, Koet, Mallen, Beers, and Witherington. On Luke's extensive use of Deuteronomy, see Christopher F. Evans, "The Central Section of St. Luke's Gospel," in *Studies in the Gospels: Essays in Memory of R. H. Lightfoot*, ed. Dennis E. Nineham (Oxford: Blackwell, 1955), 37–53; Dietrich Rusam, "Deuteronomy in Luke-Acts," in *Deuteronomy in the New Testament*, ed. Maarten J. J. Menken and Steven Moyise, NTSI, LNTS 358 (London: T&T Clark, 2007), 63–81; and Adelbert Denaux, "Old Testament Models for the Lukan Travel Narrative: A Critical Survey," in his *Studies in the Gospel of Luke: Structure, Language and Theology*, Tilburg Theological Studies (Berlin: Lit, 2010), 39–70. On the use of the Elijah–Elisha narrative, see Thomas L. Brodie, *Luke the Literary Interpreter: Luke-Acts as a Systematic Rewriting and Updating of the Elijah–Elisha Narrative in 1 and 2 Kings* (Rome: Pontifical University of St. Thomas Aquinas, 1987); and John S. Kloppenborg and Joseph Verheyden, eds., *The Elijah-Elisha Narrative in the Composition of Luke*, LNTS 493 (New York: Bloomsbury T&T Clark, 2014). See also select essays in Mogens Müller and Jesper Tang Nielsen, eds., *Luke's Literary Creativity*, LNTS 550 (London: Bloomsbury T&T Clark, 2016).

54. Sylvia C. Keesmaat, *Paul and His Story: (Re)Interpreting the Exodus Tradition*, JSNTSup 181 (Sheffield: Sheffield Academic, 1999).

55. Matthew S. Harmon, *She Must and Shall Go Free: Paul's Isaianic Gospel in Galatians*, BZNW 168 (New York: De Gruyter, 2010), 261–65; cf. the short summary in Beale, *Handbook*, 86–87.

56. Beale, *Handbook*, 80–83. Beale also argues that Dan. 7 has influenced Rev. 13 and 17; cf. G. K. Beale, *The Use of Daniel in Jewish Apocalyptic Literature and in the Revelation of St. John* (Lanham, MD: University Press of America, 1984), 178–270.

57. Calling them "motifs," Gert Steyn suggests that such large-scale uses of Scripture as structural models be recognized as a form alongside the other forms (e.g., citations, allusions, etc.); he also considers "scriptural terminology" its own category of form; Gert Jacobus Steyn, *Septuagint Quotations in the Context of the Petrine and Pauline Speeches of the Acta Apostolorum*, CBET 12 (Kampen: Kok Pharos, 1995), 26. Marshall ("Acts," 519) follows Steyn in

In addition to such conscious use of portions of the OT as models for structuring their thoughts and writings, NT authors may well have been so saturated in the Scriptures that various allusions and thematic echoes became a matter of habit. In keeping with this thought, Carson and Beale suggestively ask, "Are there instances, then, when the NT writers use biblical language simply because their minds are so steeped in Scripture that such verbal patterns provide the linguistic frameworks in which they think?"[58] Such instances are not attempts to interpret the OT per se; they merely make use of the same language.

So, sometimes a NT author may be simply using OT language without intending to interpret any particular OT text where that language is found. Perhaps this is what occurs in Luke 14:26—"If anyone comes to me and does not hate his own father and mother and wife and children and brothers and sisters . . ." (cf. Matt. 10:37, "loves more" instead of "does not hate")—with Luke's harsh phrasing a conscious allusion to the Levites' choice of God over family ties (see Deut. 33:9) and/or a subconscious utilization of the "hate" term in a familial context (as in Mal. 1:2–6; μισέω in LXX and in Luke). We find people similarly borrowing scriptural phrases today, and we extend to them the courtesy of not assuming that they are trying to interpret the particular passage of Scripture where those borrowed phrases originate.[59] We should show the same courtesy to the NT authors.

This brings us back around to the top of the list of ten function categories. In the overlapping layout of function classifications, the two broad groups of the idea usage cluster (i.e., concepts to be understood) and the declaration usage cluster (i.e., truths to be declared) overlap in sharing the ultimate truths category (item 1 above).

---

both of these suggestions and adds "language" as a form category too. While I have already admitted the possibility of overlap between these taxonomical realms, I am obviously treating these three items—"scriptural terminology," "language," and "motifs"—all as belonging in the function realm more so than in the form realm. Andrew Das also suggests a large-scale form that he labels "grand thematic narrative," but rather than its own form, I suggest that this idea as expressed by Das might be better conceived of as a collection of form classifications into a working whole. See A. Andrew Das, *Paul and the Stories of Israel: Grand Thematic Narratives in Galatians* (Minneapolis: Fortress, 2016), 13–16.

58. G. K. Beale and D. A. Carson, "Introduction," in *Commentary on the New Testament Use of the Old Testament*, ed. G. K. Beale and D. A. Carson (Grand Rapids: Baker Academic, 2007), xxv. Beale (*Handbook*, 91–92) has a separate function classification for this usage called "assimilated use."

59. For example, a commonly borrowed scriptural phrase in modern parlance is employed as a complaint about institutional disorganization: "Around here the left hand does not know what the right hand is doing!" Rarely does the complainer demonstrate awareness that Jesus used these words not to describe poor organization but to describe proper behavior regarding almsgiving (Matt. 6:1–4).

Summary on This Taxonomy of Functions

This particular taxonomy of functions for the NT use of the OT offers several benefits for those working in this field of study. One benefit is that this taxonomy has both broad usage clusters as well as more specific classifications. Thus, it allows scholars to focus at the level of their comfort, and furthermore it gives them wider areas of potential agreement even when they may disagree as they define their views more narrowly.

This leads into a second benefit. In making much of the concept of overlapping segments of broad usage clusters along a continuum, this taxonomy gives scholars the opportunity to map their disagreements in such a way as to discover more agreement. Thus, in recognizing that two scholars classify a particular NT passage's use of the OT in two different but neighboring specific function categories, they may realize that they agree on the larger, overarching usage cluster. For example, some scholars may prefer to classify all the NT uses of the servant passages of Isaiah (as well as some of the NT uses of the royal psalms) in the typological correlation category rather than having them (as I have suggested) in the promising pattern category. But noting that these two categories are right next to each other on the continuum of function classifications—both in the broad fulfillment usage cluster (see figs. 5.1 and 5.2 above)—will help scholars realize that their differences may be more arguments about emphasis of function rather than arguments about kind of function. This also brings to the fore the possibility that further research may lead scholars to suggest the migration of the classification of a particular occurrence in one direction or another along the continuum.[60]

Finally, a third benefit of this taxonomy of functions has to do with recognizing multiple levels of intentionality. While the descriptions of the function classifications in this taxonomy primarily assume some sense of conscious authorial intentionality on the part of the NT authors (and this is especially the case when they explicitly cite the OT), these same function categories fittingly apply to potentially subconscious uses as well. Living in a world that was highly influenced by the OT Scriptures, NT authors may well have utilized various allusions and thematic echoes as a matter of habit.

Yet such habitual ways of thinking, speaking, and writing need not preclude intention in some sense of the term. After all, a NT author may have

---

60. As indicated earlier, Beale notes that ongoing research on the occurrence of Hosea 11:1 in Matt. 2:15 may temper how scholars define typology, esp. with regard to the necessity of retrospection as an element in typology; Beale, *Handbook*, 57n3. But if scholars become convinced that Hosea 11:1 is sufficiently anticipatory of a new exodus, then the occurrence of Hosea 11:1 in Matt. 2:15 might simply be adjusted slightly in its classification on my taxonomy from the typological correlation category to the neighboring promising pattern category.

piled up or gathered together his various scriptural references (e.g., the many and diverse combinations of citations, allusions, recollections, and thematic echoes in Acts 7) in order to have an overall effect upon the reader that is more than the mere sum of the individual references.[61] It is this grander "function" of OT Scripture for a NT author that I mean to address in chapter 6.

61. Kenneth Duncan Litwak, *Echoes of Scripture in Luke-Acts: Telling the History of God's People Intertextually*, JSNTSup 282 (London: T&T Clark, 2005), 60–61.

6

The New Testament Use
of the Old Testament in Luke and Acts

Blessed rather are those who hear the word of God and keep it.

Luke 11:28

In examining the study of the NT use of the OT, we have looked at examples from all over the NT. Another level of this field of study is to examine the preferences and peculiarities of a particular NT writer and how that author utilizes the OT in his corpus of NT literature. To provide here a brief example of this level of study, I have selected the Lukan corpus of literature.[1] In investigations of the use of the OT in Luke-Acts, scholars regularly make observations such as these: (a) the highest concentrations of OT references are in the sections of Luke-Acts that exhibit more Jewish characteristics and tone (e.g., Luke 1–2, 4, 22–24, and Acts 1–12), (b) Luke rarely cites Scripture as the narrator in Luke-Acts; usually characters in the narrative are reported as citing the OT, and (c) not only does Luke favor the Septuagint text (LXX) over the Masoretic Hebrew text (MT) for his OT citations, but his overall Greek writing style appears to be an intentional imitation of the Greek OT. In this chapter, I pull together some further findings about Luke's use of Scripture, make some observations about how this is related to his main

1. For examples of scholarly investigations into the use of the OT in various NT corpora, see the heading in app. B titled "Book-By-Book Resources on the New Testament Use of the Old Testament."

theological themes, and from these discoveries suggest some programmatic motives for Luke's use of the OT. This chapter, then, will serve as an example of analyzing the use of the OT in the writings of one particular NT author.

Luke cites the OT authoritatively near the beginning of each of his two books (i.e., Luke 4:18–19 and Acts 2:17–21), and each of these passages indicates that a divinely intended shift in history is occurring with the Jesus event. In fact, the Gospel of Luke begins and ends with narrations about Jesus interpreting Scripture (Luke 2:41–50; 24:44–49), and Acts begins and ends with Jesus's followers doing the same (Acts 1:16–26; 28:25–28).[2] Given Luke's high view of Scripture—it is God's Word that is sure to come to pass (Luke 16:16–17; cf. 21:33)—it is not surprising that his thematic use of the OT maps onto several of his most emphasized theological themes.[3] But more than a source for his theological emphases, Luke appears to have other goals for his use of Scripture. With reference to the taxonomical outlines that I recommend for this field of study, let me begin by reviewing the forms, framings, and functions of Luke's use of the OT.

Forms, Framings, and Functions in Luke's Use of the Old Testament

The taxonomy of forms that I recommend contains eight different forms that a use of the OT can take in a NT document. Unsurprisingly, given the amount of material that Luke contributes in his two books—more than 25 percent of the NT—he has plenty of space to utilize all eight forms (see table 6.1 for the tallies; for the specific classification of each occurrence in Luke-Acts, see app. C). On the other hand, it may be surprising to see that the forms are not represented in the balance one might anticipate. The number of total OT citations, for example, is not as high as one would expect. Despite the difficulties scholars have in counting the number of OT citations in the NT (noted in chap. 2), even if we use the average number of 276 as the total number of OT citations, the 57 citations in Luke-Acts represent only about 20 percent of that total. This is less than we might expect. Furthermore, of the 57 OT citations

2. In examining the use of OT Scripture in the first and last accounts that cite Jesus teaching in the Gospel of Luke (4:16–30 and 24:13–35) and that cite Paul teaching in the book of Acts (13:14–52 and 28:16–31), Koet suggests that these central figures interpreting Scripture at crucial points in the story indicate that the Scriptures are key to understanding Luke-Acts. See Bart J. Koet, *Five Studies on Interpretation of Scripture in Luke-Acts*, SNTA 14 (Leuven: Leuven University Press, 1989), 15.

3. Barrett notes that Luke's use of the OT is "co-extensive with most of the aims and interests that he has incorporated in his book"; C. K. Barrett, "Luke/Acts," in *It Is Written: Scripture Citing Scripture; Essays in Honour of Barnabas Lindars*, ed. D. A. Carson and H. G. M. Williamson (Cambridge: Cambridge University Press, 1988), 243.

TABLE 6.1

A Tally of the Uses of the Old Testament in Luke-Acts

Forms of OT Use	Luke's Gospel	Book of Acts	Luke-Acts
Citations			
1. Introduced quotations (1-IQ)	8	14	22
2. Introduced paraphrases (2-IP)	12	19	31
3. Unintroduced quotations (3-UQ)	1	0	1
4. Unintroduced paraphrases (4-UP)	3	0	3
subtotal	**24**	**33**	**57**
Allusions and Recollections			
5. Scripture summaries (5-SS)	14	19	33
6. Historical reminiscences (6-HR)	18	36	54
7. Specific allusions (7-SA)	159	82	241
8. Thematic echoes (8-TE)	242	262	504
subtotal	**433**	**399**	**832**
Total	**457**	**432**	**889**

Note: While attempting to be more thorough than the lists provided by UBS[5] and NA[28] indexes, I must refrain from claiming this tally to be exhaustive of all OT and extrabiblical references in Luke-Acts, particularly of specific allusions and thematic echoes. Nevertheless, this is what I have counted in my years of study so far.

that I count in Luke-Acts, only four are without introductory formulas of some kind, and they all appear in the Gospel of Luke (see tables 6.2 and 6.3, where the citation forms are identified with the classifications from chap. 2).

Luke's Gospel has a few other uniquenesses with regard to OT citations. Unsurprisingly, fifteen of the twenty-four OT citations in the Gospel of Luke are framed in the mouth of Jesus, to which we can add the observation that eight of the fourteen Scripture summaries in Luke are also in the mouth of Jesus. Three of the OT citations in Luke are by the narrator (2:23–24, 3:4–6), two by the devil (4:10–11), two by a lawyer (10:27), one by some Sadducees (20:37b), and one by a multitude of disciples at the triumphal entry (19:38a). While Jesus's followers are relatively silent in citing Scripture in Luke's Gospel—the chanting of Ps. 118:26 at the triumphal entry being the one exception—the converse situation is found in Acts, where all but one of the OT citations (8:32-33) are made by Christian believers in the story (see tables 6.2 and 6.3).

Perhaps of greater curiosity, citations are overall more common in Acts than in the Gospel of Luke: almost a 2:3 ratio (see the upper portion of table 6.1). Reflecting on the nature of the story in each of Luke's two volumes, this difference is not as surprising as some might think. The Gospel of Luke focuses upon the life, death, and resurrection of Jesus. While Luke is clear that Jesus is the fulfillment of all of Scripture (e.g., Luke 24:25–27), the presence of Jesus as that fulfillment carries great weight. In the book of Acts, however, the mission of preaching Jesus is taken up. Given that Jesus commissioned his followers to serve in this witnessing role and that this witnessing role explicitly concerns what was written about Jesus as the Messiah (see Luke 24:44–48 and Acts 1:8), it is of no real surprise to see the Jesus followers actively preaching the gospel message from the OT. On the contrary, it is surprising that Acts does not have even more OT citations than it does.

It is also surprising that the OT citations in Acts are not more evenly spaced. Upon closer investigation, Luke's OT citations tend to appear in the more

TABLE 6.2

A Detailed Index of the Old Testament Citations in the Gospel of Luke

Luke Reference	OT Reference [LXX Versification]	Form	Text Tradition	Speaker	Audience	Listed in UBS[5]	Listed in NA[28]
2:23	Exod. 13:2, 12, 15	2-IP	free paraphrase	narrator	reader	✓	✓
2:24	Lev. 12:8	2-IP	LXX paraphrase	narrator	reader	✓	✓
3:4–6	Isa. 40:3–5	2-IP	LXX paraphrase (vs. MT)	narrator	reader	✓	✓
4:4	Deut. 8:3	1-IQ	LXX (vs. MT)	Jesus	the devil	✓	✓
4:8	Deut. 6:13; 10:20	2-IP	LXX paraphrase	Jesus	the devil	✓	✓
4:10	Ps. 91:11 [90:11]	1-IQ	LXX (vs. MT)	the devil	Jesus	✓	✓
4:11	Ps. 91:12 [90:12]	1-IQ	LXX (vs. MT)	the devil	Jesus	✓	✓
4:12	Deut. 6:16	1-IQ	LXX (vs. MT)	Jesus	the devil	✓	✓
4:18–19	Isa. 66:1–2	1-IQ	LXX	Jesus	synagogue	✓	✓
7:27	Mal. 3:1	2-IP	free paraphrase	Jesus	Jewish crowd	✓	✓
8:10	Isa. 6:9	2-IP	free paraphrase (vs. MT)	Jesus	disciples	✓	—
10:27	Deut. 6:5; 10:12	2-IP	LXX paraphrase	a lawyer	Jesus	✓	✓
10:27	Lev. 19:18	1-IQ	LXX	a lawyer	Jesus	✓	✓
13:35	Ps. 118:26 [117:26]	3-UQ	LXX	Jesus	Jerusalem	✓	✓
18:20	Exod. 20:12–16; Deut. 5:16–20	2-IP	LXX paraphrase	Jesus	a ruler	✓	✓
19:38	Ps. 118:26 [117:26]	4-UP	LXX paraphrase	multitude	any who listen	✓	✓
19:46	Isa. 56:7	2-IP	LXX paraphrase	Jesus	merchants	✓	✓
20:17	Ps. 118:22 [117:22]	1-IQ	LXX	Jesus	the people	✓	✓
20:28	Deut. 25:5–6	2-IP	free paraphrase	Sadducees	Jesus	✓	—
20:37	Exod. 3:6, 15, 16 (cf. 3:2)	2-IP	LXX paraphrase	Jesus	Sadducees	✓	✓
20:42–43	Ps. 110:1 [109:1]	1-IQ	LXX (vs. MT)	Jesus	scribes	✓	✓
22:37	Isa. 53:12	2-IP	LXX paraphrase	Jesus	disciples	✓	✓
23:30	Hosea 10:8	4-UP	LXX paraphrase	Jesus	Jerusalem women	✓	✓
23:46	Ps. 31:5 [30:6]	4-UP	LXX paraphrase	Jesus	God the Father	✓	✓

TABLE 6.3

A Detailed Index of the Old Testament Citations in the Book of Acts

Acts Reference	OT Reference [LXX Versification]	Form	Text Tradition	Speaker	Audience	Listed in UBS[5]	Listed in NA[28]
1:20	Ps. 69:25 [68:26]	2-IP	LXX paraphrase (vs. MT)	Peter	120 disciples	✓	✓
1:20	Ps. 109:8 [108:8]	1-IQ	LXX (vs. MT)	Peter	120 disciples	✓	✓
2:17–21	Joel 2:28–32 [3:1–5]	2-IP	LXX paraphrase (vs. MT)	Peter	Jewish crowd	✓	✓
2:25–28	Ps. 16:8–11 [15:8–11]	1-IQ	LXX (vs. MT)	Peter	Jewish crowd	✓	✓
2:34–35	Ps. 110:1 [109:1]	1-IQ	LXX (vs. MT)	Peter	Jewish crowd	✓	✓
3:22–23	Deut. 18:15–19	2-IP	LXX paraphrase (vs. MT)	Peter	Jews at temple	✓	✓
3:23	Lev. 23:29	2-IP	LXX paraphrase	Peter	Jews at temple	✓	✓
3:25	Gen. 22:13 and/or 26:4	2-IP	LXX paraphrase	Peter	Jews at temple	✓	✓
4:11	Ps. 118:22 [117:22]	2-IP	free paraphrase	Peter	Sanhedrin	✓	—
4:25–26	Ps. 2:1–2	1-IQ	LXX (vs. MT)	church	God	✓	✓
7:3	Gen. 12:1	2-IP	LXX paraphrase	Stephen	Sanhedrin	✓	✓
7:6–7	Gen. 15:13–14	2-IP	LXX paraphrase	Stephen	Sanhedrin	✓	✓
7:7	Exod. 3:12	2-IP	free paraphrase	Stephen	Sanhedrin	✓	—
7:18	Exod. 1:8	1-IQ	LXX	Stephen	Sanhedrin	✓	✓
7:26	Exod. 2:13	2-IP	free paraphrase	Stephen	Sanhedrin	—	—
7:27–28	Exod. 2:14	1-IQ	LXX (vs. MT)	Stephen	Sanhedrin	✓	✓
7:32	Exod. 3:6 (cf. 3:15–16)	2-IP	LXX paraphrase	Stephen	Sanhedrin	✓	✓
7:33–34	Exod. 3:5, 7, 8, 10	2-IP	LXX (compressed)	Stephen	Sanhedrin	✓	✓
7:35	Exod. 2:14	1-IQ	LXX (vs. MT)	Stephen	Sanhedrin	✓	✓
7:37	Deut. 18:15	2-IP	LXX paraphrase	Stephen	Sanhedrin	✓	✓
7:40–41	Exod. 32:1; 32:23	1-IQ	LXX	Stephen	Sanhedrin	✓	✓
7:42–43	Amos 5:25–27	2-IP	LXX paraphrase (vs. MT)	Stephen	Sanhedrin	✓	✓
7:49–50	Isa. 66:1–2	1-IQ	LXX	Stephen	Sanhedrin	✓	✓
8:32–33	Isa. 53:7–8	1-IQ	LXX (vs. MT)	Narrator	reader	✓	✓
13:22	Ps. 89:20 [88:21]	2-IP	free paraphrase	Paul	synagogue	✓	—
13:33	Ps. 2:7	1-IQ	LXX (vs. MT)	Paul	synagogue	✓	✓
13:34	Isa. 55:3	2-IP	LXX paraphrase (vs. MT)	Paul	synagogue	✓	✓
13:35	Ps. 16:10 [15:10]	1-IQ	LXX (vs. MT)	Paul	synagogue	✓	✓
13:41	Hab. 1:5	2-IP	LXX paraphrase (vs. MT)	Paul	synagogue	✓	✓
13:47	Isa. 49:6	2-IP	LXX paraphrase (vs. MT)	Paul	mixed crowd	✓	✓
15:16–17	Amos 9:11–12	2-IP	LXX paraphrase (vs. MT)	James	Jerusalem Council	✓	✓
23:5	Exod. 22:28 [22:27]	2-IP	LXX paraphrase (vs. MT)	Paul	Sanhedrin	✓	✓
28:26–27	Isa. 6:9–10	1-IQ	LXX (vs. MT)	Paul	Jews at Rome	✓	✓

Jewish sections of his story. In the Gospel of Luke this includes the infancy narratives of Luke 1–2, the synagogue sermon of Luke 4, and the passion and resurrection accounts of Luke 22–24. In Acts the vast majority of citations appear in the first half of the book, covering the early days of the Jerusalem church and in speeches that have primarily Jewish audiences: the selection of Matthias (1:16–24), Peter's missionary speeches (2:14–36; 3:12–26; 4:8–11), Stephen's indictment of unbelieving Jews (7:2–53), and Paul's missionary speeches in Jewish synagogues (13:16–41, 46; albeit there is a mixed crowd on the Sabbath in 13:47). Even the citation found within a prayer is by Jewish Christians (4:24–30), and James's citation of Amos is among the Jewish Christians at the Jerusalem Council (15:16–17).[4] Only two OT citations occur after Acts 15: in 23:5, where Paul cites Exod. 22:28 [27] in the Jewish council meeting, and in Acts 28:26–27, where Paul cites Isa. 6:9–10 to the Jewish leaders in Rome. Some scholars suggest that this is due to Luke's sources—a claim that is difficult to support or refute. But to me this seems to be an issue of framing. That is, as already noted, OT citations in Luke-Acts tend to be in the mouths of characters in the story, and these tend to be in speeches with Jewish audiences (and perhaps with gentile God-fearers more likely to be acquainted with the Jewish Scriptures; e.g., Acts 10:2, 22; 13:16, 26). In the latter half of Acts, however, the storyline takes us further from the center of the Jewish world and into audiences of arguably greater diversity. Thus, the speeches in the latter half of Acts have fewer citations of the OT (and in the case of Paul's address to the Areopagus in Acts 17, more citations of extrabiblical literature). But we must caution ourselves here: fewer citations does not mean an absence of OT influence.

The uneven distribution of OT citations in Acts is ameliorated by noticing the dozens of specific allusions to the OT and the scores of OT thematic echoes. Along these lines, Evans observes that Luke "punctuates his narrative with speeches that are often made up almost entirely of OT words and phrases."[5] This seems to be true not only of the speeches to Jewish audiences but even of the speeches in Acts to primarily non-Jewish audiences where no citations of the OT are made. Bruce illustrates this nicely in his analysis of Paul's speech before the Areopagus in Acts 17:12–31. The only citations in this particular speech are from extrabiblical Greek poets. And yet Bruce can

---

4. Cf. Joseph A. Fitzmyer, "The Use of the Old Testament in Luke-Acts," in *To Advance the Gospel: New Testament Studies*, 2nd ed., The Biblical Resource Series (Grand Rapids: Eerdmans, 1998; Livonia, MI: Dove, 1998), 303.

5. Craig A. Evans, "The Old Testament in the New," in *The Face of New Testament Studies: A Survey of Recent Research*, ed. Scot McKnight and Grant R. Osborne (Grand Rapids: Baker Academic, 2004), 139.

describe the speech as "good Old Testament teaching transposed into terms that were calculated to be intelligible to the Areopagites."[6] Indeed, by my count, the specific allusions and thematic echoes in Paul's Areopagus speech number no less than fourteen (and three more are found in the narrative leading up to the speech).[7]

Similarly, the speech to the Ephesian elders in Acts 20:18–35 contains no clear citation of the OT. One could wonder why a speech to a Christian audience would not utilize the OT Scriptures more explicitly. Some might suggest that, even if the believers at Ephesus were more prepared than the Areopagus audience to hear directly from the Jewish Scriptures, they generally were not fully literate with regard to the OT. But, almost ironically, Paul's speech contains a clear citation from Jesus that is not found anywhere else: "It is more blessed to give than to receive" (Acts 20:35), and this is presented as if the Ephesian believers were in a position to remember these words. Noting that Paul's Letter to the Ephesians contains only one explicit quotation of the OT, Bruce simply remarks that he is unsurprised by the absence of OT quotations in Paul's speech to the Christian audience of Acts 20.[8] Nevertheless, I count no less than ten specific allusions and thematic echoes of the OT in Paul's speech to the Ephesian elders.[9] So, as argued earlier, OT citations are not the only thing to consider when examining someone's use of Scripture.

Regarding the non-citation forms for use of the OT, Luke has more Scripture summaries and historical reminiscences than other NT writers. Both of these recollection forms are represented elsewhere in the NT.[10] Nevertheless, Joseph Fitzmyer suggests that Scripture summaries (which he calls "global references") "are almost exclusively Lucan in the NT and reveal a distinctively Lucan way of using the Scriptures of old."[11] While the distribution of Luke's Scripture summaries are balanced between his

---

6. F. F. Bruce, "Paul's Use of the Old Testament in Acts," in *Tradition and Interpretation in the New Testament: Essays in Honor of E. Earle Ellis for His 60th Birthday*, ed. Gerald F. Hawthorne with Otto Betz (Grand Rapids: Eerdmans; Tübingen: Mohr Siebeck, 1987), 74–76; quotation on 76.

7. See app. C.

8. Bruce, "Paul's Use of the Old Testament in Acts," 76; cf. E. Earle Ellis, *Paul's Use of the Old Testament* (Edinburgh: Oliver & Boyd, 1957; reprint, Grand Rapids: Baker, 1981; reprint, Eugene, OR: Wipf & Stock, 2003), 30.

9. Interestingly, Bruce suggests that all of the allusions and echoes to the OT in the speech of Acts 20 are probably unintentional; Bruce, "Paul's Use of the Old Testament in Acts," 76.

10. E.g., see Scripture summaries in Matt. 22:40; 26:56; John 1:45; 5:39, 46; 20:9; Rom. 1:2–3; 3:21; 16:26; 1 Cor. 15:3–4; and Heb. 1:1; and see historical reminiscences in Matt. 5:12; 6:28–29; 12:3–4, 39–40, 41, 42; 24:37–39; Mark 2:25–26; 8:11–12; 12:26; 1 Cor. 10:1–5; Heb. 7:1–10; and the series in Heb. 11:4–39.

11. Joseph A. Fitzmyer, *The Acts of the Apostles*, AB 31 (New York: Doubleday, 1998), 91.

Gospel and Acts, he has twice as many historical reminiscences in Acts as he does in the Gospel. Similarly, the comparable number of thematic echoes in each of Luke's two volumes contrasts with the fact that the Gospel contains twice as many specific allusions as the book of Acts. These differences may also be reflections of the slightly different intentions of his two volumes. That is to say, given the apologetic function of many specific allusions, perhaps their increased use in the Gospel of Luke is fitting with Luke's increased concern in his first book to show Christian faith as consonant with the faith of OT Israel. And given the story functions of historical reminiscences, perhaps their increased use in Acts is fitting with Luke's increased concern in his second book to show the Christian faith as not merely connected to, but as the continuation of, the historic story of God's people in the OT.

Despite the subject matter differences between the Third Gospel and the book of Acts and their few differences in the uses of the OT, Stanley Porter suggests that Luke uses the same overall pattern in both books, a pattern that helps bring the books together. "In each instance, the author introduces early on in the book a key event, in which Scripture is central, as formative for the life and mission of the individuals involved." In the Gospel of Luke, it is Jesus's citation of Isa. 61:1–2 in his Nazareth sermon in Luke 4:16–30 (vv. 18–19); and in the book of Acts, it is Peter's citation of Joel 2:28–32 [3:1–5]; Ps. 16:8–11 [15:8–11], and Ps. 110:1 [109:1] in his Pentecost sermon in Acts 2:14–41 (vv. 16–21, 25–28, and 34–35, respectively). In each case, the central figure proclaims his mission as one grounded in Scripture, and the ideas presented in those cited passages prove to be important concepts in the subsequent narrative of each book. In this way, Luke uses Scripture to justify the mission of the central figures in his work.[12] To this, I add that Luke also does something similar with his presentation of the key figure in the second half of Acts via the first sermon we have from Paul in his preaching at Pisidian Antioch in Acts 13:13–52. In all three cases, appeal is made to the Israelite Scriptures as being fulfilled in Jesus (Luke 4:17–21; Acts 2:22, 32, 36; 13:27–33, 38–39); in all three cases, there is indication that the message is to extend beyond Israel (Luke 4:25–27; Acts 2:17, 21; 13:46–48); and in all three cases, there is evidence of a mixed reception of the message (Luke 4:22–23, 28–29; Acts 2:23, 37–41; 13:40–45, 48–50). Thus, there is a unity in the diversity of Luke's contribution to the NT and in his use of the OT.

---

12. Stanley E. Porter, "Scripture Justifies Mission: The Use of the Old Testament in Luke-Acts," in *Hearing the Old Testament in the New Testament*, ed. Stanley E. Porter, McMaster New Testament Studies (Grand Rapids: Eerdmans, 2006), 109.

Theological Themes and Programmatic Motives for Luke's Use of the Old Testament

To be sure, Lukan scholars debate the primary function(s) of Scripture in Luke's writings. Nevertheless, since the 1950s scholars have come to appreciate more and more that Luke does indeed have a theological agenda for his writing. It is of no surprise that Luke's theological concerns are made evident by his use of the OT. Let me briefly touch on Luke's major theological themes in his use of Scripture as seen by other scholars before I comment on his programmatic motives for how he utilizes the OT in Luke-Acts.

Theological Themes

Scholars propose several different outlines for the theological concerns demonstrated by the use of Scripture in Luke-Acts, and these have varying overarching motifs (see table 6.4). John Carroll suggests three "theologically freighted uses" of Scripture by Luke, particularly in Acts, with something of an apologetic slant: (a) to validate that Jesus is the Messiah promised to Israel, (b) to legitimate the inclusion of gentile believers within the people of God, and (c) to demonstrate that rejection of the gospel by Jews is a continuation of the age-old pattern in Israel.[13]

With an overarching fulfillment refrain, Bart Koet also outlines three points of Luke's scriptural concerns: (a) Jesus fulfills the program revealed in Scripture, (b) the Scriptures and Jesus's fulfillment of them are programmatic for the disciples, and (c) the disciples in turn proclaim the Scriptures and Jesus's fulfillment of them to a new audience.[14] Focused on liberation and expansion, Richard Hays outlines three purposes for Luke's use of the OT: (a) to carry forward the story of the liberation of Israel, (b) to present Jesus as the agent of that liberation, the redeemer of Israel, and (c) to locate the church as a countercultural community (in relation to Jewish majority and Roman authority) to be a light for revelation to the gentiles.[15]

With a slightly different approach to Luke's use of the OT, Bock outlines three hermeneutical axioms and five central missional/scriptural themes that utilize those axioms. The hermeneutical axioms are (1) God's design and a new era of realization, (2) Christ at the center, and (3) Scripture as an

---

13. John T. Carroll, "The Uses of Scripture in Acts," in *Society of Biblical Literature 1990 Seminar Papers*, ed. David J. Lull, SBLSP 29 (Atlanta: Scholars Press, 1990), 520–28.

14. Koet, *Five Studies*, 153–56.

15. Richard B. Hays, "The Liberation of Israel in Luke-Acts: Intertextual Narration as Countercultural Practice," in *Reading the Bible Intertextually*, ed. Richard B. Hays, Stefan Alkier, and Leroy A. Huizenga (Waco: Baylor University Press, 2009), 101–17.

TABLE 6.4

Various Motifs for the Theological Themes in Luke's Use of the Old Testament

Carroll: apologetic purposes

Koet: declaring fulfillment

Hays (I): advancing liberation and expansion

Bock: hermeneutical axioms for missional themes

Hays (II): extending the narrative of the scriptural story

interpreter of divine events. The five central scriptural themes are (a) covenant and promise; (b) Christology; (c) community mission, community guidance, and ethical direction; (d) commission to the gentiles; and (e) challenge and warning to Israel.[16] Also a bit more complex, in his more recent treatment of Luke's use of the OT (esp. the Gospel of Luke), Richard Hays offers seven themes regarding Luke's narratival use of Scripture: (a) the story of Jesus is joined seamlessly to the OT story, (b) in this story God is emphatically portrayed as faithful to his covenant promises, (c) nevertheless, consistent with the larger story, suffering is a regular part of the story, (d) the poor and helpless are objects of God's concern in the story, (e) the story entails that the good news is to be offered to all nations, (f) the scriptural story places God's people in a countercultural relationship to the prevailing world structures, and (g) the story leads readers to see that Israel's OT Lord is the same as the NT Christ the Lord.[17] Certainly, these all represent fitting observations about Luke's thematic concerns in his use of Scripture, but I'd like to address a different and perhaps broader issue.

Programmatic Motives

Our quick survey of Luke's use of the OT indicates that Scripture functions in a variety of ways within the immediate contexts of Luke-Acts and furthermore that Scripture is in support of particular theological truth claims of interest in Luke-Acts. But more than this, there seem to be some larger overlapping programmatic motives for what Luke is trying to accomplish with his references to Scripture. By **programmatic motives**, I mean that there are things Luke intends to *do* by using Scripture in the whole of Luke-Acts.

16. Darrell L. Bock, *A Theology of Luke and Acts: God's Promised Program, Realized for All Nations*, Biblical Theology of the New Testament (Grand Rapids: Zondervan, 2012), 409–27.

17. Richard B. Hays, *Echoes of Scripture in the Gospels* (Waco: Baylor University Press, 2016), 277–80.

Thus, in this section I am asking not about the function of Scripture in individual passages but about Luke's goals at the larger discourse level for using Scripture as he does. I'm not so concerned here to draft a new list of Luke's theological themes related to the OT (like those outlined by others in the preceding section); rather, I am looking for what Luke wants to accomplish by using Scripture the way he does in Luke-Acts (more akin to the motifs noted above in the theological themes identified by others). While his goals for using Scripture unsurprisingly overlap with one another and with his primary theological themes, they nevertheless have a recognizably different orientation. So I highlight here five programmatic motives evidenced by the way Luke's uses of Scripture stack up (see the summary in table 6.6 below). In other words, there are five answers to the question What is Luke doing by his use of Scripture?

1. Evangelizing people to faith in Jesus Christ, the fulfiller of Scripture.

As already indicated, in several key places in his narrative, Luke uses Scripture to justify the mission of Jesus and the expansion of the gospel message about him. In fact, most of Luke's quotations of the OT have a christological importance because the OT is all about the Christ who would suffer and rise again so that all the peoples of the world would be invited to faith in him.[18] Jesus is the fulfillment—in many senses of the term—of the Israelite Scriptures.[19] This is set out early in Luke-Acts, with prophetic figures using

---

18. See François C. Bovon, *Luke the Theologian: Fifty-Five Years of Research (1950–2005)*, rev. ed. (Waco: Baylor University Press, 2006), 95.

19. Generally acknowledged as launching modern scholarship on Luke's fulfillment interests is Paul Schubert, "The Structure and Significance of Luke 24," in *Neutestamentliche Studien für Rudolf Bultmann zu seinem Siebzigsten Geburtstag am 20 August 1954*, ed. Walther Eltester, BZNW 21 (Berlin: Töpelmann, 1954), 165–86. More recent studies include Darrell L. Bock, *Proclamation from Prophecy and Pattern: Lucan Old Testament Christology*, JSNTSup 12 (Sheffield: Sheffield Academic, 1987); Mark L. Strauss, *The Davidic Messiah in Luke-Acts: The Promise and Its Fulfillment in Lukan Christology*, JSNTSup 110 (Sheffield: Sheffield Academic, 1995); and David Peterson, "The Motif of Fulfillment and the Purpose of Luke-Acts," in *The Book of Acts in Its Ancient Literary Setting*, ed. Bruce W. Winter and Andrew D. Clark, BAFCS 1 (Grand Rapids: Eerdmans, 1993; Carlisle: Paternoster, 1993), 83–104. It is noteworthy that Martin Rese argued against fulfillment as Luke's primary use of the OT in his *Alttestamentliche Motive in der Christologie des Lukas*, SNT 1 (Gütersloh: Gerd Mohn, 1969); but Bock's *Proclamation from Prophecy and Pattern* is recognized by many as a definitive refutation of Rese's thesis.

More recently others have argued against understanding proof-from-prophecy (and/or promise-fulfillment) as the primary use of Scripture in Luke-Acts, stressing rather such themes as Luke's interest to show Christianity as a continuation of the redemptive story; see Joel B. Green, "The Problem of a Beginning: Israel's Scriptures in Luke 1–2," BBR 4 (1994): 61–85; Marion L. Soards, *The Speeches in Acts: Their Content, Context, and Concerns* (Louisville: Westminster John Knox, 1994), 201; and Kenneth Duncan Litwak, *Echoes of Scripture in Luke-Acts: Telling the History of God's People Intertextually*, JSNTSup 282 (London: T&T Clark,

scriptural words to speak about Jesus (i.e., Luke 2:22–40; esp. Isa. 42:6; 49:6, 9 in v. 32) and with Jesus himself announcing his fulfillment of specific Scripture (i.e., Isa. 61:1–2; 58:6 in Luke 4:16–21; and Isa. 29:18; 35:5–6; 42:18; 26:19; and 61:1 in Luke 7:22–23). This theme comes to a climax at the hinge point of Luke-Acts when the resurrected Christ speaks about his fulfillment of all of Scripture (i.e., Luke 24:25–27, 44–47). R. T. France expresses it well:

> Thus Jesus saw his mission as the fulfilment of the Old Testament Scriptures; not just of those which predicted a coming redeemer, but of the whole sweep of Old Testament ideas. The patterns of God's working which the discerning eye could trace in the history and institutions of Israel were all preparing for the great climax when all would be taken up into the final and perfect act of God which the prophets foretold. And in the coming of Jesus all this was fulfilled. That is why he could find "in *all* the scriptures the things concerning himself."[20]

Note that Luke unmistakably designates Jesus himself as the origin of a christological reading of the OT.[21]

Moreover, Luke offers thirty-three Scripture summaries of the message of the OT Scriptures, and almost a third of these global statements center on the suffering and death of the Messiah (see esp. Luke 24:25–26, 27, 44, 46–47; Acts 3:18, 21; 10:43; 13:27, 29; 17:2–3).[22] Although the idea would be strange, and even shocking, to a Jewish mindset, Luke is insistent that a suffering Messiah who is then raised to life is actually in line with the OT Scriptures. Given the model of Luke's Gospel account and given his record of the early Christian sermons in Acts, proclamation of Jesus as the Messiah for the whole world

---

2005), 11–17. Bock offers a response in *Theology of Luke and Acts* (esp. 410n8 and 412–14), pointing out an unnecessary false dichotomy between redemptive story and promise-fulfillment motives. Years earlier, C. K. Barrett pointed out this false dichotomy between (what he called) "proof from prophecy" and "apologetic" views, suggesting, "Luke would have called it εὐαγγέλιον [gospel]"; Barrett, "Luke/Acts," 237; cf. 243. Interestingly, Paul Schubert himself noted the connection of Luke's proof-from-prophecy theme with his theology of history on the very page where Schubert introduces the fulfillment theme: see Schubert, "Structure and Significance of Luke 24," 173–74n20.

20. R. T. France, *Jesus and the Old Testament: His Application of Old Testament Passages to Himself and His Mission* (Grand Rapids: Baker, 1971), 79–80 (emphasis original); cf. 159–63, 223–26.

21. Hays, "Liberation of Israel in Luke-Acts," 111.

22. Cf. Jacob Jervell, *The Theology of the Acts of the Apostles*, New Testament Theology (Cambridge: Cambridge University Press, 1996), 73; Bock, *Theology of Luke and Acts*, 407–8, 419; Fitzmyer, "Use of the Old Testament in Luke-Acts," 308. See app. C for the Scripture summary classifications in Luke-Acts.

is the proper way to utilize the OT.[23] This is one of the primary purposes for Luke's use of Scripture.[24]

2. Extolling God's sovereign plan for history.

Luke-Acts proclaims the idea that God has a plan for history. Four Lukan texts make this especially clear, and each of them references (or at least alludes to) the Israelite Scriptures (see Luke 7:24–28; 16:16–17; Acts 10:42–43; 17:24–31).[25] Though Christianity may seem new in the first century, it has actually been God's plan all along. Thus Luke describes the very recent (in his time) events as "the things that have been fulfilled among us" (Luke 1:1 NIV). God has been bringing these things to pass in keeping with his plan. "The events are recent and the era is new, but the plan is not."[26]

Over against Marcion's disfavor for the God of the OT and his favor for (highly selective portions of) Luke's Gospel (mentioned in chap. 1 above), a proper reading of Luke's contribution to the NT makes firm the connection between the Testaments. And this consistency between the Testaments includes Luke's depiction of God. For Luke, God's character in his salvific intervention through Christ is consistent with the portrait of God displayed throughout all of Israel's history. Of Luke's characterization of God, Hays remarks, "This God who elects the people of Israel, judges their faithlessness, and still acts in unexpected ways to redeem them is recognizably the same God the reader knows from previous episodes of the story."[27] The Gospel is a continuation of the story of the OT.

Several more general statements and turns of phrase also reflect Luke's commitment to God's sovereign plan for history (see esp. Luke 7:30; Acts 2:23; 3:13–26; 4:28; 5:38–39; 10:38–41; 11:18; 13:23, 32–33, 36; 14:16–17, 27; 15:4, 12; 17:26, 30–31; 20:27; 21:19; 27:23–24). While this plan of God has reached a climax in the Jesus event, it has not yet reached its completion; but it will culminate in the future and still be centered on Jesus Christ. This was the "necessary" (Greek δεῖ) plan of God, according to the Scriptures (e.g.,

---

23. Or as Hays ("Liberation of Israel in Luke-Acts," 112) would say it, Luke models "a reading strategy that proposes the crucified and risen Jesus as the hermeneutical key to Israel's scripture."

24. For an accessible discussion about Luke's purpose(s) for writing and the difference between an evangelizing purpose and a legitimatizing purpose, see Mark L. Strauss, "The Purpose of Luke-Acts: Reaching a Consensus," in *New Testament Theology in Light of the Church's Mission: Essays in Honor of I. Howard Marshall*, ed. Jon Laansma, Grant R. Osborne, and Ray Van Neste (Eugene, OR: Cascade Books, 2011), 135–50.

25. See Bock, *Theology of Luke and Acts*, 410–11. The OT Scriptures are specifically named in Luke 7:24–28; 16:16–17; and Acts 10:42–43; on the OT allusions in Acts 17:24–31, consult app. C.

26. Bock, *Theology of Luke and Acts*, 414.

27. Hays, *Echoes of Scripture in the Gospels*, 194.

Luke 9:22; 13:33; 17:25; 22:37; 24:7, 25–27, 44–47; Acts 3:18–26; 17:1–3; cf. μέλλειν for "is to be" in Luke 9:31, 44; Acts 26:22–23).[28]

3. Authenticating the faith heritage of Christianity.

His constant use of the Israelite Scriptures is another way for Luke to stress that the story of the Christian church is the continuation of the Jesus story even as the Jesus story is the continuation of the story recorded in Israel's sacred writings.[29] Luke is the most deliberate of the Gospel writers, making this a seamless connection.[30] Nils Dahl says it even more strongly, "But whatever the Greek, Hellenistic, and Roman components of Luke's historiography may have been, his own conscious intention was to write history in biblical style or, rather, to write the continuation of biblical history. This gives him a unique place even among the New Testament writers."[31] Luke is concerned to demonstrate that faith in Christ is actually the proper carrying forward of Israelite faith. In a sociological era that considered what was older and time-tested to be better, Luke's depiction of Christianity as having the claim to heritage regarding God's acts in history was important for credibility.[32] There is perhaps a subtle hint to this in Luke's much lengthier genealogy for Jesus, which goes all the way back to Adam instead of merely to Abraham (Luke 3:23–38; cf. Matt. 1:1–17). Luke's more explicit OT citations support this claim to heritage. Faith in Jesus as the Messiah is not an attempt to break away from the ancient Israelite faith; it is a claim that the long-awaited promises of the ancient faith are now coming to pass.[33] This was Paul's regular appeal to maintaining consistency with the Israelite faith and Scriptures (Acts 23:6; 24:14–15, 21; 26:6–8, 22–23; 28:20, 23; cf. Apollos in 18:28). Thus, there is a double-edged interest for Luke here: (a) positively, to argue for the legitimacy of the Christian faith as the ancient and true faith in God, and (b) negatively, to challenge and warn his Jewish readers who have been rejecting Christ and refusing to receive the Messiah whom their religious faith had been proclaiming for centuries and who has now come.

---

28. See Charles H. Cosgrove, "The Divine ΔΕΙ in Luke-Acts: Investigations into the Lukan Understanding of God's Providence," NovT 26 (1984): 168–90.

29. See also Karl Allen Kuhn, The Kingdom according to Luke and Acts: A Social, Literary, and Theological Introduction (Grand Rapids: Baker Academic, 2015), 124–25.

30. Hays, Echoes of Scripture in the Gospels, 191.

31. Nils Alstrup Dahl, Jesus in the Memory of the Early Church (Minneapolis: Augsburg, 1976), 84.

32. Bock, Theology of Luke and Acts, 408; for ethnography as an ancient apologetic genre, Bock cites Gregory E. Sterling, Historiography and Self-Definition: Josephos, Luke-Acts and Apologetic Historiography, NovTSup 64 (Leiden: Brill, 1992), 103–310, 389–93.

33. Bock, Theology of Luke and Acts, 416. See also Peter Mallen, "Genesis in Luke-Acts," in Genesis in the New Testament, ed. Maarten J. J. Menken and Steven Moyise, LNTS 466 (London: Bloomsbury T&T Clark, 2012), 60–82.

A debated issue in Lukan theology is the question of Luke's view of Israel. Do gentile believers in Jesus replace Israel as the people of God? Are gentiles grafted into Israel, who remain the true people of God? Do believing Jews and gentiles together form a new people of God? Bart Koet provides an exegetical argument about Luke's positive view of Israel, saying that "in Luke-Acts the issue is not the rejection of Israel, but rather the salvation of the Gentiles in addition to that of Israel." He examines some of the key texts utilized in replacement theories, particularly Luke 4:16–30; Acts 13:42–52; and 28:16–31. The rejection statements in these Luke-Acts passages are aimed at those particular Jews who reject Jesus. Similar to the OT prophets (mimicked by Luke), the harsh words against the Jews rejecting Jesus are intended to provoke repentance, not to declare a finalized, permanent, all-inclusive break; using the OT, Luke rebukes the unbelieving Jews (e.g., Luke 13:34; 21:20–24; Acts 13:46; 28:26–28) *and* proclaims the salvation of Israel (e.g., Luke 1:16–17, 33, 54–55, 68, 76–77; 2:32; 4:18–19; 24:19; Acts 1:6–8; 28:20).[34] Luke utilizes the OT to demonstrate that refusal of Jesus as God's Messiah was actually in line with the Scriptures as the Christ is described there as one who "must suffer" (ἔδει παθεῖν; see particularly Luke 24:26–27, 44; cf. 18:31–33).[35]

4. Expanding the notion of God's people to include gentiles in the church.

Overlapping with the previous motifs related to evangelism, God's plan, and faith heritage is Luke's concern to appeal to the OT Scriptures to encourage the expansion of God's people to include gentile believers. One need not become a Jew first in order to be a follower of Jesus. This is not a new idea; it has been part of God's plan from of old, and the Scriptures indicate it to have been thus.[36] Luke often utilizes the words of Isaiah in addressing this particular concern (e.g., Isa. 42:6; 49:6, 9 in Luke 2:32; Isa. 40:3–5 in Luke

---

34. Koet, *Five Studies*, esp. 150–53 (quote from 150). He says further, "An investigation of Luke's use of Scripture shows that there is no pattern of rejection of Israel in Luke-Acts" (159). Cf. David L. Tiede, *Prophecy and History in Luke-Acts* (Philadelphia: Fortress, 1980), 121: "But prophetic reproofs of Israel are so much a part of the rhetorical baggage of the tradition that it would be very unlikely that they would suddenly be taken so literally." See also Robert L. Brawley, *Luke-Acts and the Jews: Conflict, Apology, and Conciliation*, SBLMS 33 (Atlanta: Scholars Press, 1987), esp. 133–54; Jacob Jervell, *Luke and the People of God: A New Look at Luke-Acts* (Minneapolis: Augsburg, 1972), 41–74; and the essays in David P. Moessner, ed., *Jesus and the Heritage of Israel: Luke's Narrative Claim upon Israel's Legacy*, Luke the Interpreter of Israel 1 (Harrisburg, PA: Trinity Press International, 1999), and in David P. Moessner, Daniel Marguerat, Mikeal C. Parsons, and Michael Wolter, eds., *Paul and the Heritage of Israel: Paul's Claim upon Israel's Legacy in Luke and Acts in the Light of the Pauline Letters*, Luke the Interpreter of Israel 2, LNTS 452 (New York: T&T Clark, 2012).

35. J. Ross Wagner, "Psalm 118 in Luke-Acts: Tracing a Narrative Thread," in *Early Christian Interpretation of the Scriptures of Israel*, ed. Craig A. Evans and James A. Sanders, JSNTSup 148, SSEJC 5 (Sheffield: Sheffield Academic, 1997), 175.

36. See also Bock, *Theology of Luke and Acts*, 417.

3:4–6; Isa. 66:1–2 in Acts 7:49–50; Isa. 49:6 in Acts 13:46–47; Isa. 42:7, 16 in Acts 26:17–18; and Isa. 6:9–10 in Acts 28:26–27). Faith heritage is not a matter of heredity but of response to God. As the OT Scriptures portray, any faithless descendants of Abraham were not recipients of the blessings of God's promises to Israel; and conversely, to be a good Jew meant that one would seek salvation for gentiles as well. As Bock says it: "Jesus is Lord of all, so the gospel can go to all. God always designed it to be so."[37]

5. Encouraging the interpretation of Scripture.

As already noted, most citations of the OT in Luke-Acts occur in speeches, primarily with Jesus speaking in the Gospel of Luke and with apostolic preaching in Acts.[38] The only four exceptions are found at the beginning of Luke-Acts when the narrator comments in Luke 2:23 and 24 (respectively citing Exod. 13:2, 12, 15, and Lev. 12:8 regarding the presentation of the baby Jesus at the temple), in Luke 3:4–6 (citing Isa. 40:3–5 regarding the role of John the Baptist), and just prior to the launching of the gentile mission in Acts 8:32 (citing Isa. 53:7–8 to clarify the passage that the Ethiopian eunuch had been reading). Hays notes that Luke's literary strategy of placing Scripture citations in the mouths of the characters in the story gives a dramatic quality to the narrative that requires the readers to interpret Luke's use of Scripture within the plot.[39] Koet suggests that Luke puts citations in the mouths of characters in the story with the intention of portraying Jesus and his followers as interpreters of Scripture.[40]

With the challenge that Jesus gives his followers in the middle of Luke-Acts—to recognize that all of Scripture is about him as Messiah (Luke 24:25–27, 32, 44–49)—it makes sense to understand Luke as concerned to encourage this proper, Jesus-centered interpretation of the OT. Charles Talbert sketches several parallels between the Third Gospel and Acts to demonstrate Luke's intentional depiction of Jesus (in the Gospel) and believers (in Acts) as parallel interpreters of Scripture (see table 6.5).[41]

---

37. Bock, *Theology of Luke and Acts*, 419; cf. 422–23.

38. Barrett ("Luke/Acts," 239–40) notes that only one of the main sermons in the first half of Acts lacks an OT citation (10:34–43; but the sermon concludes with a comprehensive reference to "all the prophets" in v. 43) and conversely that there are no citations of the OT in apostolic preaching in the last half of Acts (Acts 14–28). But as already observed, the influence of the OT is seen even in the speeches without explicit citations and even in the speeches to primarily non-Jewish audiences.

39. Hays, *Echoes of Scripture in the Gospels*, 192.

40. Koet, *Five Studies*, 149–50.

41. Charles Talbert first sketched this idea of parallel interpreters between Luke and Acts in Charles H. Talbert, *Luke and the Gnostics: An Examination of the Lucan Purpose*, Special Studies Series 5 (Nashville: Abingdon, 1966), 33–34; he then revised it in Talbert, *Reading Acts: A Literary and Theological Commentary on the Acts of the Apostles*, Reading the New

TABLE 6.5

Parallel Interpretation of Scripture in Luke-Acts

Jesus as Interpreter in Luke	Believers as Interpreters in Acts
1. John is the forerunner preparing the way for Messiah (Mal. 3:1 in Luke 7:27).	1. The accurate interpretation of Scripture sees John as Messiah's forerunner (Acts 18:24–28).
2. Jesus fulfills the hopes of Scripture (Luke 4:16–30; 20:17).	2. Jesus fulfills the hopes of Scripture (Acts 3:22–26, 30; 4:11; 10:43; 13:23; 17:2–3; 28:23).
3. Jesus's sufferings, death, resurrection, and ascension fulfill Scripture (Luke 9:22, 44; 13:33; 17:25; 18:31–34; 22:37; 24:7, 25–27, 32, 44–49).	3. Jesus's sufferings, death, resurrection, and ascension fulfill Scripture (Acts 2:25–28, 31; 3:17–18, 24–25; 8:30–35; 13:27–39; 17:2–3, 11; 26:22–23).
4. Scripture promises the coming of the Spirit (Luke 24:49; cf. Acts 1:4, 8).	4. The coming of the Spirit fulfills what Scripture promised (Acts 2:16–21).
5. Scripture points to rejection of Messiah by the Jews (Luke 20:17–18).	5. The rejection of Jesus by the Jews fulfills Scripture (Acts 13:40–41, 27; 28:25–27).
6. Scripture foretells a mission to the gentiles (Luke 24:47; cf. 4:25–27).	6. Scripture is fulfilled in the church's mission to gentiles (Acts 13:47; cf. 14:26; 15:15–18; 26:22–23).
7. Scripture teaches a general resurrection from the dead (Luke 20:37).	7. Scripture teaches a general resurrection of the dead (Acts 24:14–15; 26:6–8).

Note: This data was adapted from the work of Charles Talbert, *Reading Acts*, 2nd ed., 77–78.

Similarly, at the close of a study of Jesus's exposition of the OT in the Gospel of Luke, Charles Kimball concludes that Jesus provided the foundation for the church's theological thinking by his own exposition and choice of biblical texts and that Jesus's methodology affected the exegesis of the early believers and the NT writers.[42] Thus Luke portrays the believers as having learned proper interpretation from Jesus. Indeed, before revealing himself physically as the risen Savior to the two disciples on the road to Emmaus, Jesus is concerned that these followers learn to read the OT Scriptures as revelation of his messiahship.[43]

Testament Series (New York: Crossroad, 1997), 90–91; and it is largely the same in the second edition, Talbert, *Reading Acts* (Macon, GA: Smyth & Helwys, 2005), 77–78. Placing these observations in chart form, I have tweaked the wording in a manner similar to the chart in Craig S. Keener, *Acts: An Exegetical Commentary*, 4 vols. (Grand Rapids: Baker Academic, 2012–15), 1:489.

42. Charles A. Kimball, *Jesus' Exposition of the Old Testament in Luke's Gospel*, JSNTSup 94 (Sheffield: Sheffield Academic, 1994), 202.

43. See Ardel B. Caneday, "Biblical Types: Revelation Concealed in Plain Sight to Be Disclosed—'These Things Occurred Typologically to Them and Were Written Down for Our Admonition,'" in *God's Glory Revealed in Christ: Essays in Honor of Tom Schreiner*, ed. Denny Burk, James M. Hamilton Jr., and Brian Vickers (Nashville: B&H Academic, 2019), 135–55.

But this touches on a much-debated issue among scholars: the question of whether or not Christians today can interpret the OT in the same ways the NT writers have. Can twenty-first-century believers utilize the hermeneutical techniques that seem to be utilized by Matthew, Mark, John, Luke, Peter, Paul, and others when they interpret the OT in their NT writings? Reflecting on a variety of hermeneutical and theological issues—such as authorial intention, exegetical techniques, respect for context, inspiration, progress of revelation, canonical function, divine authority—some scholars respond in the negative, and others respond in the positive.[44]

No matter how one answers that question, however, Luke makes it abundantly clear in his writings that Jesus expected people to be able to read the OT Scriptures and see that they were all about him. Jesus says to the two disciples on the road to Emmaus, "O foolish ones, and slow of heart to believe all that the prophets have spoken! Was it not necessary that the Christ should suffer these things and enter into his glory?" (Luke 24:25–26). Luke follows this statement by noting, "And beginning with Moses and all the Prophets, he [Jesus] interpreted to them in all the Scriptures the things concerning himself" (24:27). Jesus gives a similar lesson to a larger group of his followers back in Jerusalem, "These are my words that I spoke to you while I was still with you, that everything written about me in the Law of Moses and the Prophets and the Psalms must be fulfilled" (Luke 24:44), and again Luke notes further, "Then he opened their minds to understand the Scriptures" (24:45, cf. 46–48). Indeed, between the resurrection and the ascension, Jesus was "appearing to them during forty days and speaking about the kingdom of God" (Acts 1:3), which—given what we see in the resurrection appearances of Luke 24—likely included continued lessons on understanding the Scriptures.

After Jesus ascends into heaven and as the believers prepare to move forward into ministry, a christological reading of the OT is immediately evident (e.g., Acts 1:16–22). Peter and the apostles preach faith in Christ from the OT Scriptures (e.g., Acts 3:18–21; 10:42–43; etc.). In the longest sermon synopsis of Acts, after tracing OT history, Stephen (not an apostle) holds his

---

44. See esp. Richard N. Longenecker, "Who Is the Prophet Talking About?," in *The Right Doctrine from the Wrong Texts? Essays on the Use of the Old Testament in the New*, ed. G. K. Beale (Grand Rapids: Baker Academic, 1994), 375–86; and G. K. Beale, "Did Jesus and His Followers Preach the Right Doctrine from the Wrong Texts?," in *Right Doctrine from the Wrong Texts?*, 387–404. To the question "Can we reproduce the exegesis of the New Testament?" Longenecker offers a cautious "No," while Beale offers a "Yes." See also the balanced perspective of Tremper Longman III, "'What Was Said in All the Scriptures concerning Himself' (Luke 24:27): Reading the Old Testament as a Christian," in *Evangelical Scholarship, Retrospects and Prospects: Essays in Honor of Stanley N. Gundry*, ed. Dirk R. Buursma, Katya Covrett, and Verlyn D. Verbrugge (Grand Rapids: Zondervan, 2017), 119–36.

TABLE 6.6

Programmatic Motives for the Use of the Old Testament in Luke-Acts

In addition to—or in coordination with—his particular theological truth claims, Luke is involved in accomplishing several things with his use of the OT in Luke-Acts. What is Luke doing by his use of Scripture?

1. Evangelizing people to faith in Jesus Christ, the fulfiller of Scripture.
2. Extolling God's sovereign plan for history.
3. Authenticating the faith heritage of Christianity.
4. Expanding the notion of God's people to include gentiles in the church.
5. Encouraging the interpretation of Scripture.

audience accountable for not having faith in Jesus (Acts 7:2–53, esp. 51–53). Philip begins with Isa. 53 to tell the good news about Jesus (Acts 8:35). Paul and Barnabas preach about Jesus from the OT and expect their audience to be able to understand and heed the OT warning (13:26–41, esp. 40–41) and the application of Isa. 49:6 to themselves and all Jews (Acts 13:47). Indeed, Paul expects people to be able to understand that the OT Scriptures were about Jesus (e.g., Acts 17:2–3; 28:23; cf. Apollos in 18:28), even claiming to be "saying nothing but what the prophets and Moses said would come to pass: that the Christ must suffer and that, by being the first to rise from the dead, he would proclaim light both to our people and to the Gentiles" (26:22–23).

All of Luke's readers—Jewish or gentile—can "overhear" these conversations in Luke's narrative and learn how to interpret Scripture from these models.[45] As Scripture is being fulfilled in the life, death, and resurrection of Jesus and in the lives and ministry of the Jesus followers, it makes sense for God's people to be examining the OT Scriptures for themselves and to be recognizing the fulfillment of God's plan there. Luke even provides an encouraging example in noting that the Bereans were "more noble" in that "they received the word with all eagerness, examining the Scriptures daily to see if these things were so" (Acts 17:11). So it is that, as Hays puts it, from start to finish, Luke "patiently and subtly teaches his readers how to read Israel's Scripture with new eyes."[46] Thus, by his use of Scripture, Luke means

---

45. Hays, "Liberation of Israel in Luke-Acts," 112.

46. Hays, *Echoes of Scripture in the Gospels*, 221. Hays (276–77) goes on to suggest, albeit cautiously, that Luke's Gospel would have been used in the early church as a teaching tool, with teachers explaining its intricate details for the less informed converts. See also Craig Evans, "'He Set His Face': On the Meaning of Luke 9.51," in *Luke and Scripture: The Function of Sacred Scripture in Luke-Acts*, by Craig A. Evans and James A. Sanders (Minneapolis: Fortress, 1993), 104–5.

to encourage his readers to likewise interpret the OT Scriptures as pointing to Jesus and so to forward the Scripture-based gospel message to the world.[47]

Further Observations about Luke's Use of the Old Testament

Having considered some of Luke's theological themes in his use of the OT in Luke-Acts and some of his goals for using the OT, I offer here some brief reflections on three additional areas related to Luke's use of Scripture: the relative importance of citations versus allusions, the authorship of Scripture, and the law in Luke-Acts. Observations about these matters in Luke-Acts are illustrative of how they can be approached when considering the works of other NT writers.

First, regarding the relative importance of citations versus allusions, it might be tempting to consider citations as having a particular appeal to the authority of Scripture and thus playing more significant roles in the arguments and expositions of NT writers than do allusions to the OT.[48] While this seems sensibly correct, I appreciate the caution offered by Moisés Silva specifically regarding Paul's use of the OT but applicable to Luke as well: "When Paul's citation varies from either the LXX or the MT (or both), the reason need not be significant. Just as we may sometimes refer to a passage without quoting it exactly, so might Paul." Such paraphrasing for us, as well as for all the NT authors, involves some wording differences that are due to the very character of allusory communication and other differences that intend no special significance. And, Silva adds, "nor do they imply that the speaker considers the actual words to be unimportant."[49] Thus, while citations may be used differently by different NT authors in different kinds of presentations, this does not mean that citations are somehow more important than allusions.

As it turns out, Luke uses citations of Israel's Scriptures with less frequency than the other Synoptic Gospels and Paul.[50] But Luke is nonetheless highly

---

47. See Koet, *Five Studies*, 156, cf. 160–61.

48. Barrett, "Luke/Acts," 231.

49. Moisés Silva, "Old Testament in Paul," *DPL*, 633. See the discussion in chap. 3 above for the differentiation of citations (both quotations and paraphrases) and allusions.

50. Noting that ancient biographies have more frequent use of quotations than ancient historical works, Andrew Pitts suggests that Luke's reservation in citations is evidence that he viewed himself to be writing his two volumes more closely to the history genre than that of biography; Andrew W. Pitts, "Source Citation in Greek Historiography and in Luke (-Acts)," in *Early Christianity in Its Hellenistic Context*, vol. 1, *Christian Origins and Greco-Roman Culture: Social and Literary Contexts for the New Testament*, ed. Stanley E. Porter and Andrew W. Pitts, TENTS 9 (Leiden: Brill, 2013), 349–88; here 379. Pitts also suggests that this is supported by Luke's lower frequency in naming the sources of his citations.

dependent and focused on the OT, arguing that Jesus saw himself as the ful-fillment of "all the Scriptures" (Luke 24:25–27; 45–48) and that the events of the NT era had been foretold by "all the prophets" (Acts 3:24–26). As already noted, Luke-Acts is written with something of an OT style, which seems intended to clarify for its readers that the Jesus story is a continuation of the Israelite Scriptures. Thus, despite his lower rate of explicit OT citations, for Luke the Scriptures are very important.

We can note here that Luke is aware of the possible misuse of Scripture. This is particularly evidenced in his reports of Jesus's interactions with Phari-sees and Sadducees over the interpretation and application of Scripture (e.g., Luke 5:17–6:11; 11:37–54; 13:10–17; 14:1–16:31; 20:20–47). In explicit cita-tions of Scripture, when the manner of Luke's reporting demonstrates that these are cited approvingly, one could say that in some sense the speaker's use is also Luke's use; but when cited without Luke's approval (e.g., Satan's use of Ps. 91:11–12 in Luke 4:10–11), the intended function is attributed to the referenced person (e.g., to Satan in Luke 4:9–13) but not necessarily to Luke.[51] God's Word is important to Luke, but it must be understood correctly and obeyed (e.g., Luke 6:46–49; 8:19–21; 11:27–28; cf. Prov. 8:32).

Second, regarding the authorship of Scripture, it is clear enough that Luke recognizes the involvement of human writers in the production of the OT. But, for example, while he considers David an author of Psalms (see Luke 20:42–43; Acts 1:16–20; 2:25–31, 34–35; 4:25–26; 13:33–37), for Luke even these, like all the Scriptures, are ultimately authored by God (see Acts 3:25c; 7:2–3, 5, 6, 7) or the Lord himself (Acts 13:47) or the Holy Spirit (said to be speaking "through" [διά] David in Acts 1:16 and 4:25; and "through" [διά] Isaiah in Acts 28:25).[52] Some prophets are specifically named by Luke: Moses

---

51. On the literary-critical considerations related to ascertaining an author's point of view from the narrative he writes, particularly with regard to Luke-Acts, see Bill T. Arnold, "Luke's Characterizing Use of the Old Testament in the Book of Acts," in *History, Literature and Society in the Book of Acts*, ed. Ben Witherington III (Cambridge: Cambridge University Press, 1996), 300–23; and F. Scott Spencer, "Acts and Modern Literary Approaches," in *The Book of Acts in Its Ancient Literary Setting*, ed. Bruce W. Winter and Andrew D. Clark, BAFCS 1 (Grand Rapids: Eerdmans, 1993; Carlisle: Paternoster, 1993), 381–414, esp. 391–408.

52. Nicole observes, "In a number of passages God is represented as the speaker when the quotation is not a saying of God recorded as such in the Old Testament, but the word of Scripture itself, in fact, at times a word addressed to God by man (Matt. 19:5; Acts 4:25; 13:35; Heb. 1:5–8, 13; 3:7; 4:4)"; Roger R. Nicole, "New Testament Use of the Old Testament," in *The Right Doctrine from the Wrong Texts? Essays on the Use of the Old Testament in the New*, ed. G. K. Beale (Grand Rapids: Baker, 1994), 15. Metzger also notes that, in both the Mishnah and the NT, quotations are made where a verb of saying can have either God or the Scriptures as the subject such that personality is occasionally attributed to Scripture itself; Bruce M. Metzger, "The Formulas Introducing Quotations of Scripture in the NT and the Mishnah," *JBL* 70 (1951): 306. Citing several examples, Mark Talbot has likewise observed, "Some New Testament

is named nineteen times as a prophet and/or writer of Scripture (Luke 2:22; 5:14; 16:29, 31; 20:28, 37; 24:27, 44; Acts 3:22; 6:11, 14; 7:37; 13:38–39; 15:1, 5, 21; 21:21; 26:22; 28:23); Isaiah is named five times in Luke-Acts (Luke 3:4; 4:17; Acts 8:28, 30; and 28:25); Joel is named once as a prophet (Acts 2:16); and David is once called a prophet (Acts 2:29–30) and is twice said to have been the mouthpiece of the Holy Spirit (Acts 1:16; 4:25).[53] Quite often the "prophet(s)" as writers of Scripture are mentioned but unnamed (Luke 1:70; 16:16, 29, 31; 18:31; 24:25, 27, 44; Acts 3:18, 21, 24; 7:42, 48, 52; 10:43; 13:15, 27, 40; 15:15; 24:14; 26:22, 27; 28:23). Furthermore, it is worth noting that Luke stresses Jesus functioning as a prophet himself (e.g., Luke 4:23–28; 7:16, 39–40; 13:33; 24:19; Acts 3:22–23a; 7:37; cf. Luke 9:7–9, 18–20).[54] All this to say that Luke treats the OT Scriptures as the authoritative word of God.

Third, discussion of the "law" in the NT has a long and complex history of its own about which whole books are written. I limit myself here to commenting on two basic matters regarding the law in Luke-Acts: Luke's vocabulary in writing about the OT law and Luke's idea of the relationship of Christianity to the requirements of the OT law.

As to the first matter, Luke uses the Greek term for "law" (νόμος) 26 times in Luke-Acts (194× in the NT; Luke: 9×; Acts: 17×), and most of the time this is in reference to the Torah portion of the OT Scriptures (i.e., the Pentateuch: see Luke 2:22, 23, 24, 27, 39; 10:26; 16:16; 24:44; Acts 6:13; 7:53; 13:15, 38–39; 15:5; 21:20, 24, 28; 22:12; 23:3; 24:14; 28:23). Even in this narrow sense of referring to the Torah, Luke has several descriptive phrases utilizing this term, including "Law of Moses" (e.g., Luke 2:22; 24:44; Acts 13:39; 15:5; 28:23) and "Law of the Lord" (e.g., Luke 2:23, 24, 39). To refer to the larger canon of the OT, Luke sometimes uses two-part and three-part circumlocutions, using "law" (νόμος) and/or the name of Moses: "the Law and the prophets" (Luke 16:16); "the prophets and Moses" (Acts 26:22 NIV); "in accordance with the Law and that is written in the Prophets" (Acts 24:14 NIV); "the Law of Moses,

---

passages actually obliterate the distinction between God and Scripture"; Mark R. Talbot, "Does God Reveal Who He Actually Is?," in *God under Fire: Modern Scholarship Reinvents God*, ed. Douglas S. Huffman and Eric L. Johnson (Grand Rapids: Zondervan, 2002), 55n33.

53. In the NT citations of the OT where divine and human authorship of Scripture are mentioned together, Nicole finds sufficient evidence that divine superintendence over the production of Scripture was not considered destructive of human agency: "God secured a perfectly adequate presentation of the truth through the responsible and personal agency of the men he called and prepared for this sacred task"; Nicole, "New Testament Use of the Old Testament," 16; cf. Roger R. Nicole, "The Old Testament in the New Testament," in *The Expositor's Bible Commentary*, vol. 1, *Introductory Articles*, ed. Frank E. Gaebelein (Grand Rapids: Zondervan, 1979), 621–22; Metzger, "Formulas Introducing Quotations of Scripture," 306; and Henry M. Shires, *Finding the Old Testament in the New* (Philadelphia: Westminster, 1974), 67.

54. See Koet, *Five Studies*, 144–50.

FIGURE 6.1

Luke's View of Christianity and the Old Testament Law

The first-century church struggled with the question of how the OT law applied to Christian faith now that the Messiah had come. If responses to this question are sketched on a spectrum, even a cursory reading of Luke-Acts is enough to demonstrate that the NT writer we call Luke is not to be found at either end of the continuum.

Complete continuity ——————————— **Luke** ———————————Complete discontinuity

the Prophets and the Psalms" (Luke 24:44 NIV); and (in a compound combination) "beginning with Moses and all the Prophets, he [Jesus] explained to them what was said in all the Scriptures concerning himself" (Luke 24:27 NIV). Luke uses νόμος once each in the phrases "law of our fathers" (Acts 22:3) and "law of the Jews" (Acts 25:8), and three times he uses the term in a more general way (Acts 18:13, 15; 23:29). While Luke prefers to use νόμος to refer to the Pentateuch, he is not beyond using it to refer to the whole of the Israelite Scriptures (Luke 16:17).

Whether νόμος is understood to refer to the OT in whole or in part, the second matter pertaining to the OT law is perhaps the more complex. What is Luke's view of the applicability of the various OT laws to those who put their faith in Jesus as the Christ? Here it is helpful to recognize that the various views on the relation of Christianity to the requirements of the OT law can generally be plotted on a continuum (see fig. 6.1). On one end of the continuum is the position of complete continuity, insisting that all followers of Jesus must also keep the whole of the Jewish law; in essence, one must become a Jew in order to have Jesus (the Jewish Messiah) as Lord and Savior. On the other end of the continuum is complete discontinuity, insisting that the OT law must be completely set aside by all who wish to follow Jesus; in essence, even those with cultural connections to OT practices must abandon those practices in order to have Jesus as Lord and Savior.

A cursory reading of Luke-Acts is generally enough to demonstrate that Luke is not to be found at either end of this continuum. On the one hand, Jesus did not come to abolish the law but to fulfill it (Luke 16:16; cf. Matt. 5:17), not one bit of the OT law will be destroyed (Luke 16:17), and the OT is all about Jesus (e.g., Luke 24:44). On the other hand, a major theme repeated in Acts is that God has selected gentiles to become members of his people without becoming Jews; one need not follow Jewish customs in order to follow Jesus as the Christ (e.g., Acts 11:18; 14:27; 15:7–18; 21:19). Then again, on the one hand, Luke speaks highly of people in the Luke-Acts story who keep the law (e.g., Luke 1:6; 2:22–42); and on the other hand, Luke supports the idea that people cannot save themselves by keeping the law (Acts 13:38–39; 15:10–11). And further, on the one hand, Paul is clearly a keeper of Jewish law himself (e.g., Acts 13:14; 16:3; 18:18; 21:23–24; cf. Paul's claims in Acts 24:14; 25:8; 26:22; 28:17); and on the other hand, the idea that gentiles must keep the whole law is explicitly rejected (Acts 15:1–33).

This is not to say that Luke sees some parts of the OT law continuing and other parts dropping out; indeed, not one part of the law will be destroyed. Rather, Luke recognizes that when the law is "fulfilled" and God's plan moves into the new era, the law's built-in obsolescence transforms its demands. The presence of the saving Servant-King promised by the law properly transforms the expectations placed upon the faithful.[55] This does not mean that Jews cannot continue to express their faith with OT traditions (cf. Acts 21:17–26); Luke merely notes that this is not required—either of gentile believers or even of Jewish believers.[56] The transformed view of the OT law evidenced in the NT documents—including Luke-Acts—is itself in keeping with the OT law. Luke insists on a consistent view of the law as a law that has reached the era of fulfillment; any inconsistency is only apparent inconsistency. As Craig Blomberg puts it, "The 'inconsistency,' perhaps better termed a 'tension,' is thoroughly biblical, because the very notion of the new covenant as 'fulfillment' of the old involves both a termination of temporary provisions as well as the preservation of the purposes behind those provisions, albeit sometimes in drastically altered forms." Blomberg says further, "The Law was not abolished but it was no longer directly relevant for the church apart from its fulfillment in and interpretation by the Lord Jesus."[57] For Luke, the era of fulfillment in Christ changes things, and the people of God are now

---

55. See Mark A. Seifrid, "Jesus and the Law in Acts," *JSNT* 30 (1987): 40 (39–57). Seifrid suggests that "for Luke another ethic, one based on the messianic status of Jesus, has replaced the Mosaic law as the imperative which is incumbent on both the believing community and the world at large." I wince at the use of "replace" here, for we must recognize that, in a very real way, faith in Jesus as the Messiah is in keeping with the law and not a replacement of it. In fact, Luke seems to argue that all those (Jews or otherwise) who do not believe in Jesus are going against God's plan for the ages, even as it was expressed in the law. Faith in Jesus is necessary for one to be keeping the law; abrogation of specific requirements of the Mosaic law (e.g., the OT sacrificial system) was built into God's plan from the beginning.

56. Seifrid ("Jesus and the Law in Acts," 53) observes that in Acts when Luke refers to Jewish believers keeping the law, it does not imply that Luke believes the law requires them to do so.

57. Craig L. Blomberg, "The Law in Luke-Acts," *JSNT* 22 (1984): 53–80 (quotations are from 71–72); see Blomberg's treatment focused primarily on Acts: Craig L. Blomberg, "The Christian and the Law of Moses," in *Witness to the Gospel: The Theology of Acts*, ed. I. Howard Marshall and David Peterson (Grand Rapids: Eerdmans, 1998), 397–416. Tom Schreiner argues similarly in Thomas R. Schreiner, *40 Questions about Christians and Biblical Law*, 40 Questions Series (Grand Rapids: Kregel, 2010), 171–87.

free from the regulatory nature of the law, but the changes were planned to be precisely this way. Perhaps not surprisingly, this all sounds very Pauline: the law of God is good because it points us all to faith in Jesus Christ, and now that Christ has come, we are no longer under the supervision of the law (see Gal. 3:24–25).

Concluding Thoughts on Studying the New Testament Use of the Old Testament

We have seen that, in his writing of the Third Gospel and the book of Acts, Luke seeks to maneuver his readers into alignment with the original witnesses to the fulfillment of the OT in the Jesus event. Luke-Acts is designed to persuade its audience to become believers of "the things that have been accomplished among us" (Luke 1:1) and then in turn to testify to them.[58] This is not the aim of Luke alone. We study the NT use of the OT precisely because we want to be better aligned with the NT authors and the original Jesus followers as they read the Scriptures of Israel so that we will in turn represent that same message by keeping in step with them. Despite any apparent discontinuity between the OT and the NT, they saw the Bible united in Christ, and (returning to the topic of discussion where this book began) if we want to understand the NT, we should read it with this basic unity in mind.[59]

Regarding the study of the OT Scripture, Jesus observed to some defiant listeners, "And the Father who sent me has himself borne witness about me. His voice you have never heard, his form you have never seen, and you do not have his word abiding in you, for you do not believe the one whom he has sent. You search the Scriptures because you think that in them you have eternal life; and it is they that bear witness about me, yet you refuse to come to me that you may have life" (John 5:37–40; cf. Matt. 22:29). Thus, some first-century interpreters could study Scripture and fail to understand it properly. This is no less true of Scripture readers still today. To Jesus's warning we can add Paul's cautionary comment about understanding the Scriptures: "But their minds were hardened. For to this day, when they read the old covenant, that same veil remains unlifted, because only through Christ is it taken away. Yes,

---

58. John A. Darr, *On Character Building: The Reader and the Rhetoric of Characterization in Luke-Acts*, Literary Currents in Biblical Interpretation (Louisville: Westminster John Knox, 1992), 53.

59. See Donald A. Hagner, *How New Is the New Testament? First-Century Judaism and the Emergence of Christianity* (Grand Rapids: Baker Academic, 2018), 17.

to this day whenever Moses is read a veil lies over their hearts. But when one turns to the Lord, the veil is removed" (2 Cor. 3:14–16).[60]

To this end, I hope this study of the NT use of the OT moves our hearts into better alignment with the original witnesses to the fulfillment of Scripture in the Jesus event so that we will be more willing and able to hear more clearly what the Author of Scripture is saying. While taking a somewhat meticulous "academic" approach, this investigation into the use of the OT by the NT authors is not meant to be any less "devotional" due to its scholarly bent. In my academic analysis, I make many suggestions and argue for a few specific decisions regarding how one looks at Scripture. All readers of any and all literature face interpretive decisions regarding how best to understand the authors they read. But if the literature of the Bible is indeed ultimately communication from a divine Author (as I so ascribe), then the interpretive decisions for attempting to understand that Author take on a more serious (i.e., "devotional") dimension. Investigating the NT authors' approach to reading the OT is thus more than mere discussion of methodologies and artistic presentations. A study of the NT use of the OT should help us develop into better hearers of the whole of God's Word.[61]

---

60. See Craig A. Evans, "'It Is Not as Though the Word of God Had Failed': An Introduction to Paul and the Scriptures of Israel," in *Paul and the Scriptures of Israel*, ed. Craig A. Evans and James A. Sanders, JSNTSup 83, SSEJC 1 (Sheffield: Sheffield Academic, 1993), 15.

61. See E. Earle Ellis, "Quotations in the NT," *ISBE* 4:25.

Apparent Citations Introduced in the New Testament but Difficult to Locate in the Old Testament

The following fourteen NT passages have introductory statements prefacing apparent citations that scholars have difficulty locating in the OT. As noted in chapters 2 and 3 above, however, NT authors use introductory statements not only for citations (i.e., introduced quotations and introduced paraphrases) but also for recollections (i.e., Scripture summaries and historical reminiscences). Recognizing this broader use of introductory statements is of significant help in analyzing the fourteen passages that have been problematic in researching the NT use of the OT. Given the presence of introductory statements but the absence of clear parallel wording or reference to specific OT people or events, we can expect each of these problematic passages to have the classification of introduced paraphrase (not a quotation) or Scripture summary (not a historical reminiscence). I offer here a brief analysis of each of the passages, some briefly (e.g., Acts 7:26) and some at greater length (e.g., James 4:5–6). While not slavishly sequential, these analyses will evidence the five recommended steps for studying the NT use of the OT outlined in chapter 1 above (see esp. table 1.6).

Matthew 2:23

καὶ ἐλθὼν κατῴκησεν εἰς πόλιν λεγομένην Ναζαρέτ· ὅπως πληρωθῇ τὸ ῥηθὲν διὰ τῶν προφητῶν ὅτι Ναζωραῖος κληθήσεται.

And he went and lived in a city called Nazareth, so that what was spoken by the prophets might be fulfilled, that he would be called a Nazarene.

The somewhat formal introduction here begs for this to be classified as a citation—either a quotation or a paraphrase—and scholars have suggested several possible OT referents.

a. This could represent wordplay between "Nazarene" and the Hebrew term *nēṣer* (נֵצֶר) for "branch," a messianic title in Isa. 11:1. Some might expand this wordplay to include the holiness and righteousness of the branch in Isa. 4:2–3; Jer. 23:5; 33:15, but this is less convincing here as Matthew's immediate context is not stressing Jesus's holiness as much as God's raising him up and preserving him in the face of rejection.

b. The term "Nazarene" could reflect cultural derogatory connotations (cf. John 1:46) and thus fulfill the description of the despised and rejected unattractive suffering servant of Isa. 52:13–53:12.

c. Wordplay between Nazarene and the Hebrew term *nāzîr* (נָזִיר) for "Nazirite" in the annunciation of Samson's birth in Judg. 13:3–7 seems a fitting comparison with the Matthean account of the annunciation of Jesus's birth (cf. Matt. 1:21).

With a nod to Hillel's rule 2 (and rule 4; see chap. 4 above), perhaps a choice between these suggested passages need not be made. The introductory formula used here does not necessitate a single text citation; it can introduce a Scripture summary of this constellation of OT passages. Indeed, Matt. 2:23 is the only place in Matthew's entire Gospel where he names "the prophets" in the articular plural (rather than a singular "the prophet") as his OT reference. This suggests that Matthew is aware that he is summarizing the teaching of several OT passages and not intending to cite a single text.[1] Thus I view the use of the OT in Matt. 2:23 as a Scripture summary in Matthew's oft-used promising pattern function.

1. Craig L. Blomberg, "Matthew," in *Commentary on the New Testament Use of the Old Testament*, ed. G. K. Beale and D. A. Carson (Grand Rapids: Baker Academic, 2007), 11; cf. John Goldingay, *Reading Jesus's Bible: How the New Testament Helps Us Understand the Old Testament* (Grand Rapids: Eerdmans, 2017), 62–63.

Luke 11:49

διὰ τοῦτο καὶ ἡ σοφία τοῦ θεοῦ εἶπεν· ἀποστελῶ εἰς αὐτοὺς προφήτας καὶ ἀποστό-
λους, καὶ ἐξ αὐτῶν ἀποκτενοῦσιν καὶ διώξουσιν.

Therefore also the Wisdom of God said, "I will send them prophets and apostles,
some of whom they will kill and persecute."

The apparent citation in this passage is marked by NA[28] as "unde[termined]?"
but offers Jer. 7:25–26 as an alluded to passage; UBS[5] has no indication of there
being even an allusion here, much less a citation. An examination of the wording of Jer. 7:25–26 shows a first-person dialogue perspective, a few vocabulary
similarities to Luke 11:49 (e.g., "send" and "prophets"), and some generally
synonymous terms and phrases. The LXX of Jer. 7:25–26 reads as follows:

ἀφ᾽ ἧς ἡμέρας ἐξήλθοσαν οἱ πατέρες αὐτῶν ἐκ γῆς Αἰγύπτου καὶ ἕως τῆς ἡμέρας
ταύτης καὶ ἐξαπέστειλα πρὸς ὑμᾶς πάντας τοὺς δούλους μου τοὺς προφήτας ἡμέρας
καὶ ὄρθρου καὶ ἀπέστειλα, καὶ οὐκ ἤκουσάν μου, καὶ οὐ προσέσχεν τὸ οὖς αὐτῶν,
καὶ ἐσκλήρυναν τὸν τράχηλον αὐτῶν ὑπὲρ τοὺς πατέρας αὐτῶν.

From the day your ancestors went out of the land of Egypt until this day, I
sent to you all my servants, the prophets, even by day and in the morning I
sent them. And they did not listen to me and their ear did not pay attention,
and they stiffened their neck more than their ancestors. (wooden translation)

Crediting the dialogue to "the wisdom of God" (ἡ σοφία τοῦ θεοῦ) would
not be completely foreign to Jeremiah, who refers to God as having created in
his "wisdom" (Jer. 10:12; 51:15 [28:15]) and also notes the lack of "wisdom" in
rejecting the word of the Lord (Jer. 8:9).[2] While these similarities may suggest a
paraphrasing of Jer. 7:25–26 in Luke 11:49, it is significant that Jeremiah speaks
of the sending and rejecting of the messengers as past events. This theme of
rejected messengers in the past is mentioned elsewhere in the OT, most notably
in Jer. 25:3–7 (v. 4: "You have neither listened nor inclined your ears to hear,
although the LORD persistently sent to you all his servants the prophets") and
2 Chron. 36:15–16 ("The LORD, the God of their fathers, sent persistently
to them by his messengers, because he had compassion on his people and on
his dwelling place. But they kept mocking the messengers of God, despising his
words and scoffing at his prophets, until the wrath of the LORD rose against his

2. On various options suggested for "the wisdom of God" here—including Jesus (cf. Matt.
23:34)—see I. Howard Marshall, *The Gospel of Luke: A Commentary on the Greek Text*,
NIGTC (Grand Rapids: Eerdmans, 1978), 502–3.

people, until there was no remedy"). Rather than a paraphrase of Jer. 7:25–26 in Luke 11:49, I suggest that this is a hypothetical dialogue summarized from these various Scriptures what the Lord might have said before sending his messengers. Thus, it seems that the use of the OT in Luke 11:49 is best viewed as a Scripture summary creatively phrased in hypothetical speech in keeping with Luke's promising pattern function for OT references.

Luke 24:46–47

καὶ εἶπεν αὐτοῖς ὅτι οὕτως γέγραπται παθεῖν τὸν χριστὸν καὶ ἀναστῆναι ἐκ νεκρῶν τῇ τρίτῃ ἡμέρᾳ, καὶ κηρυχθῆναι ἐπὶ τῷ ὀνόματι αὐτοῦ μετάνοιαν εἰς ἄφεσιν ἁμαρτιῶν εἰς πάντα τὰ ἔθνη. ἀρξάμενοι ἀπὸ Ἰερουσαλήμ

And said to them, "Thus it is written, that the Christ should suffer and on the third day rise from the dead, and that repentance for the forgiveness of sins should be proclaimed in his name to all nations, beginning from Jerusalem."

The Greek term οὕτως ("thus") can be understood as referring forward to the content of the written material or backward to what Jesus has just said in Luke 24:44 about the necessity of fulfilling Scripture. The sense of the first option is "This is what is written: The Messiah will suffer and . . ." (CSB and similarly in most English versions). The second option would be "So [i.e., because the Scriptures about me must be fulfilled] it is written, that the Christ would suffer and . . ." (see NASB).[3] Neither option requires us to understand the introductory formula as introducing a citation of one specific OT passage. It is quite natural to take the infinitives as indirect discourse so that the passage can be rendered simply, "Thus it is written that the Messiah is to suffer . . . and to rise. . . ." In this light, we reckon Luke 24:46–47 as a Scripture summary with such passages in view as the Suffering Servant Song of Isa. 52:13–53:12 and the promise of Hosea 6:1–2:

> After two days he will revive us;
>   on the third day he will raise us up,
> that we may live before him. (v. 2)

David Pao and Eckhard Schnabel outline several of Luke's prior OT references (citations and/or allusions) as candidates for inclusion in this summary: Ps. 118:22 [117:22] in Luke 20:17; Isa. 53:12 in Luke 22:37; Ps. 31:5 [30:6] in

---

3. Marshall (*Gospel of Luke*, 905) favors the latter understanding without ruling out the former.

Luke 23:46; Pss. 22:7, 18 [22:8, 19] and 69:21 [68:22] in Luke 23:34–36; and Isa. 49:6 in Luke 2:32 and 13:47.[4] The use of the OT in Luke 24:46–47, then, is best viewed as a Scripture summary used by Luke for a prophecy fulfillment function.[5]

John 7:38

ὁ πιστεύων εἰς ἐμέ, καθὼς εἶπεν ἡ γραφή, ποταμοὶ ἐκ τῆς κοιλίας αὐτοῦ ῥεύσουσιν ὕδατος ζῶντος.

Whoever believes in me, as Scripture has said, rivers of living water will flow from within them. (NIV)

As noted in the discussion of Scripture summaries in chapter 3, the use of the verb λέγω ("I say") in an introductory formula does not necessitate that a paraphrased citation, much less a precise quotation, must follow. In John 7, Jesus is in Jerusalem celebrating the Feast of Tabernacles, a freedom festival commemorating the exodus from Egypt to the land of promise (Lev. 23:33–43), a harvest festival celebrating the Lord's provision (Deut. 16:13–15; cf. Num. 29:12 –38), a festival renewed in Israel after Ezra read from "the Book of the Law of Moses" at the Water Gate of Jerusalem (Neh. 8:1–18). Zechariah envisions an international celebration of this festival, explicating a lack of rain as punishment for not observing it (Zech. 14:16–19). Later traditions expanded upon the festival's ceremonies and included closing water libations poured on the altar (m. Sukkah 4.1, 9–10). Indeed, just prior to his anticipatory words about the Feast of Tabernacles, Zechariah comments in 14:8, "On that day living waters shall flow out from Jerusalem, half of them to the eastern sea and half of them to the western sea. It shall continue in summer as in winter." This passage recalls the similar words of Ezekiel about the eastward flowing water from the temple that grows from a trickle to a river (Ezek. 47:1–12). These OT passages (perhaps by Hillel's rule 2 and rule 4)

---

4. David W. Pao and Eckhard J. Schnabel, "Luke," in *Commentary on the New Testament Use of the Old Testament*, ed. G. K. Beale and D. A. Carson (Grand Rapids: Baker Academic, 2007), 401; filling out Luke's perspective on scriptural support for this summary, they also point to additional related citations and/or allusions in Acts: Ps. 118:22 [117:22] (in Acts 4:11); Ps. 2:1–2 (in Acts 4:24–25); Isa. 53:7–8 (in Acts 8:32–33); Ps. 16:8–11 [15:8–11] (in Acts 2:25–28; 13:35); Isa. 55:3 (in Acts 13:34); and Isa. 49:6 (in Acts 1:8).

5. Interestingly, the Majority text tradition has an expanded, twofold reading for the introductory formula here: οὕτως γέγραπται, καὶ οὕτως ἔδει ("Thus it is written, even that it was necessary that . . ."), which would be consistent with the idea that what follows is a summary of at least two passages rather than a specific citation of a single text.

have been associated with the Feast of Tabernacles, and it would make sense that they be included in the scriptural teaching Jesus is summarizing in John 7:38. Listening to him on the last day of the Feast of Tabernacles (John 7:37), the people seem to receive Jesus's water reflections in light of the festival commanded through Moses when, upon hearing his words, some of them remark, "This really is the Prophet" (John 7:40; cf. Deut. 18:15). We must not neglect, however, that John provides his own clarifying commentary specifying that Jesus's remarks were about the Spirit to be received by those believing in Jesus (John 7:39; cf. 14:16–17, 26; 15:26; 16:7; see also 4:10–11, 14). Thus, OT passages using water imagery to picture the Holy Spirit should also be recognized as included in the Scripture summary of John 7:38 (e.g., Isa. 44:3; Joel 2:28 [3:1]; Ezek. 36:25–27; other proposed referents have included Neh. 9:15, 19–20; Prov. 18:4; Song 4:15; Isa. 43:19–20; 55:1; 58:11; Joel 4:18; Sir. 24:19–21, 30). This fits with identifying the use of the OT in John 7:38 as fitting a promising pattern fulfillment function in John's presentation.

John 12:34

ἀπεκρίθη οὖν αὐτῷ ὁ ὄχλος· ἡμεῖς ἠκούσαμεν ἐκ τοῦ νόμου ὅτι ὁ χριστὸς μένει εἰς τὸν αἰῶνα, καὶ πῶς λέγεις σὺ ὅτι δεῖ ὑψωθῆναι τὸν υἱὸν τοῦ ἀνθρώπου; τίς ἐστιν οὗτος ὁ υἱὸς τοῦ ἀνθρώπου;

So the crowd answered him, "We have heard from the Law that the Christ remains forever. How can you say that the Son of Man must be lifted up? Who is this Son of Man?"

The comment by the crowd in John 12:34 is in response to Jesus's statement, "And I, when I am lifted up from the earth, will draw all people to myself" (12:32), which the evangelist immediately interprets for the reader, "He said this to show by what kind of death he was going to die" (12:33). While clearly appealing to the OT law for the content of their question, the verb they use, "We have heard from the Law . . . ," in no way requires a citation, much less a precise quotation. Thus, it is no great tragedy that we cannot find in the OT the exact statement, "The Christ remains forever." In fact, some might even suggest that it would be odd to find such a bald statement in the OT about the Messiah.

Commenting on the Hebrew word for "messiah" (מָשִׁיחַ, māšîaḥ ≈ χριστός, christos), meaning "anointed one," John Goldingay notes that its use in the OT is to reference persons in history "anointed" by God to serve as deliverers; ironically, the OT does not utilize the title "Messiah" when referring to the coming ultimate eternal Deliverer. "When the First Testament uses the word *mashiah*, it is always referring to a king or a priest who already exists, who has been anointed with oil as a sign of his being designated by God. Paradoxically, then, the First Testament talks about the Messiah but it never calls him the *mashiah*; it does use the word *mashiah*, but it is never referring to the Messiah."[6]

Thus, to reckon the remark in John 12:34 as a summary comment about the Messiah, and not as a citation, fits with what we would expect to find—and not find—in the OT. John reports the people, in a summary fashion, appealing to an ultimate truth taught in Scripture. As a Scripture summary, this remark would have in view OT passages that teach about the eternality of the messianic figure (without necessarily using the term *māšîaḥ*) including Ps. 89:4–5, 35–37 [88:5–6, 36–38] (rooted in 2 Sam. 7:12–16); Ps. 110:1–4 [109:1–4]; Isa. 9:7; Ezek. 37:25; and Dan. 7:13–14.

Acts 7:26

τῇ τε ἐπιούσῃ ἡμέρᾳ ὤφθη αὐτοῖς μαχομένοις καὶ συνήλλασσεν αὐτοὺς εἰς εἰρήνην εἰπών· ἄνδρες, ἀδελφοί ἐστε· ἱνατί ἀδικεῖτε ἀλλήλους;

And on the following day he appeared to them as they were quarreling and tried to reconcile them saying, "Men, you are brothers. Why do you wrong each other?"

In the long narratival speech of Acts 7, Stephen provides a survey of Israelite history as a historical backdrop for his defense of Christian faith. Among his two dozen historical reminiscences and a dozen citations, in Acts 7:26 Stephen attributes to Moses (with the word "saying," εἰπών) a statement not found in the OT. In this portion of his speech, Stephen recounts a story from Moses's life and offers what I reckon to be a very free paraphrase of Exod. 2:13, which says, "When he went out the next day, behold, two Hebrews were struggling together. And he said to the man in the wrong, 'Why do you strike your companion?'" That this is intended as a paraphrase of Exod. 2:13 is supported by the simple fact that Stephen continues the reenactment of the historic scene with a precise quotation of the response of the confronted Israelite; also introduced simply with the word "saying" (εἰπών), his words from Exod. 2:14 LXX are parroted in Acts 7:27–28.

---

6. Goldingay, *Reading Jesus's Bible*, 106.

Acts 13:22

καὶ μεταστήσας αὐτὸν ἤγειρεν τὸν Δαυὶδ αὐτοῖς εἰς βασιλέα ᾧ καὶ εἶπεν μαρτυρήσας· εὗρον Δαυὶδ τὸν τοῦ Ἰεσσαί, ἄνδρα κατὰ τὴν καρδίαν μου, ὃς ποιήσει πάντα τὰ θελήματά μου.

And when he had removed him, he raised up David to be their king, of whom he testified and said, "I have found in David the son of Jesse a man after my heart, who will do all my will."

Similar to Stephen in Acts 7, in Acts 13 Paul provides a brief rehearsal of Israelite history as a historical backdrop for his defense of Christian faith. I reckon the OT reference in Acts 13:22 as an introduced ("and said"; καὶ εἶπεν) free paraphrase; it attributes to God a "testifying" (μαρτυρήσας) statement about David that appears to be an expansion of the divine testimony of Ps. 89:20 [88:21],

> Εὗρον Δαυὶδ τὸν δοῦλον μου,
>   ἐν ἐλαίῳ ἁγίῳ μου ἔχρισα αὐτόν.

> I have found David, my servant;
>   with my holy oil I have anointed him

This expansion is informed by key words and phrases in the testimony of Samuel against Saul in 1 Sam. 13:14 LXX, "The LORD has sought out a man after his own heart . . ." (καὶ ζητήσει κύριος ἑαυτῷ ἄνθρωπον κατὰ τὴν καρδίαν αὐτοῦ) and in the Lord's instructions to Samuel in the LXX of 1 Sam. 16:1, 7, and 12 ("I will send you to Jesse the Bethlehemite, for I have provided for myself a king among his sons . . . the LORD looks on the heart . . . Arise, anoint him, for this is he"). To have these two texts working together to produce the vocabulary for a free paraphrase is a reasonable framing for the OT teaching (cf. Hillel's rule 4). Thus, I see Acts 13:22 as an introduced paraphrase of Ps. 89:20 as a historical backdrop but informed by vocabulary found elsewhere in the OT.[7]

---

7. Gleason Archer and Gregory Chirichigno go further and categorize Acts 13:22 as a "quotation" of 1 Sam. 13:14 and Ps. 89:21 [88:21], listing it in their "Category A" classification, i.e., among those that are "reasonably or completely accurate renderings from the Hebrew of the Masoretic Text (MT) into the Greek of the Septuagint (LXX), and from there (apart from word order, which sometimes deviates slightly) in the New Testament passage in which the Old Testament text is cited." See Gleason L. Archer and Gregory Chirichigno, *Old Testament Quotations in the New Testament: A Complete Survey* (Chicago: Moody, 1983), 51 and xxv.

The more difficult part of the expanded paraphrase of Ps. 89:20 in Acts 13:22 is that it ends with a specific allusion to the divine testimony about Cyrus in Isa. 44:28 LXX, "And all my will he will do" (καὶ πάντα τὰ θελήματά μου ποιήσει). The difficulty occurs because Isa. 44:28 is expressly about Cyrus, but Acts 13:22 is explicitly about Jesus. Interestingly, the Aramaic Targum to 1 Sam. 13:14 does not reference "a man after God's heart" but does remark that David was "a man doing his will(s)" (גבר עביד ועותיה). Max Wilcox has suggested that Acts reflects knowledge of the OT Scriptures and the Targum commentary; there is no need to appeal to Isa. 44:28 as a source for Acts 13:22.[8] The two texts of Ps. 89:20 and 1 Sam. 13:14 are also paraphrastically combined in 1 Clem. 18.1 ("And what shall we say about the illustrious David, to whom God said, 'I have found a man after my own heart, David the son of Jesse; I have anointed him with eternal mercy'"), but without use of the Targum to 1 Sam. 13:14 or of Isa. 44:28. This omission may well indicate that 1 Clement's paraphrase of Ps. 89:20 (informed by 1 Sam. 13:14) comes from a tradition that is separate from Acts, a tradition where appeal to Isa. 44:28 is unnecessary.[9] Nevertheless, even if Acts is alluding to Isa. 44:28 here, because Cyrus is identified as God's anointed (i.e., χριστός in Isa. 45:1), he serves as a type of Christ, and thus the use of a similar descriptor for Jesus as a divinely appointed liberator of God's people is fitting.[10]

1 Corinthians 2:9

ἀλλὰ καθὼς γέγραπται·
    ἃ ὀφθαλμὸς οὐκ εἶδεν καὶ οὖς οὐκ ἤκουσεν
    καὶ ἐπὶ καρδίαν ἀνθρώπου οὐκ ἀνέβη,
    ἃ ἡτοίμασεν ὁ θεὸς τοῖς ἀγαπῶσιν αὐτόν.

But, as it is written,
    "What no eye has seen, nor ear heard,
        nor the heart of man imagined,
    what God has prepared for those who love him."

8. Max E. Wilcox, *The Semitisms of Acts* (Oxford: Clarendon, 1965), 21–24; cf. Darrell L. Bock, *Proclamation from Prophecy and Pattern: Lucan Old Testament Christology*, JSNTSup 12 (Sheffield: Sheffield Academic, 1987), 243.

9. Bock, *Proclamation from Prophecy and Pattern*, 243; cf. I. Howard Marshall, "Acts," in *Commentary on the New Testament Use of the Old Testament*, ed. G. K. Beale and D. A. Carson (Grand Rapids: Baker Academic, 2007), 583–84.

10. So Archer and Chirichigno (*Old Testament Quotations*, xxviii), who classify the use of Isa. 44:28 in Acts 13:22 in their "Category E," i.e., among those that "give the impression that unwarranted liberties were taken with the Old Testament text in the light of its context."

The presence of the introductory formula "as it is written" anticipates a citation, but here we seem to have a paraphrastic conflation of several OT texts. The first two clauses appear to come from Isa. 64:4 (MT 64:3 and LXX 64:3), where reference is made to Yahweh as the only perceivable (i.e., conceivable) deity. Interestingly, the LXX text has a two-part descriptor in first-person, "From eternity we have not heard nor our eyes seen a God except you" (ἀπὸ τοῦ αἰῶνος οὐκ ἠκούσαμεν οὐδὲ οἱ ἃ ὀφθαλμοὶ ἡμῶν εἶδον θεὸν πλὴν σοῦ), but 1 Cor. 2:9 preserves a three-part descriptor in third-person, akin to the structure and perspective of the MT text, "And from eternity they have not heard nor have they perceived by ear nor has an eye seen a God except you" (וּמֵעוֹלָם לֹא־שָׁמְעוּ לֹא הֶאֱזִינוּ עַיִן לֹא־רָאָתָה אֱלֹהִים זוּלָתְךָ). Rather than mimicking the MT's reduplicated listening clause (i.e., heard + heard + seen), however, 1 Cor. 2:9 reverses the LXX's listening and vision clauses and adds a different third clause, which seems to borrow a line found only in the LXX of Isa. 65:16, "and it will not arise in their heart" (καὶ οὐκ ἀναβήσεται αὐτῶν ἐπὶ τὴν καρδίαν; cf. Jer. 3:16), for which the MT has a vision clause: "and are hidden from my eyes" (וְכִי נִסְתְּרוּ מֵעֵינָי). It is also noteworthy that Isa. 65:17 LXX has a similar Greek phrase using a different verb (οὐδ᾽ οὐ μὴ ἐπέλθῃ αὐτῶν ἐπὶ τὴν καρδίαν), for which the MT has the Hebrew equivalent (וְלֹא תַעֲלֶינָה עַל־לֵב). This could then be a framing application of Hillel's rule 2. The final clause in 1 Cor. 2:9 might be an inference from a passage such as Exod. 20:6, "but showing love to a thousand generations of those who love me" (LXX: καὶ ποιῶν ἔλεος εἰς χιλιάδας τοῖς ἀγαπῶσίν με). Given this apparent conflation from different OT sources, I classify the OT reference in 1 Cor. 2:9 as a Scripture summary. Likewise, Archer and Chirichigno describe 1 Cor. 2:9 as presenting "a paraphrastic summary of several different texts in the Old Testament" that nonetheless "accurately brings out the teaching of each of the sources involved."[11] In Paul's argument in 1 Cor. 2, this Scripture summary serves as an illustration of the eternal truth that God's ways are inscrutable.

1 Corinthians 9:10

ἢ δι᾽ ἡμᾶς πάντως λέγει; δι᾽ ἡμᾶς γὰρ ἐγράφη ὅτι ὀφείλει ἐπ᾽ ἐλπίδι ὁ ἀροτριῶν ἀροτριᾶν καὶ ὁ ἀλοῶν ἐπ᾽ ἐλπίδι τοῦ μετέχειν.

Does he not certainly speak for our sake? It was written for our sake, because the plowman should plow in hope and the thresher thresh in hope of sharing in the crop.

11. Archer and Chirichigno, *Old Testament Quotations*, xxix–xxx (in their "Category E" grouping).

This verse continues to investigate the application of Deut. 25:4 as just formally introduced and cited in 1 Cor. 9:9, "For it is written in the Law of Moses, 'You shall not muzzle an ox when it treads out the grain.' Is it for oxen that God is concerned?" Paul's application of this OT passage to God's people and not merely to oxen is a framing for 1 Cor. 9:9 that is in line with Hillel's rule 1. Some have proposed that the repetition of the term "written" (γράφω) in 1 Cor. 9:10—along with the poetic parallelism that follows and the somewhat non-Pauline vocabulary—means that a new citation is in view. For example, NA[28] lists this as an undetermined citation and in the margin suggests Sir. 6:19, which says, "As one plowing and sowing, come to her and wait for her good fruits: for in laboring about her you will not toil much and will soon eat her fruits" (ὡς ὁ ἀροτριῶν καὶ ὁ σπείρων πρόσελθε αὐτῇ καὶ ἀνάμενε τοὺς ἀγαθοὺς καρποὺς αὐτῆς· ἐν γὰρ τῇ ἐργασίᾳ αὐτῆς ὀλίγον κοπιάσεις καὶ ταχὺ φάγεσαι γεννημάτων αὐτῆς).

Nonetheless, it seems far better to see this as a backward-looking reflection on the "written" citation already under discussion in the previous verse. This is how modern English versions tend to treat this passage (e.g., CEB, CEV, CSB, ESV, NASB, NET, NIV, NKJV, NLT, NRSV). Furthermore, 1 Cor. 9:11 continues with the *Qal wa-ḥomer* (Hillel's rule 1) framing set in reverse: "If we have sown spiritual things among you, is it too much if we reap material things among you?" This gives additional support to the proposal that no new citation is in view and that verses 10–11 are simply further reflection on the citation of Deut. 25:4 in 1 Cor. 9:9, using similar agrarian illustrations and imagery.[12]

2 Corinthians 4:6

ὅτι ὁ θεὸς ὁ εἰπών· ἐκ σκότους φῶς λάμψει, ὃς ἔλαμψεν ἐν ταῖς καρδίαις ἡμῶν πρὸς φωτισμὸν τῆς γνώσεως τῆς δόξης τοῦ θεοῦ ἐν προσώπῳ ['Ιησοῦ] Χριστοῦ.

For God, who said, "Let light shine out of darkness," has shone in our hearts to give the light of the knowledge of the glory of God in the face of Jesus Christ.

---

12. On some of the additional complexities of interpreting 1 Cor. 9:9–10, see Gordon D. Fee, *The First Epistle to the Corinthians*, rev. ed., NICNT (Grand Rapids: Eerdmans, 2014), 448–52. Interestingly, Fee questions Paul's use of a "lesser to greater" argument here (450) but then offers one as part of his explanation of Paul's argument (451). Fee notes that Paul never elsewhere uses the aorist passive ἐγράφη to *introduce* a citation (451–52n251), but uses his use of ἐγράφη in Rom. 4:23 to *comment* on an OT text, as here. An old but worthwhile defense of Paul's proper use of Deut. 25:4 in its original context—including the intended lesser-to-greater argument—is made by Frederic Louis Godet, *Commentary on St. Paul's First Epistle to the Corinthians*, 2 vols., trans. Alexander Cusins (Edinburgh: T&T Clark, 1893), 2:10–16.

The suspected citation here lies within a pendent nominative of the Greek describing the nominative phrase "the God who said" (ὁ θεὸς ὁ εἰπών), which in turn is descriptive of the pronoun ὅς in the main sentence. Thus, the grammar supports taking the questioned "shine out of darkness" line as a citation of some kind. As we know, however, citations can be paraphrases, and it is not at all difficult to see this as a paraphrase of Gen. 1:3, "Let there be light" (Γενηθήτω φῶς), especially with the mention of "darkness" (σκότος) in Gen. 1:2. Other suggestions for parallel wording in the OT include Ps. 112:4 [111:4] and Job 37:15 LXX, which both mention φῶς and σκότος; and Isa. 9:2 [9:1], which mentions both φῶς and σκότος and utilizes the verb "to shine" in the same future tense form (λάμψει). While the Isaiah passage is not primarily about God's word of creation at issue in the citation, it does address the kind of enlightenment in view in the second half of 2 Cor. 4:6 regarding the new creation that comes with faith in Christ (cf. 2 Cor. 5:17). Thus, what I understand to be Paul's paraphrase of Gen. 1:3—an expression of the ultimate truth that the Creator God is the source of all wisdom and everything else—may well be influenced by the wording of Isa. 9:2. It is noteworthy that Isa. 9:1–2 is utilized elsewhere in the NT to describe the ministry of Jesus (Matt. 4:15–16; Luke 1:79).[13]

Ephesians 5:14

πᾶν γὰρ τὸ φανερούμενον φῶς ἐστιν. διὸ λέγει·
    ἔγειρε, ὁ καθεύδων,
        καὶ ἀνάστα ἐκ τῶν νεκρῶν,
        καὶ ἐπιφαύσει σοι ὁ Χριστός.

For anything that becomes visible is light. Therefore it says,
    "Awake, O sleeper,
        and arise from the dead,
        and Christ will shine on you."

While the introductory formula used here (διὸ λέγει, "therefore it says") can point to Scripture (e.g., Eph. 4:8), it is generic enough to point to nonscriptural sources, so proposals for the mysterious citation of Eph. 5:14 have included a Christian hymn or some apocryphal work. While there is no clear OT passage as a candidate for this presumed citation, there are some verbal similarities here to several passages in the LXX of Isaiah. For

13. Peter Balla, "2 Corinthians," in *Commentary on the New Testament Use of the Old Testament*, ed. G. K. Beale and D. A. Carson (Grand Rapids: Baker Academic, 2007), 763.

example, comments about the dead rising are found in Isa. 26:19, "The dead will rise up and those in the tombs will be raised" (ἀναστήσονται οἱ νεκροί, καὶ ἐγερθήσονται οἱ ἐν τοῖς μνημείοις); and summons to awaken are found in Isa. 51:17, "Awake, awake! Rise up, Jerusalem" (Ἐξεγείρου ἐξεγείρου ἀνάστηθι, Ιερουσαλημ); and Isa. 52:1, "Awake, awake, Zion" (Ἐξεγείρου ἐξεγείρου, Σιων). Particularly parallel concepts are found in Isa. 60:1–2, "Be enlightened, be enlightened, Jerusalem, for your light has come, and the glory of the Lord is risen upon you. Behold, darkness and gloom will cover the land upon the Gentiles, but the Lord will shine upon you, and his glory will be seen upon you" (Φωτίζου φωτίζου, Ιερουσαλημ, ἥκει γάρ σου τὸ φῶς, καὶ ἡ δόξα κυρίου ἐπὶ σὲ ἀνατέταλκεν. ἰδοὺ σκότος καὶ γνόφος καλύψει γῆν ἐπ' ἔθνη· ἐπὶ δὲ σὲ φανήσεται κύριος, καὶ ἡ δόξα αὐτοῦ ἐπὶ σὲ ὀφθήσεται). In the early development of biblical theology, these OT themes could have been gathered together with their consummation viewed as in Christ. Thus, it appears that Paul may well be citing an early Christian hymn influenced by a christological reading of Isaiah; this kind of Christian hymn hypothesis for this passage has a long history and is the consensus view.[14] Such a citation of a Christian hymn would function in Paul's argument as an example of another source that also endorses the instruction he is giving in Eph. 5.

1 Timothy 5:18b

λέγει γὰρ ἡ γραφή· βοῦν ἀλοῶντα οὐ φιμώσεις, καί· ἄξιος ὁ ἐργάτης τοῦ μισθοῦ αὐτοῦ.

For the Scripture says, "You shall not muzzle an ox when it treads out the grain," and, "The laborer deserves his wages."

The introductory formula used in 1 Tim. 5:18 ("For the Scripture says," λέγει γὰρ ἡ γραφή) places the clear citation of Deut. 25:4 in the first half of the verse parallel to the mislaid citation in the second half of the verse, joined by simply "and" (καί). Thus, both citations are described as "written" (i.e., γραφή, Scripture). Because the wording of 1 Tim. 5:18b matches Luke 10:7 precisely (ἄξιος γὰρ ὁ ἐργάτης τοῦ μισθοῦ αὐτοῦ; cf. Matt. 10:10 where the synonym τῆς τροφῆς is used for τοῦ μισθοῦ), some take it as a citation of a "saying" (λόγιον) of Jesus, but this does not match its description here as

14. Clinton E. Arnold, *Ephesians*, ZECNT (Grand Rapids: Zondervan, 2010), 334. We must acknowledge that this is an attempt to solve one mystery by appealing to another.

something "written."[15] On the other hand, if 1 Tim. 5:18b is indeed a citation of Luke 10:7, it would serve as evidence of an early date for the writing of Luke's Gospel and further as evidence for early recognition of the Third Gospel as authoritative Scripture. Either way, the double citation functions as an appeal to the ultimate truth of "Scripture."

Other suggestions for possible sources include the related material in Lev. 19:13, "You shall not oppress your neighbor or rob him. The wages of a hired worker shall not remain with you all night until the morning." And Deut. 24:15 has a similar instruction, "You shall give him his wages on the same day, before the sun sets." This suggestion would render the wording of 1 Tim. 5:18b, introduced with a resumptive "and" appealing to the previous "Scripture says," as a Scripture summary, and it still functions as an appeal to authority.

An altogether simpler solution is offered by Archer and Chirichigno, who suggest that the phrase under discussion is not intended as a citation at all. Rather, joined to the citation of Deut. 25:4 by καί ("and"), it serves as an inferential comment applying the Deuteronomy text to human relationship.[16] Thus, "For the Scripture says," is thought to introduce only the citation of Deut. 25:4 in the first half of 1 Tim. 5:18, and the word "and" (καί) introduces an applicational commentary on the citation. This understanding removes the problem of identifying a citation for the second half of 1 Tim. 5:18. The question of how this line shows up in Luke 10:7 could be surmised as coming from Jesus's own reflection upon traditional teaching utilizing the same inferential and application process. This explanation, however, is unsatisfying to those who note that the purported use of a second word picture connected by "and" is not as efficient a commentary—and thus is not as convincing—as would be the use of an explanatory clause connected by an inferential or causal coordinating conjunction like "therefore" (διο) or "for" (γάρ), or a purposive or causal subordinate conjunction like "in order to" (ἵνα) or "because" (ὅτι), or some equivalent construction.[17] Thus, the non-citation view is not well received. Modern English translations tend to favor the citation view (ASV, CEV, ESV, NASB, NET, NIV, NKJV, NLT, NRSV, WEB) as opposed to the non-citation view (CJB, CSB).

15. Some might appeal to the Q hypothesis, or some other non-extant proto-Gospel document, as a written source for this citation. This would be another, and perhaps unconvincing, attempt to solve one mystery by appealing to another.

16. Archer and Chirichigno, *Old Testament Quotations*, 45.

17. See ὅτι in 1 Cor. 9:10 discussed above. As with 1 Tim. 5:18, Paul also appeals to Deut. 25:4 in 1 Cor. 9:9–10, but there he spells out the precise inferential argument that Archer and Chirichigno suggest is at work in 1 Tim. 5:18. Is Paul's earlier and more explicit inferential argument in 1 Cor. 9:9–10 well enough known that he can simply say "and" in 1 Tim. 5:18?

2 Timothy 2:19b

ὁ μέντοι στερεὸς θεμέλιος τοῦ θεοῦ ἕστηκεν, ἔχων τὴν σφραγῖδα ταύτην· ἔγνω κύριος τοὺς ὄντας αὐτοῦ, καί· ἀποστήτω ἀπὸ ἀδικίας πᾶς ὁ ὀνομάζων τὸ ὄνομα κυρίου.

But God's firm foundation stands, bearing this seal: "The Lord knows those who are his," and, "Let everyone who names the name of the Lord depart from iniquity."

The somewhat unique introductory formula found at the beginning of 2 Tim. 2:19 is in keeping with Paul's interest in architectural imagery (e.g., Rom. 15:20; 1 Cor. 3:10–13; Eph. 2:20) and is appropriate to the coming household imagery in 2 Tim. 2:20.[18] The introductory formula here places a clear citation of Num. 16:5 in the first half of verse 19b parallel to what appears to be a mislaid citation in the second half of verse 19b, joined by simply "and" (καί). The citation of Num. 16:5 is a condensed paraphrase from the LXX, focused on one phrase in the first half of the verse, "God has visited and knows those who are his" (Ἐπέσκεπται καὶ ἔγνω ὁ θεὸς τοὺς ὄντας αὐτοῦ). Paul's substitution of "Lord" (κύριος) for the LXX "God" (θεός) is fitting with the MT, which has the tetragrammaton "YHWH," which is normally rendered with "Lord" (κύριος) in the LXX (see also Nah. 1:7 LXX).[19] Possibilities for the identification of the citation in the second half of 2 Tim. 2:19b are numerous but can be grouped into three basic options.

a. This could be a Scripture summary of teaching from the OT wisdom literature. Job 36:10 (LXX) comments on God's people as those turning from wickedness (ἀδικίας), "But he will harken to the righteous: and he has said that they will turn from unrighteousness" (ἀλλὰ τοῦ δικαίου εἰσακούσεται· καὶ εἶπεν ὅτι ἐπιστραφήσονται ἐξ ἀδικίας). Similarly, but with different vocabulary, Ps. 34:14 [33:15] says, "Turn from evil and do good . . ." (ἔκκλινον ἀπὸ κακοῦ καὶ ποίησον ἀγαθόν), and Prov. 3:7 warns, "Be not wise in your own estimation, but fear God, and depart from all evil" (μὴ ἴσθι φρόνιμος παρὰ σεαυτῷ, φοβοῦ δὲ τὸν θεὸν καὶ ἔκκλινε ἀπὸ παντὸς κακοῦ).[20]

---

18. The use of "foundation" (θεμέλιος) in the introductory statement may well be an allusion to Isa. 28:16, which Paul uses elsewhere (e.g., Rom 5:5; 9:33; 10:11; cf. Matt. 21:42; Mark 12:10; Luke 20:17; 1 Pet. 2:4, 6), anticipating another allusion to Isaiah.

19. Philip H. Towner, "1–2 Timothy and Titus," in *Commentary on the New Testament Use of the Old Testament*, ed. G. K. Beale and D. A. Carson (Grand Rapids: Baker Academic, 2007), 903–4.

20. The suggestion that the language borrows from Ps. 6:8 is more doubtful. Rather than the Lord's people separating from evil, Ps. 6:8 [6:9] has the evildoers separating from the Lord,

b. Closer in vocabulary are several passages in the apocryphal book of Sirach. Sirach 17:26 encourages, "Turn again to the Most High, and turn away from wickedness" (ἐπάναγε ἐπὶ ὕψιστον καὶ ἀπόστρεφε ἀπὸ ἀδικίας); Sir. 35:5 (35:3 LXX) observes, "It is pleasing to the Lord to depart from evil, and it is atonement to depart from wickedness" (εὐδοκία κυρίου ἀποστῆναι ἀπὸ πονηρίας, καὶ ἐξιλασμὸς ἀποστῆναι ἀπὸ ἀδικίας); and Sir. 23:10 explains [with a variant addition]; "For just as a servant who is continually scrutinized will not be lacking a bruise, so also the one always swearing and naming [the name of the Lord] will not be clean from sin" (ὥσπερ γὰρ οἰκέτης ἐξεταζόμενος ἐνδελεχῶς ἀπὸ μώλωπος οὐκ ἐλαττωθήσεται, οὕτως καὶ ὁ ὀμνύων καὶ ὀνομάζων διὰ παντὸς [τὸ ὄνομα κυρίου] ἀπὸ ἁμαρτίας οὐ μὴ καθαρισθῇ). Given the brevity of shared vocabulary desirable for a citation and the possibility of a Scripture summary to canonical literature, this resorting to an apocryphal book is not convincing.

c. More convincing to me is the solution offered by George Knight that takes the larger context of Num. 16 into view. While the first half of 2 Tim. 2:19b offers a clear paraphrase of Num. 16:5a, the second half of the verse may well replace a paraphrase of Num. 16:5b with an applicational paraphrase of Num. 16:26, with the influence of verse 27 affecting Paul's choice of the phrase "turn away from" (ἀφίστημι ἀπό).[21]

This latter suggestion has several things favoring it. The framing of 2 Tim. 2:19b implies two citations separated by a simple "and" (καί) (so most English translations), and a second paraphrase from Num. 16 would certainly be fitting. Reflecting on the setting of Korah's rebellion in Num. 16, the unknown citation in 2 Tim. 2:19b does provide proper application of the lesson of the passage, and this application is expressed in Moses's words (but with different

---

"Depart from me, all you workers of evil; for the Lord has heard the sound of my weeping" (ἀπόστητε ἀπ' ἐμοῦ, πάντες οἱ ἐργαζόμενοι τὴν ἀνομίαν, ὅτι εἰσήκουσεν κύριος τῆς φωνῆς τοῦ κλαυθμοῦ μου; cf. Luke 13:27, where this passage is alluded to using ἀδικίας in place of ἀνομίαν); see Towner, "1–2 Timothy and Titus," 905–6.

21. George W. Knight III, *The Pastoral Epistles: A Commentary on the Greek Text*, NIGTC (Grand Rapids: Eerdmans, 1992), 416. Paul's paraphrase of Num. 16:26 (if that is what it is) uses language found elsewhere in the OT: "naming the name of the Lord" (ὀνομάζω τὸ ὄνομα κυρίου) is used twice in the context of blasphemy in Lev. 24:16 (see "with a curse" in Lev. 24:11); "we name your name" (τὸ ὄνομά σου ὀνομάζομεν) is used more positively as an identifier of God's people in Isa. 26:13; with different imagery for God's people, Isa. 52:11 calls for them to "depart" from evil (the same ἀφίστημι term Paul uses); and swapping "naming" (ὀνομάζων) for "call" (ἐπικαλέσηται), Paul's phrasing in 2 Tim. 2:19b looks remarkably like Joel 2:32 [3:5], "everyone who calls on the name of the Lord" (πᾶς ὃς ἂν ἐπικαλέσηται τὸ ὄνομα κυρίου; Paul favors the LXX in quoting Joel 2:32 [3:5] in Rom. 10:13).

vocabulary) in Num. 16:26, "Depart, please, from the tents of these wicked men, and touch nothing of theirs, lest you be swept away with all their sins." In the next verse, the people respond to Moses's warning by "turning away from" (ἀπέστησαν ἀπό) the tents of the rebels (v. 27). Belonging to God is displayed in how one behaves, and this is the truth being expressed in the context of 2 Tim. 2 as well (with the NT rebels following Hymenaeus and Philetus corresponding to the OT rebels following Korah, Dathan, and Abiram).

The comparison of these solutions evidences the abundant teaching of the OT that God expects his people to be separated from doing evil. If it is not actually a paraphrase of Num. 16:26 using OT language, perhaps the unknown citation of 2 Tim. 2:19b is best reckoned as a Scripture summary expressed as a proverbial saying fitting to the context of Num. 16 and functioning as an appeal to the authority of the ethical wisdom found there and in such OT passages as these others.[22]

James 4:5-6

ἢ δοκεῖτε ὅτι κενῶς ἡ γραφὴ λέγει· πρὸς φθόνον ἐπιποθεῖ τὸ πνεῦμα ὃ κατῴκισεν ἐν ἡμῖν, μείζονα δὲ δίδωσιν χάριν; διὸ λέγει· ὁ θεὸς ὑπερηφάνοις ἀντιτάσσεται, ταπεινοῖς δὲ δίδωσιν χάριν.

Or do you think Scripture says without reason that against envy he longs for the spirit he has caused to dwell in us, but he gives us more grace? Therefore it says: "God opposes the proud, but he gives grace to the humble." (my own rendering)

With no OT wording that precisely matches what is introduced as "Scripture" in James 4:5, scholars have considered several options for the target of the introduction.[23]

a. Some suggest that James is referring to an apocryphal text like the *Apocalypse of Moses* 31 or the lost *Book of Eldad and Modad* (referenced in the Shepherd of Hermas using language similar to James).[24]

---

22. Archer and Chirichigno offer a Scripture summary solution, seeing all of 2 Tim. 2:19b as one conflated quotation (in their "Category A" classification) of Num. 16:5 and Isa. 26:13 that is perhaps influenced by Job 36:10 LXX and by Sir. 35:3 as well; Archer and Chirichigno, *Old Testament Quotations*, 35.

23. For theories apart from what I discuss here, see those outlined in James B. Adamson, *The Epistle of James*, NICNT (Grand Rapids: Eerdmans, 1976), 170–71.

24. E.g., Dale C. Allison Jr., *A Critical and Exegetical Commentary on the Epistle of James*, ICC (New York: Bloomsbury T&T Clark, 2013), 622. See also E. Earle Ellis, *The Old Testament in Early Christianity: Canon and Interpretation in the Light of Modern Research* (Tübingen: Mohr

But against this view is that the term ἡ γραφή is used elsewhere in the NT only for OT "Scripture"—and in comparing the words of Jesus (1 Tim. 5:18) and Paul (2 Pet. 3:16) to the OT—and not for apocryphal works.

b. While the simple introductory formula here ("Scripture says," ἡ γραφὴ λέγει) is usually found introducing a citation of a specific OT passage— either a quotation or a paraphrase—there are exceptions. The most notable exception found in John 7:38 (see above), however, supports the possibility that the introductory formula in James 4:5 could be utilized to introduce a summary of broader scriptural teaching. Some scholars take James 4:5 in this way, proposing that it summarizes the teaching of OT passages that use ἐπιποθέω to describe how people "long for" God and/or his Word (e.g., see Pss. 42:1 [41:2]; 84:2 [83:3]; 119:20, 131, 174 [118:20, 131, 174; with v. 131 also using πνεῦμα]).[25] But these OT passages all have people longing for the divine, whereas James 4:5 seems to point in the converse direction, with God longing for his people.

c. Noting this, some scholars suggest a third possibility, which is a variation of the Scripture summary idea just mentioned. With Deut. 32:11 using ἐπιποθέω to describe God as "longing for" his people and noting that the immediate context of James 4 utilizes the widespread OT imagery of God as husband to his people (e.g., Isa. 54:5–8; Jer. 3:20; Ezek. 16:38; 23:45; Hosea), these scholars have suggested that James is charging his readers as "adulterous people" in verse 4 and speaking of God's righteous jealousy in the very next verse. Thus, James 4:5 could be a summary of OT teaching about God as a jealous God (e.g., Exod. 20:5; 34:14; Deut. 4:24) longing for his people to be faithful.[26] While this seems more likely than the first two options, I find a fourth solution most convincing.

d. The "Scripture" introduced in James 4:5–6a references an anticipatory free paraphrase of Prov. 3:34, which James goes on to quote more precisely in 4:6b (where he follows the LXX except with ὁ θεός in place of κύριος).

Siebeck, 1991; reprint, Eugene, OR: Wipf & Stock, 2003), who suggests the possibility of some unknown extracanonical writing cited as authoritative (34) or even a NT writing (153).

25. Cf. Sophie Laws, *A Commentary on the Epistle of James*, HNTC (New York: Harper & Row, 1980), 174–79; Laws, "Does Scripture Speak in Vain? A Reconsideration of James iv.5," *NTS* 20 (1974): 210–15.

26. E.g., Douglas J. Moo, *The Letter of James*, TNTC (Grand Rapids: Eerdmans, 1985), 146.; D. A. Carson, "James," in *Commentary on the New Testament Use of the Old Testament*, ed. G. K. Beale and D. A. Carson (Grand Rapids: Baker Academic, 2007), 1007.

A number of pieces of evidence support this fourth option. As a review of any critical commentary will make readily clear, what James says in 4:5–6 is complicated by several syntactical and contextual ambiguities, particularly in verse 5. I consider five of these issues to be key to understanding what "Scripture" James is referencing.[27] My translation of James 4:5–6 above shows that I understand (i) "spirit" (πνεῦμα) to be the *human* spirit (i.e., not the Holy Spirit)[28] and (ii) the *object* of (iii) the *positively oriented* verb "long for" (ἐπιποθέω) that has God as subject,[29] and that I render (iv) the prepositional phrase (πρὸς φθόνον) in a purposive *directional* manner "against"[30] (v) the "jealousy/envy" (φθόνος) displayed as a *negative human characteristic.*[31] These exegetical decisions result in the following translation for James 4:5: "against envy he longs for the spirit he has caused to dwell in us."[32]

But I have one more suggestion here, a sixth exegetical issue: I propose that exegetes follow the punctuation recommended by both NA[28] and UBS[5]

27. Although a bit different in conclusion, my analysis here follows the lead of Carson, "James," 1006–7. Naturally, the investigation could be made even more complex; for example, in arguing for a different solution, rather than a five-part analysis, Allison has an eleven-part approach; Allison, *James*, 617–22.

28. The only other place James uses the word "spirit" (πνεῦμα) is in James 2:26, and there it clearly refers to the human spirit that animates the human body. Cf. Herm. Mand. 3 (28.1–2) where a similar phrase is used in a way that clarifies the writer's intention to refer to the human spirit.

29. The subject for "he longs for" (ἐπιποθεῖ) is likely intended to be understood as God, even as God is the understood subject of the other finite verbs in the sentence, "he caused to dwell" (κατῴκισεν) and "he gives" (δίδωσιν). And the verb "long for" or "desire" (ἐπιποθέω) regularly takes an accusative noun as its object, so it seems likely that "spirit" here should be taken as the accusative of direct object. Furthermore, the verb "longs for" (ἐπιποθέω) and its cognates are always used with reference to positive desires elsewhere in the NT.

30. Most English translations render the prepositional phrase πρὸς φθόνον as descriptive of manner, "with jealousy" (≈ "jealously"); cf. BDAG, s.v. πρός 3f. In Phil. 1:8 the same verb "long for" (ἐπιποθέω) is modified by a direct object accusative and a prepositional phrase using ἐν + dative for a positive adverbial description of manner: "I long for you all with the affection of Christ Jesus" (NIV). As is attested in the NT, however, πρός + accusative of a negative concept can be used of purposive direction "against," as it does repeatedly (five times!) in Eph. 6:12, "For we do not wrestle against flesh and blood, but against the rulers, against the authorities, against the cosmic powers over this present darkness, against the spiritual forces of evil in the heavenly places."

31. The term φθόνος for "jealousy" (and its related cognates) is never used positively in the NT; in fact, it is used only negatively of "envy" everywhere else in the NT (Matt. 27:18; Mark 15:10; Rom. 1:29; Gal. 5:21, 26; Phil. 1:15; 1 Tim. 6:4; Titus 3:3; 1 Pet. 2:1) and in the LXX (Tob. 4:7, 16; 1 Macc. 8:16; 3 Macc. 6:7; Wis. 2:24; 6:23; Sir. 14:10). Allison (*James*, 611) opines, "Had James (or his source) wanted to refer to the positive quality of divine zeal, he almost certainly would have used ζῆλος."

32. This translation fits not only the grammar and syntax of James 4:5 but the context of James as well; e.g., the argument against envy in 3:13–4:3 and the biblical theme of God's positive spousal longing for his people in 4:4.

at James 4:5, surprisingly, something (to my knowledge) no modern English translation has done. In James 4:5, the writer begins with a rhetorical question, "Or do you think Scripture says without reason . . . ," and the Greek text in NA[28] and UBS[5] (contra SBLGNT) places the question mark not at the close of verse 5 but at the end of the "he gives us more grace" clause (μείζονα δὲ δίδωσιν χάριν) in 4:6a.[33] With this location of the question mark, the former "against" clause is followed immediately with a "grace" clause, and this collocation has similarity to Prov. 3:34. That is, in speaking of God, Prov. 3:34 pairs an "against" clause with a "grace" clause saying,

> Though He scoffs at the scoffers,
> Yet He gives grace to the needy. (NASB)

Making this observation, Craig B. Carpenter suggests that the "Scripture" James means to introduce in 4:5 is, in fact, Prov. 3:34.[34] To be sure, it is not an exact quotation; rather, James offers a paraphrased adaptation of Prov. 3:34 in James 4:5–6a. And this seems confirmed by the fact that immediately following, in James 4:6b, he actually quotes Prov. 3:34 more precisely. Because he has already used the term "Scripture" to introduce his paraphrase of Prov. 3:34, James now introduces his actual quotation of the passage more simply as "it." He writes, "Therefore it says, 'God opposes the proud but gives grace to the humble'" (James 4:6b). So Carpenter's suggestion is that James remarks what "Scripture says" with a paraphrase of Prov. 3:34 before he quotes "it" more precisely.

Interestingly, this same suggestion is also argued independently by Scot McKnight.[35] Although McKnight differs from me in some of his exegetical choices on the five interpretive issues discussed above, he offers a mapping of James 4:5–6 to clarify this understanding. I have adapted McKnight's mapping to fit my own recommended translation of James 4:5–6.

Paraphrase of Prov. 3:34: Or do you think Scripture says without reason that (v. 5a)

A   against envy he [God] longs for the [human] spirit he has caused to dwell in us, (v. 5b)

B   but he gives us more grace? (v. 6a)

---

33. The NA[26cor] moved the question mark from the end of James 4:5 to the end of 4:6a in 1981, and the UBS[3cor] followed in 1983.

34. Craig B. Carpenter, "James 4.5 Reconsidered," *NTS* 47 (2001): 189–205, esp. 199–203; and Craig L. Blomberg and Mariam J. Kamell, *James*, ZECNT (Grand Rapids: Zondervan, 2008), 192.

35. Scot McKnight, *The Letter of James*, NICNT (Grand Rapids: Eerdmans, 2011), 335–44. See also Chris A. Vlachos, *James*, EGGNT (Nashville: B&H Academic, 2013), 137–38.

Quotation of Prov. 3:34 (v. 6b): Therefore it says:

A′ "God opposes the proud,

   B′ but he gives grace to the humble."[36]

So I see the "Scripture" in James 4:5–6a as an anticipatory paraphrase of Prov. 3:34, which James goes on to quote more precisely in 4:6b.

---

36. Siding with the NIV 1984 translation, McKnight (*Letter of James*, 340–43) renders the first paraphrased line (A), "The human spirit yearns toward envy" in James 4:5b; my translation actually improves the parallelism for which McKnight argues.

A Select Bibliography
for the New Testament Use
of the Old Testament

Bibliographies of the literature on the NT use of the OT cannot be exhaustive; the literature is constantly changing, especially in the last few decades. Nevertheless, I have selected the items included here as a fair representation of recommended resources. This bibliography is focused primarily (but not exclusively) on items appearing in the last thirty years (with the clear exception of the first section of the bibliography). Readers interested in older items can refer to the bibliographies found within the resources listed here. Especially useful are the chapter bibliographies found in the *Commentary on the New Testament Use of the Old Testament* edited by G. K. Beale and D. A. Carson (Baker Academic, 2007), which focus on each specific NT book.

In keeping with my taxonomical approach, this listing of resources is divided into its own set of categories. First, I offer a bibliography of items discussing the unity of the OT and the NT as Christian Scripture (per the opening discussion of chap. 1 above). This is followed by a list of general resources on the NT use of the OT, which includes books and articles. After this is a list of general resources for identifying citations of the OT in the New, which has been greatly influenced by Beale's similar list in his *Handbook on the New Testament Use of the Old Testament*. Next is a list of items related to the so-called Jewish methodologies (which is particularly related to chap. 4

above). Last is a collection of book-by-book items, including a list of studies on the NT use of particular OT books and passages followed by collections of resources sorted by the NT corpora.

Resources on the Unity of the Old and New Testaments as Christian Scripture

Baker, David L. *Two Testaments, One Bible: The Theological Relationship between the Old and New Testaments.* 3rd ed. Downers Grove, IL: InterVarsity, 2010.

Barr, James. *Old and New in Interpretation: A Study of the Two Testaments.* New York: Harper & Row, 1966.

Barton, John. "Unity and Diversity in the Biblical Canon." In *Die Einheit der Schrift und die Vielfalt des Kanons = The Unity of Scripture and the Diversity of the Canon,* edited by John Barton and Michael Wolter, 11–26. BZNW 118. New York: De Gruyter, 2003.

Beale, G. K. *A New Testament Biblical Theology: The Unfolding of the Old Testament in the New.* Grand Rapids: Baker Academic, 2011.

Blomberg, Craig L. "The Unity and Diversity of Scripture." *NDBT,* 64–72.

Childs, Brevard S. "The Nature of the Christian Bible: One Book, Two Testaments." In *The Rule of Faith: Scripture, Canon, and Creed in a Critical Age,* edited by Ephraim Radner and George Sumner, 115–25. Harrisburg, PA: Morehouse, 1998.

Christensen, Duane L. *The Unity of the Bible: Exploring the Beauty and Structure of the Bible.* New York: Paulist, 2003.

Davis, John J. "Unity of the Bible." In *Hermeneutics, Inerrancy, and the Bible,* edited by Earl D. Radmacher and Robert D. Preus, 641–59. Grand Rapids: Zondervan, 1984. [with responses by James Montgomery Boice (663–68) and Robert D. Preus (671–90)]

Feinberg, John S., ed., *Continuity and Discontinuity: Perspectives on the Relationship between the Old and New Testaments: Essays in Honor of S. Lewis Johnson, Jr.* Westchester, IL: Crossway, 1988.

Filson, Floyd V. "The Unity between the Testaments." In *The Interpreter's One-Volume Commentary on the Bible,* edited by Charles M. Laymon, 989–93. Nashville: Abingdon, 1971.

Fuller, Daniel P. *The Unity of the Bible: Unfolding God's Plan for Humanity.* Grand Rapids: Zondervan, 1992.

Gaebelein, Frank E. "The Unity of the Bible." In *Revelation and the Bible: Contemporary Evangelical Thought,* edited by Carl F. H. Henry, 389–401. Grand Rapids: Baker, 1958.

Goldingay, John. *Reading Jesus's Bible: How the New Testament Helps Us Understand the Old Testament.* Grand Rapids: Eerdmans, 2017.

Goldsworthy, Graeme L. "Relationship of Old Testament and New Testament." *NDBT*, 81–89.

Kaiser, Walter C., Jr. *Recovering the Unity of the Bible: One Continuous Story, Plan, and Purpose*. Grand Rapids: Zondervan, 2009.

Longenecker, Richard N. "Three Ways of Understanding Relations between the Testaments: Historically and Today." In *Tradition and Interpretation in the New Testament: Essays in Honor of E. Earle Ellis for His 60th Birthday*, edited by Gerald F. Hawthorne with Otto Betz, 22–32. Grand Rapids: Eerdmans, 1987; Tübingen: Mohr Siebeck, 1987.

Morgan, G. Campbell. *The Unfolding Message of the Bible: The Harmony and Unity of the Scriptures*. Westwood, NJ: Revell, 1961. [see esp. 11–22]

Motyer, Steve. "Two Testaments, One Biblical Theology." In *Between Two Horizons: Spanning New Testament Studies and Systematic Theology*, edited by Joel B. Green and Max Turner, 143–64. Grand Rapids: Eerdmans, 2000.

Preus, R. D. "The Unity of Scripture." *Concordia Theological Quarterly* 54 (1990): 1–23.

Rowley, Harold Henry. *The Unity of the Bible*. London: Carey Kingsgate, 1953.

Sabourin, Leopold. *The Bible and Christ: The Unity of the Two Testaments*. New York: Alba House, 1980.

Seitz, Christopher R. *The Character of Christian Scripture: The Significance of a Two-Testament Bible*. Grand Rapids: Baker Academic, 2011.

General Resources on the New Testament Use of the Old Testament

Allen, David M. "Introduction: The Study of the Use of the Old Testament in the New." *JSNT* 38 (2015): 3–16.

Allen, David, and Steve Smith, eds. *Methodology in the Use of the Old Testament in the New: Context and Criteria*. LNTS 579. New York: Bloomsbury T&T Clark, 2020.

Allison, Dale C. "The Old Testament in the New Testament." In *The New Cambridge History of the Bible: From the Beginnings to 600*, edited by James Carleton Paget and Joachim Schaper, 479–502. Cambridge: Cambridge University Press, 2013.

Baker, David L. *Two Testaments, One Bible: The Theological Relationship between the Old and New Testaments*. 3rd ed. Downers Grove, IL: InterVarsity, 2010.

Bates, Matthew W. "The Old Testament in the New Testament." In *The State of New Testament Studies: A Survey of Recent Research*, edited by Scot McKnight and Nijay K. Gupta, 83–102. Grand Rapids: Baker Academic, 2019.

Beale, G. K. *Handbook on the New Testament Use of the Old Testament: Exegesis and Interpretation*. Grand Rapids: Baker Academic, 2012.

———. *A New Testament Biblical Theology: The Unfolding of the Old Testament in the New*. Grand Rapids: Baker Academic, 2011.

————, ed. *The Right Doctrine from the Wrong Texts? Essays on the Use of the Old Testament in the New*. Grand Rapids: Baker, 1994.

Beale, G. K., and D. A. Carson, eds. *Commentary on the New Testament Use of the Old Testament*. Grand Rapids: Baker Academic, 2007.

Beale, G. K., D. A. Carson, Benjamin L. Gladd, and Andrew David Naselli, eds. *Dictionary of the New Testament Use of the Old Testament*. Grand Rapids: Baker Academic, 2023.

Beale, G. K., and Benjamin L. Gladd. *The Story Retold: A Biblical Theological Introduction to the New Testament*. Downers Grove, IL: InterVarsity, 2020.

Berding, Kenneth, and Jonathan Lunde, eds. *Three Views on the New Testament Use of the Old Testament*. Counterpoints: Bible and Theology. Grand Rapids: Zondervan, 2008.

Bock, Darrell L. "Scripture Citing Scripture: Use of the Old Testament in the New." In *Interpreting the New Testament Text: Introduction to the Art and Science of Exegesis*, edited by Darrell L. Bock and Buist M. Fanning, 255–76. Wheaton: Crossway, 2006.

Brodie, Thomas L., Dennis R. MacDonald, and Stanley E. Porter, eds. *Intertextuality of the Epistles: Explorations of Theory and Practice*. New Testament Monographs 16. Sheffield: Sheffield Academic, 2006.

Brown, Raymond E. *The* Sensus Plenior *of Sacred Scripture*. Baltimore: St. Mary's University, 1955. Reprint, Eugene, OR: Wipf & Stock, 2008.

Collins, C. John. "How the New Testament Quotes and Interprets the Old Testament." In *Understanding Scripture: An Overview of the Bible's Origin, Reliability, and Meaning*, edited by Wayne Grudem, C. John Collins, and Thomas R. Schreiner, 181–97. Wheaton: Crossway, 2012.

Court, John M., ed. *New Testament Writers and the Old Testament: An Introduction*. London: SPCK, 2002. Reprint, Eugene, OR: Wipf & Stock, 2011.

Docherty, Susan. "'Do You Understand What You Are Reading?' (Acts 8:30): Current Trends and Future Perspectives in the Study of the Use of the Old Testament in the New." *JSNT* 38 (2015): 112–25.

Dodd, C. H. *According to the Scriptures: The Sub-Structure of New Testament Theology*. London: Nisbet, 1952.

————. *The Old Testament in the New*. The Ethel M. Wood Lecture. London: Athlone, 1952.

Evans, Craig A., ed. *From Prophecy to Testament: The Function of the Old Testament in the New*. Peabody, MA: Hendrickson, 2004.

————. "New Testament Use of the Old Testament." In *A Handbook on the Jewish Roots of the Christian Faith*, edited by Craig A. Evans and David Mishkin, 65–71. Peabody, MA: Hendrickson, 2019.

————. "New Testament Use of the Old Testament." *NDBT*, 72–80.

———. "The Old Testament in the New." In *The Face of New Testament Studies: A Survey of Recent Research*. Edited by Scot McKnight and Grant R. Osborne, 130–45. Grand Rapids: Baker Academic, 2004.

———. "Why Did the New Testament Writers Appeal to the Old Testament?" *JSNT* 38 (2015): 36–48.

Evans, Craig A., and James A. Sanders, eds. *Early Christian Interpretation of the Scriptures of Israel*. JSNTSup 148; SSEJC 5. Sheffield: Sheffield Academic, 1997.

Evans, Craig A., and H. Daniel Zacharias, eds. *"What Does the Scripture Say?": Studies in the Function of Scripture in Early Judaism and Christianity*. 2 vols. LNTS 469–70; SSEJC 17–18. New York: T&T Clark, 2012.

Foster, Paul. "Echoes without Resonance: Critiquing Certain Aspects of Recent Scholarly Trends in the Study of the Jewish Scriptures in the New Testament." *JSNT* 38 (2015): 96–111.

France, R. T. "Relationship between the Testaments." *DTIB*, 666–72.

Goldingay, John. *Reading Jesus's Bible: How the New Testament Helps Us Understand the Old Testament*. Grand Rapids: Eerdmans, 2017.

Gundry, Robert H. "Quotations in the New Testament." *ZEB* 5:11–17.

Hanson, Anthony Tyrrell. *The New Testament Interpretation of Scripture*. London: SPCK, 1980. Reprint, Eugene, OR: Wipf & Stock, 2011.

Hays, Richard B., Stefan Alkier, and Leroy A. Huizenga, eds. *Reading the Bible Intertextually*. Waco: Baylor University Press, 2009.

Hays, Richard B., and Joel B. Green. "The Use of the Old Testament by New Testament Writers." In *Hearing the New Testament: Strategies for Interpretation*, edited by Joel B. Green, 122–39. 2nd ed. Grand Rapids: Eerdmans, 2010.

Huizenga, Leroy A. "The Old Testament in the New, Intertextuality and Allegory." *JSNT* 38 (2015): 17–35.

Kaiser, Walter C., Jr. *The Uses of the Old Testament in the New*. Chicago: Moody, 1985. Reprint, Eugene, OR: Wipf & Stock, 2001.

Koptak, Paul E. "Intertextuality." *DTIB*, 332–34.

Lalleman, Pieter J. *The Hidden Unity of the Bible: The Use of the Old Testament in the New Testament*. Pontypool, Wales: Faithbuilders, 2019.

Lanier, Greg. *Old Made New: A Guide to the New Testament Use of the Old Testament*. Wheaton: Crossway, 2022.

McLay, R. Timothy. *The Use of the Septuagint in New Testament Research*. Grand Rapids: Eerdmans, 2003.

Moo, Douglas J., and Andrew David Naselli. "The Problem of the New Testament's Use of the Old Testament." In *The Enduring Authority of the Christian Scriptures*, edited by D. A. Carson, 702–46. Grand Rapids: Eerdmans, 2016.

Moyise, Steve. *Evoking Scripture: Seeing the Old Testament in the New*. London: T&T Clark, 2008.

————. *The Old Testament in the New*. 2nd ed. T&T Clark Approaches to Biblical Studies. New York: Bloomsbury T&T Clark, 2015.

————, ed. *The Old Testament in the New Testament: Essays in Honour of J. L. North*. JSNTSup 189. Sheffield: Sheffield Academic, 2000.

————. "Scripture in the New Testament: Literary and Theological Perspectives." *Neot* 42 (2008): 305–26.

Oropeza, B. J., and Steve Moyise, eds. *Exploring Intertextuality: Diverse Strategies for New Testament Interpretation of Texts*. Eugene, OR: Cascade, 2016.

Osborne, Grant R. "The Old Testament in the New Testament." In *The Hermeneutical Spiral: A Comprehensive Introduction to Biblical Interpretation*, 323–44. Rev. ed. Downers Grove, IL: InterVarsity, 2006.

Porter, Stanley E. "Allusions and Echoes." In *As It Is Written: Studying Paul's Use of Scripture*, edited by Stanley E. Porter and Christopher D. Stanley, 29–40. SymS 50. Atlanta: Society of Biblical Literature, 2008.

————, ed. *Hearing the Old Testament in the New Testament*. McMaster New Testament Studies. Grand Rapids: Eerdmans, 2006.

Porter, Stanley E., with Bryan R. Dyer. *Sacred Tradition in the New Testament: Tracing Old Testament Themes in the Gospels and Epistles*. Grand Rapids: Baker Academic, 2016.

Rodgers, Peter R. *Exploring the Old Testament in the New*. Eugene, OR: Resource, 2012.

Satterthwaite, P. E., Richard S. Hess, and Gordon J. Wenham, eds. *The Lord's Anointed: Interpretation of Old Testament Messianic Texts*. Tyndale House Studies. Grand Rapids: Baker Academic, 1995. Reprint, Eugene, OR: Wipf & Stock, 2012.

Schnittjer, Gary Edward. *Old Testament Use of Old Testament: A Book-by-Book Guide*. Grand Rapids: Zondervan Academic, 2021.

Snodgrass, Klyne. "The Use of the Old Testament in the New." In *Interpreting the New Testament: Essays on Methods and Issues*, edited by David Alan Black and David S. Dockery, 209–29. 2nd ed. Nashville: Broadman & Holman, 2001.

Swartley, Willard M. "Intertextuality in Early Christian Literature." *DLNT*, 536–42.

Vlach, Michael Joseph. *The Old in the New: Understanding How the New Testament Authors Quoted the Old Testament*. Sun Valley, CA: Master's Seminary Press, 2021.

Wall, Robert W. "Intertextuality, Biblical." *DNTB*, 541–51.

Watts, Rikk E. "How Do You Read? God's Faithful Character as the Primary Lens for the New Testament Use of Israel's Scriptures." In *From Creation to New Creation: Biblical Theology and Exegesis; Essays in Honor of G. K. Beale*, edited by Daniel M. Gurtner and Benjamin L. Gladd, 199–220. Peabody, MA: Hendrickson, 2013.

Tools and Indexes for Identifying Citations of the Old Testament in the New Testament

Aland, Barbara, Kurt Aland, Johannes Karavidopoulos, Carlo M. Martini, and Bruce M. Metzger, eds. *The Greek New Testament*. 5th rev. ed. Stuttgart: Deutsche Bibelgesellschaft/American Bible Society/United Bible Societies, 2014. [cited as UBS⁵; see esp. the footnotes and the indexes]

Archer, Gleason L., and Gregory Chirichigno. *Old Testament Quotations in the New Testament: A Complete Survey*. Chicago: Moody, 1983.

Blue Letter Bible. "Parallel Passages in New Testament Quoted from Old Testament." https://www.blueletterbible.org/study/misc/quotes.cfm.

Böhl, Eduard. *Alttestamentlichen Citate im Neuen Testament*. Wien: Wilhelm Braumüller, 1878. [accessible online]

Bratcher, Robert G. *Old Testament Quotations in the New Testament*. 3rd ed. New York: United Bible Societies, 1984.

Collins, C. John. "How the New Testament Quotes and Interprets the Old Testament." In *Understanding Scripture: An Overview of the Bible's Origin, Reliability, and Meaning*, edited by Wayne Grudem, C. John Collins, and Thomas R. Schreiner, 181–97. Wheaton: Crossway, 2012. [see esp. 191–97]

Court, John M., ed. *New Testament Writers and the Old Testament: An Introduction*. London: SPCK, 2002. Reprint, Eugene, OR: Wipf & Stock, 2011. [see esp. 98–127]

Dittmar, Wilhelm. *Vetus Testamentum in Novo: Die alttestamentlichen Parallelen des Neuen Testaments im Wortlaut der Urtexte und der Septuaginta*. Göttingen: Vandenhoeck & Ruprecht, 1903. [accessible online]

Evans, Craig A. *Ancient Texts for New Testament Studies: A Guide to the Background Literature*. Grand Rapids: Baker Academic, 2005. [see esp. 342–409]

Fairbairn, Patrick. *Hermeneutical Manual: or, Introduction to the Exegetical Study of the Scriptures of the New Testament*. Edinburgh: T&T Clark, 1858. [see esp. 354–460; accessible online]

Gough, Henry. *The New Testament Quotations Collated with the Scriptures of the Old Testament*. London: Walton & Maberly, 1855. [accessible online]

Hübner, Hans. *Vetus Testamentum in Novo*. 3 vols. Göttingen: Vandenhoeck & Ruprecht, 1997–2007.

Hühn, Eugen. *Die alttestamentlichen Citate und Reminiscenzen im Neuen Testamente*. Vol. 2 of *Die messianischen Weissagungen des israelitisch-jüdischen Volkes bis zu den Targumim, historisch-kritisch untersucht und erläutert, nebst Erörterung der alttestamentlichen Citate und Reminiscenzen im Neuen Testamente*. Tübingen: Mohr Siebeck, 1900.

McLean, Bradley H. *Citations and Allusions to Jewish Scripture in Early Christian and Jewish Writings through 180 C.E.* Lewiston, NY: Edwin Mellen, 1992.

Nestle, Eberhard, Erwin Nestle, Barbara Aland, Kurt Aland, Johannes Karavidopoulos, Carlo M. Martini, and Bruce M. Metzger, eds. *Novum Testamentum Graece.*
28th rev. ed. Stuttgart: Deutsche Bibelgesellschaft, 2012. [cited as NA^{28}; see esp.
the margin notes and the third appendix]

Toy, Crawford Howell. *Quotations in the New Testament.* New York: Scribner's,
1884. [accessible online]

Turpie, David McCalman. *The New Testament View of the Old: A Contribution to
Biblical Introduction and Exegesis.* London: Hodder & Stoughton, 1872. [acces-
sible online]

———. *The Old Testament in the New: A Contribution to Biblical Criticism and
Interpretation.* London: Williams & Norgate, 1868. [accessible online]

Resources on So-Called Jewish and Early Church Exegetical Practices

Adams, Sean A., and Seth M. Ehorn, eds. *Composite Citations in Antiquity.* 2 vols.
LNTS 525. London: Bloomsbury T&T Clark, 2016, 2018.

Bates, Matthew W. *The Birth of the Trinity: Jesus, God, and Spirit in New Testament and Early Christian Interpretations of the Old Testament.* Oxford: Oxford
University Press, 2015.

———. *The Hermeneutics of the Apostolic Proclamation: The Center of Paul's
Method of Scriptural Interpretation.* Waco: Baylor University Press, 2012.

Boersma, Hans. *Scripture as Real Presence: Sacramental Exegesis in the Early Church.*
Grand Rapids: Baker Academic, 2017.

Bowker, John W. *The Targums and Rabbinic Literature: An Introduction to Jewish
Interpretation of Scripture.* Cambridge: Cambridge University Press, 1969.

Brady, Christian M. M. "Targum." *DTIB,* 780–81.

Bray, Gerald "Allegory." *DTIB,* 34–36.

Brooke, George J. "Pesher." *DBCI,* 273–75.

———. "Shared Intertextual Interpretations in the Dead Sea Scrolls and the New
Testament." In *Biblical Perspectives: Early Use and Interpretation of the Bible in
Light of the Dead Sea Scrolls: Proceedings of the First International Symposium
of the Orion Center, 12–14 May, 1996,* edited by Michael E. Stome and Esther G.
Chazon, 35–57. STDJ 28. Leiden: Brill, 1998.

Chou, Abner. *The Hermeneutics of the Biblical Writers: Learning to Interpret Scripture from the Prophets and Apostles.* Grand Rapids: Kregel, 2018.

Docherty, Susan E. "New Testament Scriptural Interpretation in Its Early Jewish
Context: Reflections on the *Status Quaestiones* and Future Directions." *NovT*
57 (2015): 1–19.

Doeve, Jan Willem. *Jewish Hermeneutics in the Synoptic Gospels and Acts*. Assen: Van Gorcum, 1954.

Ellis, E. Earle. *The Old Testament in Early Christianity: Canon and Interpretation in the Light of Modern Research*. Tübingen: Mohr Siebeck, 1991. Reprint, Eugene, OR: Wipf & Stock, 2003.

———. *Prophecy & Hermeneutic in Early Christianity: New Testament Essays*. Grand Rapids: Eerdmans, 1978. Reprint, Eugene, OR: Wipf & Stock, 2003.

Evans, Craig A. "Jewish Exegesis." *DTIB*, 380–84.

Fitzmyer, Joseph A. "The Use of Explicit Old Testament Quotations in Qumran Literature and in the New Testament." In *Essays on the Semitic Background of the New Testament*. Vol. 1 of *The Semitic Background of the New Testament*, 3–58. The Biblical Resource Series. Grand Rapids: Eerdmans, 1997; Livonia, MI: Dove, 1997.

Glenny, W. Edward. "Typology: A Summary of the Present Evangelical Discussion." *JETS* 40 (1997): 627–38.

Goppelt, Leonhard. *Typos: The Typological Interpretation of the Old Testament in the New*. Translated by Donald H. Madvig. Grand Rapids: Eerdmans, 1982. Reprint, Eugene, OR: Wipf & Stock, 2002.

Graves, Michael. *The Inspiration and Interpretation of Scripture: What the Early Church Can Teach Us*. Grand Rapids: Eerdmans, 2014.

Hall, Christopher A. *Reading Scripture with the Church Fathers*. Downers Grove, IL: InterVarsity, 1998.

Heine, Ronald E. *Reading the Old Testament with the Ancient Church: Exploring the Formation of Early Christian Thought*. Grand Rapids: Baker Academic, 2007.

Instone Brewer, David. *Techniques and Assumptions in Jewish Exegesis before 70 CE*. TSAJ 30. Tübingen: Mohr Siebeck, 1992.

Juel, Donald. *Messianic Exegesis: Christological Interpretation of the Old Testament in Early Christianity*. Philadelphia: Fortress, 1988.

Lange, Armin, and Matthias Weigold. *Biblical Quotations and Allusions in Second Temple Jewish Literature*. JAJSup 5. Göttingen: Vandenhoeck & Ruprecht, 2011.

Lim, Timothy H. "Qumran Scholarship and the Study of the Old Testament in the New Testament." *JSNT* 38 (2015): 68–80.

Longenecker, Richard N. *Biblical Exegesis in the Apostolic Period*. 2nd ed. Grand Rapids: Eerdmans, 1999; Vancouver, BC: Regent College, 1999.

McGinnis, Claire R. Mathews. "Stumbling over the Testaments: On Reading Patristic Exegesis and the Old Testament in Light of the New." *JTI* 4 (2010): 15–31.

O'Keefe, John J., and R. R. Reno. *Sanctified Vision: An Introduction to Early Christian Interpretation of the Bible*. Baltimore: Johns Hopkins University Press, 2005.

Pickup, Martin. "New Testament Interpretation of the Old Testament: The Theological Rationale of Midrashic Exegesis." *JETS* 51 (2008): 353–81.

Simonetti, Manilo. *Biblical Interpretation in the Early Church: An Historical Introduction to Patristic Exegesis*. Edinburgh: T&T Clark, 1994.

Zimels, Abraham. "Bible Exegesis and Study: Talmudic Literature." *EncJud* 3:640–41.

Book-by-Book Resources on the New Testament Use of the Old Testament

These book-by-book lists focus on specialty studies and avoid the standard technical commentaries. The standard commentaries, of course, are helpful for explorations of broader contexts as well as for examinations of specific passages; they will also offer more detailed bibliographies for the individual book and passage under investigation.

Studies on the New Testament Use of Particular Old Testament Books and Passages

Bartholomew, Craig G. "The Intertextuality of Ecclesiastes and the New Testament." In *Reading Ecclesiastes Intertextually*, edited by Katharine Dell and Will Kynes, 226–39. LHB 587. New York: Bloomsbury T&T Clark, 2014.

Bock, Darrell L., and Mitch Glaser, eds. *The Gospel according to Isaiah 53: Encountering the Suffering Servant in Jewish and Christian Theology*. Grand Rapids: Kregel, 2012.

Chilton, Bruce. "Jesus, Levitical Purity, and the Development of Primitive Christianity." In *The Book of Leviticus: Composition and Reception*, edited by Rolf Rendtorff and Robert A. Kugler, with Sarah Smith Bartel, 358–82. VTSup 93. Leiden: Brill, 2003.

Dunn, James D. G. "The Danielic Son of Man in the New Testament." In *The Book of Daniel: Composition and Reception*, edited by John J. Collins and Peter W. Flint, with Cameron VanEpps, 2:528–49. 2 vols. VTSup 83. Leiden: Brill, 2001.

Evans, Craig A. "Daniel in the New Testament: Visions of God's Kingdom." In *The Book of Daniel: Composition and Reception*, edited by John J. Collins and Peter W. Flint, with Cameron VanEpps, 2:490–527. 2 vols. VTSup 83. Leiden: Brill, 2001.

———. "Exodus in the New Testament: Patterns of Revelation and Redemption." In *The Book of Exodus: Composition, Reception, and Interpretation*. Edited by Thomas B. Dozeman, Craig A. Evans, and Joel N. Lohr, 440–64. VTSup 164. Leiden: Brill, 2014.

———. "Genesis in the New Testament." In *The Book of Genesis: Composition, Reception, and Interpretation*, edited by Craig A. Evans, Joel N. Lohr, and David L. Peterson, 469–94. VTSup 152. Leiden: Brill, 2012.

————. "Jeremiah in Jesus and the New Testament." In *The Book of Jeremiah: Composition, Reception, and Interpretation*, edited by Jack R. Lundbom, Craig A. Evans, and Bradford A. Anderson, 303–19. VTSup 178. Leiden: Brill, 2018.

————. "Praise and Prophecy in the Psalter and in the New Testament." In *The Book of Psalms: Composition and Reception*, edited by Peter W. Flint and Patrick D. Miller Jr., with Aaron Brunell and Ryan Roberts, 551–79. VTSup 99. Leiden: Brill, 2005.

Heim, Knut M. "Proverbs in Dialogue with the New Testament." In *Reading Proverbs Intertextually*, edited by Katharine Dell and Will Kynes, 167–78. LHB 629. New York: Bloomsbury T&T Clark, 2019.

Janzen, J. Gerald. "'He Makes Peace in His High Heaven': Job and Paul in Resonance." In *Reading Job Intertextually*, edited by Katharine Dell and Will Kynes, 246–58. LHB 574. New York: Bloomsbury T&T Clark, 2013.

Lohr, Joel N. "Righteous Able, Wicked Cain: Genesis 4:1–16 in the Masoretic Text, the Septuagint, and the New Testament." *CBQ* 71 (2009): 485–96.

Menken, Maarten J. J., and Steven Moyise, eds. *Deuteronomy in the New Testament.* NTSI. LNTS 358. London: T&T Clark, 2007.

————, eds. *Genesis in the New Testament.* NTSI. LNTS 466. London: Bloomsbury T&T Clark, 2012.

————, eds. *The Minor Prophets in the New Testament.* NTSI. LNTS 377. London: T&T Clark, 2009.

Moyise, Steven, and Maarten J. J. Menken, eds. *Isaiah in the New Testament.* NTSI. New York: T&T Clark, 2005.

————, eds. *The Psalms in the New Testament.* NTSI. New York: T&T Clark, 2004.

Shepherd, Michael B. *The Twelve Prophets in the New Testament.* StBibLit 140. New York: Peter Lang, 2011.

Tait, Michael, and Peter Oakes, eds. *Torah in the New Testament: Papers Delivered at the Manchester–Lausanne Seminar of June 2008.* LNTS 401. London: T&T Clark, 2009.

Witherington, Ben, III. *Isaiah Old and New: Exegesis, Intertextuality, and Hermeneutics.* Minneapolis: Fortress, 2017.

————. *Psalms Old and New: Exegesis, Intertextuality, and Hermeneutics.* Minneapolis: Fortress, 2017.

————. *Torah Old and New: Exegesis, Intertextuality, and Hermeneutics.* Minneapolis: Fortress, 2018.

Zetterholm, Magnus. "The Books of Kings in the New Testament and the Apostolic Fathers." In *The Book of Kings: Sources, Composition, Historiography and Reception*, edited by André Lemaire and Baruch Halpern, with Matthew J. Adams, 561–84. VTSup 129. Leiden: Brill, 2010.

The Gospels and the Old Testament

Allen, David. *According to the Scriptures: The Death of Christ in the Old Testament and the New.* London: SCM, 2018.

Evans, Craig A., and W. Richard Stegner, eds. *The Gospels and the Scriptures of Israel.* JSNTSup 104, SSEJC 3. Sheffield: Sheffield Academic, 1994.

Hays, Richard B. *Echoes of Scripture in the Gospels.* Waco: Baylor University Press, 2016.

———. *Reading Backwards: Figural Christology and the Fourfold Gospel Witness.* Waco: Baylor University Press, 2014.

Holmgren, Fredrick C. *The Old Testament and the Significance of Jesus.* Grand Rapids: Eerdmans, 1999.

Marcus, Joel. "The Old Testament and the Death of Jesus: The Role of Scripture in the Gospel Passion Narratives." In *The Death of Jesus in Early Christianity*, edited by John T. Carroll and Joel B. Green, 205–33. Peabody, MA: Hendrickson, 1995.

Moyise, Steve. *Jesus and Scripture: Studying the New Testament Use of the Old Testament.* Grand Rapids: Baker Academic, 2011.

New, David S. *Old Testament Quotations in the Synoptic Gospels, and the Two-Document Hypothesis.* SCS 37. Atlanta: Scholars Press, 1993.

Pao, David W. "Old Testament in the Gospels." *DJG*², 631–41.

Subramanian, J. Samuel. *The Synoptic Gospels and the Psalms as Prophecy.* LNTS 351. New York: T&T Clark, 2007.

Swartley, Willard M. *Israel's Scripture Traditions and the Synoptic Gospels: Story Shaping Story.* Peabody, MA: Hendrickson, 1994.

Tuckett, Christopher M., ed. *The Scriptures in the Gospels.* BETL 131. Leuven: Leuven University Press, 1997.

Wenham, John W. *Christ and the Bible.* 3rd ed. Grand Rapids: Baker, 1994. Reprint, Eugene, OR: Wipf & Stock, 2009.

Matthew and the Old Testament

Allison Jr., Dale C. *The New Moses: A Matthean Typology.* Minneapolis: Fortress, 1993. Reprint, Eugene, OR: Wipf & Stock, 2013.

Beaton, Richard. *Isaiah's Christ in Matthew's Gospel.* SNTSMS 123. Cambridge: Cambridge University Press, 2002.

Gundry, Robert Horton. *The Use of the Old Testament in St. Matthew's Gospel: With Special Reference to the Messianic Hope.* NovTSup 18. Leiden: Brill, 1967.

Ham, Clay Alan. *The Coming King and the Rejected Shepherd: Matthew's Reading of Zechariah's Messianic Hope.* New Testament Monographs 4. Sheffield: Sheffield Phoenix, 2005.

Huizenga, Leroy A. *The New Isaac: Tradition and Intertextuality in the Gospel of Matthew.* NovTSup 131. Leiden: Brill, 2009.

Knowles, Michael. *Jeremiah in Matthew's Gospel: The Rejected Prophet Motif in Matthean Redaction.* JSNTSup 68. Sheffield: JSOT Press, 1993.

Menken, Maarten J. J. *Matthew's Bible: The Old Testament Text of the Evangelist.* BETL 173. Leuven: Leuven University Press, 2004.

———. "Messianic Interpretation of Greek Old Testament Passages in Matthew's Fulfillment Quotations." In *The Septuagint and Messianism*, edited by Michael A. Knibb, 457–86. BETL 195. Leuven: Leuven University Press, 2006.

Piotrowski, Nicholas G. *Matthew's New David at the End of Exile: A Socio-Rhetorical Study of Scriptural Quotations.* NovTSup 170. Leiden: Brill, 2016.

Soares-Prabhu, George M. *The Formula Quotations in the Infancy Narratives of Matthew: An Enquiry into the Tradition History of Mt 1–2.* AnBib 63. Rome: Pontifical Biblical Institute, 1976.

Stendahl, Krister. *The School of St. Matthew and Its Use of the Old Testament.* 2nd ed. ASNU 20. Lund: Gleerup, 1968; Philadelphia: Fortress, 1968.

Watts, Rikk E. "Messianic Servant or the End of Israel's Exilic Curses? Isaiah 53:4 in Matthew 8:17." *JSNT* 38 (2015): 81–95.

Mark and the Old Testament

Ahearne-Kroll, Stephen P. *The Psalms of Lament in Mark's Passion: Jesus' Davidic Suffering.* SNTSMS 142. Cambridge: Cambridge University Press, 2007.

Carey, Holly J. *Jesus' Cry from the Cross: Towards a First-Century Understanding of the Intertextual Relationship between Psalm 22 and the Narrative of Mark's Gospel.* LNTS 398. New York: T&T Clark, 2009.

Hatina, Thomas R. *In Search of a Context: The Function of Scripture in Mark's Narrative.* JSNTSup 232, SSEJC 8. Sheffield: Sheffield Academic, 2002.

Le Peau, Andrew T. *Mark through Old Testament Eyes: A Background and Application Commentary.* TOTE. Grand Rapids: Kregel, 2017.

Marcus, Joel. *The Way of the Lord: Christological Exegesis of the Old Testament in the Gospel of Mark.* Louisville: Westminster John Knox, 1992.

O'Brien, Kelli S. *The Use of Scripture in the Markan Passion Narrative.* LNTS 384. New York: T&T Clark, 2010.

Schneck, Richard. *Isaiah in the Gospel of Mark, I–VIII.* BIBAL Dissertation Series 1. Vallejo, CA: BIBAL Press, 1994.

Watts, Rikki E. *Isaiah's New Exodus in Mark.* WUNT 2/88. Tübingen: Mohr Siebeck, 1997. Reprint, Biblical Studies Library. Grand Rapids: Baker Academic, 2000.

Winn, Adam. *Mark and the Elijah-Elisha Narrative: Considering the Practice of Greco-Roman Imitation in Search for Markan Source Material.* Eugene, OR: Pickwick, 2010.

Luke-Acts and the Old Testament

Arnold, Bill T. "Luke's Characterizing Use of the Old Testament in the Book of Acts." In *History, Literature and Society in the Book of Acts*, edited by Ben Witherington III, 300–23. Cambridge: Cambridge University Press, 1996.

Beers, Holly. *The Followers of Jesus as the 'Servant': Luke's Model from Isaiah for the Disciples in Luke-Acts.* LNTS 535. New York: Bloomsbury T&T Clark, 2015.

Bock, Darrell L. "Old Testament in Acts." *DLNT,* 823–26.

Brawley, Robert Lawson. *Text to Text Pours Forth Speech: Voices of Scripture in Luke-Acts.* ISBL. Bloomington: Indiana University Press, 1995.

Fitzmyer, Joseph A. "The Use of the Old Testament in Luke-Acts." In *To Advance the Gospel: New Testament Studies,* 295–313. 2nd ed. The Biblical Resource Series. Grand Rapids: Eerdmans, 1998; Livonia, MI: Dove, 1998.

Kloppenborg, John S., and Joseph Verheyden, eds. *The Elijah-Elisha Narrative in the Composition of Luke.* LNTS 493. New York: Bloomsbury T&T Clark, 2014.

Lanier, Gregory R. *Old Testament Conceptual Metaphors and the Christology of Luke's Gospel.* LNTS 591. New York: Bloomsbury T&T Clark, 2018.

Litwak, Kenneth Duncan. *Echoes of Scripture in Luke-Acts: Telling the History of God's People Intertextually.* JSNTSup 282. London: T&T Clark, 2005.

———. "The Use of the Old Testament in Luke-Acts: Luke's Scriptural Story of the 'Things Accomplished among Us.'" In *Issues in Luke-Acts: Selected Essays,* edited by Sean S. Adams and Michael Pahl, 147–69. Gorgias Handbooks 26. Piscataway, NJ: Gorgias, 2012.

Mallen, Peter. *The Reading and Transformation of Isaiah in Luke-Acts.* LNTS 367. New York: T&T Clark, 2008.

Meek, James A. *The Gentile Mission in Old Testament Citations in Acts: Text, Hermeneutic, and Purpose.* LNTS 385. New York: T&T Clark, 2008.

Miura, Yuzuru. *David in Luke-Acts: His Portrayl in the Light of Early Judaism.* WUNT 2/232. Tübingen: Mohr Siebeck, 2007.

Moessner, David P., ed. *Jesus and the Heritage of Israel: Luke's Narrative Claim upon Israel's Legacy.* Luke the Interpreter of Israel 1. Harrisburg, PA: Trinity Press International, 1999.

———. "Luke's 'Plan of God' from the Greek Psalter: The Rhetorical Thrust of 'the Prophets and the Psalms' in Peter's Speech at Pentecost." In *Scripture and Traditions: Essays on Early Judaism and Christianity in Honor of Carl R. Holladay,* edited by Patrick Gray and Gail R. O'Day, 223–38. Leiden: Brill, 2008.

O'Day, Gail R. "The Citation of Scripture as a Key to Characterization in Acts." In *Scripture and Traditions: Essays on Early Judaism and Christianity in Honor of Carl R. Holladay,* edited by Patrick Gray and Gail R. O'Day, 207–21. Leiden: Brill, 2008.

Pao, David W. *Acts and the Isaianic New Exodus.* WUNT 2/130. Tübingen: Mohr Siebeck, 2000. Reprint, Biblical Studies Library. Grand Rapids: Baker Academic, 2002.

Smith, Steve. *The Fate of the Jerusalem Temple in Luke-Acts: An Intertextual Approach to Jesus' Laments over Jerusalem and Stephen's Speech.* LNTS 553. New York: Bloomsbury T&T Clark, 2017.

John and the Old Testament

Brendsel, Daniel J. *"Isaiah Saw His Glory": The Use of Isaiah 52–53 in John 12*. BZNW 208. Berlin: de Gruyter, 2014.

Brunson, Andrew C. *Psalm 118 in the Gospel of John*. WUNT 2/158. Tübingen: Mohr Siebeck, 2003.

Bynum, W. Randolph. *The Fourth Gospel and the Scriptures: Illuminating the Form and Meaning of Scriptural Citation in John 19:37*. NovTSup 144. Leiden: Brill, 2012.

Coxen, Paul S. *Exploring the New Exodus in John: A Biblical Theological Investigation of John Chapters 5–10*. Eugene, OR: Resource, 2014.

Daise, Michael A. *Quotations in John: Studies on Jewish Scripture in the Fourth Gospel*. LNTS 610. New York: Bloomsbury T&T Clark, 2019.

Daly-Denton, Margaret. *David in the Fourth Gospel: The Johannine Reception of the Psalms*. AGJU 47. Leiden: Brill, 1999.

Lioy, Dan. *The Search for Ultimate Reality: Intertextuality between the Genesis and Johannine Prologues*. StBibLit 93. New York: Peter Lang, 2005.

Menken, Maarten J. J. *Old Testament Quotations in the Fourth Gospel: Studies in Textual Form*. CBET 15. Kampen: Kok Pharos, 1996.

Mihalios, Stefanos. *The Danielic Eschatological Hour in the Johannine Literature*. LNTS 436. New York: T&T Clark, 2011.

Montanaro, Andrew. "The Use of Memory in the Old Testament Quotations in John's Gospel." *NovT* 59 (2017): 147–70.

Myers, Alicia D. *Characterizing Jesus: A Rhetorical Analysis on the Fourth Gospel's Use of Scripture in Its Presentation of Jesus*. LNTS 458. New York: T&T Clark, 2012.

Myers, Alicia D., and Bruce G. Schuchard, eds. *Abiding Words: The Use of Scripture in the Gospel of John*. RBS 81. Atlanta: SBL Press, 2015.

Peterson, Brian Neil. *John's Use of Ezekiel: Understanding the Unique Perspective of the Fourth Gospel*. Minneapolis: Fortress, 2015.

Sheridan, Ruth. *The Figure of Abraham in John 8: Text and Intertext*. LNTS 619. New York: Bloomsbury T&T Clark, 2020.

———. *Retelling Scripture: 'The Jews' and the Scriptural Citations in John 1:19–12:15*. Leiden: Brill, 2012.

Siliezar, Carlos Raúl Sosa. *Creation Imagery in the Gospel of John*. LNTS 546. New York: Bloomsbury T&T Clark, 2015.

Tachick, Christopher S. *"King of Israel" and "Do Not Fear, Daughter of Zion": The Use of Zephaniah 3 in John 12*. Reformed Academic Dissertations. Phillipsburg, NJ: P&R, 2018.

Westermann, Claus. *The Gospel of John in the Light of the Old Testament*. Translated by Siegfried S. Schatzmann. Peabody, MA: Hendrickson, 1998.

Pauline Epistles and the Old Testament

Abasciano, Brian J. *Paul's Use of the Old Testament in Romans 9.1–9: An Intertextual and Theological Exegesis.* LNTS 301. New York: T&T Clark, 2005.

———. *Paul's Use of the Old Testament in Romans 9.10–18: An Intertextual and Theological Exegesis.* LNTS 317. New York: T&T Clark, 2011.

———. *Paul's Use of the Old Testament in Romans 9.19–24: An Intertextual and Theological Exegesis.* LNTS 429. New York: Bloomsbury T&T Clark, 2022.

Beale, G. K. "The Old Testament in Colossians: A Response to Paul Foster." *JSNT* 41 (2018): 261–74.

Beetham, Christopher A. *Echoes of Scripture in the Letter of Paul to the Colossians.* BibInt 96. Leiden: Brill, 2008; Atlanta: Society of Biblical Literature, 2008.

Belli, Filippo. *Argumentation and Use of Scripture in Romans 9–11.* AnBib 183. Rome: Gregorian & Biblical Press, 2010.

Ciampa, Roy E. *The Presence and Function of Scripture in Galatians 1 and 2.* WUNT 2/102. Tübingen: Mohr Siebeck, 1998.

Crisler, Channing L. "The 'I' Who Laments: Echoes of Old Testament Lament in Romans 7:7–25 and the Identity of the ἐγώ." *CBQ* 82 (2020): 64–83.

Das, A. Andrew. *Paul and the Stories of Israel: Grand Thematic Narratives in Galatians.* Minneapolis: Fortress, 2016.

Ellis, E. Earle. *Paul's Use of the Old Testament.* Edinburgh: Oliver & Boyd, 1957. Reprint, Grand Rapids: Baker, 1981. Reprint, Eugene, OR: Wipf & Stock, 2003.

Evans, Craig A., and James A. Sanders, eds. *Paul and the Scriptures of Israel.* JSNTSup 83, SSEJC 1. Sheffield: Sheffield Academic, 1993.

Gignilliat, Mark S. *Paul and Isaiah's Servants: Paul's Theological Reading of Isaiah 40–66 in 2 Corinthians 5:14–6:10.* LNTS 330. New York: T&T Clark, 2007.

Gladd, Benjamin L. *Revealing the* Mysterion: *The Use of* Mystery *in Daniel and Second Temple Judaism with Its Bearing on First Corinthians.* BZNW 160. Berlin: de Gruyter, 2008.

Hafemann, Scott J. *Paul, Moses, and the History of Israel: The Letter/Spirit Contrast and the Argument from Scripture in 2 Corinthians 3.* WUNT 81. Tübingen: Mohr Siebeck, 1995.

Harmon, Matthew S. "Allegory, Typology, or Something Else? Revisiting Galatians 4:21–5:1." In *Studies in the Pauline Epistles: Essays in Honor of Douglas J. Moo,* edited by Matthew S. Harmon and Jay E. Smith, 144–58. Grand Rapids: Zondervan, 2014.

———. *She Must and Shall Go Free: Paul's Isaianic Gospel in Galatians.* BZNW 168. New York: de Gruyter, 2010.

Hays, Richard B. *The Conversion of the Imagination: Paul as Interpreter of Israel's Scripture.* Grand Rapids: Eerdmans, 2005.

———. *Echoes of Scripture in the Letters of Paul.* New Haven, CT: Yale University Press, 1989.

Heil, John Paul. *The Rhetorical Role of Scripture in 1 Corinthians.* SBLStBL 15. Atlanta: SBL Press, 2005.

Keesmaat, Sylvia C. *Paul and His Story: (Re)Interpreting the Exodus Tradition.* JSNTSup 181. Sheffield: Sheffield Academic, 1999.

Kujanpää, Katja. *The Rhetorical Functions of Scriptural Quotations in Romans: Paul's Argumentation by Quotations.* NovTSup 172. Leiden: Brill, 2018.

Lim, Timothy H. *Holy Scripture in the Qumran Commentaries and Pauline Letters.* Oxford: Clarendon, 1997.

Lincicum, David. *Paul and the Early Jewish Encounter with Deuteronomy.* WUNT 2/284. Tübingen: Mohr Siebeck, 2010.

Litwak, Kenneth Duncan. "Echoes of Scripture? A Critical Survey of Recent Works on Paul's Use of the Old Testament." *Currents in Research: Biblical Studies* 6 (1998): 260–88.

McAuley, David. *Paul's Covert Use of Scripture: Intertextuality and Rhetorical Situation in Philippians 2:10–16.* Eugene, OR: Pickwick, 2015.

Moessner, David P., et al., eds. *Paul and the Heritage of Israel: Paul's Claim upon Israel's Legacy in Luke and Acts in the Light of the Pauline Letters.* Luke the Interpreter of Israel 2. New York: T&T Clark, 2012.

Morales, Rodrigo J. *The Spirit and the Restoration of Israel: New Exodus and New Creation Motifs in Galatians.* WUNT 2/282. Tübingen: Mohr Siebeck, 2010.

Moritz, Thorsten. *A Profound Mystery: The Use of the Old Testament in Ephesians.* NovTSup 85. Leiden: Brill, 1996.

Moyise, Steve. *Paul and Scripture: Studying the New Testament Use of the Old Testament.* Grand Rapids: Baker Academic, 2010.

Osborne, Grant R. "Hermeneutics and Paul: Psalm 68:18 in Ephesians 4:7–10 as a Test Case." In *Studies in the Pauline Epistles: Essays in Honor of Douglas J. Moo,* edited by Matthew S. Harmon and Jay E. Smith, 159–77. Grand Rapids: Zondervan, 2014.

Porter, Stanley E., and Christopher D. Stanley, eds. *As It Is Written: Studying Paul's Use of Scripture.* SymS 50. Atlanta: Society of Biblical Literature, 2008.

Rosner, Brian S. *Paul, Scripture, & Ethics: A Study of 1 Corinthians 5–7.* AGJU 22. Leiden: Brill, 1994. Reprint, Biblical Studies Library. Grand Rapids: Baker Academic, 1999.

Scott, Matthew. *The Hermeneutics of Christological Psalmody in Paul: An Intertextual Enquiry.* SNTSMS 158. New York: Cambridge University Press, 2014.

Shum, Shiu-Lun. *Paul's Use of Isaiah in Romans: A Comparative Study of Paul's Letter to the Romans and the Sibylline and Qumran Sectarian Texts.* WUNT 2/156. Tübingen: Mohr Siebeck, 2002.

Stanley, Christopher D. *Arguing with Scripture: The Rhetoric of Quotations in the Letters of Paul.* New York: T&T Clark, 2004.

————, ed. *Paul and Scripture: Extending the Conversation.* ECL 9. Atlanta: Society of Biblical Literature, 2012.

Steyn, Gert J. "Observations on the Text Form of the Minor Prophets Quotations in Romans 9–11." *JSNT* 38 (2015): 49–67.

Wagner, J. Ross. *Heralds of the Good News: Isaiah and Paul in Concert in the Letter to the Romans.* NovTSup 101. Leiden: Brill, 2003.

Waters, Guy P. *The End of Deuteronomy in the Epistles of Paul.* WUNT 2/221. Tübingen: Mohr Siebeck, 2006.

Watson, Francis. *Paul and the Hermeneutics of Faith.* 2nd ed. New York: Bloomsbury T&T Clark, 2016.

Hebrews and the Old Testament

Allen, David M. *Deuteronomy and Exhortation in Hebrews: A Study in Narrative Re-presentation.* WUNT 2/238. Tübingen: Mohr Siebeck, 2008.

Bateman, Herbert W. *Early Jewish Hermeneutics and Hebrews 1:5–13: The Impact of Early Jewish Exegesis on the Interpretation of a Significant New Testament Passage.* AUS 7/193. New York: Peter Lang, 1997.

Day, Adam W. "Bearing the Reproach of Christ: The Background of Psalm 68 (LXX) in Hebrews 13:9–16." *Presbyterion* 44 (2018): 126–41.

Docherty, Susan E. *The Use of the Old Testament in Hebrews: A Case Study in Early Jewish Bible Interpretation.* WUNT 2/260. Tübingen: Mohr Siebeck, 2009.

Gheorghita, Radu. *The Role of the Septuagint in Hebrews: An Investigation of Its Influence with Special Consideration to the Use of Hab. 2:3–4 in Heb. 10:37–38.* WUNT 2/160. Tübingen: Mohr Siebeck, 2003.

Gleason, Randall C. "The Old Testament Background of the Warning in Hebrews 6:4–8." *BSac* 155 (1998): 62–91.

Guthrie, George H. "Hebrews' Use of the Old Testament: Recent Trends in Research." *CurBR* 1 (2003): 271–94.

————. "Old Testament in Hebrews." *DLNT*, 841–50.

Human, Dirk J., and Gert Jacobus Steyn, eds. *Psalms and Hebrews: Studies in Reception.* LHB 527. New York: T&T Clark, 2010.

Moyise, Steve. *The Later New Testament Writings and Scripture: The Old Testament in Acts, Hebrews, the Catholic Epistles, and Revelation.* Grand Rapids: Baker Academic, 2012.

Ounsworth, Richard Joseph. *Joshua Typology in the New Testament.* WUNT 2/328. Tübingen: Mohr Siebeck, 2012.

Steyn, Gert Jacobus. *A Quest for the Assumed LXX Vorlage of the Explicit Quotations in the Hebrews.* Göttingen: Vandenhoeck & Ruprecht, 2011.

Walser, Georg A. *Old Testament Quotations in Hebrews: Studies in their Textual and Contextual Background.* WUNT 2/356. Tübingen: Mohr Siebeck, 2013.

General Epistles and the Old Testament

Charles, J. Daryl. "Old Testament in General Epistles." *DLNT*, 834–41.

Cheung, Luke L. *The Genre, Composition, and Hermeneutics of the Epistle of James.* Paternoster Biblical Monographs. Milton Keyes: Paternoster, 2003. Reprint, Eugene, OR: Wipf & Stock, 2006.

Langford, Justin. *Defending Hope: Semiotics and Intertextuality in 1 Peter.* Eugene, OR: Wipf & Stock, 2013.

Liebengood, Kelly D. *The Eschatology of 1 Peter: Considering the Influence of Zechariah 9–14.* SNTSMS 157. Cambridge: Cambridge University Press, 2013.

Mbuvi, Andrew M. *Temple, Exile and Identity in 1 Peter.* LNTS 345. New York: T&T Clark, 2007.

Morales, Nelson R. *Poor and Rich in James: A Relevance Theory Approach to James's Use of the Old Testament.* BBRSup 20. University Park: Eisenbrauns, 2018.

Moyise, Steve. *The Later New Testament Writings and Scripture: The Old Testament in Acts, Hebrews, the Catholic Epistles, and Revelation.* Grand Rapids: Baker Academic, 2012.

Sargent, Benjamin. *Written to Serve: The Use of Scripture in 1 Peter.* LNTS 547. New York: Bloomsbury T&T Clark, 2015.

Schutter, William L. *Hermeneutic and Composition in 1 Peter.* WUNT 2/30. Tübingen: Mohr Siebeck, 1989.

Revelation and the Old Testament

Beale, G. K. *John's Use of the Old Testament in Revelation.* JSNTSup 166. Sheffield: Sheffield Academic, 1998.

Fletcher, Michelle. *Reading Revelation as Pastiche: Imitating the Past.* LNTS 571. New York: Bloomsbury T&T Clark, 2017.

Gallusz, Laszlo. "The Exodus Motif in Revelation 15–16: Its Background and Nature." *AUSS* 46 (2008): 21–43.

———. *The Throne Motif in the Book of Revelation: Profiles from the History of Interpretation.* LNTS 487. New York: Bloomsbury T&T Clark, 2014.

Jauhiainen, Marko. *The Use of Zechariah in Revelation.* WUNT 2/199. Tübingen: Mohr Siebeck, 2005.

Johns, Loren L. *The Lamb Christology of the Apocalypse of John: An Investigtion into Its Origins and Rhetorical Force.* WUNT 2/167. Tübingen: Mohr Siebeck, 2003.

Mathewson, David. *A New Heaven and a New Earth: The Meaning and Function of the Old Testament in Revelation 21.1–22.5.* JSNTSup 238. Sheffield: Sheffield Academic, 2003.

Michaels, J. Ramsey. "Old Testament in Revelation." *DLNT*, 850–55.

Moyise, Steve. "The Language of the Psalms in the Book of Revelation." *Neot* 37 (2003): 246–61.

———. *The Later New Testament Writings and Scripture: The Old Testament in Acts, Hebrews, the Catholic Epistles, and Revelation.* Grand Rapids: Baker Academic, 2012.

———. *The Old Testament in the Book of Revelation.* JSNTSup 115. Sheffield: Sheffield Academic, 1995.

Tõniste, Külli. *The Ending of the Canon: A Canonical and Intertextual Reading of Revelation 21–22.* LNTS 526. New York: Bloomsbury T&T Clark, 2016.

Applying the New Taxonomy of Forms to the UBS[5] and NA[28] Indexes of Old Testament Citations and Allusions for Luke and Acts

As an exercise in applying the recommended taxonomy of forms for the NT use of the OT, I have classified the references to the OT found in the Gospel of Luke and the book of Acts utilizing the UBS[5] and the NA[28] indexes. The indexes in these two most common editions of the Greek NT are some of the most readily available resources for identifying where the OT is referenced in the NT.[1] In addition to identifying citations and allusions at the bottom of each page (UBS[5]) or in the margins of each page (NA[28]), both critical editions of the Greek NT provide an index of the OT passages they identify. The "Index of Quotations" in UBS[5] is brief enough for the listings to be provided in both the order of the OT books (857–60) and again in the order of the NT books (860–63). The "Index of Allusions and Verbal Parallels" in UBS[5], however, is lengthier (864–83) and lists the items only in the order of the OT books. The "Loci Citati vel Allegati" ("Places Cited or Alluded to") in the

---

1. Barbara Aland, Kurt Aland, Johannes Karavidopoulos, Carlo M. Martini, and Bruce M. Metzger, eds., *The Greek New Testament*, 5th rev. ed. (Stuttgart: Deutsche Bibelgesellschaft/American Bible Society/United Bible Societies, 2014) [UBS[5]]; and Eberhard Nestle, Erwin Nestle, Barbara Aland, Kurt Aland, Johannes Karavidopoulos, Carlo M. Martini, and Bruce M. Metzger, eds., *Novum Testamentum Graece*, 28th rev. ed. (Stuttgart: Deutsche Bibelgesellschaft, 2012) [NA[28]]. See also the resources for identifying OT citations in the NT listed in app. B.

NA[28] (836–78) is a single mixed listing of citations and allusions together in the order of the OT books.[2]

The mixed index of citations and allusions provided here lists all the items of the UBS[5] and NA[28] indexes together, with some additions of my own, in the order of Luke-Acts references. In addition to comparing the classifications in the UBS[5] and NA[28] indexes, this listing offers a more precise form classification for each instance in accordance with the two-dimensional continuum suggested in this book. For simplicity, number-and-two-letter abbreviations are utilized to identify the citations and allusions in the eight types of form classifications according to the definitions presented in chapter 2.

Citations

1. Introduced quotations (1-IQ) largely retain the wording of the source text and are introduced by the NT author as citations of a prior text.
2. Introduced paraphrases (2-IP) are presented by the NT author as citations of a prior text, but reformulate the source text by means of synonym substitutions, changes to case endings, altered word order, or other adjustments.
3. Unintroduced quotations (3-UQ) largely retain the wording of their source texts but lack any introductory formulas identifying the citations as coming from a prior author; the NT author simply quotes the prior text directly as part of his own text.
4. Unintroduced paraphrases (4-UP) are places where a source text is clearly utilized in a reformulated way by means of synonym substitutions, changes to case endings, altered word order, or other adjustments but lack any introductory formulas identifying the citations as coming from a prior author.

Allusions and Recollections

5. Scripture summaries (5-SS) recollect the teachings of prior texts with limited use of similar language but with some kind of introductory statement.
6. Historical reminiscences (6-HR) recollect people and/or events recorded in prior texts with a very limited use of similar language but with some kind of introductory statement.

2. Both UBS[5] and NA[28] include select extrabiblical references. Some of the parallels suggested by NA[28] are to books likely written after the NT (e.g., 2 Esdras). In such cases, a thematic echo in the NT would not be *to* 2 Esdras but taken up *by* 2 Esdras.

7. Specific allusions (7-SA) involve intentional references to specific OT passages by means of borrowed phrases or similar wording but without any introduction.

8. Thematic echoes (8-TE) are allusions using themes or ideas or structures that occur in multiple prior texts.

While perhaps close to exhaustive with regard to citations, this list can only claim to be extensive with regard to allusions and recollections in Luke-Acts. For the most part, reading the chart is self-explanatory, but a few instructive comments are nonetheless in order. First, when the Septuagint differs from English Bible versification, the Septuagint versification is indicated in brackets (see, e.g., the allusion at Luke 1:17). Second, I use the abbreviation LXX to indicate that the citation or allusion follows the Septuagint reading (see, e.g., the citation at Luke 4:18–19). Third, "LXX (vs. MT)" indicates that the citation favors the LXX reading over against a simple Greek translation of the MT text (see, e.g., the citations at Luke 4:10 and 4:11). Fourth, for passages missing from a particular list (i.e., that of UBS⁵, the NA²⁸, or my own), the "Form Classification" column contains a dash (—). Fifth, while there are a few places where I recognize references to the OT not listed by either the UBS⁵ or the NA²⁸ (e.g., note the several places in Acts 9 where dashes appear in both the UBS⁵ and the NA²⁸ columns), for the most part I have refrained from adding Scripture references to places where one or the other of the critical texts recognizes at least one. For example, at Luke 1:11 an allusion to Judg. 6:12 is recognized by the NA²⁸, and to save space I have refrained from adding other plausible references that are not cited by either critical text, such as Exod. 3:2; Judg. 13:3; Tob. 12:22. Sixth and finally, the chart uses shaded lines to indicate where the UBS⁵ and the NA²⁸ differ in their OT reference identifications and form classifications but where I group these passages together into one form classification. For example, at Luke 1:15, what the critical texts variously recognize as allusions and citations, I cluster together as a thematic echo.

Luke				
Luke Text	**OT and Extrabiblical References**	**Form Classification**		
		UBS⁵	**NA²⁸**	**Huffman**
1:5	1 Chron. 24:10	Allusion	Allusion	6-HR
1:5	2 Chron. 8:14; Neh. 12:4, 17	—	Allusion	6-HR
1:5	Exod. 6:23 LXX	—	Allusion	8-TE
1:6	Gen. 26:5; Deut. 4:40; Ezek. 36:27	—	Allusion	8-TE
1:7	Gen. 11:30; 18:11; 25:21; 29:31; Judg. 13:2–3; 1 Sam. 1:2	—	Allusion	8-TE

Luke Text	OT and Extrabiblical References	Form Classification		
		UBS[5]	NA[28]	Huffman
1:9	Exod. 30:7–8	Allusion	Allusion	7-SA
1:10	Dan. 9:21	—	Allusion	7-SA
1:11	Judg. 6:12	—	Allusion	8-TE
1:13	Dan. 10:12	—	Allusion	8-TE
1:13	Gen. 16:11; 17:19; Judg. 13:6–7; Isa. 7:14	—	Allusion	8-TE
1:15	Lev. 10:9	—	Citation	
1:15	Num. 6:3	Allusion	Citation	8-TE
1:15	Judg. 13:4–5, 7, 14; 1 Sam. 1:11 LXX	Allusion	Allusion	
1:15	Isa. 49:1; Sir. 49:7	—	Allusion	8-TE
1:17	Mal. 3:1; 4:5–6 [3:22–23]; Sir. 48:10	Allusion	Allusion	7-SA
1:18	Gen. 18:11	Allusion	Allusion	8-TE
1:18	Gen. 15:8; 17:17; 2 Kings 20:8	—	Allusion	
1:19	Dan. 8:16; 9:21	Allusion	Allusion	7-SA
1:19	Tob. 12:15	—	Allusion	
1:22	Dan. 10:7	—	Allusion	7-SA
1:25	Gen. 30:23	Allusion	Allusion	7-SA
1:27	Isa. 7:14	—	Allusion	—
1:28	Judg. 6:12	—	Allusion	7-SA
1:30	Gen. 6:8; Exod. 33:16; Prov. 12:2	—	Allusion	8-TE
1:31	Gen. 16:11; Judg. 13:3; Isa. 7:14	Allusion	Allusion	8-TE
1:31	Gen. 17:19; Judg. 13:5	—	Allusion	
1:31	Isa. 7:14	Allusion	Allusion	7-SA
1:32	Isa. 9:6	—	Allusion	
1:32–33	Isa. 9:7	Allusion	—	8-TE
1:32–33	2 Sam. 7:12–13, 16	Allusion	Allusion	
1:33	Dan. 7:14; Mic. 4:7	Allusion	Allusion	
1:35	Isa. 4:3	—	Allusion	7-SA
1:37	Gen. 18:14	Allusion	—	7-SA
1:38	Gen. 21:1; 30:34; 1 Sam. 25:41; 2 Sam. 9:6	—	Allusion	8-TE
1:41	Gen. 25:22 LXX	Allusion	Allusion	7-SA
1:42	Deut. 28:4; Judg. 5:24	Allusion	Allusion	8-TE
1:42	Jdt. 13:18; 2 Bar. 54.10	—	Allusion	
1:43	2 Sam. 24:21	—	Allusion	7-SA
1:46–55	1 Sam. 2:1–10	Allusion	Allusion	7-SA
1:46	Ps. 34:2–3 [33:2–3]	—	Allusion	8-TE
1:47	Ps. 35:9 [34:9]; Isa. 17:10; 61:10; Hab. 2:18	—	Allusion	8-TE
1:48	1 Sam. 1:11; 9:16	Allusion	Allusion	8-TE
1:48	Gen. 29:32	—	Allusion	

Luke Text	OT and Extrabiblical References	Form Classification UBS⁵	NA²⁸	Huffman
1:48	Gen. 30:13; Ps. 72:17 [71:17] LXX; Mal. 3:12	—	Allusion	8-TE
1:49	Deut. 10:21; Pss. 44:3, 5 [43:4, 6]; 71:19 [70:19]	—	Allusion	8-TE
1:49	Ps. 111:9 [110:9]	Allusion	Allusion	8-TE
1:50	Pss. 89:1 [88:2]; 100:5 [99:5]	—	Allusion	
1:50	Ps. 103:13 [102:13]	Allusion	—	8-TE
1:50	Ps. 103:17 [102:17]	Allusion	Allusion	
1:51	Num. 10:35 [10:34]; Pss. 68:1 [67:2] LXX; 118:15–16 [117:15–16] LXX; Prov. 3:34 LXX; Isa. 51:9	—	Allusion	
1:51	2 Sam. 22:28	Allusion	—	8-TE
1:51	Ps. 89:10 [88:11] LXX; Isa. 40:10	Allusion	Allusion	
1:52	Job 5:11; 12:17–19	Allusion	Allusion	
1:52	Prov. 3:34 LXX; Ezek. 21:26 [21:31]; Sir. 10:14	—	Allusion	8-TE
1:53	1 Sam. 2:5	Allusion	—	
1:53	Job 22:9	—	Allusion	8-TE
1:53	Ps. 107:9 [106:9]	Allusion	Allusion	
1:54	Isa. 41:8–10	Allusion	Allusion	8-TE
1:54	Ps. 98:3 [97:3]	Allusion	Allusion	8-TE
1:55	Gen. 17:7; Mic. 7:20	Allusion	Allusion	
1:55	Gen. 22:17	Allusion	—	6-HR
1:55	2 Sam. 22:51	—	Allusion	
1:57	Gen. 25:24	—	Allusion	7-SA
1:58	Gen. 19:19; Ps. 126:2–3 [125:2–3] LXX	—	Allusion	8-TE
1:59	Gen. 17:12; Lev. 12:3	Allusion	Allusion	8-TE
1:64	Dan. 10:16	—	Allusion	7-SA
1:68	1 Kings 1:48	—	Allusion	
1:68	Pss. 41:13 [40:14]; 72:18 [71:18]; 106:48 [105:48]	Allusion	Allusion	8-TE
1:68	Exod. 4:31; Ruth 1:6	—	Allusion	
1:68	Ps. 111:9 [110:9]	Allusion	—	8-TE
1:69	Ps. 18:2 [17:3]	Allusion	Allusion	
1:69	1 Sam. 2:1, 10; 2 Sam. 22:3; Ps. 132:17 [131:17]; Ezek. 29:21	—	Allusion	5-SS
1:71	2 Sam. 22:18; Ps. 18:17 [17:18]	—	Allusion	
1:71	Ps. 106:10 [105:10]	Allusion	Allusion	8-TE
1:72	Gen. 17:7; Lev. 26:42	Allusion	Allusion	
1:72	Exod. 2:24	—	Allusion	
1:72	Pss. 105:8–9 [104:8–9]; 106:45–46 [105:45–46]	Allusion	—	8-TE
1:73	Gen. 26:3; Jer. 11:5	—	Allusion	
1:73–74	Gen. 22:16–17	Allusion	—	
1:74	Ps. 97:10 [96:10]; Mic. 4:10	—	Allusion	8-TE

Luke		Form Classification		
Text	OT and Extrabiblical References	UBS[5]	NA[28]	Huffman
1:74	Josh. 24:14	—	Allusion	8-TE
1:75	Wis. 9:3	—	Allusion	8-TE
1:76	Isa. 40:3; Mal. 3:1	Allusion	Allusion	7-SA
1:78	Jer.23:5 LXX; Zech. 3:8 LXX; 6:12 LXX; T. Zeb. 7.3; 8.2; T. Naph. 4.5	—	Allusion	8-TE
1:78	Mal. 4:2 [3:20]	Allusion	—	8-TE
1:78	Isa. 60:1–2	Allusion	Allusion	8-TE
1:78–79	Isa. 9:2 [9:1]; 58:8	Allusion	Allusion	8-TE
1:79	Ps. 107:10, 14 [106:10, 14]; Isa. 42:7; 59:8	—	Allusion	8-TE
1:80	Judg. 13:24–25	—	Allusion	7-SA
2:6	Gen. 25:24	—	—	7-SA
2:7	Ezek. 16:4; Wis. 7:4	—	—	8-TE
2:8	1 Sam. 16:11, 19; 17:15, 28, 34; Ps. 78:70–72 [77:70–72]	—	Allusion	8-TE
2:11	Mic. 5:1	—	Allusion	—
2:12	1 Sam. 10:1 LXX; Isa. 38:7	—	Allusion	8-TE
2:13	1 Kings 22:19	—	Allusion	8-TE
2:14	Pss. 51:18 [50:20]; 89:17 [88:18] LXX; Isa. 9:5–6; 57:19; Mic. 5:4	—	Allusion	8-TE
2:19	Gen. 37:11; Dan. 7:28	—	Allusion	8-TE
2:21	Gen. 17:12; Lev. 12:3	Allusion	—	8-TE
2:22	Exod. 13:12; 22:28–29	—	Allusion	
2:22	Lev. 12:3	Allusion	—	5-SS
2:22	Lev. 12:6	Allusion	Allusion	
2:23	Exod. 13:2, 15	Citation	Citation	2-IP
2:23	Exod. 13:12	Citation	—	2-IP
2:24	Lev. 12:8 LXX	Citation	Citation	2-IP
2:25	Isa. 40:1	Allusion	Allusion	8-TE
2:25	Isa. 49:1; 61:2	—	Allusion	8-TE
2:26	Ps. 89:48 [88:49]	—	Allusion	7-SA
2:26	Lam. 4:20 LXX; Pss. Sol. 17.32; 18.5	—	Allusion	8-TE
2:27	Lev. 12:6–8; Exod. 13:2, 11–16	—	—	5-SS
2:29	Gen. 15:15; 46:30; Tob. 11:9	—	Allusion	8-TE
2:29	Dan. 3:37; 8:16–17; 2 Macc. 15:22	—	Allusion	8-TE
2:30	Job 19:27; 42:5; Isa. 52:10	—	Allusion	8-TE
2:30–31	Isa. 40:5 LXX	Allusion	Allusion	8-TE
2:32	Isa. 42:6; 49:6	Allusion	Allusion	8-TE
2:32	Isa. 46:13	Allusion	Allusion	8-TE
2:34	Isa. 8:14	Allusion	—	7-SA
2:34	Isa. 8:18	—	Allusion	7-SA

Luke Text	OT and Extrabiblical References	UBS⁵	NA²⁸	Huffman
2:37	Jdt. 8:6	—	Allusion	7-SA
2:38	Isa. 52:9	Allusion	Allusion	8-TE
2:39	Lev. 12:6–8; Exod. 13:2, 11–16	—	—	5-SS
2:40	1 Sam. 3:19	—	Allusion	7-SA
2:41	Exod. 12:24–27; Deut. 16:1–8	Allusion	Allusion	8-TE
2:41	Exod. 23:14–17; Deut. 16:16	—	Allusion	
2:43	Exod. 12:15, 18	—	Allusion	8-TE
2:51	Gen. 37:11; Dan. 7:28	—	—	8-TE
2:52	Judg. 13:24; Prov. 3:3	—	Allusion	8-TE
2:52	1 Sam. 2:26; Prov. 3:4	Allusion	Allusion	
3:2	1 Sam. 15:10; Jer. 1:1–2; Ezek. 1:3; Hosea 1:1	—	Allusion	8-TE
3:4–6	Isa. 40:3–5 LXX (vs. MT)	Citation	Citation	2-IP
3:6	Pss. 67:2 [66:3]; 98:3 [97:3]	—	Allusion	8-TE
3:11	Job 31:16–20; Isa. 58:7; Ezek. 18:7; Tob. 1:17; 4:16	—	Allusion	8-TE
3:21	Ezek. 1:1	—	—	7-SA
3:22	Isa. 11:2	—	Allusion	8-TE
3:22	Ps. 2:7	—	Allusion	7-SA
3:22	Gen. 22:2	Allusion	Allusion	7-SA
3:22	Isa. 42:1	—	Allusion	7-SA
3:23	Gen. 41:46; 2 Sam. 5:4; Ezek. 1:1	—	Allusion	8-TE
3:27	1 Chron. 3:17	Allusion	—	
3:27	Ezra 3:2	Allusion	Allusion	
3:27	1 Chron. 3:19; Ezra 5:2	—	Allusion	
3:31	2 Sam. 5:14	Allusion	Allusion	
3:31	1 Chron. 3:5; 14:4	—	Allusion	
3:31–32	1 Sam. 16:1, 13	Allusion	Allusion	
3:31–33	Ruth 4:17–22; 2 Chron. 2:1–14	Allusion	Allusion	
3:32	Ruth 4:18–22; 2 Chron. 2:15	—	Allusion	
3:33	Gen. 29:35	Allusion	Allusion	6-HR
3:33	Gen. 38:29; Ruth 4:12	—	Allusion	
3:34	Gen. 21:2	—	Allusion	
3:34	Gen. 21:3; 25:26	Allusion	Allusion	
3:34	1 Chron. 1:28, 34	Allusion	—	
3:34–36	Gen. 11:10–26	Allusion	Allusion	
3:34–36	1 Chron. 1:24–27	Allusion	—	
3:36–38	Gen. 4:25–5:32; 1 Chron. 1:1–4	Allusion	Allusion	
3:38	Gen. 2:7	—	Allusion	

Luke Text	OT and Extrabiblical References	Form Classification UBS[5]	NA[28]	Huffman
4:1	Deut. 8:2	—	Allusion	8-TE
4:2	Exod. 24:18; 34:28; Deut. 9:9; 1 Kings 19:8	—	Allusion	
4:4	Deut. 8:3 LXX (vs. MT)	Citation	Citation	1-IQ
4:8	Deut. 6:13 LXX; 10:20 LXX	Citation	Citation	2-IP
4:9	Ezek. 8:3	—	Allusion	8-TE
4:10	Ps. 91:11 [90:11] LXX (vs. MT)	Citation	Citation	1-IQ
4:11	Ps. 91:12 [90:12] LXX (vs. MT)	Citation	Citation	1-IQ
4:12	Deut. 6:16 LXX (vs. MT)	Citation	Citation	1-IQ
4:12	Isa. 7:12	—	Allusion	8-TE
4:18–19	Isa. 61:1–2 LXX	Citation	Citation	1-IQ
4:18–19	Isa. 58:6 LXX	Allusion	Citation	7-SA
4:19	Lev. 25:10	—	Allusion	8-TE
4:22	Deut. 8:3	—	Allusion	7-SA
4:25	1 Kings 17:1; 18:1	Allusion	Allusion	
4:25	1 Kings 17:7	Allusion	—	6-HR
4:26	1 Kings 17:9	Allusion	Allusion	
4:27	2 Kings 5:1–13	Allusion	—	6-HR
4:27	2 Kings 5:14	Allusion	Allusion	
4:34	Judg. 16:17 LXX; 1 Kings 17:18	—	Allusion	8-TE
4:34	Ps. 106:16 [105:16]	—	Allusion	7-SA
5:10	Jer. 16:16	—	Allusion	7-SA
5:11	1 Kings 19:19–21	—	Allusion	7-SA
5:14	Lev. 13:19	—	Allusion	5-SS
5:14	Lev. 14:2–32	Allusion	Allusion	
5:21	Isa. 43:25	Allusion	Allusion	8-TE
5:21	Isa. 44:22; 55:7	—	Allusion	
5:24	Dan. 7:13–14	—	—	7-SA
5:29	Gen. 21:8	—	Allusion	8-TE
5:35	Isa. 53:8; Amos 8:11; 9:13	—	Allusion	8-TE
5:37	Job 32:19	—	Allusion	7-SA
5:39	Sir. 9:10	—	Allusion	7-SA
6:1	Deut. 23:25	Allusion	—	7-SA
6:1	Deut. 23:26	—	Allusion	
6:2	Exod. 34:21	—	Allusion	8-TE
6:3–4	1 Sam. 21:1–6	Allusion	—	6-HR
6:4	1 Sam. 21:7	—	Allusion	
6:4	Lev. 24:5–9	Allusion	Allusion	7-SA
6:5	Dan. 7:13–14; cf. Luke 5:24	—	—	7-SA

Luke Text	OT and Extrabiblical References	Form Classification		
		UBS[5]	NA[28]	Huffman
6:12	Exod. 19:3; 24:1–3, 12–18; 34:2	—	Allusion	8-TE
6:20	Isa. 61:1	—	Allusion	8-TE
6:21	Ps. 126:5–6 [125:5–6]; Isa. 61:3	Allusion	Allusion	
6:21	Jer. 31:25	Allusion	—	8-TE
6:21	Isa. 61:2; 65:18–19	—	Allusion	
6:22	Dan. 7:13–14; cf. Luke 5:24	—	—	7-SA
6:23	2 Chron. 36:16	Allusion	—	6-HR
6:23	Neh. 9:26; Jer. 2:30	—	Allusion	6-HR
6:25	Isa. 65:13	—	Allusion	8-TE
6:26	Isa. 30:10–11; Jer. 5:31; Mic. 2:11	—	Allusion	6-HR
6:27	Exod. 23:4–5; Prov. 25:21	—	Allusion	8-TE
6:29	Isa. 50:6; Lam. 3:30	—	Allusion	8-TE
6:35	Lev. 25:35–36	Allusion	Allusion	8-TE
6:35	Pss. 25:8 [24:8]; 86:5 [85:5]; Sir. 4:10; Wis. 15:1–2; Pss. Sol. 17.30	—	Allusion	8-TE
6:36	Lev. 19:2	—	Allusion	7-SA
6:38	2 Sam. 12:8; Ps. 79:12 [78:12]; Isa. 65:7	—	Allusion	8-TE
6:46	Mal. 1:6	Allusion	Allusion	7-SA
6:49	Isa. 28:17–19; Ezek. 13:10–15	—	Allusion	8-TE
7:11	1 Kings 17:9–10	—	Allusion	7-SA
7:12	1 Kings 17:17	Allusion	Allusion	7-SA
7:12	1 Kings 17:17–24; 2 Kings 4:32–37	—	Allusion	7-SA
7:15	1 Kings 17:23; 2 Kings 4:36	Allusion	—	7-SA
7:18	Deut. 19:15	—	Allusion	8-TE
7:19	Mal. 3:1	Allusion	Allusion	8-TE
7:19	Ps. 40:7 [39:8]	Allusion	—	8-TE
7:19	Zech. 14:5	—	Allusion	
7:22	Isa. 29:18–19; 42:7, 18	—	Allusion	8-TE
7:22	Isa. 35:5	Allusion	Allusion	8-TE
7:22	Isa. 35:6	Allusion	Allusion	7-SA
7:22	Isa. 26:19	—	Allusion	7-SA
7:22	Isa. 61:1	Allusion	Allusion	7-SA
7:24	1 Kings 14:15 LXX	—	Allusion	7-SA
7:27	Mal. 3:1	Citation	Allusion	2-IP
7:27	Exod. 23:20	Allusion	Citation	7-SA
7:28	Job 14:1; 15:14; 25:4	—	Allusion	8-TE
7:30	Ps. 33:11 [32:11]	—	Allusion	8-TE
7:34	Dan. 7:13–14; cf. Luke 5:24	—	—	7-SA

Luke Text	OT and Extrabiblical References	Form Classification UBS⁵	NA²⁸	Huffman
7:34	Deut. 21:20; Prov. 23:19–20	—	Allusion	8-TE
7:35	Prov. 8:32–33; Sir. 4:11	—	Allusion	8-TE
7:44	Gen. 18:4	Allusion	Allusion	8-TE
7:46	Ps. 23:5 [22:5]	Allusion	Allusion	8-TE
8:5	2 Esd. 8:41; 9:31–33	—	Allusion	8-TE
8:6	Jer. 17:8; Sir. 40:15	—	Allusion	8-TE
8:7	Jer. 4:3	—	Allusion	8-TE
8:8	Gen. 14:35; 26:12	—	Allusion	7-SA
8:10	Isa. 6:9 LXX (vs. MT)	Citation	Allusion	2-IP
8:11	2 Esd. 9:31–33	—	Allusion	8-TE
8:18	Prov. 1:5; 9:9	—	Allusion	8-TE
8:24	Pss. 65:7 [64:8]; 89:9 [88:10]; Nah. 1:4; 2 Macc. 9:8; T. Naph. 6	—	Allusion	8-TE
8:28	Judg. 11:12; 2 Sam. 16:10; 19:23; 1 Kings 17:18; 2 Kings 3:13; 2 Chron. 35:21; 1 Esd. 1:24	—	—	8-TE
8:28	Gen. 14:18	—	Allusion	8-TE
8:32	Lev. 11:7–8; Deut. 14:8	—	Allusion	8-TE
8:35	Deut. 33:3; 2 Kings 4:38	—	—	8-TE
8:44	Num. 15:38–39	—	Allusion	8-TE
8:55	1 Kings 17:22	—	Allusion	7-SA
9:8	Sir. 48:10	—	Allusion	7-SA
9:13	Num. 11:21–22; 2 Kings 4:42, 43	—	Allusion	7-SA
9:16	Ps. 123:2 [122:2]	—	Allusion	7-SA
9:17	2 Kings 4:44	Allusion	Allusion	7-SA
9:22	Dan. 7:13–14; cf. Luke 5:24	—	—	7-SA
9:22	Ps. 118:22 [117:22]	—	—	7-SA
9:22	Hosea 6:2	—	Allusion	7-SA
9:24	Gen. 19:17; 1 Sam. 19:11	—	Allusion	8-TE
9:26	Dan. 7:13–14; cf. Luke 5:24	—	—	7-SA
9:28	Lev. 23:36	—	—	7-SA
9:28	Exod. 24:1	—	Allusion	8-TE
9:29	Exod. 34:29–30, 35	—	Allusion	7-SA
9:31	Exod. 19:1; Num. 33:38; 1 Kings 6:1; Pss. 105:38 [104:38]; 114:1 [113:1]	—	—	8-TE
9:33	Lev. 23:33–43	—	—	7-SA
9:34	Exod. 16:10; 24:15–18	—	Allusion	7-SA
9:35	Isa. 42:1	Allusion	Allusion	
9:35	Ps. 2:7	Allusion	—	8-TE
9:35	Pss. 89:19 [88:20]; 106:23 [105:23]	—	Allusion	

Luke		Form Classification		
Text	OT and Extrabiblical References	UBS⁵	NA²⁸	Huffman
9:35	Deut. 18:15	—	Allusion	7-SA
9:41	Num. 14:27; Deut. 32:4, 20; Isa. 65:2	—	Allusion	8-TE
9:44	1 Sam. 21:12 [21:13]; Jer. 12:11	—	Allusion	8-TE
9:44	Dan. 7:13–14; cf. Luke 5:24	—	—	7-SA
9:49	Num. 11:28	—	Allusion	7-SA
9:51	Ezek. 21:2 [21:7]	—	—	7-SA
9:54	2 Kings 1:10, 12	Allusion	Citation	7-SA
9:58	Dan. 7:13–14; cf. Luke 5:24	—	—	7-SA
9:59	Tob. 4:3; 6:15	—	Allusion	8-TE
9:60	Jer. 16:5–7; Ezek. 24:15–24	—	Allusion	8-TE
9:61	1 Kings 19:20	Allusion	Allusion	7-SA
9:62	Gen. 19:17, 26	—	—	7-SA
10:1	Gen. 10; Exod. 24:1; Num. 11:16	—	Allusion	8-TE
10:1	Exod. 32:34; 33:2	—	Allusion	8-TE
10:2	Isa. 27:12	—	Allusion	7-SA
10:3	Sir. 13:15–17	—	Allusion	8-TE
10:4	2 Kings 4:29	Allusion	Allusion	7-SA
10:5	1 Sam. 25:5–6	—	Allusion	7-SA
10:7	Num. 18:31	—	—	7-SA
10:12	Gen. 19:4–9	—	Allusion	7-SA
10:12	Gen. 19:24–25	Allusion	—	
10:13	Esther 4:3; Job 2:8; Isa. 58:8; Dan. 9:3; Jon. 3:5–6	—	Allusion	8-TE
10:13–14	Isa. 23; Ezek. 26–27; Joel 3:4–8 [4:4–8]; Amos 1:9–10; Zech. 9:2–4	Allusion	—	8-TE
10:14	Ezek. 28:1–23	Allusion	Allusion	
10:14	Ezek. 26:20	—	Allusion	
10:15	Isa. 14:13, 15	Allusion	Allusion	7-SA
10:15	Isa. 14:14	—	Allusion	
10:18	Isa. 14:12	Allusion	Allusion	7-SA
10:19	Gen. 3:15	Allusion	—	
10:19	Ps. 91:13 [90:13]	Allusion	Allusion	8-TE
10:19	Deut. 8:15	—	Allusion	
10:20	Exod. 32:32	Allusion	Allusion	8-TE
10:21	Ps. 136:26 [135:26]; Tob. 7:17; Sir. 51:1	—	Allusion	8-TE
10:21	Isa. 29:14; 44:25	—	Allusion	8-TE
10:22	Dan. 7:14	—	Allusion	7-SA
10:27	Deut. 6:5 LXX	Citation	Citation	2-IP
10:27	Deut. 10:12 LXX	Allusion	Allusion	

Luke		Form Classification		
Text	OT and Extrabiblical References	UBS[5]	NA[28]	Huffman
10:27	Lev. 19:18 LXX	Citation	Citation	1-IQ
10:27	Josh. 22:5	Allusion	Allusion	8-TE
10:27	Jub. 36.7–8; T. Iss. 5.2; 7.6; T. Ben. 3.3	—	Allusion	
10:28	Lev. 18:5	Allusion	Allusion	8-TE
10:28	Deut. 4:1; 8:1; Neh. 9:29; Ezek. 20:11, 21	—	Allusion	
10:29	Lev. 19:16, 33–34; Deut. 10:19	—	Allusion	8-TE
10:34	2 Chron. 28:15; Isa. 1:6	—	Allusion	8-TE
10:39	Deut. 33:3; 2 Kings 4:38	—	—	8-TE
10:41	Ps. 55:22 [54:23] LXX	—	Allusion	8-TE
10:42	Pss. 16:5–6 [15:5–6]; 73:26 [72:26]; 119:57 [118:57]	—	Allusion	8-TE
11:2	Isa. 63:16; 64:7	—	Allusion	8-TE
11:2	Isa. 5:16; Ezek. 20:41; Zech. 14:9	—	Allusion	8-TE
11:3	Exod. 16:4–5	—	Allusion	7-SA
11:4	Sir. 28:2	—	Allusion	8-TE
11:20	Exod. 8:19 [8:15]	Allusion	Allusion	8-TE
11:21–22	Pss. Sol. 5.4	Allusion	—	8-TE
11:22	Isa. 49:24–25; 53:12	—	Allusion	
11:23	Isa. 40:11	—	Allusion	—
11:29–30	Jon. 1:17	—	—	6-HR
11:30	Dan. 7:13–14; cf. Luke 5:24	—	—	7-SA
11:31	1 Kings 10:1–10	Allusion	Allusion	6-HR
11:31	2 Chron. 9:1–12	Allusion	—	
11:32	Jon. 3:1–10	Allusion	Allusion	6-HR
11:42	Lev. 27:30	Allusion	Allusion	8-TE
11:42	Deut. 14:22	—	Allusion	
11:42	Eccles. 7:18	—	Allusion	7-SA
11:44	Num. 19:16	—	Allusion	7-SA
11:49	Jer. 7:25–26	—	Allusion	5-SS
11:51	Gen. 4:8; 2 Chron. 24:20–21	Allusion	Allusion	6-HR
11:51	Gen. 4:10; 2 Chron. 24:22; Zech. 1:1	—	Allusion	
12:2	Eccles. 12:14	—	Allusion	7-SA
12:4	Isa. 8:12–13; 4 Macc. 13:14	—	Allusion	8-TE
12:5	Ps. 119:120 [118:120]	—	Allusion	
12:7	1 Sam. 14:25; 2 Sam. 14:11; 1 Kings 1:52	—	Allusion	8-TE
12:8–10	Dan. 7:13–14; cf. Luke 5:24	—	—	7-SA
12:14	Exod. 2:14	Allusion	Allusion	7-SA
12:15	T. Naph. 3.1	—	Allusion	8-TE

Luke Text	OT and Extrabiblical References	Form Classification		
		UBS⁵	NA²⁸	Huffman
12:19	Eccles. 8:15; Tob. 7:10; 1 En. 97.8–10	—	Allusion	8-TE
12:19–20	Sir. 11:19	Allusion	Allusion	
12:20	Ps. 39:6 [38:7]; Jer. 17:11; Wis. 15:8	—	Allusion	8-TE
12:21	Ps. 49:16–20 [48:17–21]	—	Allusion	7-SA
12:24	Job 38:41	—	Allusion	8-TE
12:24	Ps. 147:9 [146:9]	Allusion	Allusion	
12:27	1 Kings 10:4–7; 2 Chron. 9:3–6	Allusion	Allusion	6-HR
12:28	Pss. 37:2 [36:2]; 90:5–6 [89:5–6]; 102:11 [101:12]; Isa. 40:6–7	—	Allusion	8-TE
12:32	Isa. 41:14	—	Allusion	8-TE
12:32	Dan. 7:18, 27	—	Allusion	7-SA
12:33	Tob. 4:8–10; Sir. 29:10–12	—	Allusion	8-TE
12:35	Exod. 12:11	Allusion	Citation	
12:35	1 Kings 18:46;	Allusion	Allusion	8-TE
12:35	2 Kings 4:29; 9:1; Job 38:3; 40:7; Prov. 31:17; Jer. 1:17	Allusion	—	
12:40	Dan. 7:13–14; cf. Luke 5:24	—	—	7-SA
12:49	Jer. 5:14; 23:29; Amos 5:6; Mal. 3:2–3; Sir. 48:1	—	Allusion	8-TE
12:53	Mic. 7:6	Allusion	Citation	7-SA
12:53	Zech. 13:3	—	Allusion	—
12:53	2 Esd. 6:24; Jub. 23.16, 19; 1 En. 100.1–2	—	Allusion	—
12:54	1 Kings 18:44	—	Allusion	7-SA
13:3	Ps. 7:12 [7:13]	Allusion	Allusion	8-TE
13:3	Jer. 12:17 LXX	—	Allusion	
13:5	Ps. 7:12 [7:13]	Allusion	—	8-TE
13:6	Hab. 3:17	Allusion	Allusion	
13:6	Ps. 80:8–16 [79:9–17]; Isa. 5:1–7; Jer. 8:13; 24:2–10; Hosea 10:16–17; Mic. 7:1–4	—	Allusion	8-TE
13:14	Exod. 20:9–10; Deut. 5:13–14	Allusion	Allusion	8-TE
13:16	Isa. 45:11	—	Allusion	—
13:17	Isa. 45:16	—	Allusion	7-SA
13:17	Exod. 34:10 LXX	—	Allusion	8-TE
13:19	Ps. 104:2 [103:2]; Dan. 4:9, 18	—	Allusion	
13:19	Ezek. 17:23; 31:6	Allusion	Allusion	8-TE
13:19	Dan. 4:12, 21	Allusion	—	
13:23	2 Esd. 7:47; 8:3; 9:15	—	Allusion	7-SA
13:27	Ps. 6:8 [6:9] LXX	Allusion	Citation	7-SA
13:27	1 Macc. 3:6	—	Allusion	

Luke		Form Classification		
Text	OT and Extrabiblical References	UBS[5]	NA[28]	Huffman
13:29	Ps. 107:3 [106:3]	Allusion	Allusion	
13:29	Isa. 25:6–8; 43:5–6; 49:1; 59:19; Mal. 1:11; Bar. 4:37; 1 En. 62.14	—	Allusion	8-TE
13:31	Amos 7:12	—	Allusion	7-SA
13:34	Deut. 32:11; Pss. 36:7 [35:8]; 91:4 [90:4]; Isa. 31:5	—	Allusion	8-TE
13:35	1 Kings 9:7–8; Ps. 69:25 [68:26]; Jer. 12:7; Tob. 14:4	—	Allusion	8-TE
13:35	Ps. 118:26 [117:26] LXX	Citation	Citation	3-UQ
14:1	2 Sam. 9:7, 10; 2 Kings 4:8	—	Allusion	8-TE
14:5	Deut. 22:4	—	Allusion	7-SA
14:8–10	Prov. 25:6–7	Allusion	Allusion	7-SA
14:11	Ezek. 17:24; 21:31	—	—	8-TE
14:13	Deut. 14:29; Tob. 2:2	—	Allusion	8-TE
14:20	Deut. 24:5	—	Allusion	7-SA
14:26	Deut. 33:9	Allusion	Allusion	7-SA
14:32	Ps. 122:6 [121:6]	—	Allusion	—
15:4	Ezek. 34:11, 16	Allusion	—	8-TE
15:5	Isa. 49:22	—	Allusion	8-TE
15:12	1 Macc. 10:30; Tob. 3:17; Sir. 33:20–24	—	Allusion	8-TE
15:13	Prov. 29:3	Allusion	Allusion	7-SA
15:18	Exod. 10:16	—	Allusion	8-TE
15:18	Ps. 51:4 [50:6]	Allusion	Allusion	8-TE
15:20	2 Sam. 14:33	—	Allusion	8-TE
15:20	Tob. 11:9	Allusion	Allusion	8-TE
15:22	Gen. 41:42	—	Allusion	8-TE
15:25	Dan. 3:5, 10, 15	—	Allusion	8-TE
16:3	Isa. 22:19	—	Allusion	7-SA
16:9	1 En. 63.10	Allusion	Allusion	8-TE
16:9	1 En. 39.4; Sir. 27:1–2	—	Allusion	8-TE
16:13	Gen. 29:29–31	—	Allusion	8-TE
16:15	1 Kings 8:39; 1 Chron. 28:9	—	Allusion	8-TE
16:15	Prov. 24:12 LXX	Allusion	Allusion	8-TE
16:17	Bar. 4:1	—	Allusion	8-TE
16:18	Deut. 24:1	—	Allusion	7-SA
16:19	Prov. 31:22	—	Allusion	8-TE
16:20	2 Kings 20:3; Job 2:7	—	Allusion	8-TE
16:22	4 Macc. 13:17; 1 En. 103.5–8	—	Allusion	8-TE
16:23	4 Macc. 13:15	—	Allusion	8-TE
16:26	2 Esd. 7:36; 1 En. 22.9–13	—	Allusion	8-TE

Luke Text	OT and Extrabiblical References	Form Classification UBS⁵	NA²⁸	Huffman
17:3	Lev. 19:17	—	Allusion	7-SA
17:4	Ps. 119:164 [118:164]	—	Allusion	8-TE
17:10	2 Sam. 6:22	—	Allusion	8-TE
17:12	Lev. 13:45; Num. 5:2–3	—	Allusion	8-TE
17:12	Lev. 13:46	Allusion	Allusion	
17:14	Lev. 14:2–3	Allusion	—	8-TE
17:14	2 Kings 5:14	—	Allusion	
17:15	2 Kings 5:15	—	Allusion	7-SA
17:22–30	Dan. 7:13–14; cf. Luke 5:24	—	—	7-SA
17:25	Ps. 118:22 [117:22]	—	—	7-SA
17:26	Gen. 6:5–12	Allusion	Allusion	6-HR
17:27	Gen. 7:6–23	Allusion	Allusion	
17:28	Gen. 18:20–21	Allusion	Allusion	
17:28	Gen. 19:1–14	Allusion	—	6-HR
17:29	Gen. 19:15–29	Allusion	Allusion	
17:29	Ezek. 16:49–50; Sir. 16:8	—	Allusion	
17:31	Gen. 19:17	Allusion	Allusion	6-HR
17:32	Gen. 19:26	Allusion	Allusion	
17:37	Job 39:30	Allusion	Allusion	7-SA
18:2–8	2 Kings 8:1–6	—	—	7-SA
18:3	Exod. 22:22; Deut. 10:18; Ps. 79:9 [78:9]; Isa. 1:17	—	Allusion	8-TE
18:7	Judg. 11:36 LXX	—	Allusion	8-TE
18:7	Ps. 22:2 [21:3]	—	Allusion	8-TE
18:7	Bar. 4:25; Sir. 35:23	—	Allusion	8-TE
18:8	Dan. 7:13–14; cf. Luke 5:24	—	—	7-SA
18:9	Ezek. 33:13	—	Allusion	8-TE
18:11	Pss. Sol. 16:5	—	Allusion	8-TE
18:12	Gen. 14:20	Allusion	—	8-TE
18:13	2 Kings 5:18 LXX; Ps. 25:11 [24:11] LXX; Dan. 9:19	—	Allusion	8-TE
18:13	Ps. 51:1 [50:3]	Allusion	—	
18:19	Deut. 6:4; Ps. 25:8 [24:8]	—	Allusion	8-TE
18:20	Exod. 20:12–16 LXX; Deut. 5:16–20 LXX	Citation	Citation	2-IP
18:20	Exod. 20:13–16; Deut. 5:17–20	Allusion	—	
18:22	Sir. 29:11	Allusion	—	—
18:31	Dan. 7:13–14; cf. Luke 5:24	—	—	7-SA
18:32	Isa. 50:6	—	Allusion	5-SS
19:8	Exod. 22:1 [21:37]	Allusion	Allusion	8-TE
19:8	Num. 5:6–7	—	Allusion	

Luke Text	OT and Extrabiblical References	Form Classification		
		UBS⁵	NA²⁸	Huffman
19:10	Dan. 7:13–14; cf. Luke 5:24	—	—	7-SA
19:10	Ezek. 34:16	Allusion	Allusion	7-SA
19:27	1 Sam. 15:33	—	Allusion	7-SA
19:30	Num. 19:2; 1 Sam. 6:7; Zech. 9:9	—	Allusion	8-TE
19:36	2 Kings 9:13	Allusion	Allusion	7-SA
19:37	Zech. 14:4	—	Allusion	7-SA
19:37	Ps. 118:15–16 [117:15–16]	—	—	7-SA
19:38	Ps. 118:26 [117:26] LXX	Citation	Citation	4-UP
19:38	Zech. 9:9	—	—	7-SA
19:40	Hab. 2:11	—	Allusion	7-SA
19:41	2 Kings 8:11	—	Allusion	7-SA
19:42	Deut. 32:28	—	Allusion	8-TE
19:42	Deut. 32:29; Isa. 6:9–10	Allusion	Allusion	8-TE
19:43	Isa. 29:3; Ezek. 4:2	—	Allusion	8-TE
19:44	Ps. 137:9 [136:9]	Allusion	Allusion	8-TE
19:44	2 Sam. 17:13; Hosea 10:14; 13:16 [14:1]; Nah. 3:10	—	Allusion	8-TE
19:44	Job 10:12 LXX; Jer. 6:15 LXX; Wis. 3:7	—	Allusion	8-TE
19:46	Isa. 56:7 LXX	Citation	Citation	2-IP
19:46	Jer. 7:11	Allusion	Citation	7-SA
20:2	Exod. 2:14	—	—	7-SA
20:9	Isa. 5:1	Allusion	Allusion	7-SA
20:10–12	2 Chron. 36:15–16	Allusion	Allusion	7-SA
20:13	Isa. 5:4	—	Allusion	7-SA
20:14	1 Kings 21:19 [20:19]	—	—	7-SA
20:17	Ps. 118:22 [117:22] LXX	Citation	Citation	1-IQ
20:17	Isa. 28:16	—	Allusion	8-TE
20:18	Isa. 8:14–15; Dan. 2:34–35, 44–45	—	Allusion	8-TE
20:21	Ps. 82:2 [81:2] LXX; Mal. 2:9	—	Allusion	8-TE
20:28	Deut. 25:5	Citation	Allusion	2-IP
20:28	Deut. 25:6	—	Allusion	2-IP
20:28	Gen. 38:8	Allusion	Allusion	8-TE
20:29	Tob. 7:11; As. Mos. 9.1	—	Allusion	8-TE
20:36	Gen. 6:2; Job 1:6	—	Allusion	8-TE
20:37	Exod. 3:1, 15–16 LXX	—	Allusion	6-HR
20:37	Exod. 3:2	Allusion	Allusion	6-HR
20:37	Exod. 3:6 LXX	Citation	Citation	2-IP
20:38	4 Macc. 7:19; 16:25	—	Allusion	8-TE
20:42–43	Ps. 110:1 [109:1] LXX (vs. MT)	Citation	Citation	1-IQ

Luke Text	OT and Extrabiblical References	UBS⁵	NA²⁸	Huffman
20:47	As. Mos. 8.1	—	Allusion	8-TE
21:1	2 Kings 12:9 [12:10]	—	—	7-SA
21:5	2 Macc. 9:16	—	Allusion	7-SA
21:6	Hag. 2:15	—	—	7-SA
21:8	Jer. 14:14; 29:8 [36:8]	—	—	8-TE
21:8	Dan. 7:22	Allusion	Allusion	8-TE
21:9	Dan. 2:28–29	Allusion	Allusion	7-SA
21:9	Dan. 2:45	—	Allusion	
21:10	2 Chron. 15:6; Isa. 19:2	Allusion	Allusion	8-TE
21:11	Isa. 19:17; Ezek. 38:19; 2 Macc. 5:2–3	—	Allusion	8-TE
21:15	Exod. 4:12; Jer. 1:9	—	—	8-TE
21:16	Mic. 7:6; Zech. 13:3; cf. Jub. 23.16, 19; 1 En. 100.1–2; 2 Esd. 6:24	—	—	8-TE
21:18	1 Sam. 14:45	Allusion	—	8-TE
21:20	Ps. 118:10–12 [117:10–12]; Isa. 29:3; Jer. 6:6; Ezek. 4:1–2; 26:8	—	—	8-TE
21:20	Dan. 9:27	—	—	7-SA
21:22	Deut. 32:35; Hosea 9:7	Allusion	Allusion	5-SS
21:22	1 Kings 9:6–9; Jer. 46:10 [26:10]; Dan. 9:26; Mic. 3:12	—	Allusion	
21:24	Gen. 34:26	—	Allusion	8-TE
21:24	Jer. 21:7; Sir. 28:18	Allusion	Allusion	
21:24	Deut. 28:64; Isa. 63:18; Jer. 25:29 [32:29]; Ezek. 32:9; Pss. Sol. 17.25	—	Allusion	8-TE
21:24	Ezra 9:7; Ps. 79:1 [78:1]; Dan. 12:7; Tob. 14:4–6	Allusion	Allusion	
21:24	Dan. 9:26; Zech. 12:3 LXX; 1 Macc. 3:45, 51	Allusion	—	
21:25	Isa. 13:10; Ezek. 32:7	Allusion	—	8-TE
21:25	Joel 2:30–31 [3:3–4]	Allusion	Allusion	
21:25	Pss. 46:2–3 [45:3–4]; 65:7 [64:8]; Isa. 24:19 LXX; Wis. 5:22	Allusion	Allusion	8-TE
21:25	Ps. 89:9 [88:10]	—	Allusion	
21:26	Isa. 34:4; Joel 2:10	—	Allusion	8-TE
21:26	Hag. 2:6, 21	Allusion	Allusion	
21:27	Dan. 7:13	Citation	Citation	7-SA
21:28	1 En. 51.2	Allusion	Allusion	8-TE
21:33	Ps. 119:89 [118:89]; Isa. 40:8	—	Allusion	8-TE
21:34	Isa. 5:11–13; 2 Bar. 32.1; 83.8; 85.4	—	Allusion	8-TE
21:35	Isa. 24:17	Allusion	Allusion	8-TE
21:35	Jer. 25:29 [32:29]	—	Allusion	8-TE
21:36	Dan. 7:13–14; cf. Luke 5:24	—	—	7-SA
22:1	Exod. 12:1–27	Allusion	—	6-HR

Luke Text	OT and Extrabiblical References	Form Classification		
		UBS[5]	NA[28]	Huffman
22:3	Mart. Ascen. Isa. 3.11	—	Allusion	8-TE
22:7	Exod. 12:6, 14, 15	Allusion	Allusion	8-TE
22:8	Exod. 12:8–11	Allusion	—	
22:10	1 Sam. 10:2–7	—	Allusion	7-SA
22:15	Gen. 31:30	—	Allusion	8-TE
22:19	Isa. 53:10–12	—	Allusion	7-SA
22:19	Exod. 12:14; Deut. 16:3	—	Allusion	8-TE
22:20	Isa. 53:10–12	—	Allusion	7-SA
22:20	Exod. 24:8; Jer. 31:31; 32:40; Zech. 9:11	Allusion	Allusion	8-TE
22:21	Ps. 41:9 [40:10]	Allusion	Allusion	7-SA
22:22	Dan. 7:13–14; cf. Luke 5:24	—	—	7-SA
22:30	Dan. 7:9–10	—	Allusion	7-SA
22:31	Job 1:6–12	—	Allusion	7-SA
22:31	Amos 9:9	Allusion	Allusion	8-TE
22:32	Ps. 51:13 [50:15]	—	Allusion	7-SA
22:37	Isa. 53:12 LXX	Citation	Citation	2-IP
22:37	Pss. 22:1–11 [21:1–12]; 69:1–36 [68:1–36]; Isa. 50:6; 52:13–53:12; Dan. 9:26; Zech. 12:10; 13:7	—	—	5-SS
22:37	Pss. Sol. 16.5	—	Allusion	
22:38	Deut. 3:26	—	Allusion	8-TE
22:43	Dan. 10:18–19	—	Allusion	8-TE
22:44	2 Macc. 3:14, 16; 15:19	—	Allusion	8-TE
22:48	Dan. 7:13–14; cf. Luke 5:24	—	—	7-SA
22:49	Sir. 48:25	—	Allusion	8-TE
22:62	Isa. 22:4	—	Allusion	8-TE
22:67	Jer. 38:15	—	Allusion	8-TE
22:69	Dan. 7:9, 13–14; cf. Luke 5:24	—	—	7-SA
22:69	Ps. 110:1 [109:1]	Citation	Allusion	7-SA
22:70	Exod. 3:14	—	—	7-SA
23:2	1 Kings 18:17	—	Allusion	8-TE
23:12	Ps. 2:2; cf. Acts 4:27	—	—	7-SA
23:27	Zech. 12:10–14	—	Allusion	7-SA
23:28	Song 2:7; 3:5, 10	—	Allusion	8-TE
23:28	Jer. 9:20–21 [9:19–20]	—	Allusion	8-TE
23:29	Isa. 54:1	—	Allusion	7-SA
23:30	Hosea 10:8 LXX	Citation	Citation	4-UP
23:31	Prov. 11:31	—	Allusion	8-TE
23:33	Isa. 53:12	Allusion	—	7-SA

Luke		Form Classification		
Text	OT and Extrabiblical References	UBS⁵	NA²⁸	Huffman
23:34	Isa. 53:12	Allusion	Allusion	7-SA
23:34	Ps. 22:18 [21:19]	Allusion	Citation	7-SA
23:35	Ps. 22:7–8 [21:8–9]	Allusion	Allusion	7-SA
23:35	Pss. 89:19 [88:20]; 106:23 [105:23]; Isa. 42:1; 49:7; cf. Luke 9:35a	—	—	8-TE
23:36	Ps. 69:21 [68:22]	Allusion	Allusion	7-SA
23:42	Gen. 40:14; Ps. 106:14 [105:14]; Jer. 15:15	—	Allusion	8-TE
23:44	Amos 8:9	Allusion	Allusion	7-SA
23:45	Exod. 26:31–33	Allusion	Allusion	8-TE
23:45	Exod. 36:35	Allusion	—	8-TE
23:46	Ps. 31:5 [30:6] LXX	Citation	Citation	4-UP
23:48	3 Macc. 5:24	—	Allusion	8-TE
23:49	Pss. 38:11 [37:12]; 88:8 [87:9]	Allusion	Allusion	8-TE
23:53	Deut. 21:22–23	—	Allusion	8-TE
23:53	Isa. 53:9	—	—	7-SA
23:56	Exod. 12:16	Allusion	—	
23:56	Exod. 20:10; Deut. 5:14	Allusion	Allusion	5-SS
23:56	Exod. 20:11; Deut. 5:12–13	—	Allusion	
24:4	2 Macc. 3:26	Allusion	—	—
24:7	Dan. 7:9, 13–14; cf. Luke 5:24	—	—	7-SA
24:7	Hosea 6:2; cf. Luke 9:22	—	—	7-SA
24:11	Gen. 45:26	—	Allusion	8-TE
24:12	Num. 24:25 LXX	—	Allusion	7-SA
24:19	Judg. 6:8	—	Allusion	7-SA
24:21	Isa. 41:14; 43:14; 44:24	—	Allusion	8-TE
24:25–26	Deut. 18:15; Pss. 22:1–11 [21:1–12]; 69:1–36 [68:1–36]; Isa. 49:6; 50:6; 52:13–53:12; Dan. 9:24–27; 12:2; Mic. 5:2 [5:1]; Zech. 12:10; 13:7; Hosea 6:1–2	—	—	5-SS
24:27	Deut. 18:15; Ps. 22:1–18 [21:2–19]; Isa. 53	Allusion	—	5-SS
24:29	Gen. 19:3; Judg. 19:9; 1 Sam. 28:23	—	Allusion	8-TE
24:31	2 Kings 6:17	—	Allusion	8-TE
24:31	Judg. 6:21; 2 Macc. 3:34	—	Allusion	8-TE
24:32	Ps. 39:2 [38:3]; Jer. 20:9	—	Allusion	8-TE
24:44	See the texts listed at Luke 24:25–26.	—	—	5-SS
24:45	Job 33:16; Ps. 119:18 [118:18]; 2 Macc. 1:4	—	—	8-TE
24:46	Isa. 53	Allusion	—	5-SS
24:46	Hosea 6:2	Allusion	Allusion	
24:49	Job 29:14; Ps. 132:9, 16 [131:9, 16]; Prov. 31:26 LXX; Isa. 51:9; 52:1; 59:17; 61:10; Wis. 5:18; Sir. 17:3	—	—	8-TE

Luke Text	OT and Extrabiblical References	Form Classification UBS⁵	NA²⁸	Huffman
Luke Text	**OT and Extrabiblical References**	**UBS⁵**	**NA²⁸**	**Huffman**
24:50	Lev. 9:22; Sir. 50:20	—	Allusion	8-TE
24:51	2 En. 67.1–3	—	Allusion	8-TE
24:52	Sir. 50:17	—	Allusion	8-TE
24:53	Sir. 50:22	—	Allusion	8-TE

Acts

Acts Text	OT and Extrabiblical References	UBS⁵	NA²⁸	Huffman
1:3	2 Bar. 76.4	—	Allusion	8-TE
1:4–6	Joel 3:28–3:21 [3:1–4:21]	—	—	7-SA
1:6	Isa. 49:6; Mal. 4:6 [3:23]	—	Allusion	8-TE
1:8	Isa. 32:15	—	Allusion	7-SA
1:8	Isa. 43:9–13	—	—	7-SA
1:8	Isa. 49:6	—	Allusion	8-TE
1:9	2 Kings 2:11; 2 Bar. 76; Sir. 48:9; 1 En. 70.1–2	—	Allusion	8-TE
1:10	2 Macc. 3:26	—	Allusion	8-TE
1:16	Ps. 41:9 [40:10]	Allusion	Allusion	7-SA
1:18	Wis. 4:19	—	Allusion	8-TE
1:20	Ps. 69:25 [68:26] LXX (vs. MT)	Citation	Citation	2-IP
1:20	Ps. 109:8 [108:8] LXX (vs. MT)	Citation	Citation	1-IQ
1:21	Num. 27:17; Deut. 31:2; 1 Sam. 18:13; 2 Chron. 1:10	—	—	8-TE
1:24	1 Sam. 16:7; 1 Kings 8:39; 1 Chron. 28:9; Prov. 21:2; 24:12	—	—	8-TE
1:25	Deut. 9:16; 17:20	—	Allusion	8-TE
1:26	Prov. 16:33	Allusion	Allusion	8-TE
2:1	Lev. 23:15–21; Deut. 16:9–11	Allusion	—	8-TE
2:2	Exod. 14:21; 1 Kings 19:11; Job 38:1; Ps. 48:7 [47:8]; Ezek. 1:4	—	—	8-TE
2:2	Job 27:3; 32:8; 33:4; Isa. 42:5; 57:16	—	—	8-TE
2:3	Num. 11:25	—	Allusion	8-TE
2:4	Sir. 48:12	—	Allusion	8-TE
2:4	Num. 11:25; 1 Sam. 10:6, 10; 19:23–24	—	—	8-TE
2:4	2 Sam. 23:2; Ps. 104:4 [103:4]; Isa. 48:16	—	—	8-TE
2:5–11	Isa. 43:9–13; Dan. 7:27	—	—	8-TE
2:11	Sir. 36:7	—	Allusion	8-TE
2:14	Job 32:11 LXX	—	Allusion	8-TE
2:17–21	Joel 2:28–32 [3:1–5] LXX (vs. MT)	Citation	Citation	2-IP
2:18	Num. 11:29	—	Allusion	8-TE

Acts Text	OT and Extrabiblical References	UBS⁵	NA²⁸	Huffman
			Form Classification	
2:19	Exod. 7:3, 9; 11:9–10; Deut. 4:34; 6:22; 7:19; 11:3; 26:8; 28:46; 29:3; 34:11; Pss. 78:43 [77:43]; 105:27 [104:27]; 135:9 [134:9]; Isa. 8:18; Jer. 32:20–21 [39:20–21]	—	—	8-TE
2:20	Isa. 2:12–22; Ezek. 30:2–3; Joel 1:15; Amos 5:18	—	Allusion	8-TE
2:21	Gen. 4:26; 12:8; 13:4; 21:33; 26:25; 1 Kings 18:24; Pss. 116:4 [114:4]; 116:13 [115:4]; Jon. 2:32 [3:5]; Zeph. 3:9	—	—	8-TE
2:22	See the texts listed at Acts 2:19.	—	—	8-TE
2:24	2 Sam. 22:6 LXX; Pss. 18:6 [17:7]; 116:3 [114:3]	Allusion	Allusion	8-TE
2:25–28	Ps. 16:8–11 [15:8–11] LXX (vs. MT)	Citation	Citation	1-IQ
2:29	1 Kings 2:10	Allusion	—	6-HR
2:30	2 Sam. 23:2	—	—	7-SA
2:30	2 Sam. 7:12–13	Allusion	Allusion	
2:30	Ps. 89:4–5 [88:5–6]	—	Allusion	6-HR
2:30	Ps. 132:11 [131:11]	Citation	Allusion	
2:31	Ps. 16:10 [15:10]	Citation	—	5-SS
2:33a	Exod. 15:6; Pss. 98:1 [97:1]; 110:1 [109:1]; 118:15–18 [117:15–18]	—	—	8-TE
2:33b	Num. 11:17, 25, 29; Isa. 32:15 MT; 44:3 MT; Joel 3:28–3:21 [3:1–4:21]; Zech. 12:10; cf. Acts 2:17–18	—	—	8-TE
2:34	Gen. 28:12; Deut. 30:12; 1 Sam. 2:10 LXX; 2 Kings 2:1, 11; Ps. 139:8 [138:8]; Prov. 30:4; Ezek. 8:3; Sir. 48:9; 1 En. 70.1–2; cf. 2 En. 67.1–3; 2 Bar. 76.1–5	—	—	8-TE
2:34–35	Ps. 110:1 [109:1] LXX (vs. MT)	Citation	Citation	1-IQ
2:37	Ps. 109:16 [108:16]	—	Allusion	8-TE
2:39	Isa. 44:3; 54:13	—	—	8-TE
2:39	Isa. 57:19	Allusion	Allusion	8-TE
2:39	Sir. 24:32	—	Allusion	
2:39	Joel 2:32 [3:5]	Allusion	Allusion	7-SA
2:40	Deut. 32:5; Ps. 78:8 [77:8]	Allusion	Allusion	8-TE
2:43	See the texts listed at Acts 2:19.	—	—	8-TE
2:46	Eccles. 9:7	—	Allusion	8-TE
3:8	Isa. 35:6	—	Allusion	7-SA
3:13	Exod. 3:6	Citation	Citation	7-SA
3:13	Exod. 3:15–16	Citation	Allusion	
3:13	Isa. 52:13	Allusion	Allusion	7-SA
3:13	Isa. 53:11	—	Allusion	
3:15	Isa. 43:9–13; cf. Acts 1:8	—	—	7-SA
3:18	Gen. 3:15; Num. 21:9; Pss. 22:1–11 [21:1–12]; 69:1–36 [68:1–36]; Isa. 50:6; 52:13–53:12; Dan. 9:24–27; Zech. 12:10; 13:7; Hosea 6:1–2	—	—	5-SS

Acts		Form Classification		
Text	OT and Extrabiblical References	UBS[5]	NA[28]	Huffman
3:19a	Deut. 4:30; 30:2, 10; 2 Chron. 19:4; Job 33:23 LXX; Ps. 85:8 [84:9]; Isa. 55:7; Jer. 3:12; 24:7; Hosea 3:5; Joel 2:13; Sir. 17:29	—	—	8-TE
3:19b	Ps. 51:1, 9 [50:3, 11]; Isa. 43:25; 44:22	—	—	8-TE
3:21	Gen. 3:15; 12:3; 22:18; Num. 21:9; 24:17; Deut. 18:15; 2 Sam. 7:12–16; Pss. 22:1–11 [21:1–12]; 69:1–36 [68:1–36]; Isa. 7:14; 9:6–7 [9:5–6]; 49:6; 50:6; 52:13–53:12; 61:1; Jer. 23:5–6; Dan. 7:13–14; 9:24–27; 12:2; Mic. 5:2 [5:1]; Zech. 6:12; 9:9; 12:10; 13:7; Hosea 6:1–2	—	—	5-SS
3:22	Deut. 18:15–16 LXX (vs. MT)	Citation	Citation	2-IP
3:23	Deut. 18:18–19 LXX (vs. MT)	Citation	Citation	2-IP
3:23	Lev. 23:29 LXX	Citation	Citation	2-IP
3:24	See the texts listed at Acts 3:21.	—	—	5-SS
3:25	Pss. Sol. 17:15	—	Allusion	8-TE
3:25	Gen. 12:3; 18:18	Allusion	Allusion	6-HR
3:25	Gen. 22:18 LXX; 26:4 LXX	Citation	Citation	2-IP
3:26	Ezek. 3:19; 18:21, 27; 33:12, 19	—	—	8-TE
4:1	1 Chron. 9:11; Neh. 11:11	—	—	8-TE
4:11	Ps. 118:22 [117:22]	Citation	Allusion	2-IP
4:20	Num. 22:20, 35, 38; 23:12, 26; 24:13; 1 Kings 22:14; 2 Chron. 18:13; Amos 3:8	—	—	8-TE
4:24	Jdt. 9:12	—	Allusion	8-TE
4:24	Exod. 20:11	Allusion	Citation	8-TE
4:24	2 Kings 19:15; Neh. 9:6; Ps. 146:6 [145:6]; Isa. 37:16	—	Citation	8-TE
4:25–26	Ps. 2:1–2 LXX (vs. MT)	Citation	Citation	1-IQ
4:27	Ps. 2:2	—	Allusion	7-SA
4:27	Isa. 61:1	Allusion	—	7-SA
4:28	Isa. 46:10	—	—	7-SA
4:30	Exod. 3:20; Ps. 138:7 [137:7]; Isa. 1:25; Jer. 1:9; Zeph. 1:4	—	—	8-TE
4:30	See the texts listed at Acts 2:19.	—	—	8-TE
4:31a	Exod. 3:1; 35:1; Num. 27:18; Ezek. 36:27; 37:14; Mic. 3:8; Sir. 48:12; cf. Acts 2:4	—	—	8-TE
4:31b	Prov. 1:20 LXX; Wis. 5:1	—	—	8-TE
4:32	1 Chron. 12:39; 2 Chron. 30:12; Ezek. 11:19	—	—	8-TE
4:33	4 Macc. 6:32	—	Allusion	8-TE
4:34	Deut. 15:4	—	Allusion	7-SA
5:2	Josh. 7:1; 2 Macc. 4:32	—	Allusion	7-SA
5:4	Deut. 23:22–24	—	Allusion	8-TE
5:5	Ezek. 11:13	—	—	7-SA
5:7	3 Macc. 4:17	—	Allusion	8-TE
5:12	See the texts listed at Acts 2:19.	—	—	8-TE

Acts Text	OT and Extrabiblical References	Form Classification UBS⁵	NA²⁸	Huffman
5:15	Ps. 57:1 [56:2]; Song 2:3; Isa. 51:16; Ezek. 17:23; 31:6	—	—	8-TE
5:21	Exod. 12:21; 1 Macc. 12:6; 2 Macc. 1:10	—	Allusion	8-TE
5:24	1 Chron. 9:11; Neh. 11:11	—	—	8-TE
5:29	Num. 22:20, 35, 38; 23:12, 26; 24:13; 1 Kings 22:14; 2 Chron. 18:13; Amos 3:8	—	—	8-TE
5:30	Deut. 21:22	—	Allusion	8-TE
5:31	Exod. 15:6; Pss. 98:1 [97:1]; 110:1 [109:1]; 118:15–18 [117:15–18]	—	—	8-TE
5:31	Wis. 12:10, 19	—	—	7-SA
5:32	Isa. 43:9–13; cf. Acts 1:8	—	—	7-SA
5:39	2 Macc. 7:19	—	Allusion	8-TE
5:41	4 Macc. 18:3	—	—	8-TE
6:2	Exod. 18:17–23	—	Allusion	7-SA
6:3	See the texts listed at Acts 4:31a.	—	—	8-TE
6:5	See the texts listed at Acts 4:31a.	—	—	8-TE
6:6	Num. 27:18, 23	—	Allusion	7-SA
6:8	See the texts listed at Acts 2:19.	—	—	8-TE
6:13	Exod. 20:26; Prov. 14:5	—	Allusion	8-TE
6:13	Jer. 26:11	Allusion	—	
6:14	Gen. 17:1–27; 21:4; Exod. 12:43–49; Lev. 12:3; 17:8–9, 10–12, 13–14; 18:6–26; cf. Gen. 9:4; Exod. 4:24–26; Josh. 5:2–8	—	—	5-SS
7:2	Ps. 29:3 [28:3]	Allusion	Allusion	7-SA
7:2	Gen. 11:31; 15:7	—	Allusion	6-HR
7:3	Gen. 12:1 LXX	Citation	Citation	2-IP
7:4	Gen. 11:31–12:1, 5	Allusion	Allusion	6-HR
7:5	Deut. 2:5	Allusion	Allusion	7-SA
7:5	Gen. 16:1	Allusion	Allusion	
7:5	Gen. 17:8; 48:4	Citation	Citation	6-HR
7:5	Deut. 32:49	—	Allusion	
7:6	Exod. 2:22	—	Allusion	7-SA
7:6–7	Gen. 15:13–14 LXX	Citation	Citation	2-IP
7:7	Exod. 3:12	Citation	Allusion	2-IP
7:8	Gen. 17:10–14	Allusion	Allusion	6-HR
7:8	Gen. 21:4	Allusion	Allusion	6-HR
7:8	Gen. 25:26; 35:22–26; 1 Chron. 1:34; Jub. 16.14	—	Allusion	
7:9	Gen. 37:11, 28; 45:4	Allusion	Allusion	6-HR
7:9	Gen. 39:2–3, 21, 23	Allusion	Allusion	
7:10	Gen. 41:37–46; Ps. 105:21 [104:21]	Allusion	Allusion	6-HR
7:10	Gen. 45:8	—	Allusion	
7:10	Ps. 34:19 [33:20]	—	Allusion	8-TE

Acts		Form Classification		
Text	OT and Extrabiblical References	UBS⁵	NA²⁸	Huffman
7:11	Gen. 41:54; 42:5	Allusion	Allusion	6-HR
7:12	Gen. 42:1–2	Allusion	Allusion	
7:13	Gen. 45:1, 3–4, 16	Allusion	Allusion	6-HR
7:14	Gen. 45:9–11, 18–19; 46:27 LXX; Exod. 1:5 LXX	Allusion	Allusion	6-HR
7:14	Deut. 10:22 LXX	Allusion	—	
7:15	Gen. 46:3–4; 49:33; Exod. 1:6	Allusion	Allusion	
7:15	Deut. 26:5	—	Allusion	6-HR
7:16	Gen. 23:3–20; 33:19; 50:7–13; Josh. 24:32	Allusion	Allusion	
7:16	Gen. 49:29–30	Allusion	—	
7:17	Gen. 47:27; Ps. 105:24 [104:24]	—	Allusion	6-HR
7:17	Exod. 1:7	Allusion	Allusion	
7:18	Exod. 1:8 LXX	Citation	Citation	2-IP
7:19	Exod. 1:9–11, 22	Allusion	Allusion	6-HR
7:19	Exod. 1:16	—	Allusion	
7:19	Exod. 2:3	—	Allusion	
7:20	Exod. 2:2	Allusion	Allusion	6-HR
7:21	Exod. 2:3–10	Allusion	Allusion	
7:21	Jub. 47.8	—	Allusion	
7:22	1 Kings 4:30 [5:10]	—	Allusion	—
7:23–24	Exod. 2:11–12	Allusion	Allusion	6-HR
7:26	Jub. 47.11–12	—	Allusion	
7:26	Exod. 2:13	Allusion	Allusion	2-IP
7:27–28	Exod. 2:14 LXX (vs. MT)	Citation	Citation	1-IQ
7:29	Exod. 2:15, 21–22; 18:3–4	Allusion	Allusion	6-HR
7:30	Exod. 3:2	Citation	Allusion	6-HR
7:31	Exod. 3:3–4	Allusion	Allusion	
7:32	Exod. 3:6 LXX	Citation	Citation	2-IP
7:32	Exod. 3:15–16 LXX	—	Allusion	
7:33	Exod. 3:5 LXX	Citation	Citation	1-IQ
7:34	Exod. 3:7, 8, 10 LXX	Citation	Citation	
7:35	Exod. 2:14 LXX (vs. MT)	Citation	Citation	1-IQ
7:35	Pss. 19:14 [18:15]; 78:35 [77:35]	—	Allusion	8-TE
7:35	Exod. 3:2	Allusion	—	
7:35	Deut. 33:16	—	Allusion	6-HR
7:36	Exod. 14:21; Num. 14:33–34	Allusion	Allusion	
7:36	Exod. 15:4; Neh. 9:12–21; As. Mos. 3.11	—	Allusion	
7:36	Exod. 7:3	Allusion	Allusion	8-TE
7:37	Deut. 18:15 LXX	Citation	Citation	2-IP

Acts Text	OT and Extrabiblical References	UBS⁵	NA²⁸	Huffman
7:38	Exod. 19:1–6; 20:1–17; Deut. 5:4–22; 9:10	Allusion	—	6-HR
7:38	Deut. 4:10; 32:47	—	Allusion	
7:39	Num. 14:3	Allusion	Allusion	6-HR
7:39	Neh. 9:17	—	Allusion	
7:40–41	Exod. 32:1 LXX; 32:23 LXX	Citation	Citation	1-IQ
7:41	Exod. 32:4–8	Allusion	Allusion	6-HR
7:41	Neh. 9:18; Ps. 106:19 [105:19]	—	Allusion	
7:41	Deut. 31:29; 1 Kings 16:7; 2 Kings 22:17; 2 Chron. 34:25; Ps. 9:16 [9:17]; Isa. 2:8; 17:8; Jer. 1:16; 25:6	—	—	8-TE
7:42	Jer. 7:18 LXX; 8:2; 19:13	Allusion	Allusion	8-TE
7:42	Hosea 13:4 LXX	—	Allusion	
7:42–43	Amos 5:25–27 LXX (vs. MT)	Citation	Citation	2-IP
7:44	Exod. 25:9, 40; Num. 1:50	Allusion	—	
7:44	Exod. 25:29	—	Allusion	6-HR
7:44	Exod. 27:21	Allusion	Allusion	
7:45	Josh. 3:14–17; 23:9; 24:18	Allusion	Allusion	6-HR
7:45	Josh. 18:1	Allusion	—	
7:45–46	2 Sam. 7:2–16; 1 Kings 8:17–18; 1 Chron. 17:1–14; 2 Chron. 6:7–8; Ps. 132:1–5	Allusion	—	
7:46	Ps. 132:5 [131:5]	Allusion	Allusion	6-HR
7:47	2 Sam. 7:13; 1 Kings 6:2; 8:20	—	Allusion	
7:47	1 Kings 8:19–20	Allusion	Allusion	
7:47	1 Kings 6:1, 14; 2 Chron. 3:1; 5:1; 6:2, 10	Allusion	—	
7:48	Isa. 16:12	—	Allusion	8-TE
7:49	1 Kings 22:19; 2 Chron. 18:18; Pss. 11:4 [10:4]; 103:19 [102:19]; Prov. 8:27; Wis. 9:10; 18:15	—	—	8-TE
7:49–50	Isa. 66:1–2 LXX	Citation	Citation	1-IQ
7:51	Exod. 32:9	Allusion	—	8-TE
7:51	Exod. 33:3, 5	Allusion	Allusion	
7:51	Lev. 26:41; Jer. 6:10	Allusion	Allusion	8-TE
7:51	Jer. 9:26	Allusion	—	
7:51	Num. 27:14	—	Allusion	7-SA
7:51	Isa. 63:10	Allusion	Allusion	
7:52	1 Kings 19:10, 14	—	Allusion	6-HR
7:52	2 Chron. 36:16	Allusion	—	
7:53	Deut. 33:2 LXX	—	Allusion	6-HR
7:54	Job 16:9; Pss. 35:16 [34:16]; 37:12 [36:12]	Allusion	Allusion	8-TE
7:54	Ps. 112:10 [111:12]	Allusion	—	
7:55	See the texts listed at Acts 4:31a.	—	—	8-TE

Acts Text	OT and Extrabiblical References	Form Classification UBS[5]	NA[28]	Huffman
7:55	Ps. 63:2 [62:3]; Isa. 6:1	—	Allusion	8-TE
7:55–56	1 Kings 22:19; 1 Chron. 6:39; 2 Chron. 18:18; Ps. 109:6 [108:6]; Zech. 3:1	—	—	8-TE
7:56	Ezek. 1:1; cf. Luke 3:21	—	—	7-SA
7:56	Dan. 7:13–14; cf. Luke 5:24	—	—	7-SA
7:58	Lev. 24:14; Num. 15:35–36; Deut. 17:7	—	Allusion	8-TE
7:59	Ps. 31:5 [30:6]	Allusion	—	7-SA
8:15–19	See the texts listed at Acts 2:33b.	—	—	8-TE
8:17–19	Num. 27:18, 23; cf. Deut. 34:9; Acts 6:6	—	—	7-SA
8:20	Jer. 44:12 [51:12]; 49:2 [30:18]; Dan. 2:5; 3:29 [3:96]	—	Allusion	8-TE
8:20	2 Kings 5:16; Dan. 5:17 Theod.; Isa. 55:1	—	—	8-TE
8:21	Deut. 12:12; 14:27, 29	—	Allusion	8-TE
8:21	Ps. 78:37 [77:37]	Allusion	Allusion	8-TE
8:23	Deut. 29:18 [29:17] LXX; Lam. 3:15 LXX	Allusion	Allusion	8-TE
8:23	Lam. 3:19	—	Allusion	8-TE
8:23	Isa. 58:6	Allusion	Allusion	7-SA
8:24	Exod. 8:4, 24; 9:28	Allusion	Allusion	8-TE
8:24	Exod. 10:17	—	Allusion	8-TE
8:26	1 Kings 19:7; 2 Kings 1:3, 15	—	—	8-TE
8:26	Dan. 8:4, 9	—	Allusion	8-TE
8:27	1 Kings 8:41–42; Ps. 68:30–32 [67:31–33]; Isa. 18:7; 56:3–7; Zeph. 3:10	—	Allusion	8-TE
8:27	Jer. 34:19	—	Allusion	—
8:31	Wis. 9:11	—	Allusion	8-TE
8:31	1 Kings 20:33 [21:33]; 2 Kings 10:15	—	—	8-TE
8:32–33	Isa. 53:7–8 LXX (vs. MT)	Citation	Citation	1-IQ
8:39	1 Kings 18:12	Allusion	Allusion	7-SA
8:39	2 Kings 2:16; Ezek. 11:24	—	Allusion	7-SA
9:1	2 Macc. 3:24–40; 4 Macc. 4:1–14	—	Allusion	8-TE
9:2	1 Macc. 15:21	—	Allusion	8-TE
9:2	Isa. 35:8	—	—	7-SA
9:4	Gen. 46:2; Exod. 3:4	—	Allusion	8-TE
9:4–5	Zech. 2:8 [2:12]	—	—	7-SA
9:6	Ezek. 3:22	—	Allusion	8-TE
9:7	Deut. 4:12; Dan. 10:7	—	Allusion	8-TE
9:8	Deut. 28:28–29	—	—	7-SA
9:10	Gen. 22:1, 11; 27:1, 18; 37:13; 1 Sam. 1:8; 3:4–8, 16; 22:12; 2 Sam. 1:7; Isa. 6:8	—	—	8-TE
9:12	Num. 27:18, 23; cf. Deut. 34:9; Acts 6:6	—	—	7-SA

Acts Text	OT and Extrabiblical References	UBS⁵	NA²⁸	Huffman
9:14	See the texts listed at Acts 2:21.	—	—	8-TE
9:17	Num. 27:18, 23; cf. Deut. 34:9; Acts 6:6	—	—	7-SA
9:17	See the texts listed at Acts 4:31a.	—	—	8-TE
9:21	See the texts listed at Acts 2:21.	—	—	8-TE
9:25	Josh. 2:15; 1 Sam. 19:12	—	—	8-TE
9:28	See the texts listed at Acts 1:21.	—	—	8-TE
9:35	See the texts listed at Acts 3:19a.	—	—	8-TE
9:37	1 Kings 17:19	—	Allusion	7-SA
9:38	Num. 22:16	—	Allusion	8-TE
9:40	2 Kings 4:33, 35	—	Allusion	7-SA
9:40	1 Kings 8:54	—	—	7-SA
10:2	Tob. 12:8	—	Allusion	8-TE
10:4a	Dan. 4:26; Tob. 12:8; 14:2; Sir. 7:10; Pss. Sol. 15.13	—	—	8-TE
10:4b	Exod. 28:12, 29; 30:16; Lev. 6:15; Num. 31:54; Isa. 23:18 LXX	—	—	8-TE
10:9	2 Kings 23:12; Jer. 19:13; 32:29 [39:29]; Zeph. 1:5	—	—	8-TE
10:10	Gen. 15:12	—	Allusion	8-TE
10:11	Ezek. 1:1	—	Allusion	7-SA
10:12	Gen. 1:24; Lev. 11	—	Allusion	8-TE
10:14	Lev. 11	Allusion	—	
10:14	Ezek. 4:14	Allusion	Allusion	8-TE
10:14	1 Macc. 1:62	—	Allusion	
10:22a	Gen. 22:12; Lev. 19:32; 25:36; Neh. 7:2; Esther 2:20 LXX; Ps. 66:16 [65:16]; Prov. 24:21; Eccles. 7:18; 8:12; Jdt. 8:8; Tob. 4:21	—	—	8-TE
10:22b	1 Macc. 10:25; 11:30, 33	—	Allusion	8-TE
10:25	2 Kings 4:37	—	—	7-SA
10:26	Wis. 7:1	—	Allusion	8-TE
10:31	See the texts listed at Acts 10:4a.	—	—	8-TE
10:31	See the texts listed at Acts 10:4b.	—	—	8-TE
10:34	Dan. 2:8	—	Allusion	8-TE
10:34	Deut. 10:17; 2 Chron. 19:7; Sir. 35:12–13	—	Allusion	8-TE
10:35	Ps. 15:2 [14:2]	—	Allusion	7-SA
10:36	Pss. 107:20 [106:20]; 147:18 [147:7]	Allusion	Allusion	8-TE
10:36	Isa. 52:7; Nah. 1:15 [2:1]	Allusion	Allusion	8-TE
10:36	Dan. 7:14	—	—	7-SA
10:36	Wis. 6:7; 8:3	—	Allusion	7-SA
10:38	1 Sam. 16:13; Isa. 61:1	—	Allusion	8-TE
10:38	Isa. 58:11 LXX	—	Allusion	8-TE

Acts Text	OT and Extrabiblical References	UBS⁵	NA²⁸	Huffman
10:39	Isa. 43:9–13; cf. Acts 1:8	—	—	7-SA
10:39	Deut. 21:22	Allusion	—	8-TE
10:41–42	Isa. 43:9–13; cf. Acts 1:8	—	—	7-SA
10:43	Isa. 33:24; 53:5–6; Jer. 31:34 [38:34]; Dan. 9:24	Allusion	—	5-SS
10:44–47	See the texts listed at Acts 2:33b.	—	—	8-TE
10:46	Deut. 11:2 LXX; Ps. 71:17–19 [70:17–19]; Tob. 11:15; 2 Macc. 3:34; 7:22; Sir. 17:8–9; 18:4; 36:7; cf. Acts 2:11	—	—	8-TE
11:5	Gen. 2:21; 15:12; cf. Acts 10:10	—	—	8-TE
11:6	Gen. 1:24, 30	—	Allusion	8-TE
11:8	Lev. 20:25; Ezek. 4:14; Dan. 1:8; 1 Macc. 1:62; cf. Acts 10:14	—	—	8-TE
11:15–16	See the texts listed at Acts 2:33b.	—	—	8-TE
11:18	Wis. 12:19	—	Allusion	7-SA
11:21	2 Sam. 3:12	—	Allusion	8-TE
11:21	See the texts listed at Acts 3:19a.	—	—	8-TE
11:22	Isa. 5:9	—	Allusion	8-TE
11:24	See the texts listed at Acts 4:31a.	—	—	8-TE
12:3	Exod. 12:6, 14–15; 23:15; Lev. 23:6; Num. 9:1–14; 28:17; Deut. 16:1–8; cf. Luke 22:7	—	—	8-TE
12:7	1 Kings 19:5	—	Allusion	7-SA
12:11	Dan. 3:28 [3:95 Theod.]	—	Allusion	8-TE
12:11	Exod. 18:4	—	Allusion	8-TE
12:17	Ps. 107:10–16 [106:10–16]	—	Allusion	7-SA
12:20	1 Kings 5:11 [5:25]; Ezek. 27:17	Allusion	Allusion	8-TE
12:22	Ezek. 28:2	Allusion	Allusion	8-TE
12:23	2 Kings 19:35; 1 Macc. 7:41; Sir. 48:21	—	Allusion	8-TE
12:23	Dan. 5:20	Allusion	—	8-TE
12:23	Jdt. 16:17; 2 Macc. 9:9	—	Allusion	8-TE
13:3	Num. 27:18, 23; cf. Deut. 34:9; Acts 6:6	—	—	7-SA
13:9	See the texts listed at Acts 4:31a.	—	—	8-TE
13:10	Jer. 5:27; Sir. 1:30; 19:26	—	Allusion	8-TE
13:10	Prov. 10:9	Allusion	Allusion	8-TE
13:10	Hosea 14:9 [14:10]	Allusion	Allusion	8-TE
13:10	Sir. 39:24	—	Allusion	8-TE
13:11	Judg. 2:15; 1 Sam. 12:15	—	Allusion	8-TE
13:11	Deut. 28:28–29; cf. Acts 9:8	—	—	7-SA
13:16	See the texts listed at Acts 10:22a.	—	—	8-TE
13:17	Isa. 1:2	—	Allusion	—

Acts Text	OT and Extrabiblical References	Form Classification		
		UBS⁵	NA²⁸	Huffman
13:17	Exod. 6:1, 6	Allusion	Allusion	
13:17	Exod. 12:51	Allusion	—	
13:17	Deut. 4:34, 37; 5:15; 9:26, 29; 10:15; Wis. 19:10	—	Allusion	
13:18	Exod. 16:35	—	Allusion	6-HR
13:18	Num. 14:33–34; Deut. 1:31	Allusion	Allusion	
13:19	Deut. 7:1; Josh. 14:1–2	Allusion	Allusion	
13:20	1 Kings 6:1	—	Allusion	
13:20	Judg. 2:16; 1 Sam. 3:20	Allusion	Allusion	
13:20	Sir. 46:13	—	Allusion	6-HR
13:21	1 Sam. 8:5, 10; 10:20–21, 24	Allusion	Allusion	
13:21	1 Sam. 8:10; 11:15	Allusion	—	
13:22	Ps. 89:20 [88:21]	Citation	Allusion	2-IP
13:22	1 Sam. 13:14	Citation	Allusion	7-SA
13:22	1 Sam. 15:23; 16:1	—	Allusion	6-HR
13:22	1 Sam. 16:12–13	Allusion	Allusion	
13:22	Isa. 44:28	Allusion	Allusion	7-SA
13:23	2 Sam. 7:12; 22:51	Allusion	Allusion	
13:23	2 Sam. 22:51	—	Allusion	5-SS
13:23	Isa. 11:1	Allusion	—	
13:26	See the texts listed at Acts 10:22a.	—	—	8-TE
13:26	Pss. 107:20 [106:20]; 147:18 [147:7]; cf. Acts 10:36	—	—	8-TE
13:27	Pss. 22:1–11 [21:1–12]; 69:1–36 [68:1–36]; Isa. 50:6; 52:13–53:12; Dan. 9:26; Zech. 12:10; 13:7	—	—	5-SS
13:29	Pss. 22:1–11 [21:1–12]; 69:1–36 [68:1–36]; Isa. 50:6; 52:13–53:12; Dan. 9:26; Zech. 12:10; 13:7	—	—	5-SS
13:32–33	2 Sam. 7:12; 22:51; Pss. 89:28–37 [88:29–38]; 132:10–12 [131:10–12]	—	—	5-SS
13:33	Ps. 2:7 LXX (vs. MT)	Citation	Citation	1-IQ
13:34	Isa. 55:3 LXX (vs. MT)	Citation	Citation	2-IP
13:35	Ps. 16:10 [15:10] LXX (vs. MT)	Citation	Citation	1-IQ
13:36	1 Kings 2:10	Allusion	Allusion	6-HR
13:36	2 Sam. 7:12	—	Allusion	
13:36	Judg. 2:10	Allusion	—	8-TE
13:41	Hab. 1:5 LXX (vs. MT)	Citation	Citation	2-IP
13:43	Josh. 4:24; 22:25; Job 1:9; Isa. 66:14 LXX; Jon. 1:9; cf. 3 Macc. 3:4; 4 Macc. 5:24	—	—	8-TE
13:47	Isa. 49:6 LXX (vs. MT)	Citation	Citation	2-IP
13:47	Isa. 42:6; 51:4; cf. Luke 2:32	—	—	8-TE

Acts Text	OT and Extrabiblical References	Form Classification UBS⁵	NA²⁸	Huffman
13:47	Pss. 67:2 [66:3]; 98:2–3 [97:2–3]; Isa. 45:21–22; 62:11; cf. Luke 3:6	—	—	8-TE
13:47	Isa. 8:9; 45:21–22; 48:20; 62:11; Jer. 16:19; 31:8 [38:8]; cf. Acts 1:8	—	—	8-TE
13:50	See the texts listed at Acts 13:43.	—	—	8-TE
13:51	Neh. 5:13	—	—	7-SA
13:52	See the texts listed at Acts 4:31a.	—	—	8-TE
14:3	See the texts listed at Acts 2:19.	—	—	8-TE
14:10	Ezek. 2:1	—	Allusion	7-SA
14:10	Isa. 35:6	—	—	7-SA
14:14	Jdt. 14:16–17	—	Allusion	8-TE
14:15	4 Macc. 12:13; Wis. 7:3	—	Allusion	8-TE
14:15	See the texts listed at Acts 3:19a.	—	—	8-TE
14:15	Jer. 2:5	—	Allusion	8-TE
14:15	2 Kings 19:4, 16; Ps. 42:2 [41:3]; Dan. 6:20 [6:21]; Hosea 1:10 [2:1]	—	Allusion	8-TE
14:15	Exod. 20:11; Ps. 146:6 [145:6]	Allusion	Citation	8-TE
14:16	2 Kings 17:29–41; cf. Ps. 81:12 [80:13]; Mic. 4:5	—	—	6-HR
14:17	Lev. 26:4; Ps. 145:16 [144:16]	—	Allusion	8-TE
14:17	Ps. 147:8 [146:8]; Jer. 5:24	Allusion	Allusion	8-TE
14:19	Lev. 24:14–16; Num. 15:35; Deut. 13:1–11; 17:7; 1 Kings 21:13 [20:13]; cf. Acts 7:58	—	—	8-TE
15:1	Lev. 12:3	Allusion	—	5-SS
15:4	Jdt. 8:26	—	Allusion	8-TE
15:8	1 Sam. 16:7; 1 Kings 8:39; 1 Chron. 28:9; Prov. 21:2; 24:12; cf. Acts 1:24	—	—	8-TE
15:8	See the texts listed at Acts 2:33b.	—	—	8-TE
15:10	Exod. 17:2	—	Allusion	7-SA
15:10	Gen. 27:40, 25; 29; Isa. 9:4 [9:3]; Jer. 27:8, 11 [34:8, 11]; 28:11, 14 [35:11, 14]; 30:8 [37:8]	—	—	8-TE
15:12	See the texts listed at Acts 2:19.	—	—	8-TE
15:14	Deut. 7:6; 14:2; 26:19; 28:9; 1 Sam. 12:22; Isa. 43:21	—	—	8-TE
15:16	Jer. 12:15	—	Allusion	7-SA
15:16–17	Amos 9:11–12 LXX (vs. MT)	Citation	Citation	2-IP
15:17	Isa. 43:7; Jer. 7:10–14, 30; 14:9; 32:34 [39:34]; 34:15 [41:15]; Dan. 9:19	—	—	8-TE
15:18	Isa. 45:21	—	Allusion	7-SA
15:19	See the texts listed at Acts 3:19a.	—	—	8-TE

Acts Text	OT and Extrabiblical References	Form Classification		
		UBS⁵	NA²⁸	Huffman
15:20	Gen. 9:4; Lev. 17:10–14	Allusion	Allusion	
15:20	Lev. 3:17	Allusion	—	5-SS
15:20	Lev. 18:6–18, 26	—	Allusion	
15:23–29	2 Chron. 30:1; 1 Esd. 4:47–48; 6:7; Ezra 4:6, 8; Esther 9:29; 1 Macc. 10:17; 11:29, 31; 12:5; 13:35; 15:15; 2 Macc. 9:18; 11:16; 3 Macc. 3:11, 30; 6:41; cf. Acts 15:23–29	—	—	8-TE
15:29	Gen. 9:4; Lev. 3:17; 17:10–14	Allusion	—	5-SS
15:33	Gen. 26:29; Exod. 18:23; Judg. 18:6; 1 Sam. 1:17; 20:42; 2 Sam. 3:21; 1 Esd. 5:2; 1 Macc. 10:66; 12:4, 52; 16:10; cf. 3 Macc. 6:27; 7:19	—	—	8-TE
16:13	Ezra 8:15–21; Ps. 137:1–4 [136:1–4]	—	—	8-TE
16:14	See the texts listed at Acts 13:43.	—	—	8-TE
16:14	2 Macc. 1:4	—	Allusion	8-TE
16:16	Deut. 18:10–14; 1 Sam. 28:3–9; Isa. 8:19	—	—	8-TE
16:17	Dan. 3:26 [3:93]	—	—	7-SA
16:20	1 Kings 18:17	Allusion	Allusion	8-TE
16:20	Amos 7:10	—	Allusion	
16:24	Jer. 20:2–3 MT; 29:26 MT [36:26]; T. Jos. 8.5; cf. Job 13:27; 33:11	—	—	7-SA
16:25	T. Jos. 8.5	—	Allusion	8-TE
16:26	Ps. 107:13–16 [106:13–16]	—	Allusion	7-SA
16:34	Pss. 9:14 [9:15]; 16:9–11 [15:9–11]; 20:5 [19:5]; 21:1 [20:2]; 35:9 [34:9]; 40:16 [39:17]; 51:14 [50:16]; 53:6 [52:7]; Isa. 25:9	—	—	8-TE
16:36	Judg. 18:6	—	Allusion	8-TE
17:2–3	Pss. 22:1–11 [21:1–12]; 69:1–36 [68:1–36]; Isa. 50:6; 52:13–53:12; Dan. 9:26; Zech. 12:10; 13:7; Hosea 6:1–2.	—	—	5-SS
17:4	See the texts listed at Acts 13:43.	—	—	8-TE
17:5	Judg. 9:4; 11:3; 1 Sam. 22:2; 2 Chron. 13:7	—	—	8-TE
17:6–8	1 Kings 18:17–18; Ezra 4:12–13; Esther 3:8; Amos 7:10; cf. Luke 23:2	—	—	8-TE
17:16	Isa. 63:10	—	—	7-SA
17:16	Isa. 2:8	—	—	7-SA
17:17	See the texts listed at Acts 13:43.	—	—	8-TE
17:23	Wis. 14:20; 15:17	—	Allusion	—
17:24	2 Macc. 7:23; 4 Macc. 5:25; Wis. 9:9	—	Allusion	8-TE
17:24	Gen. 24:3; Deut. 10:14; Ps. 115:15–16 [113:23–24]; Tob. 7:17	—	—	8-TE
17:24	1 Kings 8:27	Allusion	—	8-TE
17:25	Ps. 50:9–13 [49:9–13]	Allusion	Allusion	8-TE

Acts		Form Classification		
Text	OT and Extrabiblical References	UBS⁵	NA²⁸	Huffman
17:25	Isa. 42:5	Allusion	Allusion	8-TE
17:25	Isa. 57:15–16	—	Allusion	
17:26	Gen. 9:19; 10	—	Allusion	6-HR
17:26	Gen. 1:14, 28; Ps. 74:17 [73:17]; Wis. 7:18	—	Allusion	8-TE
17:26	Deut. 32:8	Allusion	Allusion	
17:27	Deut. 4:29; Jer. 29:13–14; Wis. 13:6	—	Allusion	8-TE
17:27	Isa. 55:6	Allusion	Allusion	
17:27	Ps. 145:18 [144:18]; Jer. 23:23	Allusion	Allusion	8-TE
17:28–29	Gen. 1:26–27	Allusion	Allusion	8-TE
17:28–29	Ps. 8:6–7	—	Allusion	
17:29	Deut. 4:28; Wis. 13:10–19	—	Allusion	8-TE
17:29	Isa. 40:18–20; 44:9–20	Allusion	Allusion	
17:30	Sir. 28:7	—	Allusion	6-HR
17:30	Isa. 59:20; Jer. 15:19; Ezek. 14:6; 18:30–32; cf. Acts 2:38; 3:19	—	—	8-TE
17:31	Pss. 9:8 [9:9]; 96:13 [95:13]; 98:9 [97:9]	Allusion	Allusion	8-TE
18:5	Job 32:18; Jer. 6:11; 20:9; 23:9; Amos 3:8	—	—	8-TE
18:6	Neh. 5:13; cf. Acts 13:51	—	—	7-SA
18:6	Ezek. 33:4	—	Allusion	8-TE
18:7	See the texts listed at Acts 13:43.	—	—	8-TE
18:9	Josh. 1:9; Jer. 1:19	—	Allusion	8-TE
18:9	Isa. 41:10; 43:5; Jer. 1:8	Allusion	Allusion	
18:13	1 Kings 18:17–18; Ezra 4:12–13; Esther 3:8; Amos 7:10; cf. Luke 23:2	—	—	8-TE
18:18	Num. 6:2–21	Allusion	Allusion	8-TE
19:2–7	See the texts listed at Acts 2:33b.	—	—	8-TE
19:4	Pss. 40:7 [39:7]; 118:26 [117:26]; Mal. 3:1; Zech. 14:5; cf. Luke 7:19–20	—	—	8-TE
19:6	Num. 27:18, 23; cf. Deut. 34:9; Acts 6:6	—	—	7-SA
19:9	Isa. 35:8; cf. Acts 9:2	—	—	7-SA
19:19	Deut. 18:10–14	—	Allusion	8-TE
19:23	Isa. 35:8; cf. Acts 9:2	—	—	7-SA
19:26	Deut. 4:28; Isa. 40:18–25; 44:9–20; 46:5–7; Wis. 13:10–19; cf. Acts 17:29	—	—	8-TE
19:27	Isa. 40:17; Wis. 3:17	—	Allusion	8-TE
19:28	Bel 18, 41	—	Allusion	8-TE
19:34	Exod. 18:11; 2 Sam. 7:22; 2 Chron. 2:5 [2:4]; Pss. 48:1 [47:2]; 77:13 [76:14]; 95:3–4 [94:3–4]; 135:5 [134:5]; Dan. 9:4; Bel 18, 41	—	—	8-TE

Acts Text	OT and Extrabiblical References	Form Classification UBS⁵	NA²⁸	Huffman
20:6	Exod. 12:6, 14–15; 23:15; Lev. 23:6; Num. 9:1–14; 28:17; Deut. 16:1–8; cf. Luke 22:7	—	—	8-TE
20:10	1 Kings 17:21	Allusion	Allusion	7-SA
20:10	2 Kings 4:34–35	—	Allusion	
20:16	Lev. 23:15–21; 2 Macc. 12:32; Tob. 2:1	—	Allusion	8-TE
20:26	Sus. 46	—	Allusion	8-TE
20:27	Deut. 1:17; Hab. 2:4 LXX; cf. Jer. 26:2 [33:2]; Ezek. 3:17–21; 33:2–9	—	—	8-TE
20:27	Pss. 66:5 [65:5]; 107:11 [106:11]; Isa. 4:2 LXX; Jer. 32:19 [39:19]; Wis. 6:4; Jdt. 8:16	—	—	8-TE
20:28	Ps. 74:2 [73:2]	Allusion	Allusion	8-TE
20:28	Isa. 31:5; 43:21	—	—	8-TE
20:28	Gen. 22:2, 16	—	—	7-SA
20:29	Ezek. 22:27	—	Allusion	8-TE
20:32	Deut. 33:3–4; Wis. 5:5	Allusion	Allusion	8-TE
20:33	1 Sam. 12:3	Allusion	Allusion	7-SA
20:35	Sir. 4:31	—	Allusion	8-TE
20:37	Gen. 33:4; 45:14–15; Tob. 7:6	—	Allusion	8-TE
21:9	Joel 2:28 [3:1]	Allusion	—	7-SA
21:11	1 Sam. 15:27–28; 1 Kings 11:30; Jer. 13:1–11	—	—	8-TE
21:13	Pss. 34:18 [33:19]; 51:17 [50:19]; 147:3 [146:3]; Prov. 17:10 LXX; Isa. 57:15; 61:1; Jer. 23:9	—	—	8-TE
21:21	See the texts listed at Acts 6:14.	—	—	5-SS
21:23–24	Num. 6:5, 13–18, 21	Allusion	—	8-TE
21:24	Num. 6:9, 18	—	Allusion	
21:26	Num. 6:2–4, 14–21	Allusion	—	
21:26	Num. 6:5, 13	Allusion	Allusion	
21:25	Lev. 17:8–9, 10–12, 13–14; 18:6–26; cf. Gen. 9:4; cf. Acts 15:20–21, 29	—	—	8-TE
21:28	Ezek. 44:7	Allusion	Allusion	8-TE
21:30	Exod. 21:14; 1 Kings 2:28–34; 2 Kings 11:15	—	—	8-TE
22:3	Deut. 33:3; 2 Kings 4:38; cf. Luke 8:35; 10:39	—	—	8-TE
22:4	Isa. 35:8; cf. Acts 9:2			7-SA
22:4–5	Deut. 13:12–18; 1 Macc. 15:21; cf. 2 Macc. 3:24–40; 4 Macc. 4:1–14; Acts 9:2	—	—	8-TE
22:6	Dan. 8:4, 9; cf. Acts 8:26	—	—	8-TE
22:7	Gen. 46:2; Exod. 3:4; cf. Acts 9:4	—	—	8-TE
22:7–8	Zech. 2:8 [2:12]; cf. Acts 9:4–5	—	—	7-SA
22:9	Deut. 4:12; Dan. 10:7; cf. Acts 9:7	—	—	8-TE

Acts		Form Classification		
Text	**OT and Extrabiblical References**	**UBS[5]**	**NA[28]**	**Huffman**
22:10	Isa. 32:9; Jer. 18:2; Ezek. 2:1; 3:22–23; cf. Acts 9:6	—	—	8-TE
22:11	Deut. 28:28–29	—	Allusion	7-SA
22:14	Isa. 32:9; Jer. 18:2; Ezek. 2:1; 3:22–23; cf. Acts 9:6	—	—	8-TE
22:15	Isa. 43:9–13; cf. Acts 1:8; 4:20	—	—	7-SA
22:16	Joel 2:32 [3:5]	Allusion	—	8-TE
22:17	Gen. 2:21; 15:12; cf. Acts 10:10	—	—	8-TE
22:21	Isa. 57:19; Zech. 6:15; 10:9; Sir. 24:32; cf. Acts 2:39	—	—	8-TE
23:2	1 Kings 22:24; Lam. 3:30; Mic. 5:1 [4:14]	—	—	8-TE
23:3	Deut. 28:22	—	Allusion	8-TE
23:3	Ezek. 13:10–15	Allusion	Allusion	7-SA
23:3	Lev. 19:15	Allusion	Allusion	8-TE
23:4	Exod. 17:2; 21:18–19; Num. 20:3, 13; Deut. 33:8	—	—	8-TE
23:5	Exod. 22:28 [22:27] LXX (vs. MT)	Citation	Citation	2-IP
23:25	1 Macc. 11:29; 3 Macc. 3:30	—	Allusion	8-TE
24:2	2 Macc. 4:6	—	Allusion	8-TE
24:5	1 Sam. 25:25 LXX; Ps. 1:1 LXX; Prov. 22:10; 29:8 LXX	—	Allusion	8-TE
24:6	Lev. 19:8; 20:3; Neh. 7:64; Ezek. 23:38–39; 28:18; 44:7; cf. Acts 21:28	—	—	8-TE
24:14	Isa. 35:8; cf. Acts 9:2	—	—	7-SA
24:14	4 Macc. 12:17	—	Allusion	8-TE
24:15	Dan. 12:2	Allusion	Allusion	5-SS
24:16	Prov. 3:4	—	Allusion	8-TE
24:22	Isa. 35:8; cf. Acts 9:2	—	—	7-SA
26:6–8	2 Sam. 7:12; 22:51; Pss. 89:28–37 [88:29–38]; 132:10–12 [131:10–12]	—	—	5-SS
26:11–12	Deut. 13:12–18; 1 Macc. 15:21; cf. 2 Macc. 3:24–40; 4 Macc. 4:1–14; cf. Acts 9:2	—	—	8-TE
26:14	Gen. 46:2; Exod. 3:4; cf. Acts 9:4	—	—	8-TE
26:14–15	Zech. 2:8 [2:12]; cf. Acts 9:4–5	—	—	7-SA
26:16	Ezek. 2:1	Allusion	Allusion	7-SA
26:16	Isa. 43:9–13; cf. Acts 1:8; 4:20	—	—	7-SA
26:17	1 Chron. 16:35; Jer. 1:8	Allusion	Allusion	8-TE
26:17	Jer. 1:19	—	Allusion	8-TE
26:18	Isa. 42:7, 16	Allusion	Allusion	7-SA
26:18	Isa. 35:5; 61:1 LXX	Allusion	—	7-SA
26:18	See the texts listed at Acts 3:19a.	—	—	8-TE
26:18	Deut. 33:3–4; Wis. 5:5	Allusion	—	8-TE
26:20	See the texts listed at Acts 3:19a.	—	—	8-TE

Acts		Form Classification		
Text	OT and Extrabiblical References	UBS⁵	NA²⁸	Huffman
26:22–23	Deut. 18:15; Pss. 22:1–11 [21:1–12]; 69:1–36 [68:1–36]; Isa. 49:6; 50:6; 52:13–53:12; Dan. 9:24–27; 12:2; Mic. 5:2 [5:1]; Zech. 12:10; 13:7; Hosea 6:1–2	—	—	5-SS
26:23	Isa. 42:6; 49:6	Allusion	—	8-TE
26:24–25	2 Kings 9:11; Jer. 29:26 [36:26]; Hosea 9:7–8; Wis. 14:28; cf. 4 Macc. 10:13	—	—	8-TE
27:9	Lev. 16:29	Allusion	Allusion	8-TE
27:19	Jon. 1:5	—	Allusion	7-SA
27:23	1 Kings 19:7; 2 Kings 1:3, 15; cf. Acts 8:26	—	—	8-TE
27:24	Deut. 31:6–8; Josh. 1:9; Isa. 41:10, 13; 43:5; Jer. 1:8, 17–19; 42:11 [49:11]; 46:28 [26:28]; cf. Acts 18:9–10	—	—	8-TE
27:24	Gen. 18:23–32; 19:21–29; Ezek. 14:12–23	—	—	8-TE
27:34	1 Sam. 14:45; 2 Sam. 14:11	Allusion	—	8-TE
28:4	Job 4:7; Num. 32:23; Amos 5:19; 9:3	—	—	8-TE
28:8	Num. 27:18, 23; cf. Deut. 34:9; Acts 6:6	—	—	7-SA
28:23	See the texts listed at Acts 26:22–23.	—	—	5-SS
28:26–27	Isa. 6:9–10 LXX (vs. MT)	Citation	Citation	1-IQ
28:27	See the texts listed at Acts 3:19a.	—	—	8-TE
28:28	Pss. 67:2 [66:3]; 98:3 [97:3]	Allusion	Allusion	8-TE
28:28	Isa. 40:5 LXX	Allusion	—	

Glossary

Common Terms in the Study of the New Testament Use of the Old Testament

allegory: A cluster of metaphors woven together. Allegorical interpretive practices focus on extracting symbolic meanings from Scripture passages even when such symbolism is not indicated.

allusion(s) or **allusions and recollections:** A term used in a broad sense to refer to any reference to a prior work accomplished by borrowed terms and/or concept(s). As an overarching label, it encompasses other categories with labels such as *recollection, Scripture summary, historical reminiscence, specific allusion,* and *thematic echo.* Some scholars might even refer to a paraphrase as a kind of allusion in this broad sense. In addition to these terms, see also **echoes,** which is likewise used by some as an umbrella term for any and all references to prior texts. In a narrower sense, *allusion* is the name of a subcategory of the broader category *allusions and recollections* and contains the form classifications of *specific allusion* and *thematic echo.*

antitype: In God's providential dealings in history, a later and greater figure, place, event, or institution that corresponds to an earlier one, which is called the "type" that was foreshadowing this subsequent escalated reality. *See also* **typology.**

See also the *Dictionary of the New Testament Use of the Old Testament*, ed. G. K. Beale, D. A. Carson, Benjamin L. Gladd, and Andrew David Naselli (Grand Rapids: Baker Academic, 2023). While this dictionary was not yet available to me as I finished the present book, I can only imagine that its articles will be significantly helpful for those studying the NT use of the OT.

appropriation technique: Another term for "framing," describing the way a NT author selects an OT text and puts it on display in his NT writing; often used to compare and contrast the practices of NT writers with those of other first-century interpreters.

canon of Scripture: The list of books recognized by the church as measuring up (the term *canon* means "measure") to be God's authoritative word to humanity. The content of the Protestant OT of thirty-nine books is the same as the Hebrew Bible, but Roman Catholics and Orthodox Christians include the Apocrypha (or parts of it) in the OT canon. Nevertheless, all branches of the Christian church agree on the twenty-seven books of the NT canon.

citation: An authorially intended excerpt (either a **quotation** or **paraphrase**) of a specific passage from a prior text. Such an excerpt is considered a citation whether or not it occurs with an **introductory formula** and whether it is a word-for-word rendering (i.e., an introduced quotation or an unintroduced quotation) or a reworded rendering (i.e., an introduced paraphrase or unintroduced paraphrase) of the prior text.

composite citation: When two (or more) different passages of Scripture are referenced together as if they are one passage; aka **conflation**.

compressed citation: When an author quotes several key phrases from a particular prior text while eliminating extraneous intervening parts of the quotation so as to shorten the quotation.

conflation: *See* **composite citation**.

Dead Sea Scrolls: A collection of ancient writings (numbering over 980 documents) discovered in caves along the northwestern edge of the Dead Sea in the 1940s and associated with the first-century Jewish community at **Qumran**; these have been hailed as the most important archaeological discovery of the twentieth century.

echo(es): Similar to **allusion**, a term that is utilized by some in a broad sense to refer to any and all references to prior works accomplished by borrowed terms and/or concept(s). But some utilize the *echo* label for more subtle—intentional or unintentional—references to prior texts and the *allusion* label only for clearer and authorially intended references. I take a narrow approach and qualify it with the more descriptive two-word label **thematic echo** over against the label **specific allusion**.

features: The characteristics or criteria used for identifying a particular **form** of a NT writer's reference to the OT.

figural reading: Another name for recognizing **typology**—i.e., divinely intended symbolism in history whereby historical figures, places, events, or institutions foreshadow subsequent greater realities. Due to abuses of typological thinking that have resulted in overinterpretation of biblical texts, some scholars prefer the label *figural reading* when speaking of the proper use of typology.

First Testament: Another term for the Old Testament, or Hebrew Bible. *See* **canon of Scripture.**

form: The means by which a NT author references an OT passage or theme (e.g., by means of a citation, specific allusion, recollection, thematic echo, etc.).

formal citations: Citations that have introductory statements—i.e., introduced quotations and introduced paraphrases.

framing: The method by which a NT author presents a particular form of referring to an OT passage; distinct from the selected form (e.g., citation or allusion) and from its function (i.e., the way in which the OT passage works in the NT argument), the framing is the manner in which an OT passage is displayed in the NT.

fulfillment: The completion in history of some prior scriptural indication. Rather than mere achievement of some predictive prophecy, it is better to think of fulfillment as having at least three possible implications: (a) when a prediction comes true, or (b) when a promise is still kept or some other pattern is still followed, or (c) when a typological prefigurement comes to light.

function: The discourse purpose for which the NT writer intends to utilize an OT passage or theme (e.g., making a declaration, referring to history, demonstrating fulfillment of prophecy, etc.).

Hebrew Bible or **Hebrew Scriptures:** The Scriptures of the Jewish people, equivalent in content to the Protestant OT. *See* **canon of Scripture.**

hermeneutical axiom: An underlying theological presupposition or commitment of a NT author that leads to a particular use of the OT Scriptures and/or to a particular conclusion drawn from the OT Scriptures.

historical reminiscence: A recollection focused on people and/or events in a prior text but with a very limited use of similar language and yet some kind of introductory statement; a form classification within the broad category of **allusions and recollections.**

informal citations: Citations that occur without introductory statements—i.e., unintroduced quotations and unintroduced paraphrases.

inner-biblical exegesis or **inner-biblical allusion:** The use of prior Scripture in later Scripture, whether that is the NT use of the OT, the OT use of prior OT texts, or the NT use of prior NT texts; this term is suggested by some scholars as more fitting for biblical studies than the broader term **intertextuality**.

interpretive gloss: An author's attempt to interpret and/or apply what appears to be a cited passage and/or his use of a prior text to explain (or otherwise ground) his own comments.

intertextuality: A term coined in wider postmodern reader-oriented literary studies to refer to the creation of new contexts for understanding previous texts when they are referenced by later texts. In biblical studies the term is often used in a narrower sense simply to mean that one text is using another text. *See* **inner-biblical exegesis**.

introduced paraphrase: A paraphrase of an OT passage that is introduced by the author as a citation using an introductory formula but reformulates the source text by means of synonym substitutions, changes to case endings, altered word order, or other adjustments; a form classification within the broad category of **citation**. *See* contra **unintroduced paraphrase**.

introduced quotation: A quotation of a prior text that is introduced by the author as a citation using an introductory formula and largely retains the wording of the source text; a form classification within the broad category of **citation**. *See* contra **unintroduced quotation**.

introductory formula: One of several phrases, whether detailed and official or simple and vague, used by NT authors to introduce a citation of an OT passage, whether an introduced quotation or an introduced paraphrase. Examples of such introductory formulas include "it is written" and "David said about him."

LXX: *See* **Septuagint**.

manuscripts: Handwritten copies of ancient documents, like those of the OT and those of the NT.

Masoretic Text (MT): The traditional Hebrew text form of the Hebrew Bible or Old Testament (with some portions of Daniel and Ezra in Aramaic). This **text form** gets its name from the group of Jews known as the Masoretes (seventh–tenth centuries CE), who were responsible for copying and preserving biblical manuscripts and supplying them with diacritical markings of vowel points and accents to preserve proper pronunciation.

midrash: Jewish interpretation and/or commentary resulting from searching the scriptural text itself.

MT: *See* **Masoretic Text**.

network: A group of intentionally interconnected interpretive passages within the OT such that a NT author might appeal to the whole network by referencing one of its members.

parallel wording: Where the wording of a passage substantially mimics that of another by more than a simple phrase, although the wording may incorporate synonyms and other paraphrasing alterations.

paraphrase: An intentional citation of a prior text that significantly modifies the vocabulary, verb tenses, case endings, and/or word order of the cited passage and yet still renders the sense of that passage. An **introduced paraphrase** is presented by the author as a citation; an **unintroduced paraphrase** is simply cited without any introduction. *See also* **citation**; **quotation**.

peshat: In Jewish exegetical tradition, the practice of understanding a passage to mean plainly and exactly what it says—i.e., literal interpretation.

pesher: In Jewish exegetical tradition, the practice of explaining eschatological mysteries.

proem: In Jewish homiletical tradition, a sermonic format for discussing several Scripture passages together. *See also* ***yelammedenu rabbenu***.

programmatic motives: The larger reasons an author has for writing the things he does, beyond the particular functions of individual sections including the particular functions of Scripture references within those individual passages.

prooftexting: Appealing to a passage of Scripture as an authoritative voice to prove one's viewpoint even while taking that passage of Scripture out of context.

quotation: An intentional and almost verbatim citation of a prior text; in distinction from a paraphrase, which significantly modifies the vocabulary, verb tenses, case endings, and/or word order of the cited passage. An **introduced quotation** is presented by the author as a citation; an **unintroduced quotation** is simply cited without any introduction. *See also* **citation**; **paraphrase**.

Qumran: A Jewish community (ca. 100 BCE–100 CE) along the northwestern shore of the Dead Sea that likely produced and/or stored the **Dead Sea Scrolls**. Most scholars believe the Qumran community was made up of Essenes who thought they were living in the end times.

rabbinic literature or **rabbinic writings:** Discussions and interpretations of the Jewish law produced by rabbis in the centuries after the destruction of Jerusalem and eventually committed to writing, beginning with the

Mishnah (ca. 200 CE). While there are questions of continuity between the first century and the era when the rabbinic teachings were finally codified, cautious appeal to rabbinic writings remains informative, and at least illustrative, for the study of the NT.

recollection: A reference to a prior text that does not have any blatantly shared language structures with that prior text, but where the NT author, nevertheless, makes his reference to the prior text clear enough with something of an introduction focused on either a **historical reminiscence** or a **Scripture summary**; a subcategory of the broad form category of **allusions and recollections**.

Scripture summary: A recollection of the teachings of prior Scriptures but with a very limited use of similar language and yet some kind of introductory statement; a form classification within the broad category of **allusions and recollections**.

sensus plenior: A "fuller sense" that could be divinely intended for Scripture beyond the recognition of its original writers and made available only via revelation; some scholars understand NT authors to be revealing the *sensus plenior* of OT passages by their use of those passages in new contexts, but others see it as a variation on **typology**.

Septuagint (LXX): The Old Greek translations of the Hebrew Scriptures (i.e., the OT) from ca. 250 BCE, abbreviated with the Roman numerals for seventy (LXX), as a tradition suggests that seventy (or rather, seventy-two) was the number of scribes who worked for seventy-two days to produce the translation.

specific allusion: An intentional reference to a particular OT passage by means of a borrowed phrase or similar wording but without any introduction; a form classification within the broad category of **allusions and recollections**. *See* contra **thematic echo**.

syntactical tension: When an author's use of a prior text maintains that prior text's syntactical point of view (e.g., with its verb tenses and pronominal references) as something separate from his own syntactical point of view; adjusting the wording so as to remove all the syntactical tension moves an author's use of a prior text from a citation classification toward an allusion classification.

targum: The practice of translating a scriptural text by way of interpretive and applicational paraphrase. Regarding the official Aramaic translations of the Hebrew Scripture, see **Targums**.

Targums: The Aramaic interpretive and applicational paraphrases of, and expansions upon, Hebrew Scripture used in the liturgy of Jewish synagogues.

text type or **text form:** The textual model or tradition for an OT passage that appears to be lying behind a particular usage of that passage in the NT, specifically the **Masoretic Text** (MT), the **Septuagint** (LXX), or **Targums.**

textual criticism: The process of sorting through the variations within the extant manuscripts so as to reconstruct the original reading of the ancient literary work that has survived only in handwritten copies of the original. *See also* **variant reading.**

thematic echo: When a NT author uses themes or ideas or structures from the OT Scriptures in such a vague and mixed way that it seems to point to a variety of OT passages rather than a single one; a form classification within the broad category of **allusions and recollections.** *See* contra **specific allusion.**

type: In God's providential dealings in history, a historical figure, place, event, or institution that foreshadows a subsequent greater reality, which is called the "antitype." *See also* **typology.**

typology. Divinely intended symbolism in history whereby historical figures, places, events, or institutions (the "types") foreshadow subsequent greater realities (the "antitypes"). Typological investigations of Scripture are focused on making connections between the biblical facts of history found within the text of Scripture more so than on interpreting biblical texts. Due to abuses of typological thinking that have resulted in overinterpretation of biblical texts and have given typology a bad name, some scholars prefer the label **figural reading** when speaking of the proper use of typology.

unintroduced paraphrase: A paraphrase of an OT passage reformulating the source text by means of synonym substitutions, changes to case endings, altered word order, or other adjustments that is not introduced by the author as a citation; a form classification within the broad category of **citations.** *See* contra **introduced paraphrase.**

unintroduced quotation: A quotation of an OT passage that is not introduced by the author as a citation but largely retains the wording of the source text; a form classification within the broad category of **citations.** *See* contra **introduced quotation.**

variant reading: When the wording for a particular passage in one manuscript varies from the wording for the same passage as recorded in the other manuscripts. *See also* **textual criticism.**

yelammedenu rabbenu: In Jewish homiletical tradition, a dialogical sermonic format for discussing several Scripture passages in a dialogue setting. *See also* **proem.**

Index of Modern Authors

Index of Scripture
and Other Ancient Texts

John

Acts